Not Built in a Day

NOT BUILT IN A DAY

EXPLORING THE

ARCHITECTURE

OF

ROME

GEORGE H. SULLIVAN

Carroll & Graf Publishers
New York

Not Built in a Day
Exploring the Architecture of Rome

Carroll & Graf Publishers
An Imprint of Avalon Publishing Group, Inc.
245 West 17th Street, 11th Floor
New York, NY 10011

AVALON

First Carroll & Graf edition 2006

The list of illustrations begins on p. 371 and serves as a continuation of this copyright page.

Library of Congress Cataloging-in-Publication Data is available.

ISBN-13: 978-0-78671-749-1
ISBN-10: 0-78671-749-1

9 8 7 6 5 4 3 2

Printed in the United States of America

INTERIOR DESIGN BY PAULINE NEUWIRTH, NEUWIRTH & ASSOCIATES, INC.
MAPS BY SUZANNE SERVICE

Distributed by Publishers Group West

FOR JONATHAN AND ROSANNE
amici del cuore

CONTENTS

INTRODUCTION

———•———

I STARTED WORKING on this book many years ago, without realizing it, during my first sightseeing visit to Rome. In college I had received a modicum of preparation — Introduction to the History of Art 101, taught by a celebrated professor whose lectures were famous for their passion and erudition — so I thought I knew a thing or two. And I did know, mostly, what I was supposed to be looking at and where it was located. But when I arrived at the prescribed destination, I was almost invariably disappointed. Far from being transported by the beauty or power of this painting or that building, I usually ended up scratching my head, wondering what all the fuss was about. To my great dismay, I found myself failing the appreciation test.

When it came to architecture, the leading guidebooks of the day did not help. "Turning right at the corner," they always seemed to be saying, "we note the striking façade of S. Susanna, one of the city's finest Baroque churchfronts. Moving down the street . . ." But wait, I would protest. What, exactly, makes S. Susanna's façade so striking? And why, exactly, is there no mention of what looks like the equally striking façade of that other church across the street? Why is only one of them worthy of attention, when they are so clearly similar in style? What complexities or subtleties of design set the one above the other? I was, it seemed, already supposed to know how to assess these matters. Cryptic utterances offered without elaboration — "the capitals repay study" (said of the nave columns at S. Maria in Cosmedin) or "the church interior is both affected and austere, bizarre and elegant" (describing S. Carlino) — added to my confusion, and left me feeling ignorant and excluded. They seemed to presume an automatic, fully-formed aesthetic response — a response that I entirely lacked.

Since that initial trip I have returned to Rome many times, and exploring the city, both on foot and in books, became first a hobby and then a passion. But in gradually learning to understand and appreciate the city's architecture, I never did find a guide that offered the kind of help I had needed on that first visit. I found architectural history textbooks — some of them very fine — that analyzed Rome's best-known buildings in detail. But these were for study, not for sightseeing, and were usually limited in scope to a single architectural era. I found traditional guidebooks, overflowing with facts. But these were primarily (often overwhelmingly) historical in emphasis. Even the few specialized guides that dealt exclusively with the city's architecture failed to do the job, for they seemed to be aimed at architects, and favored technical description over aesthetic reaction. There was nothing out there that described — *explained* — what makes the architecture of Rome (of Bramante, of Michelangelo, of Borromini and Bernini and Cortona) so special. There was nothing out there that considered the varied architectural personalities of Rome's individual buildings (not to mention its fountains and piazzas and ancient ruins), or that addressed the issue of why a given building was considered important by the experts. In short, there was nothing to help me see what I was missing.

This book is an attempt to fill that gap. It is also an attempt to move beyond the traditional guidebook form to create something that is at once more personal and more instructive. The "facts" — the names and dates and vital statistics that are the sum and substance of most guidebooks — are of course necessary and important, up to a point. But by themselves they will not help the sightseer look at and respond to architecture; they will not explain the stylistic questions that obsessed the leading architects of the day; they will not point out the innovations that set the pioneering buildings of each new style apart from their predecessors. So where other guides offer historical fact, I have tried to supply historical perspective — background about the prevailing architectural style of the era and the artistic beliefs that produced it. Where other guides offer cursory glances, I have tried to supply detailed visual analysis — analysis that will help readers see and appreciate the special character of Roman architecture. And where other guides shy away from presenting a strong personal viewpoint, I have nowhere hesitated to express my opinion. My aim is to convey not only information but also vision and conviction and enthusiasm. In the end, my hope is to give readers a set of tools — tools that will allow them, when looking at architecture, to formulate informed personal responses entirely on their own.

On the practical side, the book requires walking, and reading, and look-ing; it does not require any previous knowledge of architectural history. To keep sightseeing frustrations to a minimum, I have made it a rule to include only buildings that are accessible to the public on a regular basis without special arrangements. With a few irresistible exceptions — Bernini's incom-parable *Ecstasy of St. Theresa* and the remarkable medieval frescoes in the Oratory of St. Sylvester at SS. Quattro Coronati, to name two — I have not discussed paintings or sculpture in detail; however, important pieces of art are either mentioned in passing or listed at the end of the appropriate entry, and I have noted the presence of important museums as they occur within the walking tours. A reasonably thorough exploration of the city takes a week at the least, but for visitors with limited time or specialized interests I have included as appendices a three-day itinerary and a chronological index that groups the individual sights by artist and era.

Finally, Rome itself. Despite its long-standing renown — it has been called "The Eternal City" for centuries — many first-time visitors find it distinctly off-putting. Compared to Florence or Venice, it is just too crowd-ed, too noisy, too dirty, too chaotic. At some times and at some locations, this is certainly true. But Florence and Venice, for all their glories, are living off the past, while Rome is very much a city of the present. It is a thriving mod-ern capital, the hub of Italy. Yet its visible architectural history stretches back an astonishing twenty-five hundred years; of the great epochal European styles — Classical, Medieval, Gothic, Renaissance, Baroque, Historicist, Modern — only the Gothic (essentially a northern European phenomenon) is not present in its most compelling form. This combination of contemporary vitality and historical variety produces an urban dialogue between past and present — an urbanity, if you will — that is nothing less than unique. And for anyone wishing to experience firsthand the history of European architecture in its full panoply and glory, it makes Rome the per-fect place to start.

ORIENTATION

—◆—

*T*HIS BOOK IS divided into twelve walking tours; the general titles (such as "Baroque Rome" or "Ancient Rome") refer to the most important entries within a given tour, and are not meant to imply that sites from other eras along a given route are excluded. The tours are ordered geographically, starting at the city's center (the Piazza Venezia) and then moving from the Tiber Bend clockwise around the area within the ancient city walls, ultimately crossing the river to Trastevere and the Borgo (Vatican City). Within each tour, no route between individual sites is specified, but the order of the entries implies a route that will minimize backtracking.

Tour 1 covers the Capitoline Hill and its immediate environs, and is meant to serve as an introduction to the city and its architecture. Tours 2–5 cover the Campus Martius and Corso areas, the historic center of the city bounded roughly by the Capitoline Hill to the south, the Tiber Bend to the west, the Piazza del Popolo to the north, and the Spanish Steps to the east. Tours 6–9 cover the remaining ancient hills (the Quirinal, the Viminal, the Palatine, the Esquiline, the Caelian, and the Aventine); Tours 10 and 11 cover Trastevere and the Borgo (including St. Peter's and the Vatican); Tour 12 covers a handful of favorite sites outside the ancient city walls. Readers who wish to explore the city chronologically (that is, starting with ancient and medieval Rome) should begin with Tour 1 as an introduction to the city, then skip to Tour 7 (mostly ancient sites), then to Tours 8 and 9 (mostly medieval sites), and then to Tours 2–6 and Tours 10–12 (although Tour 11 — St. Peter's — could be inserted at any point after Tour 9 if desired).

In planning the sightseeing day, it is always worth remembering that except for the major basilicas (St. Peter's, S. Giovanni in Laterano, S. Maria Maggiore, and S. Paolo fuori le Mura), churches mostly close at noon and reopen from 4:00 P.M. to dusk. This temporary inaccessibility can be frustrating; one possible remedy (other than a siesta) is to devote the hours immediately after lunch to one of the city's major museums: the Capitoline Museums, the antiquities museums at the Palazzo Massimo alle Terme and the Palazzo Altemps, the National Gallery of Art in the Palazzo Barberini, the Etruscan museum in the Villa Giulia, or the Galleria Borghese. The Vatican Museums should if possible be visited first thing in the morning to avoid the worst of the crush.

Readers who wish to depart from the prescribed walking route and visit sites in a different order of their own choosing should feel free to do so. The avid sightseer can certainly finish each of the tours in a full morning or afternoon (excluding time spent in museums), but a warning is in order: the pace and duration of each outing should be determined by the reader, not by the text. These are walking tours, not marching orders, and they are meant to aid and encourage further exploration, not constrain it.

Getting around the city is not so difficult as it might initially seem; for the first-time visitor, here are a few pointers:

Maps. Some readers may prefer to carry a separate city map for ease of consultation; the best is probably the spiral-bound Michelin pocket atlas (*"atlante tascabile"*), sold at most major news kiosks in the main squares and at the main subway entrances.

Traffic. Over the past twenty years, nonessential traffic (including tour buses) has been banned from large sections of the old city within the walls, but the lack of traffic lights can still make crossing the street an intimidating exercise. Bear in mind that pedestrians possess the right of way at all zebra-stripe street crossings. As a general rule, however, automobile drivers will not stop for pedestrians *waiting* to cross at a zebra stripe; they will only stop for pedestrians *in the act of* crossing at a zebra stripe. Native pedestrians are therefore adept at plunging ahead in the face of approaching traffic, which then (most of the time) comes to a halt. For visitors, this interaction can take some getting used to; the most stimulating place to practice (or to study the native behavior amid a whirl of traffic) is around the Piazza Venezia. If discomfort persists, it is best to wait for a Roman headed in the same direction and then follow his or her example.

Public Transportation. The distances in downtown Rome are not nearly so great as might be expected; within the ancient walls, it is possible to walk from one end of town to the other in less than an hour. This, happily, makes it feasible to explore Rome entirely on foot. The subway system can be handy, but it is not extensive (it is limited to two lines that cover only the eastern half of the downtown area). The bus system is more useful, although some effort may be required to master its intricacies (detailed bus maps are sold at most news kiosks in the main squares and at the main subway entrances). Tickets for individual bus rides can be purchased at tobacco shops throughout the city; weeklong passes allowing an unlimited number of rides can be purchased from multilingual machines in subway stations and at major bus stops. In theory (and sometimes in practice), bus etiquette works as follows: one-trip ticketholders enter by the back door (so they have easy access to the machine that validates their tickets upon entry); passholders enter by the front door (since they need not validate their passes); everyone exits by the center door. Since taxis seeking passengers always drive to the nearest taxi stand, it is usually not possible to flag down an empty taxi on the street.

Pickpockets. There is very little serious street crime in downtown Rome, but pickpockets are all too common (particularly on crowded buses) and they can be extremely dexterous. It is advisable, always, to carry a minimum amount of cash or valuables, and women who carry purses should wear the strap across the body, if possible.

Drinking Water. Among sightseers, the most underutilized amenity in Rome is the sidewalk fountain. These small, hydrant-like conveniences can be found all over the city, but since they continually pour water down into street drains, many visitors do not realize that they are designed for drinking as well as for container fill-up (the faucet pipe out of which the water flows can be stopped up with a finger, causing the water to shoot up out of a small hole near the top of the pipe). The water is famous for its high quality — nondrinkable water is labeled *non potabile* — and it is cold and delicious. On hot summer days it is memorably refreshing, and during the afternoon a series of short drinks taken at regular intervals supplies ample protection against dehydration.

Ice Cream. Admittedly, *gelato* (Italian for "frozen" as well as for "ice cream") is not a necessity on the order of drinking water. But in Rome it is a luxury that must not be overlooked. For many decades, Giolitti's (located on the Via degli Uffici del Vicario, three blocks north of the

Pantheon) has claimed to make the best ice cream in the city, if not all of Italy, if not the entire world. They will not get any argument from this quarter. Payment for the cone or cup is made first, to the cashier; the receipt is then taken to the counter (which can be mobbed, since Italians do not believe in orderly lines) and traded for ice cream. The hazelnut — *nocciola,* pronounced "noh-choh-lah," with the accent on the "choh" — is especially delicious. A free dollop of whipped cream (*panna*) will be supplied upon request.

A Note on the Illustrations
———•———

THE ILLUSTRATIONS IN this book are mostly etchings by Giuseppe Vasi, who in the mid-1700s produced some two hundred views of Rome that included almost all of the city's famous buildings, fountains, monuments, and piazzas. In part, these etchings are meant to function in the same manner as conventional guidebook photographs: to help the reader quickly locate the site in question. But they are also meant to serve a purpose that goes beyond mere identification. Most of the illustrations depict not only specific single structures, but also the surrounding Roman cityscape of the years 1746–1761. So they are genuine historical documents. They can function as time machines, transporting the sightseer back to the end of the Baroque era, when the basic character of modern Rome had already been established but the crowded infill of the nineteenth and twentieth centuries had not yet appeared. This pictorial journey back in time is interesting in its own right, offering historical sidelights that no modern photograph could possibly provide.

TOURS
1 – 4

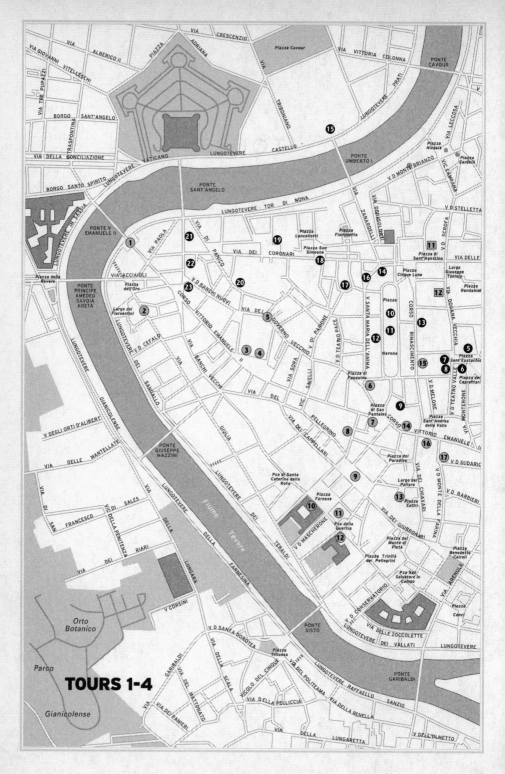

MAP #1
TOURS 1 — 4

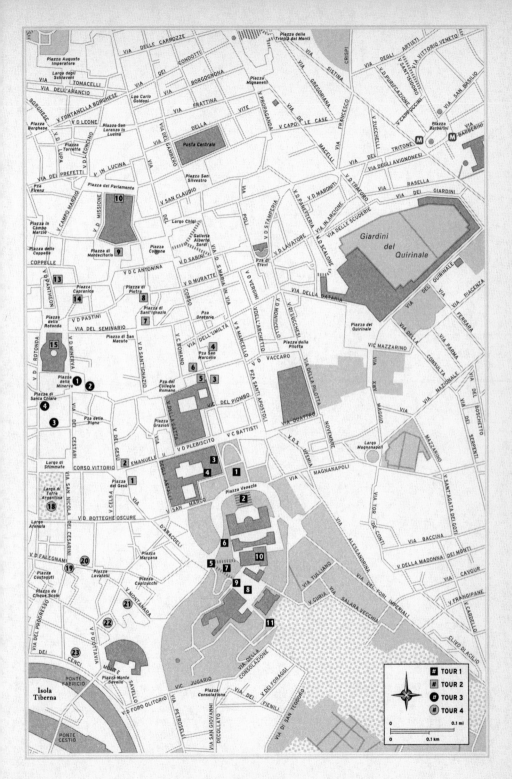

MAP #1

TOURS 1 — 4

TOUR 1

—•—

OVERVIEW OF THE CITY:
THE CAPITOLINE HILL

ROME'S UNUSUAL GEOGRAPHY has long been defined by a single famous phrase: "the Seven Hills of Rome." The hills in question — the Capitoline, Palatine, Quirinal, Viminal, Esquiline, Caelian, and Aventine — form a circle (more or less) around the valley that contains the ruins of the ancient Roman Forum; they gained their identity as a group when they were all enclosed by a single long defensive city wall, probably erected in the sixth century B.C.E. and rebuilt in the fourth century B.C.E. when Rome was a republic. Imperial Rome, like modern Rome, grew to incorporate three additional hills (the Pincian to the north, and the Janiculum and Vatican across the river to the west and northwest). In the popular imagination, however, it is the original seven hills that define Rome to this day.

The Capitoline Hill is the smallest of the seven, but it is by no means the least important. Its steepness, its location overlooking the central Piazza Venezia, and its conspicuous architectural extravagance — the massive Victor Emmanuel Monument covers its entire northern slope — all give it special prominence. In ancient times, the hill's southern peak was the site of the city's preeminent building: the Temple of Jupiter, dedicated to the most powerful of the Roman gods. Today the temple is long gone, supplanted by the Palazzo dei Conservatori and Michelangelo's incomparable Campidoglio (pictured on previous page), the first of Rome's great planned modern cityspaces. Beyond the Campidoglio, the hill and its immediate environs offer a fine cross-section of Roman architecture, including a modern square, a Renaissance palazzo, a large medieval church, a small neighborhood church, excavated ruins, and a famous ancient execution site. It is a jumble, but as an introduction to a great and varied city — the finest architectural jumble in Europe — it could not be more appropriate.

The history of the Capitoline Hill mirrors the history of the city as a whole: a thousand years of increasing importance, a thousand years of decline, and five hundred years of renewed growth. In ancient times, the main approach to the hill was from the southeast, through the complex of forums where the daily business of the city and its empire was conducted. But during the Middle Ages the city's center of gravity shifted. The destruction of the ancient aqueducts forced the medieval populace toward the river, and the rebirth of the city during the Renaissance was centered in the low-lying Tiber Bend area. As a result, Michelangelo's renovations at the Campidoglio required an entirely new approach route — from the northwest instead of the southeast — and the hill did a complete about-face. Today, with the modern metropolis grown up on every side and the Victor Emmanuel Monument visible from every direction, it is once again the key geographic element in the Roman cityscape.

1-1 PIAZZA VENEZIA
(Best viewed from the south end, on the sidewalk in front of the Victor Emmanuel Monument at the point where the whole of the long vista up the northbound Via del Corso to the obelisk in the center of the Piazza del Popolo becomes visible.)

The geographic center of Rome, with exactly the right bull's-eye center-of-town feel. The present layout evolved out of a much smaller square at the foot of the Via del Corso that dated back to the Renaissance. Plans for enlargement were first drawn up in 1883; by 1911, when the huge marble pile that is the Victor Emmanuel Monument was inaugurated, the entire area between the Monument and the Corso had been opened up, its buildings either razed or moved to other locations.

To its builders, the Piazza Venezia was a modern urban showplace — Rome's answer to the new boulevards and squares that had so dramatically transformed Paris in the 1860s. But in the 1940s and 1950s opinion began to change, and the piazza became a symbol of everything that the twentieth century deemed wrong with nineteenth-century city planning. Scholars deplored the razing of the Renaissance buildings as a shameful historical loss; architects denounced the Palazzo delle Assicurazioni Generali (constructed in 1907 on the piazza's east side to mirror the shape of the fifteenth-century Palazzo Venezia opposite) as retrograde pastiche untrue to the dictates of Modern architecture; everyone reviled the Victor Emmanuel Monument as a monstrous Neoclassical wedding cake. But to condemn the square because of the Monument is hardly fair. And today, with the achievements of twentieth-century Modern architecture under reassessment, the Palazzo delle Assicurazioni Generali looks more respectful than retrograde — a deferential exercise in contextualism that serves both to complement and compliment its much older peer across the square.

Admittedly, the piazza's historical cost in lost architecture may have been high. But its compensating virtues cannot be dismissed lightly. With its open space and enlivening touches of greenery, the piazza brings breathing room to the center of the city, offering a welcome contrast to the labyrinthine complexities of the nearby street layout. The cannily placed landscaping, especially, does its work with understated grace; to either side of the Victor Emmanuel Monument, islands of oleander and umbrella pines soften the square's southern corners, and in the center more islands of grass and flowers attract the eye and lead it toward the square's northern edge, where the Via del Corso begins its long, enticing journey toward the city's ancient northern gate at the Piazza del Popolo. And the non-Baroque feel of the nineteenth-century layout yields an extra dividend: for once, Rome's unnerving automobile traffic, with all its clamor and confusion, does not seem a jarring intrusion.

Most cities are fortunate if they possess even a single unique open urban space. Rome possesses four: the Piazza Navona, the Spanish Steps, St. Peter's Square, and the Piazza Venezia. The first three are Baroque, and incomparable. But the pulse of the *modern* city — the contemporary, rackety, chaotic, electric energy that sets Rome apart from its great rivals Florence and Venice — is best felt here in the Piazza Venezia, at the very heart of the Roman maelstrom.

1-2 VICTOR EMMANUEL MONUMENT
Giuseppe Sacconi, 1884–1927
(Piazza Venezia, south side)

Rome's centerpiece, built at the end of the nineteenth century in celebration of Italy's unification and named after the new nation's first king (reigned 1861–1878). The Monument took forty years to build, sprawling all over the north slope of the Capitoline, and what finally emerged was a cityscape split personality: what it *is* is lamentable, what it *does* is admirable.

Aesthetically, it is difficult to view the Monument as anything other than a calamity. Pompous, vainglorious, overwrought, overblown — if ever a piece of architecture deserved to be cut down to size, this is it. Architecturally, the mountain of antiseptically white Brescia marble* serves primarily to support a massive colonnade, thrust high into the air in a coarse gesture of heavy-handed triumph. Thematically, the Monument is similarly overloaded: a grab bag of allegorical sculptural groupings meant to represent variously Law, Sacrifice, Concord, Strength, Action, Thought, Victory, the Triumph of Patriotism, the Triumph of Labor, the Seas of Italy, and Rome. In the midst of it all is the grave of Italy's Unknown Soldier, marked by an eternal flame and guarded by two live sentries. The center of Italy's capital city is the perfect location for such a memorial, but the grave is all but invisible amid the welter of marble, and the simple and moving message it expresses is lost in the clamor of the surrounding bombast.

Given a larger perspective, however, the Monument possesses some unexpected compensating virtues. Soulless it may be, but as the keystone element in Rome's cityscape it undeniably works, and works well. At any other spot such a man-made mountain would probably be impossible for the city to assimilate, but here, bang in the center of Rome, it somehow seems to hold the whole city down. For tourists, it is an immensely helpful orienting device: climb any of Rome's hills and it comes into view, definitively marking the heart of the city. For natives, it is the hub of the city's wheel, the visible center around which everyday life in Rome continually whirls.

---

*From H. V. Morton's *A Traveller in Rome:* "The story in Rome — a typical pasquinade, by the way — is that when the Monument was built, the Prime Minister was deputy for Brescia, and that the contract for marble kept his seat safe for over a quarter of a century."

The climb up to the top is arduous — particularly on a hot day — but the crowning colonnade offers shelter from the sun, and the pavilions at either end catch and amplify even the smallest breeze. The views in all directions are fine, and include one startling close-up: at the western pavilion (on the right when climbing) the monument runs smack up to the medieval façade of S. Maria in Aracoeli and seems ready to swallow up the defenseless church the same way it did the hillside. In other directions, panoramic photographs with labels can be found at key viewing points; the labels identify the city's most prominent structures, including St. Peter's to the northwest, looking much closer and smaller than it actually is. The photographs are effectively placed and doubly useful — a tool that can serve both to introduce the city at the beginning of a visit and to sum it up at the end.

And then there is the biggest surprise of all: nighttime. After darkness falls, the floodlights around the Piazza Venezia come on, and an astonishing transformation takes place. The gold of the colonnade mosaics shines forth with unexpected splendor, and the heightened contrast of light and shadow produces an increase in three-dimensionality that renders the whole massive composition both more real and more fantastical. Set against the pitch-black sky, the ponderous lump of marble finally becomes what its builders meant it to be: a mighty cast-of-thousands Roman-triumph extravaganza that carries all aesthetic objections before it. This is no longer just architecture, this is theater, and the dramatic jump in voltage is dazzling. At night the Victor Emmanuel Monument is, quite simply, a sight to behold.

Interior Museums: The interior of the monument — newly restored — is capacious and imposing, and contains two museum spaces, one on the ground floor devoted to temporary exhibitions (entrance on the Piazza d'Aracoeli, to the right of the monument) and one at the upper terrace level (accessible by interior stairs or by climbing the exterior steps). The latter houses the *Museo del Risorgimento*, containing historical exhibits illustrating (with explanatory labels in English as well as Italian) the nineteenth-century struggle for Italian independence and unification.

The Piazza Venezia (north end looking west), with the Palazzo Venezia on the left.

1-3 PALAZZO VENEZIA
Probably Francesco del Borgo, 1466
(Piazza Venezia, west side)

The extensive nineteenth-century demolitions that produced the Piazza Venezia left one major building untouched: the austere and monolithic Palazzo Venezia, on the piazza's west side. The new setting greatly enhanced the structure's visibility, giving it a special prominence that, historically speaking, is entirely fitting and proper. This was Rome's first Renaissance palazzo.

Built (probably) by Francesco del Borgo for Pope Paul II during the mid-1400s, the Palazzo Venezia served first as a papal residence, then as a foreign embassy (to both the Venetians and the Austro-Hungarians), and finally — after major interior restoration in the early twentieth century — as headquarters for the fascist dictator Benito Mussolini, who loved to make preening speeches from his office balcony facing the piazza. Today it houses a large and rather forlorn museum devoted to the decorative arts (entered from the Via del Plebiscito).

As architecture, the exterior is harsh and forbidding — more a fortress than a palace — with awkwardly spaced windows and a medieval battle-mented parapet above. Only the carved window frames suggest the revolution in architecture to come, and then only in the most rudimentary man-ner. But the façade is worth noting because it so forcefully illustrates the embryonic state of Roman palazzo architecture at the very beginning of the Renaissance.

As the Renaissance took hold in Florence during the 1420s, Rome was just emerging from a century of neglect and decay. The papacy had removed itself to Avignon in 1309 — the so-called Babylonian Captivity — and its ill-starred return to Rome in 1377 had ignited the infamous pope-antipope hostilities of the Great Western Schism (1378–1417). But in 1417, when Rome at last regained its position as the undisputed seat of papal power, the city began to revive, and its reestablished ecclesiastical aristocracy soon came to require new and appropriately aristocratic housing. Massive structures containing long suites of rooms with high ceilings became the order of the day, giving rise to Rome's first genuine building boom in over a thousand years. At the same time, investigation of the city's ancient Classical ruins became a passion among scholars and architects. The two fashions soon combined to produce the central problem of Renaissance palazzo design: how to dress up the imposing new structures in dignified Classical clothing. How could the Classical vocabulary — most notably the Doric, Ionic, and Corinthian orders that ancient Rome had inherited from ancient Greece — be modified for use on the façades of urban palaces? Various solutions (more than four hundred years' worth) can be seen all over Rome, beginning with the Palazzo della Cancelleria (1486) off the Campo dei Fiori and ending with the Camera dei Deputati (1918) on the Piazza del Parlamento. The façade of the Palazzo Venezia is so crude that it does not even address the problem, but if surfeit eventually sets in — if all the city's palazzi begin to look numbingly alike — it will be worth remembering just how nakedly ugly the oldest of them all really was.

1-4   SAN MARCO
833 and after
(Piazza di S. Marco, entrance on the south side of the Palazzo Venezia)

The little church of San Marco is noted more for its venerability than its architecture, but after the enormity of the Victor Emmanuel Monument and the austerity of the Palazzo Venezia, its small size and human scale offer a welcome respite. Conveniently, it also serves as a timely introduction to a typically Roman phenomenon: the architectural palimpsest.*

---

*A palimpsest is an ancient writing tablet or parchment that was imperfectly erased before being reused; the subsidiary layers of writing below the primary text on palimpsests are a major source of historical documents from Classical antiquity. Obscure as the term is, its use in relation to Roman churches has in recent times become widespread to the point of cliché.

Founded in 336, S. Marco is a *titulus,* or titular church, one of twenty-five ancient Roman churches from which twenty-five cardinal priests have taken their titles since the fourth century. The original structure was almost entirely rebuilt (retaining its original ground plan) in 833 by Pope Gregory IV; the apse mosaics, which date from this reconstruction, show the Pope being introduced to Christ by St. Mark and holding a model of the church in symbolic offering. The carved wooden ceiling and the exterior double-story portico date from a renovation in the 1460s; most of the interior was redecorated during the 1650s and again around 1740. The church that exists today is thus an architectural hybrid of very mixed pedigree, and a similar pattern of structural and decorative renovation can be seen again and again in older churches throughout the city. The typical early Roman church, it turns out, was rebuilt during the Middle Ages, extensively renovated during the Renaissance, and then given a superficial overlay of elaborate interior decoration during the Baroque era.

Interesting as such an architectural palimpsest may be for historians, for architectural purists it is often an aesthetic nightmare — an indigestible hodgepodge that combines wildly incompatible elements of different styles from different eras. The Baroque decoration, especially, is liable to offend. In a fully Baroque church the surface ornamentation grows logically out of the underlying structure, but in many older Roman churches (as here) the Baroque additions are merely grafted on. The ornate displays of colored marble and gilded stucco had a religious origin: they were meant to reflect the riches of the hereafter and the glory of the kingdom of God. But the Baroque renovators tended to fall back on glitter when unable to convey glory, and too often their flamboyant embellishments ended up smothering the restrained pre-Baroque architecture under a suffocating layer of ostentatious frippery. Critics have found these decorative extravagances irritating — if not irreverent — ever since the Baroque era ended, and over the years many a visitor has left Rome feeling that its churches are more numerous than numinous.

As Baroque interiors go, S. Marco is fairly subdued. The decorative scheme is applied consistently throughout, with the columns of red Sicilian jasper (added in the 1740s) adding an appealing note of glistening color to the nave. Happily, the general effect is not excessive. Despite its overlay of Baroque pretensions, S. Marco has not lost its fundamentally intimate architectural character, and it remains, like all good neighborhood churches, a place of quiet refuge that seems to welcome all who enter.

1-5 STAIRCASES: SANTA MARIA IN ARACOELI AND CAMPIDOGLIO

S. Maria in Aracoeli Staircase: 1348
Campidoglio Staircase: Michelangelo, 1538 onward
(Piazza d'Aracoeli; best viewed from the sidewalk in front of the
entrance to the Syrian Embassy, Piazza d'Aracoeli 1)

From the Piazza in Aracoeli, two adjacent sets of steps ascend the Capitoline Hill, one leading to the church of S. Maria in Aracoeli, the other to Michelangelo's Campidoglio. The contrast between the two is extreme, and more than a simple matter of steepness. To those who first ascended them, they served very different purposes: the goal of the Aracoeli staircase was the medieval kingdom of God, while the goal of the Campidoglio staircase was the Renaissance city of man.

The climb to S. Maria in Aracoeli is perhaps the most physically challenging in the entire city: 124 steep steps of hard, unforgiving marble. The staircase was constructed in 1348, and it met an obvious need in improving access to the church above. But its deeper purpose was urgently felt by its builders. Italy had recently been ravaged by plague, and the steps were constructed in propitiation; survivors gave thanks for their deliverance by ascending to the church on their knees. For the fourteenth-century Romans, the staircase was a penitential offering to a wrathful God who had scourged the land with pestilence, and the long, arduous climb to the top was a punishing reminder that the wages of sin is death.

Michelangelo's famous approach to the Campidoglio — known to Italians as *la cordonata* — was designed not to punish but to invite. Its gentle slope prompts an easy and measured pace that produces a slow, majestic unveiling of the revolutionary cityscape at the top.* That cityscape is rigorously secular in design; for all its decorative statuary, the Piazza del Campidoglio possesses not a single Christian religious element, and its buildings completely hide S. Maria in Aracoeli from view. As designed by Michelangelo, the piazza and its seductive, theatrical approach reflect not God's power but man's — the newfound Renaissance ability of the human imagination to shape the urban environment in a way that, Godlike, creates order out of chaos.

---

*An unveiling that is unfortunately marred by the presence of the oversized and much restored Dioscuri (late Roman statues of the mythical twins Castor and Pollux, with their horses) at the top of the stairs. The statues were probably not part of Michelangelo's design, and are clumsily out of scale with their surroundings.

1-6 PIAZZA D'ARACOELI RUINS
Early second century C.E.
(Piazza d'Aracoeli, to the left of the staircase leading up to S. Maria in Aracoeli)

A large mound of picturesquely dilapidated brickwork, nestled into the angle between the west side of the Victor Emmanuel Monument and the steep flight of steps leading up to S. Maria in Aracoeli. The ruin looks like an outsized sand castle in the process of being washed away by the tide, and as a symbolic thorn-in-the-side deflator of the Monument's overblown pretensions, it is perfectly placed. But its jumble of rectangular niches and round arches (bizarrely punctuated by the remains of a medieval religious fresco and a tiny out-of-scale tower) makes no apparent architectural sense. What could have produced such a muddle?

The answer, in part, lies underfoot. As can be seen from the adjacent sidewalk railing, the below-ground excavations reveal a startling fact: the ruins' underpinnings are not underpinnings at all. In fact, they are the original structure's lower floors, on top of which medieval and Baroque buildings were later built. Modern downtown Rome, it turns out, is built upon the collapsed remains of its own previous incarnations, and the layer of rubble — usually embedded in the sediment left behind by centuries of recurrent Tiber flooding — is often shockingly deep.

The ruin here began as an apartment building during the second century C.E. The medieval religious fresco and the tiny medieval tower are remnants of the church of S. Biagio del Mercato, which was incorporated into the aboveground remnants of the apartment building during the Middle Ages. Both sets of remains were discovered in 1927, when the seventeenth-century church of S. Rita da Cascia — S. Biagio's successor — was torn down as part of the plan to open up and landscape the areas to either side of the Victor Emmanuel Monument.

1-7 COLA DI RIENZO MEMORIAL
1887
(Halfway up the ramp leading to the Campidoglio, on the left)

A patchy, equivocal monument to a patchy, equivocal leader. Viewed as a hero in the nineteenth century (he is the subject of Wagner's opera *Rienzi*) and as a megalomaniac today, Cola di Rienzo was in many ways a fourteenth-century precursor of the twentieth-century Italian dictator Benito Mussolini. Aligning himself with the people against the nobility, Cola styled himself "tribune" and promised the Roman populace a new era and a new empire.

But his reign as dictator lasted only six months. In the end, so the story goes, he was cornered atop the Capitoline by an angry, disillusioned mob; when he attempted to escape in disguise, he was recognized because he had failed to remove his ostentatious jeweled rings, and was stabbed to death.*

In 1887, the supposed spot of Cola's execution was marked by this oddly shy little statue. The hooded figure stands next to a symbol of Roman decline — a decapitated Corinthian capital upended to serve as a simple stool — and exhorts the city to greatness; the entire ensemble is set on a patchwork pedestal cobbled together, like Cola's dreams of glory, out of fragments of left-over antiquities. In its quiet way, the memorial evinces not only a sense of history but a sense of irony as well — a rare quality in a civic monument.

1-8 THE CAMPIDOGLIO
Michelangelo, 1538 onward
(On the Capitoline Hill; best approached from the Piazza d'Aracoeli, up the long, sloping ramp known as *la cordonata*)

In concept, the Campidoglio is simple. Set into the depression between the two peaks of the Capitoline Hill, it is nothing more than three buildings and a statue arranged to create a small, quiet square. But its historical importance can scarcely be overstated, for in its day it represented a tremendous leap forward for both urbanism and architecture.

The raw materials were not promising. In 1537, when Pope Paul III first proposed renovating the piazza and transferring the bronze equestrian statue of Marcus Aurelius from the Lateran,† the site was a gully-scarred, mud-prone open space bordered by a church (S. Maria in Aracoeli, ca. 1250) and two medieval palazzi (the Palazzo del Senatore, a much-rebuilt twelfth-century Senate hall constructed during one of the city's periodic ill-fated spasms of

---

*In Luigi Barzini's *The Italians*, socialist Aldo Parini describes pleading with Mussolini at the height of his power: "I said, 'This regime of yours, I am afraid, will end badly. Such things always do. Benito, you'll die like Cola di Rienzo.' Mussolini made one of his grimaces, expressing mock horror, then laughed and looked at his hands, spread out in front of him, fingers wide apart, the thick and short hands of a peasant. What he said I will never forget. He said: 'I wear no rings, you see. It will not happen to me.' " In April 1945, a deposed Mussolini attempted to flee Italy across the Austrian border disguised as a German soldier; he was recognized and summarily executed, and his body, hung by its heels, was put on public display.

†The statue now in place is a copy. The famous original survived the vicissitudes of time and history for eighteen centuries — it escaped being melted down during the Middle Ages because it was thought to be a statue of Constantine, the first Christian emperor — but in recent decades Rome's acid-air pollution began to take a deadly toll. The statue was therefore removed and restored, and is now on display in a newly opened wing of the Capitoline Museums, in the identical pair of buildings that flank the square.

republican self-government, and the Palazzo dei Conservatori, a fifteenth-century meeting hall for city magistrates).

Stylistically, the buildings were chaotic, and their placement around the central space was haphazard: the façades of the two palazzi formed an awkward 80-degree angle as they faced the square, while the façade of the church — a short distance away on the north peak — did not face the square at all. Moreover, the renovation problems were formidable. All the buildings were still in use and funds for rebuilding were limited, so any new scheme had to leave the existing structures intact and allow for their continued use during remodeling. Finally, the site lacked paved access from the northwest, which isolated it from the working city.

Recognizing the difficulties these problems presented, Pope Paul called in Michelangelo. Sixty-two years old and turning his hand to Roman architecture for the first time, the sculptor took this jumble of leftovers and constraints and produced Rome's first true modern piazza.

(Top) *The Campidoglio around 1555, with the statue of Marcus Aurelius and the new Palazzo del Senatore staircase already in place;* (Bottom) *Michelangelo's design before modifications by Della Porta (the positioning of the side palaces has been distorted by the artist — canted outward rather than inward — so as to make the façades visible in the drawing).*

Michelangelo's basic idea was revolutionary. Up to that time, Renaissance architecture had been very much a matter of single, isolated buildings. Occasionally several important structures were purposely placed around a central open space, but the aim was to display each individual building to maximum advantage, not to relate it to its neighbors and create an aesthetically unified whole. Michelangelo's concept of a building ensemble — an outdoor interior, as it were, where the exterior walls of a group of buildings shape an outdoor space the way interior walls shape a room — was utterly new.

The details of Michelangelo's design were every bit as revolutionary as its underlying idea. Ignoring the pervasive Renaissance belief that the circle and the square were the most philosophically "perfect" and therefore the most aesthetically pleasing geometric forms, Michelangelo took as his ruling ground-plan shapes a trapezoid (the area enclosed by the building's façades and the balustrade at the top of the approach ramp) and an oval (the area delimited by steps set into the ground around the central statue). Moreover, he used these forms in a way that earlier Renaissance architects would probably have deplored: despite their disparate shapes, he placed the one inside the other and — more important — he gave each its own separate focal point. In so doing, he rejected the traditional central, single-point focus that had been the obsession of Renaissance vision ever since the invention of one-point perspective in painting.

The first focal point (and the most obvious to anyone approaching the square up Michelangelo's long, sloping *cordonata*) is the façade of the Palazzo del Senatore. To emphasize it as the dominant side of his trapezoid, Michelangelo redesigned the façade and moved the building's existing bell tower from off-center-left to the building's center, directly over the main doorway and in line with the *cordonata*. To deemphasize the Palazzo dei Conservatori on the right, he gave it a new façade; though similar in many details to the façade of the Palazzo del Senatore, the new design employed a ground-floor portico to hide the building's main doorway in deep shadow so its entrance would not compete with the Palazzo del Senatore.

To complete the trapezoid, Michelangelo placed an entirely new building opposite the Palazzo dei Conservatori. The purpose of this new structure was purely aesthetic: to hide the side of S. Maria in Aracoeli and to supply the Palazzo dei Conservatori with a mirror-image twin. The new building had no practical function and was only one room deep (the small Capitoline Museum courtyard behind it today is a much later addition). Michelangelo never even gave it a name, and to this day it is known only as the "Palazzo Nuovo" — the new palazzo. Its lack of function notwithstanding, it is a critical element in the trapezoidal composition, for when entering the square from the *cordonata,* the two identical façades function as an extension of the approach ramp, opening out to focus attention firmly on the Palazzo del Senatore.

The second focal point is the statue of Marcus Aurelius in the middle of the square. The statue is set in the center of its own spatial composition: the oval within the trapezoid. The shallow steps that define the oval serve two purposes: they give the oval a strong border by impressing the shape into the ground, and they highlight the statue by allowing the ground to rise back to its original level as it approaches the statue. Inside the oval, the pavement is decorated with an elegant curvilinear grid; the grid's lines become tighter and narrower toward the center, where they reach their point of origin, a twelve-pointed star surrounding the statue's pedestal (which Michelangelo himself designed). As with the Palazzo Nuovo, the oval's steps and decorative pavement have no practical purpose; they merely serve to give the statue an architectural framework of its own — to expand the oval space commanded by the statue so that it is commensurate with the trapezoidal space created by the buildings.

The use of two focal points creates a tension — where does the eye settle to rest? — that pervades the entire piazza. Where the eye is drawn when first entering the square depends upon which entrance is used: from the main entrance, the façade of the Palazzo del Senatore will dominate; from the side entrances, the statue of Marcus Aurelius. Once inside the piazza, however, the relative weight of the focal points will vary as the viewer moves around the square. Yet no matter what the vantage point, the competition between statue and façade is never lopsided, never unbalanced; no matter where the viewer stands, the one is never overwhelmed by the other. It is a superb spatial juggling act.

Michelangelo's radical architectural thesis — that tension is not incompatible with balance — was by no means limited to multistructure compositions. He applied it to single buildings as well. The matching façades of the side palaces, for instance, employ the Classical vocabulary in a double-edged way that was distinctly unconventional. To Michelangelo's eye, Rome's most important Renaissance palazzi probably looked ponderous and overbearing, weighted down by the excessive horizontality produced by their long, tiered rows of regularly placed windows. To counterweight his own design's horizontal elements, he introduced something rarely seen before in Rome: giant pilasters that cut cleanly through the ground-floor entablature and soar straight up to the building's cornice. Earlier architects had experimented with giant pilasters, but the resulting mix of scales — two-story pilasters next to one-story columns — tended to look chaotic, almost as if the parts of two different-sized buildings had been combined willy-nilly. Michelangelo succeeded in combining these apparently disparate elements in a way that appears orderly and logical; indeed, his giant pilasters are a key feature of the design, for they give his façade the strong vertical emphasis that earlier façades lack. And again, a double focus results. It is possible to read the façade in the traditional way, as a composition of three dissimilar horizontals (open ground floor, closed upper floor, cornice), but it is also possible to read it in the opposite way, as seven similar two-story verticals (the bays delimited by the eight pilasters). Paradoxically, this duality increases rather than decreases the façade's overall unity, for it locks all the elements together, and what would otherwise be a sedate arrangement of static horizontals becomes a far more powerful latticework of crisscrossed horizontals and verticals.

As a closer look at the giant pilasters reveals, Michelangelo modeled that latticework with special care. The pilasters (as James Ackerman points out in *The Architecture of Michelangelo*) depart from prevailing convention in a subtle but critical way. Rather than being set directly into the wall, they are set into slightly wider piers, which are in turn set into the wall behind. This small but crucial adjustment — a tiny extra step forward from the underlying wall — produces an increase in slimness and relief that gives the pilasters both added elegance and added power. As a result, the pilasters possess a special (and unprecedented) sculptural presence, a presence that was shortly to become one of the defining characteristics of the new Baroque style in architecture.

With the façade of the central Palazzo del Senatore, Michelangelo faced an added problem: how to relate the three-story building in the center of the composition to the two two-story buildings on either side. His solution was typically ingenious: he hid the building's ground floor behind a double staircase running most of the length of the building. The staircase is a visual masterstroke, for it transforms a three-story building into a two-story building raised on a podium and thereby allows the use of two-story giant pilasters on the rest of the façade, just as on the side palaces. Moreover, the staircase itself serves to tie the three buildings together, for its two wings seem to reach out to the side palaces like outspread arms.

Michelangelo's unconventional use of geometric forms and Classical detailing ran counter to most of the accepted theory of the High Renaissance, which sought to revive and improve upon the architecture of ancient Rome as outlined in the newly rediscovered writings of the ancient architect

Vitruvius. But the goal of historical and philosophical correctitude, with its rigorous rules and regulations governing the use of the Classical orders, meant little to Michelangelo. His vision was ruled by something else entirely: his sculptor's eye. With his architecture, the question, "Is it correct?" was overruled, for the first time, by the question, "How does it look?" This was a radical shift in emphasis — a shift that signaled the end of the Renaissance era in architecture. As Michelangelo's compatriot (and biographer) Giorgio Vasari stated, "He proceeded quite differently in proportion, composition, and rules from what others had done . . . whence artisans have been infinitely and perpetually indebted to him because he broke the bonds and chains of a way of working that had become habitual by common usage."

When Michelangelo died in 1564, construction of the Campidoglio was far from complete, and his successor architect, Giacomo della Porta, changed the design in two significant ways. First, he altered Michelangelo's side-palace window scheme by redesigning and enlarging each palace's central window, giving the façades a central focus. The windows themselves are far from displeasing, but their impact on the façades is unfortunate: they effectively punch a large hole into the middle of Michelangelo's carefully constructed network of balanced verticals and horizontals. Second, Della Porta radically altered the design for the façade of the Palazzo del Senatore. Michelangelo's scheme called for an upper story that was almost identical to the upper stories of the side palaces; Della Porta substituted a simple row of plain, small, rectangular windows placed high on the façade. The new window design created an awkward empty space below, which Della Porta partially filled with a decorative plaque and two carved crests. Michelangelo's design, by contrast, employed no such decoration because it contained no such awkward empty space. Happily, Della Porta's modifications are not critical to the overall effect of the piazza. But the familial likeness between the Palazzo del Senatore and the two side palaces is considerably reduced — the twins' older brother, as it were, is now merely a distant cousin.*

When it was built, the Campidoglio was an unprecedented architectural *tour de force*, and it remains one of Western architecture's greatest urban set pieces to this day. And from a historical point of view, Michelangelo's

---

*Other departures from Michelangelo's design: the Palazzo del Senatore's single-story campanile set on a rusticated pedestal (an echo of the façade design) was redesigned by Martino Longhi when it was finally constructed in 1583; the one-story baldacchino at the top of the Palazzo del Senatore stairs — a sort of *porte-cochère* for pedestrians — was never built; the complicated curvilinear grid set into the piazza paving was rejected in favor of a much simpler radial (wheel-spoke) pattern. The piazza paving was relaid and Michelangelo's grid restored in 1940.

two-fold achievement is unique. With his overall plan, he created Europe's first aesthetically unified multistructured urban enclosure; with his innovative use of Classical detail, he overthrew the "objective" dictates of Renaissance architectural theory in favor of the subjective vision of his artist's eye. He broke through to a new vision on two artistic fronts at the same time, and he became, as a result, the father of both modern city planning and the Baroque style of architecture.

Interior Museums: The museums in the two buildings flanking the Campidoglio (one entrance ticket for both) are among the finest in the city, and can make a fair claim to being the oldest public museums in Europe, if not the entire world (they date back to 1471, when Pope Sixtus IV donated a collection of antique bronzes to the people of Rome and put them on display here). The Palazzo Nuovo (on the left at the top of the *cordonata*) is devoted entirely to antiquities; the larger Palazzo dei Conservatori (on the right) contains both antiquities and a fine collection of paintings, including notable works by Bellini, Titian, Tintoretto, Veronese, Caravaggio (*St. John the Baptist*), Rubens, Guercino (the vast *St. Petronilla*, formerly in St. Peter's), and Van Dyck, among others. The highlight is perhaps the roomful of busts of the Caesars (in the Palazzo Nuovo), some of which are far from flattering: Caracalla's infamous thuggishness and Heliogabalus's infamous nastiness ("to confound the order of seasons and climates, to sport with the passions and prejudices of his subjects, and to subvert every law of nature and decency, were in the number of his most delicious amusements," says Gibbon) are abundantly apparent. Other notable antiquities include Marforio (a giant river god reclining in the Palazzo Nuovo courtyard), two superb small mosaics (one of doves and the other of theatrical masks), the famous Capitoline *Venus,* the *Satyr Resting* (the statue that inspired Nathaniel Hawthorne's novel *The Marble Faun*), and the *Dying Gaul* (all in the Palazzo Nuovo), plus the *Spinario (Boy with Thorn,* one of the most engaging depictions of innocent self-absorption ever created) and the *She-Wolf of Rome* (both in the Palazzo dei Conservatori).

1-9 ROOFTOP VILLAGE

The full, formal splendor of the Campidoglio is best experienced at the top of the *cordonata,* where all the compositional elements can be taken in at once. One special feature of the view, however, is not immediately apparent.

A literal turnabout is required: when standing at the top of the staircase facing the Palazzo del Senatore, turn around and look across the street.

Atop the building opposite, some forgotten architect (builder? owner?) has transformed a chaotic cluster of utilitarian chimneys into a miniature hilltop village. Amid the grandeur of the Campidoglio, the sight is completely unexpected, and the surprise is wholly captivating. In most settings such a conceit would be little more than a gracious urban pleasantry, but placed just here — set apart from the Campidoglio by nothing more than an intervening void — the gesture produces one of the most unusual and unexpected architectural dialogues in the entire city. All sorts of fundamental architectural oppositions suddenly snap into focus: Renaissance vs. Medieval, Classical vs. picturesque, order vs. disorder, function vs. decoration, noble vs. humble. Compared to the grand declamation of the Campidoglio, the voice of the rooftop village is the merest of whispers, but its beguiling message — "this, too, is architecture" — is at this particular spot especially appropriate and especially welcome.

1-10 SANTA MARIA IN ARACOELI
Thirteenth century
(North peak of the Capitoline Hill, accessible from the Campidoglio through the church's side entrance behind the Palazzo Nuovo)

On October 15, 1764, Edward Gibbon was sitting in the church of S. Maria in Aracoeli listening to the friars sing vespers when he was unexpectedly inspired (as the ancient Romans might have put it) by Clio, the muse of history. Some twenty-three years later he finished writing what is perhaps the most famous historical treatise ever published: the vast 3,000-page *History of the Decline and Fall of the Roman Empire*.

The site of Gibbon's inspiration is splendidly apt, for if any church in Rome can stand as a metaphor for the city itself — a reflection of all the city's myriad past glories and ignominies — it is S. Maria in Aracoeli. Like the city, the church's origins are lost in legend, and (also like the city) the church is an artistic and architectural potpourri, full of poignant bits and pieces left behind by time and history. The façade was never finished, and the interior, by any conventional aesthetic standard, is far too haphazard and jumbled to be considered important. But S. Maria in Aracoeli wears its motley dress with remarkable dignity, and its interior possesses an aura of venerable old age — of history endured and survived — that sets it apart from its more architecturally polished Renaissance and Baroque successors.

Situated on the north peak of the Capitoline Hill, the church occupies the site of the ancient Temple of Juno Moneta — the Roman mint. It was here, according to legend, that the Roman sibyl foretold the coming of Christ to the emperor Augustus, who was granted a heavenly vision of the Virgin Mary standing on an altar holding the Christ child. Augustus supposedly built an altar on the spot — the altar of heaven, or *ara coeli* — and the church rose around it. The original structure cannot possibly date from the time of Augustus (Rome did not become officially Christian until the fourth century), but by the sixth century the existing church was already considered old. The present structure dates from the thirteenth century, when its predecessor was completely rebuilt.

The interior's most ancient feature is the set of columns on either side of the nave. As in so many medieval churches, S. Maria in Aracoeli's nave supports were mostly scavenged from deteriorating Roman buildings; one of the columns — the third on the left, inscribed with the words "a cubicolo Augustorum" — may even have come from the Imperial Palace on the Palatine. (The column capitals are remarkably varied, and will repay study; anyone who thinks that Roman capital decoration was rigidly confined to the canonical Doric, Ionic, and Corinthian designs is in for a shock.)

Next oldest are the floors. The decorative marble patterns were meticulously laid out by the Cosmati, an extended family — in fact several families — of marble workers active in Rome between 1100 and 1300. The Cosmati's distinctive geometric designs will appear relatively primitive to the modern eye, but in their day they caused a sensation, and the renown of the Cosmati eventually became so great that in 1268 they were summoned to London by England's King Henry III to work in Westminster Abbey. As might be expected, Cosmatesque marble work turns up in many of Rome's older churches; the most intricate floor designs here are located at the right-hand side of the crossing (near the right-hand *ambo* — staired lectern — which is also inlaid with Cosmatesque decoration and dates from the same period).

The church's side chapels vary widely in date and style. When viewed individually, only the first chapel on the right stands out, and its unusual beauty is artistic (the Pinturicchio frescoes) rather than architectural. But four of the chapels off the right-hand aisle, when viewed as a group, offer a timely object lesson in the history of architectural style. Nowhere else in Rome can the progression from Gothic to Renaissance to Baroque be seen with such succinct clarity.

The oldest chapel is the seventh toward the altar (the Cappella di S. Diego d'Alcala); the Gothic tradition is clearly evident in the architectural skeleton of the ceiling, with its pointed arches and ribbed vault. At the fifteenth-century Cappella del Crocifisso (three chapels away toward the main entrance door), the Gothic style is on the wane; the vault is still ribbed but less steep, and the side arches approach a true semicircle. In the sixteenth-century Cappella di S. Matteo (next toward the altar), the Renaissance has arrived; the vault has become a hemispherical dome, unribbed, and the Renaissance obsession with "perfect" shapes — squares, circles, cubes, spheres — can be seen on all sides. Finally, the seventeenth-century Cappella di S. Pietro d'Alcantara (next toward the altar) bursts out in full Baroque flower. Much of the Renaissance geometry from next door is retained, but the chapel's architectural elements are broken up and overlaid with exuberantly theatrical sculpture and decoration.

The nave ceiling dates from 1575, and its central Madonna and Child suggest a conventionally religious decorative scheme full of gentle piety. But the rest of the composition, with its unusual and unexpected collection of naval motifs, is anything but gentle in its meaning. In fact, the ceiling is a war trophy. It was constructed to celebrate the papal victory at the Battle of Lepanto in 1571 (when a fleet of allied papal, Venetian, and Spanish ships repelled an Ottoman Turk invasion of the Venetian island of Cyprus), and it was meant to be read — Madonna and Child notwithstanding — as a bellicose architectural manifestation of the Church Militant and Triumphant.

The stained-glass window on the entrance wall displays an even more curious motif: bees. Such decorative bees are far from unusual in Rome; they can be found all over the city, and the game of searching them out in unexpected places has become something of a tradition among historical-minded (and eagle-eyed) sightseers. They date from the seventeenth-century heyday of the powerful Barberini family, when Cardinal Maffeo Barberini was elected Pope Urban VIII (1623–1644) and became, famously, the foremost patron of the most versatile artistic genius of the entire Baroque era, the great Gianlorenzo Bernini. The bee was the Barberini family emblem, and its presence at a fountain or on a building or in a painting is a sure sign of Barberini largesse and patronage.

Notable Works of Art: In addition to the Pinturicchio frescoes illustrating the life of St. Bernardine (ca. 1486, in the first chapel on the right), two works of art stand out: the tomb of the twelfth-century senator Luca Savelli, attributed to Arnolfo di Cambio and incorporating as a base a third-century pagan sarcophagus (set into the left wall of the right transept), and the Temple of St. Helena, a seventeeth-century shrine in the center of the left transept that incorporates a medieval altar picturing the apparition of the Virgin to Augustus (visible below the shrine on the side facing the crossing).

Off the right wall of the left transept is the Chapel of the Santissimo Bambino, erstwhile home to a much-revered doll-sized figure of the infant Christ, said to have been carved from the wood of an olive tree in the Garden of Gethsemane. The world-famous figure — letters have arrived addressed simply to "Il Bambino, Rome" — was long thought to possess miraculous healing powers, and was formerly a regular visitor to the hospitals of Rome. It was stolen in 1994 (not for the first time), and has been replaced by a copy.

1-11 VIEW OF THE ROMAN FORUM
(One block southeast of the Campidoglio; when facing the double staircase of the Palazzo del Senatore, follow the street that exits the square to the palazzo's right)

View of the Roman Forum before modern excavations, with the Arch of Septimius Severus at the right and the columns of the Temple of Saturn in the left center.

On its southeast side the Capitoline Hill drops off sharply, forming a bluff that overlooks the Roman Forum. The view is justly famous, and unforgettable.*

---

*Slightly to the west, overlooking the backwater Piazza della Consolazione, is the probable location of a second and equally famous bluff: the Tarpeian Rock, from which traitors were hurled to their deaths during Republican times. The modern cliff face is worth a look from below; the unpretentious beauty of its plantings (which soften a terraced retaining wall that is all sharp crazy angles and cubist dislocations) put the aesthetic tub-thumping of the Victor Emmanuel Monument to shame.

The ruins of the Forum are perhaps Rome's greatest treasure; among Rome's European rivals only Athens, with its revered Acropolis, can claim a comparable monument. In her memoir *Rome and a Villa,* Eleanor Clark called it "a lake of time" — a vast historical oasis that stands apart in the heart of the city as an extraordinary memorial to a lost and glorious past. Its importance as a civic and ceremonial center ended more than fifteen centuries ago; during the thousand years of Rome's decline it was abandoned and silted in, and even as late as the nineteenth century cows grazed in its grassy rubble-strewn fields. Today most of it is excavated down to its Imperial level, and the route followed by the Roman conquerors on their stately progress up the Via Sacra toward the Capitoline can once again be traced.

The famous triumphal processions approached the Forum from the Colosseum (visible in the distance beyond the white façade and brown tower of S. Maria Novella), passed over the crest of the hill topped by the Arch of Titus (to the right of S. Maria Novella), veered slightly to the left at the bottom of the hill, and passed up the middle of the Forum; at the near end the processions turned left after passing the portico of the Temple of Saturn, with its eight tall columns, and wound their way up the face of the Capitoline Hill to the Temple of Jupiter, located on the west peak of the Capitoline where the Palazzo dei Conservatori now stands.

Gibbon, in his *Decline and Fall of the Roman Empire,* gives a detailed description of one such triumph, awarded to the emperor Aurelian in 274 C.E. in celebration of his victory over the forces of the rebellious Zenobia, Queen of Syria:

> Since the foundation of Rome no general had more nobly deserved a triumph than Aurelian; nor was a triumph ever celebrated with superior pride and magnificence. The pomp was opened by twenty elephants, four royal tigers, and above two hundred of the most curious animals from every climate of the North, the East, and the South. They were followed by sixteen hundred gladiators, devoted to the cruel amusement of the amphitheater. The wealth of Asia, the arms and ensigns of so many conquered nations, and the magnificent plate and wardrobe of the Syrian queen, were disposed in exact symmetry or artful disorder. The ambassadors of the most remote parts of all the earth, of Ethopia, Arabia, Persia, Bactriana, India, and China, all remarkable by their rich or singular dresses, displayed the fame and power of the Roman emperor, who exposed likewise to the public view the presents that he had received, and particularly a great number of crowns of gold,

the offerings of grateful cities. The victories of Aurelian were attested by the long train of captives who reluctantly attended his triumph — Goths, Vandals, Sarmatians, Alemanni, Franks, Gauls, Syrians, and Egyptians. Each people was distinguished by its peculiar inscription, and the title of Amazons was bestowed on ten martial heroines of the Gothic nation who had been taken in arms. But every eye, disregarding the crowd of captives, was fixed on ... the queen of the East. ... The beauteous figure of Zenobia was confined by fetters of gold; a slave supported the gold chain which encircled her neck, and she almost fainted under the intolerable weight of jewels. She preceded on foot the magnificent chariot in which she once hoped to enter the gates of Rome. ... The triumphal car of Aurelian (it had formerly been used by a Gothic king) was drawn, on this memorable occasion, either by four stags or by four elephants. The most illustrious of the senate, the people, and the army closed the solemn procession. Unfeigned joy, wonder, and gratitude swelled the acclamations of the multitude. ... So long and so various was the pomp of Aurelian's triumph, that, although it opened with the dawn of day, the slow majesty of the procession ascended not the Capitol before the ninth hour; and it was already dark when the emperor returned to the palace.

By the time of Aurelian's triumph, the use of the Forum had become mainly social; its role as the seat of Roman government ended with the Republic in the first century B.C.E., when power passed irrevocably into the hands of the Caesars. But its ceremonial importance endured. It was the acknowledged hub of the city — the nucleus around which first the Roman metropolis and then the Roman Empire had grown — and it remained, as it remains today, the symbolic center of all things Roman.

TOUR 2

— • —

OLD ROME I:
THE CAMPUS MARTIUS (NORTHEAST)
FROM THE PIAZZA VENEZIA TO THE PANTHEON

Il Panteon di Agrippa, è via la Chiesa di S. Maria della Rotonda 2 Fontana con Obelisco di Granito di Egitto 3 Palazzo Crescenzi.

Piazza della Rotonda.

*T*HE COURSE OF the Tiber River changes directions several times as it passes through downtown Rome, and as it happens those shifts are marked by antiquities: the Tomb of Augustus at the point where the river bends to the west, the Tomb of Hadrian (the Castel S. Angelo) just before the second bend back to the southeast, and the Theater of Marcellus at the final bend to the southwest. The area thus encompassed — basically delimited by the Via del Corso to the east and the river to the west — is sometimes called *Tiber Bend.* But more commonly it is known by its antique name, the *Campus Martius* (in modern Italian *Campo Marzio,* in English *Field of Mars*), after the Roman god of war, whose favor was invoked because the area's open fields were the site of regular military exercises in the city's early days.

The Campus Martius was outside the walls that enclosed the Seven Hills during Republican Times; in addition to serving as a military training ground, it was the site of public town meetings and (once every five years) the city census taking. Intensive urban development arrived late — not until the Imperial era — but ultimately the entire area was built up so thickly that it was possible to walk from one end to the other under covered porticoes. The buildings were almost exclusively public, including temples, baths, theaters, a stadium, an odeon (outdoor concert hall), a water reservoir, and a huge obelisk-centered sundial. Despite the area's urbanization, however, the city's center remained to the east, in the complex of forums just to the north of the central Palatine Hill. The public buildings of the Campus Martius were secondary, and were not enclosed within the city defenses until the construction of the Aurelian walls in 271–275 C.E.

During the Middle Ages, when the destruction of the aqueducts forced the populace to abandon the hills, the Campus Martius grew in population as the rest of the city shrank (ultimately the total population of the city decreased to fewer than 20,000 inhabitants in the fourteenth century, from a peak that may have reached 1.5 million at the height of the Imperial era). Throughout the long thousand-year decline, however, the Campus Martius remained continually inhabited, and when the city finally began to revive during the Renaissance, the area became the nucleus around which the modern city grew. As a result, its present-day character is defined by a unique mixture of urban elements: a substructure (sometimes visible) of ancient ruins overlaid by a medieval street pattern that is dotted with Renaissance and Baroque buildings. It is a heady mixture that no other city in Europe can match.

Because the Campus Martius is so densely packed with important sites and buildings, it requires three separate walking tours, the last two of which start where their predecessors leave off. The first tour begins with the Gesù (the mother church of the Jesuit Order, two blocks west of the Piazza Venezia), and the last tour ends with the Jewish Ghetto, just a few blocks to the south of the starting point. Connecting those two sites is a great counterclockwise circuit that covers the entire Tiber Bend area — the "old Rome" section of the modern metropolis, where the city's long and varied architectural history is most richly on display.

The Campus Martius's most celebrated building is undoubtedly the Pantheon, built as a temple to all the gods. As a Classical survivor — it is almost two thousand years old — it is second only to Athens's Parthenon in architectural importance, and (unlike the Parthenon) it remains entirely intact. The previous engraving depicts both the temple and its forecourt piazza (created in 1711, when Pope Clement XI cleared the area and ordered construction of a new fountain centerpiece). It also depicts an anomaly that is no longer to be seen: the distinctly non-Classical twin bell towers that top the entrance portico. Needless to say, they were not original to the building. They were added during a restoration under Pope Urban VIII that began in 1626, and they later became known as "Bernini's ass's-ears" (an unwarranted slur, since they were probably designed by Carlo Maderno, and Bernini is known to have been critical of them). They were removed during the restoration of 1882.

2-1   IL GESÙ
Body and interior: Giacomo da Vignola, 1568–1584
Façade: Giacomo della Porta, 1575
(Piazza del Gesù, west of the Piazza Venezia)

The Gesù is one of Rome's best-known churches, but it is not what it might have been, or once was. Bad luck and the vagaries of taste intervened, and the original architect's plans were severely compromised, both outside and in. Still, the Gesù's influence on future church architecture was immense, for it offered definitive solutions to the two main problems of Renaissance church design: how to adapt the time-honored cross-shaped ground plan to the needs of the newly revised Counter-Reformation liturgical service, and how to employ the Classical vocabulary on the façade.

The ground plan was the result of a close collaboration between architect Giacomo da Vignola and Cardinal Alessandro Farnese, who was financing the church's construction. Farnese knew what he wanted. As the mother church of the burgeoning Society of Jesus — and as a potential model for new Jesuit churches around the world — the Gesù had to be large and imposing. Moreover, it had to be functional in a new way that required radical changes in traditional design. The reforms of the Council of Trent, concluded in 1563, had introduced a new emphasis on liturgical sermons preached to large congregations, but the most common longitudinal Renaissance church ground plan — a Latin cross, with aisles on either side of the nave and a chancel and transepts of equal size — was neither visually nor acoustically suited to such preaching. Yet the Latin cross plan could not be ignored entirely, since its symbolic significance as a reminder of the crucifixion of Christ made it far too important to reject. A classic architectural dilemma resulted: form was at war with function.

Vignola's solution to the problem was highly ingenious. He truncated the transepts, widened the nave, and replaced the side aisles with a series of small chapels. The result is very nearly a simple rectangle with a semicircular apse attached to one end. But the Latin cross shape is retained: it is now *inside* the rectangular building shell, abutted and defined by the side chapels, which fill in the leftover space. Traditional form is thus preserved, while function is improved on all counts: the lack of side aisles increases audibility, the truncated transepts increase visibility, and the widened nave increases congregation space. Moreover, the high dome over the crossing allows a flood of light to fall on the apse and transepts, intensifying the visual impact of the altars.

In designing the façade, Vignola faced a different kind of problem. Renaissance taste prescribed the architectural vocabulary: columns (or pilasters), entablatures, and pediments, as in the Roman temples of old. But the overall shape of the façade raised a difficult question. Given its central nave and side aisles, the prototypical Christian church possessed an exterior front wall that was high in the middle and low over the sides, with sloped roofs over the sides to boot. How could the ancient Classical orders — so pleasingly regular on the uniformly curved exteriors of the Colosseum and the nearby Theater of Marcellus — be arrayed across such an irregularly shaped surface?

Renaissance architects had been wrestling with this problem for a hundred years, but no consensus had emerged. Vignola's solution — known only from drawings (see next page), since it was never carried out — was inspired. He hid the side roofs behind statuary pedestals, and then continued the pedestals across the center of the façade, where they support the upper-story pilasters. The pedestals are a critical element in the overall design, for they supply extra space between the upper-story and lower-story pilasters, and thereby allow for the insertion of a strong focal centerpiece — a secondary curved pediment over the central door that echoes the primary triangular pediment at the façade's peak.

In the hands of a lesser architect, such pedestals might have been mere space fillers, but Vignola ties them inseparably to the other façade elements. At either end they read as a visual continuation of the ground-floor pilasters; in the center they become part of the upper-floor composition. Thus they serve to unify rather than disrupt the overall design, and the awkward sloped side roofs are completely disguised.

Vignola's unbuilt design for the Gesù façade.

Vignola's plan for the façade was to become one of the most widely copied designs of all time, but apparently it did not appeal to Farnese. He rejected it and turned the project over to Giacomo della Porta. It is Della Porta's design, not Vignola's, that was finally constructed.

It is difficult to see it as an improvement. The revised design is unquestionably more in keeping with the Renaissance taste for clarity of organization (Della Porta's pilasters are clearly and unambiguously paired, whereas Vignola's can be read as either single and unevenly spaced or double and evenly spaced). But in eliminating Vignola's outer upper-story pedestals and replacing Vignola's statuary with a ponderous pair of decorative scrolls, Della Porta diminishes the visual connection between the upper and lower stories. Moreover, the elimination of Vignola's ground-floor niches produces an increase in the amount of blank wall surface on the façade, and Della Porta's new double pediment over the central door looks both out of scale with the main pediment above and disconnected from the columns and pilasters below (which should visually support it). As a result, the façade as a whole has a patchwork look to it, as if the pilasters and pediment were merely pasted onto the wall behind. When compared with Vignola's façade — in which the Classical elements themselves dominate, with the wall merely filling in — it looks clumsy and inert.*

Inside, the decoration is also not as Vignola planned. When it was first built, the interior was quite plain, in keeping with the Counter-Reformation's spirit of religious asceticism. But the fashion for austerity eventually passed, replaced by a passion for decorative resplendence meant to reflect the riches of God's heavenly kingdom. Embellishment of the interior began with the chapels in 1584 and ended with the marbling of the nave pilasters in 1858 — a relentless three-hundred-year onslaught seemingly bent on decorating the place to death. The welter of haphazard ornamentation drains all strength from the interior's architectural elements, and everything mixes and merges and blends until the walls become merely an undifferentiated shell encrusted with suffocating decorative barnacles. Even Andrea Pozzo's imposing monument to S. Ignatius in the left transept loses its impact, and what might in another setting emerge as a tightly controlled *tour de force* here seems just another exhausting exercise in Baroque overkill.

The frescoed ceilings, too, deserve a less competitive environment. Painted between 1672 and 1683 by Giovanni Battista Gaulli, known as Baciccio, they are among the most dramatic in the city — a full-blown Baroque response to Michelangelo's famous frescoes in the Sistine Chapel across town. The nave ceiling, especially, combines architectural, sculptural, and painterly elements with great assurance and ingenuity. The subject

---

*Many (perhaps most) critics do not prefer Vignola's façade to Della Porta's. The opposing point of view is summarized by James Ackerman in his essay "The Gesù in the Light of Contemporary Church Design," in which he criticizes Vignola's design as "an intricate, even ambiguous interplay of forms that lacks the cohesion of the inspired plan [of the interior]." Comparing the two designs, Ackerman sees Della Porta's façade as "brilliantly knit together in a fashion which focuses attention at the center in a dramatic way. While Vignola's suggests a rectangular center with subsidiary wings, Della Porta's creates a crescendo, accentuating the main portal by the invention of a pediment within a pediment, and, by drawing all the niches into the central area, leaving the outer wings bare. His volutes [scrolls], moreover, softly link the two stories and emphasize their oneness."

("The Adoration of the Name of Jesus") might seem a dry and unpromising theme, but Baciccio has here created a variation on the traditional Last Judgment that pulls out all the Baroque stops. Refusing to be contained by its gilded framing medallion, the fresco bursts out to obliterate the surrounding architecture in three separate places: on the two sides, where the saved ascend to heaven in triumph, and at the crossing end, where the damned tumble down in agony. These potentially disruptive explosions are visually counterbalanced by the eccentric placement of the fresco's main focal point — the lambent void of light containing the glowing letters "IHS"* — which is positioned off-center within the fresco's frame. The end result is paradigmatically Baroque both in its flamboyance and its formal control, achieving a balanced effect while rejecting symmetrical design.

2-2   PALAZZO ALTIERI
Façade: Giovanni Antonio de' Rossi, ca. 1670
(Across the Via del Plebiscito from and at a right angle to the Gesù façade)

Late seventeenth century, despite appearances. Giovanni Antonio de' Rossi, the designer of the Palazzo Altieri façade, was capable of designing in a flamboyant mode — his altar niche for the Lancellotti Chapel in S. Giovanni in Laterano is thoroughly Baroque in style — but his façade here is one of the most conservative works of its era. In its stripped-down simplicity, it barely acknowledges the developments that had dominated Roman architecture since the early 1600s; only the scrolls, shells, and stars that decorate the overhanging cornice suggest the freedom of invention typical of the Baroque.

The ground floor is notable for a structural oddity that de' Rossi must have found irksome in the extreme. He was hired by the Altieri family to enlarge the existing palazzo and to design a new façade in 1670, immediately following the election of Cardinal Emilio Altieri as Pope Clement X. But when the necessary adjacent land was acquired, one neighbor refused to sell: an elderly woman whose little house was located just at the point where the palazzo façade makes a slight angle to follow the line of the Via

---

*The first three letters of the name "Jesus" in Greek, which the Jesuits adopted as their symbolic device. The letters are often (but erroneously) thought to refer to the religious conversion of Constantine the Great, who on the eve of military victory over his rival Maxentius in 312 C.E. supposedly beheld the vision of a cross in the sky bearing the legend *In Hoc Signo Vinces* — "By This Sign You Shall Conquer." As the Gesù's interior was first being decorated, its unprecedented richness caused the Grand Duke of Tuscany to suggest that the letters in fact stood for *Iesuiti Habent Satis* — "The Jesuits Have Enough."

del Plebiscito. The Pope, who was scandalized by the amount of money his relatives were spending on the expansion, refused to intervene. So the old woman and her house remained, swallowed up by the enlarged palazzo on all sides. The remnants of her windows can still be seen, punching incongruous holes through the façade wall above the third and fourth windows to the right of the main entrance.

2-3   PALAZZO ODESCALCHI
Façade: 1887
(Via del Corso 260–269, north of the Piazza Venezia)

PALAZZO DORIA-PAMPHILI
Façade: Gabriele Valvassori, 1731–1734
(Via del Corso 303–305, north of the Piazza Venezia)

The Corso façade of the Palazzo Odescalchi was built in 1887, but it derives from fifteenth-century models and reasonably approximates the look of Italy's earliest full-blown Renaissance palazzi, constructed in Florence during the mid-1400s. The façade of Palazzo Doria-Pamphili across the street was built in the mid-1700s, at the tail end of the Baroque era. The contrast between the two points show both how much and how little Roman palazzo façade design changed over the course of three hundred years.

The underlying principles changed very little. The archetypal façade is organized as a series of horizontals laid on top of one another without interacting; the bottom floor is the heaviest, and the upper stories decrease in visual weight as they ascend. Each window, no matter how elaborate its decoration, remains isolated from its neighbor, and the rows of windows are arrayed with military precision, as if standing at attention for parade review. In Rome, this design derives from the monumental Palazzo Farnese (begun in 1516), an architectural prototype that was so forceful in its effect that Roman palazzo design never fully emerged from its shadow, the occasional innovations of visionary architects like Michelangelo and Borromini notwithstanding.

If the organizational schemes of the two façades are similar, the decorative details clearly are not. Over the course of three hundred years, solemnity gave way to high-spirited invention, and architects all over Europe began to create decorative motifs of their own that departed dramatically from Classical models. Northern European architects reveled in the challenge, but most Roman architects, perhaps inhibited by the remains of antiquity to be seen on all sides, never went so far as their German and Austrian contemporaries. Valvassori's decoration for the Palazzo Doria-Pamphili is about as uninhibited as Roman palazzo embellishment ever got, and it cannot exactly be described as licentious. It is usually characterized as Rococo, but the term "Rococo" conjures up so many connotations of lightness and grace and verve and vivacity — all the qualities Roman palazzo design so emphatically lacks — that the use of the term here seems downright perverse. Better to characterize the Palazzo Doria-Pamphili façade as late Baroque (or, as the Italians do, *Barocchetto*); there is, alas, no real Rococo architecture in Rome, and very little Rococo interior decoration.

Interior Museum: The interior of the Palazzo Doria-Pamphili is open to the public (entrance at the back side of the palazzo, on the Piazza del Collegio Romano), and contains one of the largest private art collections in Italy. Hundreds of paintings are on display (along with a good deal of sculpture), including notable works by Giovanni di Paolo, Mantegna, Memling, Massys, Raphael, Titian, Corregio, Parmigianino, Tintoretto, Pieter Bruegel, Annibale Carracci, Caravaggio, Domenichino, Guercino, Claude Lorraine, and Allesandro Algardi (a Bernini contemporary who sculpted a superb no-nonsense bust of the formidable seventeenth-century matriarch of the Pamphili family, Donna Olimpia). The unquestioned highlight of the collection — well worth the price of admission even if all the other art is ignored — is a study in artistic contrast: Bernini's marble bust (ca. 1647) and Velasquez's oil painting (1650) of the Pamphili Pope Innocent X. The Bernini bust, despite its brilliant execution and beautiful finish, remains an official portrait. Innocent is portrayed as a dignified and commanding figure, with an unflinching glance and a suggestion of asceticism in the sunken cheeks and eyes. The Velasquez painting, on the other hand, is fearless in its realism, and possesses far greater psychological depth and presence than Bernini's bust. The look in Innocent's eye — suspicion? wariness? threat? — is caught with masterly authority, and is none too flattering. This is a portrait of a real man, and a dangerous one.

2-4 SAN MARCELLO
Façade: Carlo Fontana, 1682–1683
(Piazza di S. Marcello, on the Via del Corso just south of the Via dell' Umiltà)

S. Marcello.

A small Baroque set piece, with its own tiny piazza to set it back from the bustle of the Corso. The church proper dates from the 1500s (a much older church on the site burned in 1519), but construction was not completed until 1682, when Carlo Fontana was called in to design the façade. Its basic ideas — the concave curve, the step forward into the third dimension, the receding center-outward progression from bold columns to flat pilasters — were not new. But Fontana employs these fundamental Baroque conventions with great skill, and adds a few ingenious touches all his own. The result is one of the most original and sophisticated Baroque façades in the entire city.

Visually, the façade can be split into two separate compositions, constructed one in front of the other. The first, and smaller of the two, is the portal surrounding the front door: double columns supporting an entablature supporting a broken, rounded pediment supporting a square sculpture frame with a triangular pediment of its own. The second composition, echoing and enveloping and incorporating the first, is the conventional wide-lower-story-with-narrower-upper-story façade that originated with the Gesù and was copied all over Rome. Viewed together, the two compositions merge into a conventional façade that exhibits an unconventional twist: the upper story reverses the visual pattern of the lower, exhibiting its weaker elements (the flat pilasters) in the center rather than at the sides. Such a reversal might be considered an arbitrary exercise in rule-flouting, but in fact it serves a crucial visual purpose: it allows the upper story to serve as an uncompetitive backdrop for the square sculpture frame rising out of the lower-story pediment — the frame that is the central element of the whole composition.

Fontana's design, then, can be viewed in two ways. On the one hand, it can be seen as a traditional Gesù-type façade, with the narrower upper story offering a variation of the theme established by the lower. On the other hand, it can been seen as a highly theatrical framing device: an arrangement of foreground and background elements that unites the two stories into a single composition and thereby focuses the viewer's attention on the religious message presented by the sculpture enframed at its center.

So where is the sculpture? Sadly, the frame has been empty ever since the façade was constructed. Visually and thematically, the resulting void is one of the most exasperating decorative lapses in all Rome, for it robs the façade of its central focus, and offers up an enfeebling absence just at the point where the entire composition should achieve maximum presence.

2-5 SANTA MARIA IN VIA LATA
Façade and loggia: Pietro da Cortona, 1658–1662
(Via del Corso, at the Via Lata)

The church proper (as opposed to the façade) dates from 1491, but it replaced an earlier church, which replaced a still earlier church, which replaced a chapel that had been established in the fifth century. The original ancient Roman building housing the chapel — now belowground — was said to contain the cell in which St. Paul was held while awaiting trial.

The façade was designed by a great Baroque architect (Pietro da Cortona) for an important location (the Corso), and therefore demands attention. But it confounds expectations. As Baroque churches go, it is sober and restrained, almost subdued; in comparison with the dazzling wealth of invention at S. Marcello just up the street, the overall design seems quite tame. Contrary to popular myth, however, Baroque architects were on occasion perfectly capable of understatement, and Cortona's façade is no less powerful for its simplicity.

Cortona probably took his basic idea — a ground-floor loggia fronted by a screen of paired columns flanked by pairs of pilasters — from Peruzzi's Palazzo Massimo alle Colonne, some six blocks to the west on the Corso Vittorio Emanuele. He added a second loggia above, and gave the upper story extra strength and verticality by topping its central opening with an arch that intrudes into the façade's triangular pediment. Except for the elaborately carved capitals on the columns and pilasters, decoration is kept to a minimum; in the end, the façade's most dramatic feature is the striking contrast between the light color of the central columns and the darkness of the void behind them. The columns themselves seem to revel in the effect; their exaggerated entasis — the swell in the middle, here so pronounced as to be easily visible — makes them seem compressed by the weight they support, and the combination of unusual shape and spotlit placement gives them a bold, muscular presence that is distinctively Baroque.

If Cortona's design for the façade is unusually restrained (at least by Baroque standards), his design for the interior of the ground-floor loggia — the open-air vestibule inside the façade but *not* inside the church proper — is just the opposite. Far more complicated than it looks at first glance, the narrow loggia offers one of the most challenging displays of Baroque virtuosity in the entire city.

The basic architectural problem is clear enough: how to create a unified, satisfying interior space when the space's doorway and most of its entrance wall have been replaced by a screen of columns. Cortona's solution was radical. Instead of giving the loggia conventional flat walls and a flat ceiling — as might be expected from the ground floor's boxy exterior — he molds the interior space into an entirely new and unexpected shape using columns and curves. He places the flat wall of the church proper behind a second screen of columns, sets a curved barrel vault directly atop the column capitals, and inserts apse-like curved walls at either end. And he combines these heterogeneous architectural elements with such polished assurance that their coherence seems obvious and inevitable.

The apses, particularly, are a marvel of ingenuity, both in placement and design. At first glance, they may appear unexpectedly narrow for the room as a whole, for two reasons. First, instead of hiding the plain vertical apse edges behind the outermost columns, Cortona frankly exposes them, setting them just inside the perimeter defined by the columns; second, instead of closing off the decorative pattern of the main barrel-vaulted ceiling at the ends (where it meets the apse arches), Cortona leaves the pattern open-ended, as if unexpectedly interrupted by the upper section of the apse. These seemingly minor details combine to produce a startling visual effect: when viewed from the center of the loggia, the apses look almost as if they could be pushed back — slid along the horizontal molding above the column capitals — to reveal columns and barrel vault stretching on to infinity.

Once noticed, the suggestion of spatial expansion is very strong, and it invests the modest loggia with a visual impact far beyond its scale. But Cortona keeps the effect under rigorous control. Here, yet another minor design detail becomes key: the molding immediately above the column capitals. Cortona could have made the suggestion of spatial expansion even stronger by handling this molding differently; if the molding had been allowed to end abruptly at the points where it meets the apse, it would then function visually in the same open-ended way as the interrupted ceiling pattern above it. But the molding does not end; instead, it detours out from the columns and continues along the curved walls of the apses to run around the entire perimeter of the space. The molding as a whole thus serves to unify the entire composition, almost as if it were a riveted metal band that holds all the design's constituent parts — columns, apses, vault — together from the inside.

Cortona's achievement in fitting these architectural elements together was typically Baroque, both in its originality and in its ingenuity. And it was historically significant as well, for (as Rudolf Wittkower notes in his survey *Art and Architecture in Italy 1600–1750*) Cortona's design resolved an architectural problem that had plagued architects for two hundred years. As many of Cortona's predecessors had discovered, the use of columns within an enclosed rectangular space produces a difficult design problem: an interior row of columns set against a wall tends to lose visual force at the ends when it runs up against the perpendicular walls that enclose it. Extra authority — some sort of emphatic closure at the ends — is thus required to keep the column row from petering away to nothing. But how can this authority be achieved? If the columns are respaced so that the last column is merged with the perpendicular wall — if it becomes an inset half column, say, or a flat pilaster — it will look flimsy compared to its peers; if the last column remains freestanding, it will look as if it is about to run into the wall with a knockhead thunk. Architects had puzzled over this problem ever since the beginning of the Renaissance, but no definitive solution had emerged.

Cortona's solution, of course, eliminates the perpendicular wall entirely and replaces it with a cunningly inserted curved apse. The resulting design transforms a simple room — four walls and a ceiling — into something radically new and quintessentially Baroque: spatially complex, suggestive of movement, illusionistic. In the process, it gives the lie to the old canard that Baroque architecture is merely Renaissance architecture run amok. For Cortona here brings off a definitively Baroque coup: in inventing an innovative new synthesis of old architectural elements, he addresses a technical problem that Renaissance architects were unable to solve and produces a solution that is both conceptually daring and visually elegant.

2-6 IL FACCHINO
Fifteenth century
(Via Lata, west of the Via del Corso)

Set into the wall of the palazzo across the Via Lata from S. Maria in Via Lata, Il Facchino ("the porter") is one of the city's oldest and most beloved curbside drinking fountains. The man carrying the water barrel is sometimes said to represent a humbled Martin Luther — the porter's cap recalls a famous painting of Luther by Lucas Cranach the Elder — but the sculpture is in fact a portrait of one Abbondio Rizzi, head of the porters' guild during the fifteenth century. In a city full of grandiloquent commemorative monuments, the simplicity of the tribute here is especially compelling: no elaborate carving, no Classical references, no aggrandizing fuss, just a plain man remembered, continuing to carry out his work in death as he did in life.

2-7 PIAZZA DI SANT' IGNAZIO
Filippo Raguzzini, 1727

SANT' IGNAZIO
Orazio Grassi, 1628
Vault frescoes: Andrea Pozzo, 1684–1694
(West of the Via del Corso along the Via del Caravita)

A big early Baroque church and a little late Baroque square. Each is fine in its way; together they unexpectedly produce one of the most eccentric odd-couple juxtapositions in the entire city. The designer of the piazza, Filippo Raguzzini, must have loved the theater, for he here created a stage set come to life. His buildings are far from fancy — these were plebeian apartment houses, not aristocratic town palaces — but their gracefully interlocking shapes are placed around the square with the skill of a master set designer. Viewed from the steps of the church, the five buildings and six streets combine to make eleven onstage exits and entrances, enough for even the most dizzyingly complicated of Roman comic plots. At any moment, it seems, the performance will begin, with a cast of neighborhood characters tumbling out of doorways and shouting out of windows.

The church — one of Rome's many variations on the Gesù — was built a hundred years before the piazza, and in another setting its sober façade might possess great dignity. But set against Raguzzini's *jeu d'esprit* it looks pompous and stuffy, like an old fogey who has come to the play but refuses to laugh.

Inside the church, theatricality unexpectedly returns — and with a blazing burst of painterly glory that is one of the summits of monumental

Baroque art. Andrea Pozzo's vast, vertiginous ceiling fresco is best viewed from the circular ocher marker set into the nave floor, where all the tricks of perspective overhead click into place; like Baciccio's nave fresco in the Gesù, the work is a go-for-broke response to the challenge laid down by Michelangelo in the Sistine Chapel almost two hundred years earlier. Representing St. Ignatius's ascent into Paradise, Pozzo's sweeping vision engulfs the entire nave ceiling; its painted columns and arches grow straight out of the real columns below, opening the roof of the church to the sky, where all of heaven seems to have turned out in welcome. Architecturally, the Baroque swing of the pendulum away from the Renaissance values of structural clarity and balance here reaches its farthest extreme, for the aim of the ceiling is nothing less than to deny its own existence.

Pozzo's false painted dome over the crossing is equally artful in its illusionism, though in a less flamboyant way. It should be viewed from two different spots, first from the circular marker set into the floor where the nave meets the crossing, and then, after moving forward without looking up, from as close to the main altar as possible. A mere artistic trick, to be sure, but one of the most entertaining tricks in Rome.

2-8   TEMPLE OF THE DEIFIED HADRIAN
Constructed 145 C.E.
(Piazza di Pietra, north of the Piazza di S. Ignazio)

The Temple of the Deified Hadrian was constructed by Hadrian's successor, Antoninus Pius, in 145 C.E., and the columns of its northside colonnade are still visible today, their presence diminished but not destroyed by incorporation into the exterior wall of an ordinary building. Originally the first four columns on the left formed the side of the temple's entrance portico (the temple faced east, toward the Corso); the side of the *cella*, or main temple chamber, was behind the seven remaining columns on the right. Today the colonnade still functions to support the building's roof, but its appearance — unrestored, ravaged by time, in places brutally bruised and hacked — is worlds away from the serene nobility its builders intended. This is one of Rome's most poignant ruins, and all the more evocative for being still in everyday use.

2-9 PIAZZA DI MONTECITORIO
Obelisk: Egyptian, sixth century B.C.E.

PALAZZO DI MONTECITORIO
Façade: Gianlorenzo Bernini, 1653 onward; ground-floor entranceway and
bell tower added by Carlo Fontana, 1694
(Northwest of the Piazza di Pietri)

Of the forty-eight obelisks that dotted the ancient city, only thirteen have
been rediscovered and reassembled. Happily, most of them are not isolated in
parks or museums; instead, they are woven into the fabric of the functioning
city, serving as focal points for piazzas and centerpieces for fountains — an
integral part of the new Baroque city that rose from the ancient ruins during the sixteenth and seventeenth centuries. Originally brought to Rome to
stand as symbols of Imperial conquest, the reerected obelisks now stand —
far more humanely — as symbols of the city's rebirth and regeneration after
a decline that lasted more than a thousand years.

The obelisk in the center of the Piazza di Montecitorio dates from the
sixth century B.C.E.; it was brought to Rome from Egypt by Augustus in 10
B.C.E. to commemorate his victory over Cleopatra. Originally raised in a
public park (where it served as the gnomon of a giant sundial), it was
unearthed in pieces in 1748, and in 1792 it was reconstructed by Pius VI
near the spot where it stood in Imperial times.

The Palazzo di Montecitorio, on the piazza's north side, is the seat of the
Chamber of Deputies (the lower house of the Italian Parliament). The building's hulking façade was designed — mostly — by Bernini (the ground-
floor entranceway and the bell tower above the clock were later additions by
Carlo Fontana). The palazzo possessed an unusually broad expanse of
frontage, so Bernini departed from Roman convention in three ways: he set
the side wings at angles to the central block, he introduced giant pilasters at
the points where the façade shifts direction, and he gave the outer pilasters
giant single-story bases cut to resemble natural rock. These novelties were
no doubt meant to alleviate the façade's relentless horizontality, but the setback angles are too timid and the giant pilasters too sparsely placed to supply the needed counterbalance. In the end (as is so often the case in Rome) it
is the monotonous arrangement of windows that dominates, and the innovations come off as distinctly halfhearted. This is perhaps Bernini's least
ingratiating piece of Roman architecture.

Classicism's last hurrah. Beginning in 1902, the seventeenth-century Palazzo di Montecitorio was expanded toward the rear to fill an entire city block, and the extension was ultimately given a grandiose entrance facing the Piazza del Parlamento. The façade inevitably attracts attention because of its size and its distinctly non-Roman (and often criticized) use of red brick. Certainly it is very full of itself, and open to the charge of pastiche, but it is not unlikable for all that. And in its overloaded nineteenth-century way it is quite respectful of the long tradition of Roman palazzo design.

The ground floor (floors, really, since the grand staircase leading to the main entrance turns the actual ground floor into a basement) follows Renaissance precedent by eschewing carved decoration in favor of rustication; the lower levels thus become a podium supporting the display of Classical motifs above. The upper floors' giant pilasters recall Michelangelo's designs for the Campidoglio, and the short twin towers at each end — joined by a roof parapet derived from a medieval battlement — recall the oldest of all the great Roman palaces, the Palazzo Venezia. The wealth of decorative detail, however, is pure nineteenth-century, from the clichéd heroism of the statuary flanking the front door to the unexpected (and certainly unintentional) whimsicality of the parapet carving — a row of arms that from the street looks like a family of amiable, bug-eyed frogs. The decorative carving, in fact, is first-rate throughout, with a strong suggestion of Art Nouveau that adds a welcome lighter touch to the overall weight of the façade as a whole.

There is considerable irony here. Very soon after this façade was finished, the long tradition of European architecture based on the examples of Greek and Roman antiquity came to an abrupt end. After four uninterrupted centuries of varied Classical styles — from the Renaissance through Mannerism to the Baroque and then on to the Neoclassicism of the eighteenth and nineteenth centuries — the twentieth century arrived on the scene and declared: no more. In Italy and Germany, the fascist architects of Mussolini and Hitler stripped Classicism bare in their desire to show off flexed muscles; elsewhere in Europe, the increasingly powerful dogma of Modern architecture dictated that the Classical vocabulary be banished utterly from the architectural lexicon. Henceforth, form was to follow function, and function did not require pilasters on walls and pediments above windows. So the new Camera dei Deputati façade, meant when it was built to show the health and vigor of a long architectural tradition, turned out instead to be the last of a dying line. And in paying its respects to the very first of the city's Renaissance palazzi, the façade brings the history of Classical Roman palazzo design not only to an end but also full circle, back where it began. It is an unexpectedly fitting valediction.

2-11 SANT' AGOSTINO
Façade: Giacomo di Pietrasanta, 1483
(Via di S. Agostino, southeast of the Piazza del Parlamento)

One of the earliest Renaissance façades in Rome, and a more awkward arrangement of architectural elements it would be hard to imagine. Its picture-frame moldings are stuck onto the wall like notices on a bulletin board, its ground-floor pediment is squashed almost out of existence by its upper-story rose window, and its decorative scrolls possess all the delicacy of a weight lifter's barbells, overpowering the spindly 97-pound-weakling pilasters below. The basic architectural problem — how to employ pagan architectural elements borrowed from Classical antiquity on a Christian church façade — is recognized, but a definitive solution is clearly a long way off. It was not to arrive until the construction of the Gesù, nearly a hundred years later.

The interior is no less rudimentary in its use of the Classical vocabulary than the exterior. The half columns set into alternate pillars along the nave support protruding and isolated chunks of entablature; the chunks are visually unrelated to the horizontal bands (set with rosettes over the center of each arch) that connect them, and are made to support weak and incongruous pilasters out of which the vault ribs spring. But if the interior architecture is clumsy, the interior art is not. It includes a Baroque high altar (1628) with two angels designed (but not carved) by Bernini, a set of frescoes of prophets on the nave pillars that includes *Isaiah* by Raphael (1512, third pillar on the left), a *Madonna and Child* sculpted by Andrea Sansovino (1512, below the Raphael), and Caravaggio's *Madonna dei Pelligrini* (1603, in the first chapel to the left).

2-12 SAN LUIGI DEI FRANCESI

Façade: Domenico Fontana or Giacomo della Porta, ca. 1585
Interior: Giovanni Mangone, ca. 1530;
redecorated 1756–1764 by Antoine Dérizet
(Piazza di S. Luigi dei Francesi, south of the Via di S. Agostino
along the Via della Scrofa)

S. Luigi dei Francesi.

The façade of S. Luigi dei Francesi* is large and imposing, and oddly discomfiting. The architect — probably Domenico Fontana working under the supervision of Giacomo della Porta — rejected the narrow-upper-story-on-wider-lower-story precedent established by the nearby churches of S. Agostino and the Gesù, and opted instead for equal upper and lower stories. The boxy shape that results creates a bulked-up and broad-shouldered mass of wall that borders on the oppressive. The wall decoration — a network of vertical pilasters and horizontal cornices — exacerbates the problem by dividing the wall-surface into a grid of ten separate rectangular cells, each with its own

---

* As the name of the church implies, S. Luigi dei Francesi is the national church of the French, ministering especially to travelers from France. S. Antonio dei Portoghesi serves a similar function for the Portuguese, S. Andrea degli Scozzesi for the Scottish, S. Giovanni dei Fiorentini for the Florentines, and so forth. But — this being Rome — not all national churches reveal their nationalities in their names (the American church in Rome is S. Susanna, and the English church is S. Silvestro in Capite), and not all nationalized names are reliably significant (the official Spanish church in Rome is S. Maria di Monserrato, not SS. Trinità dei Spagnoli).

architectural centerpiece framing a door, window, or niche. The organizational principle is logical enough, but it produces a scaffold-like skeleton that accentuates the façade's ponderous squareness and makes the individual windows and niches appear isolated and free-floating, unrelated to each other or to the façade as a whole. Even the façade's conventional triangular pediment suffers; instead of capping the composition with authority, it sits awkwardly atop the façade looking squat and outgrown.

The façade is sometimes characterized as High Renaissance, even though it dates from a decade (the 1580s) when the Mannerist rebellion against Renaissance correctitude and clarity of form was in full swing. In fact, some of its individual elements are typically Mannerist in their willingness to experiment with conventional Classical forms (the pediments atop the upper-story niches, for instance, hung with elegant earring-like pendants carved with freely adapted Classical motifs). But the prosaic organization of the wall surface robs these adventurous details of their visual force, and gives the façade as a whole the feel of a throwback to an earlier time and style.

Inside, the architecture is considerably more successful, with the deep side chapels and the narrow nave giving the space a taut power that the façade lacks. The most immediately conspicuous feature of the interior, however, is its Baroque decorative scheme of marble, paint, and gilded stucco, added by Antoine Dérizet around 1760, almost two hundred years after the church was built. For once the Baroque overlay does not smother the architecture it decorates. The gilding, as usual, is extensive and elaborate, but the overall effect is tempered by the logical and consistent use of marble and paint. The warm pinks, roses, and maroons of the marbled nave pilasters and entablature frieze, the lighter ochers of the chancel, the cool gray of the vault background that sets off the elaborate gilded decoration — these three predominant colors contrast with and complement each other, emphasizing the three main building parts and keeping the decorative scheme as a whole from agglomerating itself into the usual clamorous hodgepodge. The end result is luxurious rather than garish, opulent rather than gaudy — an effect that, sadly, is all too rare in Roman Baroque churches.

Appealing as it may be, the decorative scheme pales beside S. Luigi's most famous attraction, found in the Contarelli Chapel (the last on the left, with a coin machine for lighting the interior). Here, painted expressly for the chapel and set into the walls with a simplicity and magnificence that is without peer in Rome, are Caravaggio's three great masterpieces illustrating the life of St. Matthew, painted 1599–1602: *The Calling* (on the left), *The Martyrdom* (on the right), and *The Inspiration* (in the center). Caravaggio's dramatic, almost hallucinatory use of intense light and murky dark was a new development in art and hugely controversial in its day. To many seventeenth-century eyes, these scenes made no visual sense. Was Caravaggio omitting the traditional realistic backgrounds because he was perverse, or merely inept? But the modern eye, growing up with movies, has no difficulty accepting the style as a heightening as well as a distortion of reality. The effect is most powerful (and most powerfully cinematic) in *The Calling*, where the play of light and dark — and the brilliant colors illuminated and highlighted by that play — produces a visual intensity that had never before been achieved in art, and has rarely been achieved since.

2-13   SANTA MARIA MADDALENA
Façade: Giuseppe Sardi (?), 1735
Interior: Carlo Fontana, 1673; Giovanni Antonio de' Rossi or
Carlo Quadri, ca. 1695
(Piazza della Maddalena, northeast of the Piazza di S. Luigi dei Francesi)

Whoever designed the façade of La Maddalena — the traditional (but recently questioned) attribution is to Giuseppe Sardi — owed a great debt to Borromini. The concave wall curve, the convex upper-story window-surround, the crisp zigzag pediment above the doorway, the sinuous pediment on top — these are typical Borrominian motifs, most of which he invented. They are used here with great authority, but without the cunning three-dimensional jigsaw interlock of Borromini at his best. Here the basic organization of architectural elements is quite straightforward, functioning more to frame and set off the façade's stucco decoration than to create a sophisticated architectural design.

But with decoration like this, who could complain? La Maddalena's swirls and swoops and swags possess a lyricism that is unusual for Rome and that approaches the lilting, singing quality of Rococo design across the Alps. All of the façade's exuberant carving is worth examining in detail, but first prize must surely go to the elaborately carved top-hat pile (it can hardly be called a pediment) above the entrance door. Its two superbly carved angels seem to hover miraculously in midair as they put the façade's final bits of decoration in place.

Inside, the ground plan is of considerable interest. The east end of the church — the chancel and its side chapels — was completed first, designed by Carlo Fontana around 1673 in a straightforward, traditional manner. But when a successor architect (G.A. de' Rossi, or possibly Carlo Quadri) was called in to finish the job twenty years later, he broke with convention.

Rather than design the expected straight nave with three deep chapels on each side, he pushed back the nave walls to form an oval, and gave each wall two wide, shallow chapels set at an angle to the nave. The oval shape considerably intensifies the nave's presence, giving it its own distinct spatial identity, and suggesting — erroneously, as it turns out — that the transepts and chancel beyond may have surprises of their own in store. Critics have complained that the design lacks unity, but the overall composition as viewed from the entranceway — graceful, swelling curves in every direction, with the prosaic crossing hidden from view — is difficult to fault, even if exploration proves disappointing.

The decoration, unfortunately, is another matter. As with so many Roman churches, La Maddalena's interior architectural elements are slathered with marble, gilding, stucco, and fresco, and the feeling of ornamental assault is overwhelming. Occasional bits and pieces stand out from the confusion; in the second nave chapel on the left, for instance, a pair of carved memorials over the doorways — cherubs setting medallions into the wall above draped coffins — exploit their cramped spaces with unfaltering virtuosity. But for every such success there is a countermanding excess, and in the end it is the excesses that win out. The decorative contrast with S. Luigi dei Francesi — so similiar in style, so different in effect — is striking. This is the sort of interior that gave the Baroque a bad name.

2-14 VIA DEGLI ORFANI
(Piazza Capranica, east of the Piazza della Maddalena)

A short, crooked street that offers the best visual approach to the city's most important Classical antiquity, the Pantheon. From the Piazza Capranica, where the street begins, the Pantheon looks almost like a painted backdrop, a mere sliver of portico and dome filling the narrow space between the buildings at the street's far end. But with every approaching step the Pantheon gains in three-dimensionality, and gradually — irrevocably — the full magnitude of its astonishing architectural presence is revealed. As the street debouches into the Piazza della Rotunda, the Pantheon commands absolute, riveting attention.

2-15 PANTHEON
Architect unknown, constructed 118–128 C.E.
(Piazza della Rotonda)

The Pantheon is Rome's preeminent architectural survivor. Built in the second century C.E. as a temple to all the gods, it is today the best-preserved of all monumental Roman buildings, not just in Rome but anywhere. Its survival throughout the Middle Ages was assured in the early seventh century, when Pope Boniface IV removed the temple's decorative "pagan filth" and reconsecrated it as a Christian church dedicated to all martyred saints. Since then, fourteen centuries of urban transformation — decay during bad times and modernization during good — have eradicated every other ancient building on the Campus Martius. Only the Pantheon remains, and it stands today almost exactly as it stood eighteen centuries ago.

The ancient Latin inscription on the entablature of the portico ("Marcus Agrippa, son of Lucius, three times consul, built this") would seem a typically Roman boast — straightforward, self-confident, and proud. In fact, the inscription is a bold-faced lie. Agrippa — lieutenant, friend, and son-in-law to the *emperor* Augustus — constructed the original Pantheon on the site around 25 B.C.E. But Agrippa's temple burned twice, and ultimately it was replaced (as the date-stamped bricks uncovered during modern restoration attest) by the present structure, built by the emperor Hadrian around 125 C.E. Hadrian, it is currently thought, left no trace of the original temple beyond the intentionally misleading inscription.

Hadrian's reasons for lying so audaciously about his building's origin are unclear and much debated. Perhaps they were personal: he was a true connoisseur of architecture, and he may have wanted to honor the memory of Agrippa, who had overseen the construction of so many buildings in the Campus Martius area. Perhaps they were political: Agrippa was associated in the popular mind with the deified Augustus, and a public reminder of the dynastic connection between Hadrian and Augustus would have served Hadrian well. But whatever Hadrian's motives may have been, the inscription remains unique — a bold and highly visible declaration by a Roman emperor (a species not exactly noted for its modesty) that cedes the credit for one of Rome's most important buildings to someone else.

Today the Pantheon occupies an entire block to itself, but originally its relation to the surrounding cityscape was more complicated. Modern research suggests that in ancient times the forecourt piazza was enclosed by a low-roofed colonnade. Moreover, the building itself was raised on a podium approached up a wide flight of five marble steps (since covered over by the rise of the ground level in the area), and various other buildings probably crowded up against the entire structure on at least two of its three remaining sides. The effect of this less-open setting would have been twofold: the podium and forecourt would have dramatized the rectangular portico from the front, and the abutting buildings would have deemphasized the exterior walls of the circular rotunda behind (and disguised what today appears as a distinctly awkward transition between the two).*

Beyond the change in setting, the exterior of the building remains largely unaltered, marred only by the loss of its original decorative accents. All the sculpture — Pope Boniface's pagan filth — is long gone, and its original placement and character remain a matter of speculation (the remains of a statuary base can be seen at the peak of the pediment, and the pattern of surviving clamp-holes in the tympanum — the triangular space within the pediment — has suggested to recent scholars the outline of a sculpted Imperial eagle with outspread wings). The sunlit glitter and shaded sheen of metal has disappeared as well: in 663, the Byzantine emperor Constans II carted off the gilded bronze tiles that covered the exterior of the rotunda dome — the drab replacement covering is lead, probably dating from the eighth century — and in the 1620s, Pope Urban VIII, in need of metal for cannons, tore away some two hundred tons of ancient bronze that encased the supporting beams and underside of the portico roof (he commented, notoriously, that the metal was better employed keeping enemies away from the Holy See than keeping rain out of the Pantheon porch).

The basic architectural forms remain, however, and upon entering the building it is still possible to feel some of the shock that the interior must have produced eighteen centuries ago. An ancient visitor, approaching the temple from the far end of the long forecourt, would have seen the exterior portico as irreproachably Greek in both form and feel, and would have expected more of the same inside. The interior, the portico would have suggested, was to be a secret and privileged space accessible only on special occasions, rectangular, timbered over with a flat ceiling, and dimly lit only by whatever light managed to find its way under the portico and through the entrance doors.

Those huge bronze-covered doors are still intact, and the interior beyond them belies all Greek expectations. Far larger than the entrance portico implies, expansively circular rather than narrowly rectangular in form,

---

*One current explanation for this awkwardness suggests that the original design called for the portico to be considerably higher (with the roofline reaching to the level marked out on the transitional block), but that practical considerations — possibly the failure to obtain monolithic columns of the necessary height on schedule — forced a reduction in size.

capped by a vast floating dome instead of a flat ceiling, amply lit by light streaming in through the oculus at the dome's peak, elaborately decorated with colored marbles, granites, and Imperial porphyry: this is a space that leaves the time-honored conventions of Greek temple architecture far behind. The Pantheon interior is wholly Roman, and it was in its day an unprecedented architectural statement, proclaiming with stentorian authority both the power of the gods and the power of the Roman Empire.

In part, the unprecedented size and character of the interior reflects a revolutionary development in construction technique. In earlier times, circular temples were not unknown, but they tended to be small and specialized. Larger structures became feasible when the Imperial Romans discovered that by mixing stones and small rocks with a particular brand of mortar (lime and a local volcanic sand known today as *pozzolana*) they could produce a new building material — concrete — that was thickly liquid when first mixed but solid and durable when set. This revolutionary material made it possible to construct massive walls without massive stone, and also (not incidentally) to vault large spaces with nonflammable roofing, molded during construction by temporary wooden forms. The Pantheon's dome was constructed in just this manner: some 5,000 tons of concrete poured over an immense wooden hemisphere supported by scaffolding and checkered over with the 140 convex molds that shaped the ceiling's concave coffers. At 142 feet across — a dimension not even approached in Rome until the dome of St. Peter's was built some fifteen centuries later — it remains today one of the largest domes in the world, and one of the most impressive engineering feats of all time.[*]

But the significance of the Pantheon interior goes beyond mere size. Prior to the Romans, Western architecture had been very much an exterior matter. For the Greeks particularly, large and important buildings were defined primarily by the way they looked on the outside, and especially by the way they related to the landscape or cityscape in which they were set. Interior rooms were usually limited in size and of distinctly subsidiary importance;

---

[*] It is for engineering reasons that the dome, which is revealed as a half sphere inside, appears so much shallower outside, where it looks like an inverted saucer supported by a high cylindrical wall. If the interior and the exterior elevations are compared, the interior dome begins two-thirds of the way up the exterior cylindrical wall — at the second protruding ring — and not (as might be expected from the shape on the outside) at the top of the cylindrical wall on which the exterior inverted saucer rests. The purpose of this additional vertical rise on the exterior is to supply pressure on the interior dome; the upper part of the exterior cylinder acts as a shoulder-like buttress that keeps the interior dome from bursting outward. The massive-seeming wall, however, is not monolithic; it is honeycombed with hollows made possible through the use of a network of brick arches behind the thin exterior skin (some of the arches can be seen on the outside of the building in the patterns of the exterior brickwork).

large interior halls, when they were constructed at all, were broken up by intrusive rows of roof-supporting columns.

The Romans changed all that. Over a long period of gradual but persistent architectural experiment, they invented and perfected a host of new building types — most famously the public bath and the basilica — that placed unprecedented emphasis on the character of the interior. For the first time in the history of Western architecture, the manipulation of interior space became more important than the shaping of exterior mass. The Pantheon, with its rigorously traditional entrance portico opening into a stunningly unexpected and innovative interior, is the preeminent architectural expression of this epochal shift in emphasis. The exterior is now secondary, and the primary experience is to be found inside.

For the ancient visitor, that experience would have been uniquely powerful. Traditional Greek and Roman temple interiors were basically simple rectangular containers, and what they contained was the statue of the god to whom the temple was dedicated. It was this statue, and not the surrounding architecture, that served as the primary interior focal point. But the Pantheon contains no such central cynosure. The presence of the gods has here been relegated to the periphery — inside the series of chapel-like openings and enframing aedicules that are alternately carved out of and set against the circular wall — and the center of the interior is conspicuously, dramatically empty.

Empty, that is, of statuary. But not empty of light. Even on cloudy days, the oculus at the peak of the dome ushers in ample light to illuminate the entire interior. And on clear days, the sun — the eye of Zeus, according to the ancients — produces an extraordinarily luminous added presence: a circular beam of brighter light, shaped by the oculus and carved out of pure air, that moves gradually across the interior from west to east as the earth rotates on its axis. Among other things, the interior of the Pantheon is a giant clock face, marking the daily passage of light and time.

When the Pantheon is first entered, then, the absence of a central statue and the presence of the light streaming in through the oculus focus attention inexorably on the interior's most dramatic architectural feature: the dome. The temple's architect — his identity is not known, though Hadrian himself may have had more than a passing hand in the building's overall conception and design — shaped the dome with extraordinary precision. It is a perfect half sphere, and if the half sphere were extended downward, the full sphere would just touch the floor of the interior exactly at its center. The lower two-thirds of the dome is inset with five rings of coffers, each coffer consisting of four receding levels of squares that are nested off-center (that is, scrunched together toward the upper edge of each coffer). The visual effect of this purposefully skewed coffer design, when combined with the overall decrease in size of the coffers as they move up the dome, is one of ever-increasing intensity — of forces being compressed, like a coiled spring, as they rise. When the coffering abruptly stops near the peak, the remainder of the dome seems suspended as if by magic, hovering weightlessly over the floor below. The accumulated visual tension created by the coffers finds its ultimate release at the oculus, and the modern eye, conditioned to seeing domes with ribs locked into place at their peaks by crowning lanterns, cannot but be shocked by the unexpected open space. It is as if the keystone of the entire composition has been suddenly and daringly removed, dissipating the dome's accumulated forces into thin air.

Inevitably and powerfully, the great dome calls to mind the far greater vault of the heavens outside. The parallel would have been even more forceful in ancient times, when each coffer almost certainly contained at its center a gilded bronze rosette that caught and reflected the incoming light, the rosettes as a group arrayed like planets in precisely ordered orbit around the sun of the dome's oculus. The identity of the deities represented by statuary around the floor periphery is not known, but the coffer orbits above suggest obvious celestial candidates: Jupiter (as Zeus was known to the Romans), Saturn, Venus, Mars, Mercury, Apollo (god of the sun), and Diana (goddess of the moon). The gods' sculptural presence below, however, must always have remained secondary to the dome above. In the Pantheon, the ruling image is the great hemispherical vault — an architectural sky — that floats above the floor below as a metaphor not for any individual god but for the entire cosmos that the gods inhabit, order, and control.

A more mundane and earthbound type of control came into play as well. In ancient times, the Pantheon was far more public in its function than most temples. Hadrian himself held judicial court here, and his presence would have turned the entire building into a declaration of Imperial power. When court was in session, the surrounding architectural cosmos would have taken on a political character, and the order it implies would have been civic as well as sacred — the order of the Roman Empire, with the emperor at its center dispensing Roman justice. Thus the Pantheon, at least in part, was designed to serve as a monumental piece of political propaganda. As a setting for judicial ritual, the cosmological character of its interior would have imparted a celestial stature to its occupants and their actions; as a temple to all the gods, the sunlit void at the interior's center waited to be filled by the nearest thing to a god on Earth, the emperor.

With the fall of the Roman Empire, the Pantheon lost forever its aura of political and civic importance. But a thousand years later it emerged from the Middle Ages with its architectural significance intact. During the Renaissance, it was extravagantly admired and endlessly studied; the sixteenth-century architect and theorist Sebastiano Serlio, whose famous treatise, *L'Architettura*, analyzed and codified the ancient architectural orders for the first time since antiquity, called it "the fairest, the most whole ... the most perfect piece of work I ever saw." As a thousand-year-old Christian church, the Pantheon was for Renaissance builders an architectural text-book uniquely preserved by God, a holy writ in which they could find the rules by which they might create an architecture that would equal and per-haps even surpass the ruined architecture of the ancients.

Foremost among these rules was the Pantheon's mathematically elegant geometry. The perfect hemisphere of the dome generates a perfect circle below, and the placement of the ground-level architectural elements — the chapels, the aedicules, the columns, even the pattern of the marble squares and circles on the floor (relaid in 1873, preserving the ancient design) — follows logical-ly from a division of that circle into equal parts. To the Renaissance eye, such clarity of organization was the very definition of architectural beauty.

One feature of the interior, however, does not relate obviously to the over-all geometric scheme and is much discussed among architects and scholars even today. At ground level, the arrangement of columns and pilasters around the perimeter divides the walls into sixteen equal segments; logically, such a division would give rise, in the dome, to rings of thirty-two coffers, each cof-fer aligning vertically with the arrangement below. But the rings in the dome possess twenty-eight coffers each, not thirty-two. As a result, the dome coffer-ing system possesses an organizational scheme that is unrelated (except at the four cardinal points of the circle) to the plan of the walls below.

It was probably this geometric discrepancy that produced the only major change in the Pantheon's interior since antiquity. In the 1740s, the entire attic section of the wall — the upper story, below the dome — was redesigned, and the original marble pilasters and rectangular grilled windows were replaced with blind pedimented windows and stucco panels. In the late nineteenth century, a short segment of the original attic was restored (opposite the entrance to the right), and when the two designs are compared, the reasons for the "improvement" can easily be surmised. The modern decoration is more obviously scaled to match the architectural elements above and below, and the elimination of the pilasters would have served, in the minds of the eighteenth-century renovators, to disguise the troubling discontinuity between walls and dome. From a strictly geometric point of view, the change is understandable (if historically regrettable). But it begs the fundamental question: why does the original design, otherwise so precisely and perfectly ordered, fail to align its upper and lower elements?

The answer can only be a matter of speculation, but it is entirely possible — even probable — that the discontinuity was carefully planned. If the coffers were aligned with the architectural elements below, the overall effect of the dome would be quite different. Visually, it would then seem to grow naturally and logically out of the walls, and the interior as a whole would appear more uniform and more unified. But it would also appear more static. The dome would no longer seem to hover so magically over the space below, and its visual effectiveness as a metaphor for the vault of the heavens would be substantially reduced. The sky outside, after all, is nowhere connected to the earth; like the discontinuous Pantheon dome, it overarches and encompasses the world below without being part of it.* The misalignment of coffers and columns heightens this heavenly effect, giving the dome an independent identity it would not otherwise possess. Architectural regularity is purposely sacrificed, and in the process visual geometry becomes visual poetry.

Today the Pantheon is much reduced in function (although it is still a church, and it contains the tombs of Raphael and of Italy's two nineteenth-century kings, Victor Emmanuel II and Umberto I). But as an architectural memorial to the ancient Romans it remains incomparable, and its influence on Western architecture since the Renaissance can scarcely be overstated. In the words of architectural historian William L. MacDonald:

> Symbolically and ideologically the Pantheon idea survived because it describes satisfactorily, in architectural form, something close to the core of human needs and aspirations. By abstracting the shape of the earth and the imagined form of the cosmos into a grand, immediately assimilated image, the architect of the Pantheon gave mankind a symbol that transcends religion, class, and political conviction.... Because it was not freighted with any sectarian or localized meaning, and because of the universality inherent in its forms, it was unendingly adaptable. It is one of the very few archetypal images in western architecture.

---

*The arrangement of the coffers could symbolically refer to the sky as well, with the twenty-eight coffers in each ring representing the lunar cycle, the five rings representing the orbits of the known planets, and the oculus representing the sun.

TOUR 3

—•—

OLD ROME II:
THE CAMPUS MARTIUS (NORTHWEST)
FROM THE PANTHEON TO THE TIBER BEND

Piazza Navona allagata solito farsi nelle Feste di Agosto.
1 Obelisco e Fontana 2 Altre Fontane 3. Chiesa di S. Agnese, e Palazzo Panfilj 4. Chiesa ed Ospitale di S. Giacomo degli Spagnuoli

*T*HE SECOND OF the Campus Martius tours continues west from the Pantheon, and includes the Piazza Navona, the most famous and beloved of all Rome's great cityspaces (depicted above at manmade flood tide and in full August-festival array). It also includes, at S. Ivo della Sapienza and S. Maria della Pace, an introduction to the work of Bernini's two great contemporaries Francesco Borromini and Pietro da Cortona. The three architects are generally considered something of a triumvirate; they all came of age around 1620, and the boldness and confidence with which they employed the Classical vocabulary in their buildings established a new style and a new era in architecture: the Baroque.

In passing, a word of explanation about the courtyard at S. Ivo is perhaps in order. Borromini incorporated the small church of S. Ivo into a larger and earlier building (designed by Giacomo della Porta some forty years before the beginning of the Baroque era) known as the Palazzo della Sapienza. Although it is necessary to pass through the Sapienza courtyard in order to gain access to the church, discussion of the courtyard is postponed until Tour 4 (the Sapienza is located on the border between Tours 3 and 4). The delay is not arbitrary. The architectural problems that are so beautifully resolved in the Sapienza courtyard are first encountered — and not solved — in two earlier courtyards, at S. Maria della Pace and at the Palazzo della Cancelleria (discussed in Tours 3 and 4, respectively). From both a historical and an aesthetic point of view, it is useful to view the other courtyards before examining the Sapienza; the elegant refinements of the latter are much easier to appreciate after having viewed the experimental clumsinesses of the former. But readers who are particularly struck by the Sapienza courtyard may certainly jump ahead to the Tour 4 entry on the Palazzo della Sapienza if they wish.

3-1   ELEPHANT WITH OBELISK
Designed by Gianlorenzo Bernini, executed by Ercole Ferrata, 1667
(Piazza della Minerva, southeast of the Pantheon)

A typical Bernini impromptu. The little Egyptian obelisk was unearthed in the garden of S. Maria sopra Minerva in 1665, and Alexander VII commissioned Bernini and his studio (Ercole Farrata did the actual carving) to erect it in the church square. The elephant was traditionally a symbol of divine wisdom; here, as the inscriptions on the base state, it serves to honor and consecrate the wisdom of the ancient Romans and Egyptians. In its own small way, the gesture epitomizes the entire Renaissance.

3-2   SANTA MARIA SOPRA MINERVA
Fra Sisto and Fra Ristoro, 1280
(Piazza di Minerva, southeast of the Pantheon)

The art inside is exceptional, but the architecture, both inside and out, is a disappointment. Begun near the site of an ancient Temple of Minerva during the thirteenth century, S. Maria sopra Minerva is famous as the only example of Gothic architecture in Rome. But the exalted, soaring verticality of the Gothic cathedrals of northern Europe is nowhere to be seen. The façade was never finished; its only notable feature is its collection of small marble plaques marking three hundred years of Tiber floodwater levels. The interior possesses the necessary ribbed vaults and pointed arches — hallmarks of the Gothic style — but they are so flattened that almost all the Gothic feel is lost. Nor does the brightly painted nave ceiling help matters; like the marble facings of the nave piers, it is the product of a well-meant but overzealous nineteenth-century restoration, and adds a look of Victorian Gothic Revival to an interior that was never all that Gothic to begin with.

> *Notable Works of Art:* Michelangelo and Bernini are both present, but it is the luminously delicate Filippino Lippi frescoes in the Carafa Chapel (right transept) that stand out. The cycle was painted between 1488 and 1492, and commemorates the life and works of St. Thomas Aquinas: *St. Thomas Presenting Cardinal Carafa to Our Lady of the Annunciation* (altar), *Assumption of the Virgin* (back wall), *The Triumph of St. Thomas over Heresy* (right wall), *The Miracle of the Crucified Christ Praising St. Thomas* (the lunette above the right wall), and *Sybils* (in the vault). Other noteworthy works include Baciccio's *St. Louis Bertrand in Ecstasy* (over the altar in the first chapel to the right after the small baptistry); Antoniazzo Romano's *Annunciation* (1508, fourth chapel to the right); Barocci's *Institution of the Eucharist* (1594, fifth chapel to the right); Michelangelo's *Christ Bearing the Cross* (1519, standing to the left of the chancel and incorporating bronze drapery that is a later addition); the pavement tomb of Fra Angelico, attributed to Isaia da Pisa (1455, first chapel to the left of the chancel); *Hercules and the Lion*, an antique bas-relief incorporated into the fifteenth-century tomb of Giovanni Arberini (second chapel to the left of the chancel); Bernini's *Monument to the Venerable Maria Raggi* (1643, left side of the nave on the second pillar back from the crossing); and Bernini's bust of Giovanni Vigevano (1630, on the tomb between the third and fourth chapels to the left).

3-3   BATHS OF AGRIPPA REMNANT
Constructed 25 B.C.E.
(North side of Via dell' Arco della Ciambella, south of the Pantheon)

Contrary to common belief, the barbarians were not the sole ravagers of ancient Rome. The great architects of the Renaissance were equally destructive, plundering the city of building materials and demolishing a great deal of ancient architecture in the process. The depredations under Pope Urban VIII, of the Barberini family, were especially notorious, and gave rise to a famous epigram: *Quod non fecerunt barbari, fecerunt Barberini* ("What the barbarians started, the Barberini finish").

Occasionally, a visible piece of the ancient urban fabric turns up as part of a newer building. The curved wall here, into which three small houses are set, once enclosed the central hall of the Baths of Agrippa, the first of the famous Roman public baths. In ancient times, the complex occupied an entire city block, but this isolated fragment is the only trace remaining. As ruins go it is hardly worth noticing, but Christian Rome has singled it out nonetheless: as if to ward off any lingering pagan spirits, a street shrine dedicated to the Virgin has been incorporated into the left side of the ancient Roman wall.

3-4 SANTA CHIARA
Façade: Luca Carimini, late nineteenth century
(Via di S. Chiara, north of the Via dell' Arco della Ciambella
but south of the Pantheon)

A façade of bits and pieces, rather haphazardly arranged on the lower half but rigorously regimented above. The overall organization is something of a puzzle, resembling neither the seminal Gesù (with its wide lower story and narrow scroll-flanked upper story) or the later Baroque churches on the Corso. The crude Early Renaissance façade of S. Agostino might spring to mind — the pretty round-arched row of seven windows looks at first glance distinctly pre-Renaissance — but the main doorway and the niches flanked by pilasters to either side are far from primitive, even if awkwardly placed in relation to one another. What style is this? The answer (as is so often the case when a Roman church façade departs markedly from the expected models) is a simple one: nineteenth century. The S. Chiara façade is an example of Historicism, the catchall category that embraces the several revivalist "neo" or "revival" styles that came into fashion in the 1800s.

These new styles arose concurrently with — and in part stemmed from — the development of art history as a modern academic discipline. For the first time, scholars began in a systematic way to investigate the long history of European architecture, producing in due course the descriptive architectural classifications that are still in general use today: Classical, Medieval, Romanesque, Gothic, Renaissance, Mannerist, Baroque, Rococo. And just as architects during the Renaissance became fascinated with the Classical architecture of antiquity, Historicist architects of the 1800s became fascinated with the entire history of European building. The elaborate architectural costume ball that followed lasted more than a century, from the decline of the Baroque style in the late 1700s to the advent of Modernism in the early 1900s.

With two millennia's worth of architecture to draw on, nineteenth-century Historicism was nothing if not eclectic, and any past style was fair game for revival. Over a period of time, national preferences emerged. England, under the spell of the Victorian art critic John Ruskin, favored the Gothic; France favored the Renaissance, producing the elaborate Belle Epoch style of Neoclassicism that came to be known as Second Empire. Austria, when it tore down the medieval city walls of Vienna and replaced them with a broad boulevard studded with new civic buildings, created a veritable smorgasbord: Greek Revival for the government buildings (Greece signifying the cradle of democracy), Gothic Revival for the church (Gothic signifying the great medieval cathedrals), and Renaissance Revival for the museum and theater (the Renaissance signifying a flowering of art and culture).

In Italy, the medieval antipathy toward the Gothic was renewed. Just as the Gothic style never flourished in Rome during the Middle Ages, the Gothic Revival style never really caught on during the nineteenth century. When new churches were built or old churches renovated, it was the styles that immediately preceded and followed the Gothic that were most commonly adopted. Hence the hybrid that is S. Chiara: a façade that combines elements of both the Romanesque (the medieval-looking round-arched windows) and the Renaissance (the niches and main doorway). As is often the case with nineteenth-century hybrids, the mingling of styles is uncomfortable, and the lower half is clumsy in its own right, with an unhappy overall organization of elements that fails to cohere into a unified whole. Still, the historical impulse is typical of the era. Such backward glances are especially common among Rome's smaller neighborhood churches (there are several nearby, including S. Pantaleo, S. Ivo dei Bretoni, and S. Salvatore in Lauro), many of which received drastic face-lifts in the nineteenth century.

3-5 SANT' EUSTACHIO
Portico capitals: early 1700s
Apse and dome: Antonio Canevari, 1724–1730
(Piazza di S. Eustachio, west of the Pantheon)

*S. Eustachio (on the right), with the lantern of S. Ivo della Sapienza
in the background behind the Palazzo Stati-Maccarani.*

The bar at No. 82 is said to serve the best coffee in Rome; a less-celebrated attraction can be found across the street at the portico of S. Eustachio, which serves the best Baroque capitals. Their basic design is not original — they are close copies of Michelangelo's capitals at the Campidoglio — but the carving is superb. The usual Ionic papyrus scrolls are here utterly transformed, bursting to life as soft, sensuous, bell-shaped flowers at the peak of bloom. It is a splendid feat, and all the more unexpected given the humble surroundings. As an added attraction, each capital sports its own tiny stag's head, symbol of St. Eustace (probably a legendary figure, said to have been a Roman general under the emperor Trajan who converted to Christianity while hunting near Tivoli, where he encountered a stag that carried a shining cross between its antlers).

The prize of the small interior is the vaulted ceiling, on which the decoration is partly painted and partly stuccoed, but consistently applied throughout. The nave vault is straightforward in structure, but at the crossing it gives way to a profusion of softly billowing, pillowy shapes that seem to sit atop the cornice like great dollops of whipped cream. The contrast between the lower and upper areas of the interior is extreme, with the lower area, defined by its conventional cross shape, somehow giving rise to a dome ceiling that puffs itself out in every direction. Nor is the effect merely a matter of decoration, since it is the window openings that give rise to the unusual shapes. It is very late Baroque (the apse and dome were entirely rebuilt in the 1720s), and very fine.

3-6 PALAZZO STATI-MACCARANI
Giulio Romano, ca. 1520
(Piazza di S. Eustachio 81–85, west of the Pantheon)

Mannerism. As a classification used to describe sixteenth-century Italian art and architecture, the term was first applied to painting, where it signified a "mannered" style that was self-consciously artificial and exaggerated, and a reaction against the "ideal" beauty and balanced equanimity so prized by the High Renaissance. In architecture, the name denotes against-the-grain experimentation — a willingness (sometimes a willful willingness) to employ the Classical vocabulary in new and unexpected ways that deliberately contravene the historical rules and aesthetic theories of the previous era. Giulio Romano, who designed the Palazzo Stati-Maccarani around 1520, was a leading practitioner of the style, and went on to design what is perhaps the most famous Mannerist building in Italy, the Palazzo del Te in Mantua.

On the façade here, the most intriguing Mannerist element is the front-door surround. Rather than employ an aedicule design — the traditional arrangement of side columns and top pediment that is so common as a frame for doorways and windows all over town — Giulio has surrounded the entranceway with stone blocks that continue the groove pattern of the rustication on the rest of the ground floor. These blocks are "mannerist" because they are visually ambiguous, purposely lacking the clarity of form that characterized the architecture of the High Renaissance. Are the blocks to be read horizontally, as rustication? Or are they to be read vertically, as pilasters that support capitals? In fact, capitals of a sort *are* present (but reduced to a single molding), as is a rudimentary entablature (reduced to a single frieze-like band below a protruding cornice that doubles as the bottom of the triangular pediment). But the "entablature" does not read as a traditional Classical element because — like the bottom of the pediment — it is not allowed to continue across the top of the entranceway opening in the normal manner. Instead it is broken by a set of five vertical rusticated blocks, which push their way into the interior of the pediment as if trying to explode it into pieces from within.

Once these details are noticed, the door-surround does come to look like a conventional aedicule — if an unusual one — in form and effect. And in the process, the block-stacks flanking the doorway pull off a cunning visual trick. Because they are visually ambiguous, the stacks can read two ways: as a horizontal continuation of the rustication on the ground-floor wall (in which case the stacks seem to want to disappear back into the wall surface) or as vertical supports for the entablature and broken pediment above (in which case the stacks seem to step forward from the wall surface). To the casual eye, however, this double reading will not be obvious, and the broken pediment will just seem to have been placed rather arbitrarily and clumsily atop two stacks of stone blocks. The "trick" requires a closer look, and it is the need for this sort of close looking that is responsible for Mannerism's reputation as a difficult style, appealing mainly to specialists and to highly educated (some would say overeducated) connoisseurs.

The rest of the façade is considerably more straightforward than the door surround, with the power of the ground-floor rustication petering away to nothing as the building rises. On the middle story, strong alternating triangular and curved pediments above the windows contrast markedly with weak, paired pilasters in between, and on the top story the pilasters disappear altogether, turning into simple moldings that frame the windows. The vertical progression from great strength on the ground floor to almost minimalist flatness on the top floor seems logical enough, but it is Mannerist nonetheless because it departs from the standard Roman palazzo façade model, on which the *piano nobile* — the "noble story" located above the ground floor — is visually the most prominent design element (meant to denote the location of the principal reception rooms).

Across the piazza, the southern façade of the block-long extension to the seventeenth-century Palazzo Madama (the building that houses the Italian Senate) echoes the Palazzo Stati-Maccarani's look of Mannerist experiment, and with a force that makes the Stati-Maccarani doorway look downright timid. On the Palazzo Madama façade, the doorway-surround has expanded to occupy three-fifths of the ground-floor façade, and the massive paired columns look as if they are being held prisoner, riveted to the wall surface with straitjacket straps. The composition cannot be characterized as truly Mannerist, however, and it is the boldness of the conception that is the giveaway. This is not sixteenth-century Mannerism; this is nineteenth-century (actually twentieth-century, although the spirit is nineteenth-century) Mannerist Revival, dating from 1931.

3-7 LANTERN, S. IVO ALLA SAPIENZA
Francesco Borromini, 1643
(Overlooking the Piazza di S. Eustachio, west of the Pantheon)

The nondescript façade at the west end of the Piazza di S. Eustachio is the back side of the sixteenth-century Palazzo della Sapienza, the seat (until 1935) of the University of Rome; above it rises the oddly shaped dome of S. Ivo alla Sapienza, topped by the most unusual lantern in the city. The designer was Francesco Borromini, the most inventive and original Roman architect of the Baroque era.

Unlike his contemporaries Gianlorenzo Bernini and Pietro da Cortona — the other two towering figures of seventeenth-century Roman architecture — Borromini was not equally famous as a sculptor or a painter. Throughout his fifty-year career, he devoted his attentions solely to architecture. As a man he was notoriously suspicious and antisocial, but as an architect he was an idealist and a visionary. He pushed the edge of the Baroque envelope more persistently and more imaginatively than any of his peers, and his designs remain to this day uniquely individual.

The lantern of S. Ivo is no exception. When it was constructed in the 1640s, the lantern's lower half might just conceivably have been viewed as merely very bold (witness those audacious bites chomped out of the encircling cornice). But the lantern's upper half could only have been seen as wildly unconventional. The traditional hemispherical lantern cap is here stretched upward into a tall cone — almost a spire — and then fitted out with a ramp ascending to a carved crown of flames, out of which rises a single wrought-iron flame that supports an orb topped by a wrought-iron cross. The whole is elaborately carved, and possesses a fantastical quality — a look of a make-believe fairy-tale castle — that sets it apart from every other lantern in Rome.

What could have produced such an unusual design? Renaissance architecture offered no precedent whatsoever, and Borromini's rationale is unrecorded. In Renaissance literature, however, flames commonly symbolized the desire for knowledge, so it is possible that Borromini simply meant his lantern to stand as a symbol for the University. The spiral ramp would thus imply a journey — the journey of study — that culminates in the true goal of learning: knowledge of a world ruled by God (the flame supporting an orb dominated by a cross).

But architectural historians have never been wholly satisfied with this explanation. The unusual lack of historical precedent for the spiral design was seen as a challenge, and over the years Borromini's lantern has stimulated more academic speculation than any other post-Classical monument in Rome. Many possible sources have been suggested: the papal tiara, the Old Testament Pillar of Fire, ancient Mesopotamian ziggurats, the ruins of the Temple of Venus at Baalbek in Lebanon, contemporary drawings of the Tower of Babel, Dante's description of Mount Purgatory, and even Mount Olympus. Perhaps the most appealing theory centers around another famous (but long lost) piece of architecture: the ancient lighthouse of Alexandria.

Built around 280 B.C.E. and still standing as late as the twelfth century, the lighthouse was one of the Seven Wonders of the Ancient World. It was said to be more than 440 feet high — almost as high as the modern St. Peter's — and it stood at the entrance to the harbor of the ancient Egyptian port founded by Alexander the Great. Described by contemporary travelers as a spiral tower, the lighthouse was fancifully illustrated in 1572 by Maerten van Heemskerck, best known today for his drawings of the construction of the new St. Peter's. Van Heemskerck's engraving of the lighthouse (which Borromini might well have seen) bears a striking resemblance to the S. Ivo dome and lantern.

Martin van Heemskerck, The Pharos of Alexandria
(from Septem Orbis Miracula, published 1572).

Symbolically, the lighthouse and the lantern form an aptly matched pair. Both are emblems of refuge and safe haven meant to be seen from afar, and both overlooked centers of learning (Alexandria was famous as the site of the largest and most comprehensive library of Classical antiquity). One was dedicated to sailors, the other to scholars, but both connoted journeys — of the body or the mind — and both served to embody a destination, whether it be in this world or the next. And the obvious architectural connection should not be overlooked: what architectural form could be more appropriate for a symbolic "lantern" atop a dome than the world's most famous lighthouse?

Iconography aside, Borromini's lantern remains the most distinctive in Rome. As a crowning visual element, it is both elegant and fanciful — a typically Borrominian combination. And when its probable iconography is taken into account, the lantern stands revealed as something more than just a memorable architectural *divertissement*. As is so often the case with Borromini's architecture, an idiosyncratic and apparently iconoclastic design turns out to be deeply rooted in — and deeply respectful of — the traditions and creations of the ancient past.

The two nearby fountains, it should perhaps be noted, are respectful of the past as well, and make a fine complement to Borromini's lantern. The gigantic antique granite basin at the east end of the Via degli Staderari was uncovered in the neighborhood, and probably came from the Baths of Nero, which were located just to the north on the site of the Palazzo Madama and S. Luigi dei Francesi. As the accompanying wall plaque states, the basin was restored and presented by the Senate to the Roman electorate in 1987, in celebration of the fortieth anniversary of the signing of the Italian constitution. Beyond the basin (set into the wall of the Palazzo della Sapienza) is a more modest fountain dating from the 1920s, when each of the city's twenty-two *rioni* (wards) was given a sidewalk fountain reflecting its own special character. The pile of books here symbolizes scholarly learning — a particularly appropriate motif for a building and a *rione* that were once home to Rome's university.

3-8   SANT' IVO DELLA SAPIENZA
Francesco Borromini, 1643–1660
(Corso Rinascimento, west of the Piazza di S. Eustachio)

Rome is full of inventive Baroque church façades, but there is very little argument about which of them is the most dramatic. Time and time again, sightseers heading up the Corso Rinascimento walk by the Palazzo della Sapienza, glance offhandedly through the open front doors, and stop dead in their tracks. Their reaction is understandable, for at the far end of the Sapienza courtyard stands one of the city's most arresting view-stoppers: Francesco Borromini's S. Ivo della Sapienza. With its curved façade, bulging drum, stepped dome, and spiral lantern, the little church is like no other in Rome, and possesses a visual impact far beyond its size.

Borromini was the Baroque era's preeminent iconoclast, famous for ignoring Classical conventions and breaking Classical rules. But the exterior of S. Ivo is not so much an exercise in unorthodox Classicism as an essay in contrasting curves. From the concave curve of the entrance wall up through the convex billowings of the dome to the tall circular lantern (with its concave bites taken out of base and cornice), there is barely a flat surface or a right angle in sight. And at the dome's peak, the crown of the lantern introduces a new and highly unconventional curved motif: an ascending spiral. When the spiral is viewed as the climax of the façade's upward movement, the entire composition becomes a geometric progression that increases in tension as it decreases in size, beginning with the broad curve of the lower stories, progressing through the increasingly tense curves of the drum, dome, and lantern, and ending with the tight-as-a-spring spiral of the crown, which gathers all the forces into a single compact surge that shoots straight up into the sky.

Renaissance correctitude is here entirely overthrown. The canonical Renaissance arrangement of exterior parts — façade topped by drum topped by dome topped by lantern — is still present, but the Renaissance obsession with "perfect" circles, squares, cubes, and spheres is nowhere to be seen. The drum is not circular, but instead bulges out at its windows as if pushed from within; the dome is not hemispherical, but instead is stepped and flattened, almost disappearing from view. Only the lantern retains its expected cylindrical shape, but then it is elongated and topped with that most anti-Classical of crowning features, a spire. The ensemble as a whole is almost sculptural in character — molded rather than carved, as if modeled in clay rather than constructed out of stone.

Something very unusual is going on here. At S. Ivo it is not the elegant arrangement of Classical elements that impresses, it is the visual power of the *shapes* that underlie those elements. The composition's Classical details are of secondary importance, subservient in every way to the curving, billowing, spiraling surfaces they adorn. Such a departure from geometric simplicity — extreme even by Baroque standards — shocked many of Borromini's contemporaries. But Borromini was quite open about his desire to experiment and explore. "I would not have joined this profession," he once said, "with the aim of being merely an imitator." He was, in the seventeenth century, in some ways comparable to Frank Lloyd Wright in the twentieth, and S. Ivo was the Guggenheim Museum of its day — a radical new building shape that had never been seen before.

Inside, the surprises continue. Again, shape is paramount, and again the overall design is built up out of contrasting convex and concave curves, curves that produce an almost dizzying effect as they rollick their way around the perimeter of the centralized space. The ruling shape is most force-fully expressed by the main entablature, between the ground-floor pilaster capitals and dome: a six-pointed star with the points modified to become alternately convex and concave bays. This intricate ground plan is the most unusual in Rome, and a contemporary engraving suggests that Borromini may have conceived it as a geometric reference to that most ubiquitous of Roman insects, the Barberini bee (it was the Barberini pope Urban VIII who appointed Borromini to the post that produced the S. Ivo commission).

A seventeenth-century engraving summarizing the decoration of the S. Ivo dome, showing a Barberini bee in the center; the dome as constructed centers on a Holy Dove rather than a bee, and it has been suggested that the purpose of the bee in this engraving is to show that the form of the dome (and the ground plan of the church as a whole) follows logically from the shape of the bee, with the bee's head, body, and four wings generating the alternately concave and convex perimeter bays and the bee's six legs generating the ribs of the dome.

Many architectural historians dispute the bee thesis, but no one disputes the geometric rigor of the overall design. The S. Ivo ground plan was meticulously thought out. To generate the shape of the interior space, Borromini began with a "star-hexagon" — two interpenetrating equilateral triangles — on which he superimposed six circles possessing a diameter the same length as the sides of the star's points. He then arrived at the ground plan by drawing a perimeter that jumped between star and circles, alternating short straight star segments with alternately convex and concave circle segments.

Historically speaking, there is a certain irony here. After S. Ivo was completed, the unconventionality of its ground plan — all those walls changing direction every few feet — led some critics to condemn Borromini as the ultimate corrupter of all things Renaissance. When the general reaction against the Baroque style set in during the eighteenth century, the negative verdict became virtually universal. In so ardently embracing an arbitrary and undisciplined Baroque complexity (the argument went), Borromini had sacrificed Renaissance rigor, and had betrayed the orderly ideals of his illustrious predecessors. Yet the geometry that produced the S. Ivo ground plan is not in the least arbitrary or undisciplined; with its emphasis on circles and equilateral triangles, it is as ordered and as "perfect" as any Renaissance purist could wish. The results may be spatially complex, but the underlying idea is elegantly simple.

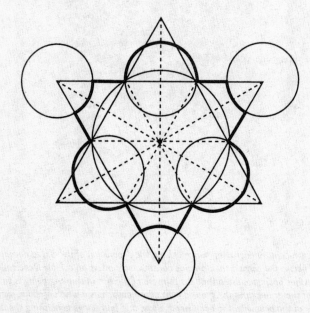

Diagram showing the geometric genesis of the S. Ivo ground plan.

The overall plan of the S. Ivo interior, then, is not so capricious as its unorthodox wall curves might at first suggest, and the rigor of its geometry can be viewed as continuing a Renaissance tradition, even if in a highly complex and Baroque manner. What cannot be viewed as traditional, however, is S. Ivo's extraordinary dome. With characteristic audacity, Borromini chooses not to limit the unique perimeter shape to the ground floor, as might be expected. Instead he opts *to continue the plan of the walls into the dome.* Here Borromini was venturing onto entirely new ground, and his vision was utterly without precedent.

Prior to the construction of S. Ivo, domes had always been either circular or oval, and in departing from this tradition Borromini faced a formidable technical challenge. At the base of the dome (at the level of the windows), the complicated convex-concave alternation of the ground plan remains entirely intact. But at the peak of the dome (at the ring around the lantern), the convex-concave alternation has disappeared, and the dome is conventionally shaped (that is, uniformly concave). This transition from complexity to simplicity is structurally straightforward in the three uniformly concave lobes of the dome, where the wall surface starts out concave at the base and remains concave all the way up to the peak. But in the other three lobes — the convex lobes, with their straight sides and convex center — the progression is anything but straightforward. At the level of the windows, the wall decoration curves inward toward the viewer; at the level of the winged cherubim (just below the lantern ring), the wall decoration curves outward away from the viewer. Somewhere in between the wall surface *reverses shape,* and in the process the straight-convex-straight form of the base morphs into the simple concave curve of the peak.*

Given the radical nature of this design, it would be reasonable to expect a certain awkwardness in the result. But Borromini handles the problem so skillfully that it is impossible to see exactly where the transition from convex to concave takes place, and to the casual eye the concave lobes appear similar in structure to their convex neighbors. To the more attentive eye, however, the subtle transformations of shape impart to the dome surfaces a look of extraordinary plasticity; like the church exterior, the dome interior appears molded rather than constructed, a shape more sculptural than architectural.

---

*The six dome ribs (which run from the base of the dome to the circle of stars surrounding the lantern at the peak) undergo a similar transformation. At the base of the dome each rib possesses two distinct sides that form a sharp 90-degree angle, but as the rib rises the sides gradually flatten out, and at the peak of the dome the rib has actually become slightly concave, following the uniform overall curve of the upper portion of the dome.

The same plasticity can be seen on the ground-floor level, where the Classical pilasters do not so much decorate the walls as react to them. Far from being a collection of uniform verticals (as in earlier centralized churches), Borromini's pilasters expand and contract as the wall surface moves in and out. Where the walls protrude into the central space, the pilasters are doubled; where the walls draw back from the central space, the pilasters are halved and compressed together. The resulting rhythm of contraction and expansion — of tension and release — produces an effect that is almost organic, as if the scrunched pilasters could at any moment be swallowed up by the walls and disappear entirely.

It is, in the end, the antithesis of Renaissance simplicity and stability, full of exhilarating movement. Yet — and this is the paradox that makes the interior so extraordinary — in Borromini's hands the unprecedented complexity of design ultimately serves to produce what is probably the most unified interior space of the entire Baroque era. When read horizontally, S. Ivo's walls seem to shrink and swell as they dance their way around the perimeter of the space. But when read vertically, the walls gather themselves together into a single uprush of movement that begins at ground level and then continues straight up into the dome, uniting ground floor and dome into a single, unified, soaring whole. At the peak of the dome, complexity and simplicity are reconciled as the complicated ground plan finally resolves itself into a simple circle surrounding the lantern.

The peak of the dome also supplies another climax: the lantern, with its flood of light illuminating the Dove of Heaven. The Dove caps a decorative scheme that grows more complex as it rises, and that is based not upon the Barberini bee but upon the oak branches, stars, and piled-up *monti* (mounds or mountains) of the Chigi coat of arms.* As always with Borromini, the carved decoration is unconventional, and worth examining down to the minutest detail. Within the pediments crowning the two subsidiary ground-floor doorway frames, for instance, cherub heads peer out, supported by outstretched wings that — a typically enlivening Borrominian touch

---

*The change in ruling motif reflects the fact that the interior decoration was not carried out until the pontificate of the Chigi pope Alexander VII. Today the overall look of the decoration may not be quite as Borromini planned. The interior of the church was renovated in the 1850s; the gallery openings in the convex bays were modified slightly, the bay containing the high altar was modified dramatically (it originally possessed a window), and an elaborate scheme of false painted marbling was added throughout. In the 1960s, the false marbling was painted over, but the evidence concerning Borromini's original plans was inconclusive. The current uniformly white-paint scheme is thus open to question, and some authorities suggest that Borromini would have preferred certain of the interior's decorative elements to be set off in shades of off-white or gray.

— reach out beyond the allotted space to rest at their tips on the door-frame molding below. In the convex bays of the dome, the decorative moldings above the windows (and above the cherub heads) do double duty as part of a larger, elastically deformed triumphal-arch motif that supports the Chigi *monti*. Similarly inventive details can be found throughout the interior, all leading the eye up to the crowning lantern. With its round columns supporting a crisp miniature entablature — the theme of convex-concave explored one last time — the lantern sits atop the dome like a tiny temple, a fitting frame for the Dove of Heaven, whose rays form (in Borromini's own words) "tongues of fire signifying the coming of the Holy Spirit, bringer of true Wisdom."

Borromini as an architect was audacious and rebellious, and his fundamental insight — that the primary purpose of architecture is the molding of exterior form and the shaping of interior space — was not well received in Italy. But his work was a revelation to the less Classical-minded architects of northern Europe, most of whom visited Rome as part of their training and then went home to produce the great swelling, singing Baroque church interiors of Germany and Austria. More recently, Borromini has come to seem astonishingly prescient; his love of pure form anticipates the architectural developments of the twentieth century, which began with the wholesale rejection of Classical decoration and ended with a succession of buildings — Frank Gehry's Guggenheim Museum in Bilbao is the most famous — that are frankly and unabashedly sculptural in effect. Such buildings, when they succeed, create an artful balance between order and disorder, simplicity and complexity, expectation and surprise. The struggle to achieve this balance is fundamental to Borromini's work, and it led him to produce the most original and inventive architecture of the entire Baroque era.

3-9   SINGLE COLUMN, PIAZZA DEI MASSIMI
(Piazza dei Massimi, west of the Corso Rinascimento one block north of the Corso Vittorio Emanuele)

Rome is full of anonymous fragments of antiquity, but few catch the eye as poignantly as this single unmarked and unemployed column, worn and battered, standing all by itself in an apparent cul-de-sac off the busy Corso Rinascimento. The surrounding city goes about its business, and does not acknowledge (or even seem to care) where the column came from or why it remains behind. But for once the lack of an informative historical label feels altogether appropriate, for the orphaned column, standing alone in a sequestered corner of the teeming city, is made instantly memorable by its aura of isolated loneliness.

In fact, the reerected column was once part of the Odeon of Domitian (the outdoor theater that occupied the site in ancient times), and it proves, upon further examination, to be not quite so solitary as it at first seems. Viewed from inside the piazza — where the faded remains of the original sixteenth-century painted decoration can still be made out on the wall of the Palazzo Massimo alle Colonne to the left — the column turns out to possess an unexpected companion. To the north from the piazza's entrance edge, visible in the distance at the end of one of the city's happiest acciden- tal vistas, stands a second antiquity: one of the thirteen ancient obelisks reerected (beginning in the sixteenth century) by Rome's modern popes.

The contrast between the two eye-catching verticals could hardly be more striking. The column, detached and ignored, survives as a forlorn reminder of a glorious past forever lost. But the distant obelisk was raised — and raised atop a gloriously sculpted pile — specifically to present the oppo- site view: to proclaim a great city revived and renewed, its past glories recap- tured and its future glories assured. This is Bernini's celebrated Fountain of the Four Rivers, the *tour de force* centerpiece of the finest of all Rome's city- spaces, the incomparable Piazza Navona.

3-10   PIAZZA NAVONA

There are seven entrances to the Piazza Navona, but two are special, and it is a toss-up as to which entrance a first-time visitor should favor. The best long-view entrance — and the hardest to find — is from the Piazza dei Massimi to the south. From the eastern edge of that tiny backwater the build- ings on either side of the block-long Via della Posta Vecchia enticingly frame the Fountain of the Four Rivers in the distance and invite exploration of the piazza's long north-south axis. The best short-view entrance is from the Corso Rinascimento to the east, opposite the Palazzo Madama. Here the approach along the very short Corsia Agonale ends quickly and abruptly, all but dump- ing the piazza's splendors into the visitor's lap. Both entrances are effective in their opposite ways, and both should be experienced.

The individual characters of Rome's four other great cityspaces can be traced to a single mind or structure: the Campidoglio and St. Peter's Square are architectural masterpieces laid out by the greatest artists of their era, Michelangelo and Bernini; the Piazza di Spagna basks in the glow of its famous steps; the Piazza Venezia takes the problematical Victor Emmanuel Monument in stride because of its centrality, size, and greenery. But the Piazza Navona is different. It is not defined by a single dominating element, nor was it planned by a single genius. Indeed, it was hardly planned at all. It is in large part an accident of history.

The piazza began not as a piazza but as a stadium, constructed by Domitian in the first century C.E. as part of the complex of public buildings that covered the entire Campus Martius area. The stadium seated some 30,000 people and was used primarily for athletic contests (known as *agoni,* a word which in corrupted form eventually supplied the name for both the square — *agoni* became *in agona* became *navona* — and its main church, S. Agnese in Agone). The stadium was stripped of its marble in the mid-fourth century, and by the fifth century it was in ruins. But it retained its visible structure for more than a thousand years, until Pope Sixtus IV in 1477 chose the site for a market transferred from the base of the Capitoline Hill. The new makeshift piazza flourished, and by the end of the century the stadium's seats had disappeared completely, covered over by taverns and shops serving the market's patrons.

Rescued from ruin and transformed by its new commercial use, the stadium served a purely utilitarian purpose for some 150 years; its transformation into the showplace it is today did not begin until 1644, when Cardinal Giambattista Pamphili was elected Pope Innocent X. The Pamphili family possessed a modest palazzo on the west side of the square, and Innocent set out to turn the enclosure into a family enclave similar to the one his predecessor Urban VIII had created across town in the Piazza Barberini. First came an expansion of the family residence, combining the original palazzo with adjacent buildings and building over several small streets in the process. Next came the fountains: Bernini designed the centerpiece Fountain of the Four Rivers in 1647, and modified the pre-existing fountain at the piazza's southern end by adding the figure of the Moor in 1653 (the balancing northern fountain was constructed during the sixteenth century, but the sculpture of Neptune battling a sea monster was not added until 1878). Finally, and most importantly, came the church of S. Agnese in Agone, designed (mostly) by Borromini, which began to rise adjacent to the much-expanded Palazzo Pamphili in 1652.

It is the church that is the key to the piazza's power. The curved, recessed, and stepped front façade is the only architectural element around the square that steps back from the perimeter line of the central space; in doing so it marks the façade as the most important in the piazza, increases the prominence of the church dome, and creates distinctive wings — towers, really —

on either side. At the same time, the dome and twin towers form a powerful architectural trinity that dominates the square without threatening it. All the other buildings defer to the church in height, giving the perimeter a prominent and distinguished primary focus that balances and complements the piazza's fountain centerpiece.

Everything works together, and works splendidly. The size and shape of the original stadium turn out to be ideal: large and open enough to offer breathing room, small and enclosed enough to retain a human scale and furnish a sense of safe haven from the crowded jumble of streets nearby.* The central church and fountain, despite being oddly placed in relation to each other, work together to give the overall space a strong Baroque identity. And the combination of sidewalk cafés and street performers — caricaturists, puppeteers, and magicians have replaced the acrobats and mountebanks of earlier centuries — adds the activity necessary to spark the whole magnificent composition to vibrant, pulsating life.

In a sense, the piazza is the creative antithesis of the Campidoglio, Michelangelo's great architectural masterpiece atop the Capitoline Hill. At the Campidoglio, all the elements — the general layout, the individual buildings, the central statue — were carefully planned by a single brilliant mind. At the Piazza Navona, the minds at work (most notably Bernini at the fountain and his archrival Borromini at the church) paid no attention to each other, creating their own works in their own way on their own turf. Such a history — weird origins, weird shape, hodgepodge growth, rivalry between architects, no overall planning — should by rights have produced a disaster. Instead, the Piazza Navona bumbled its way to glory, ultimately emerging from the ruins of Domitian's stadium as Rome's most memorable and beloved outdoor cityspace. Go figure.

3-11 FONTANA DEI QUATTRO FIUMI
Gianlorenzo Bernini, 1647–1651
(Piazza Navona)

The twin towers, curved façade, and dome of S. Agnese in Agone dominate the Piazza Navona with commanding confidence, but — happily —

---

*And enclosed enough to be intentionally flooded. During summers in the eighteenth century, the aristocracy of Rome regularly entertained itself by filling the piazza with water and staging water jousts, mock sea battles, and horse-and-carriage soak-your-neighbor free-for-alls whose only point seems to have been to generate a maximum amount of splashing.

they never overpower the piazza's centerpiece, the famous Fountain of the Four Rivers. The fountain's creator, Gianlorenzo Bernini, was the preeminent Italian sculptor of the Baroque era, and the special circumstances surrounding the commissioning and construction of the fountain shed a good deal of light on both his talent and his personality.

Bernini's gifts were prodigious and multifaceted. Like Michelangelo, he was primarily a sculptor, but — again like Michelangelo — he was also an architect, a painter, and a poet. The most famous description of his wide-ranging abilities comes from a contemporary, the English writer John Evelyn, who on a visit to Rome in 1644 noted with astonishment in his *Diary* that Bernini had staged an opera for which he "painted the scenes, cut the statues, invented the engines, composed the music, writ the comedy, and built the theater all himself." Bernini was also (unlike his neurotic contemporary Borromini) polished and self-assured socially, and adept at playing the courtier when circumstances required. In his work he was possessed of boundless energy; as Howard Hibbard describes it in his biography *Bernini*:

> He would work the marble for hours at a stretch without stopping; when he was old and his assistants wanted him to stop work he resisted, saying, "Let me stay here, since I'm in love with it." ... When working, he seemed to be in an ecstasy and it sometimes seemed to observers that he was animating the statue by sending his own soul into it with his eyes. Cardinals and princes came and went without saying a word in order to leave him undisturbed. In Bernini's time ... these gifts were considered God-given. Bernini constantly disclaimed any praise given his works, saying that whatever gifts he had came from God. He often said that the more he worked the less he knew, and this was more than rhetoric. The Idea (from God) always excited Bernini; its execution left him increasingly dissatisfied. In this respect he is similar to Michelangelo, with the important difference that Michelangelo was an introverted neurotic who left most of his works unfinished while Bernini, a typical extrovert, often let his assistants finish the job.

Born in 1598, Bernini spent all but a few months of his working life in Rome; he served eight different popes before dying in 1680 at the age of eighty-one. His most enthusiastic supporter was undoubtedly Pope Urban VIII, the greatest sculptural patron in papal history. While still a cardinal, Urban had become one of Bernini's closest personal friends, and on the day of his elevation, correctly convinced that Bernini's renown as an artist in ages to come would outshine even his own fame as pontiff, he supposedly called the sculptor to him and pronounced what must be the greatest compliment in all of art history: "Your luck is great, Cavaliere, to see Cardinal Maffeo Barberini become Pope, but ours is much greater to have Cavaliere Bernini alive in our pontificate." Bernini was only twenty-three years old at the time, but he had already received the three commissions from Cardinal Scipione Borghese that made him famous (*Pluto and Persephone, Apollo and Daphne,* and *David,* all today in the Galleria Borghese museum in the Villa Borghese park).

Bernini's friendship and partnership with Urban VIII lasted until the pope's death in 1644; during the second half of Urban's papacy, Bernini controlled virtually all of the pope's artistic and architectural projects. But Urban VIII's profligacy ultimately left the papacy near bankruptcy, and his successor, Innocent X — a member of the Pamphili family, notorious rivals of the Barberinis — was in no mood to continue Urban's lavish artistic patronage. Under the new regime, papal commissions declined drastically, and the sculptural and architectural projects that previously would have been Bernini's went instead to his rivals Alessandro Algardi and Francesco Borromini. Bernini was ostracized from the papal inner circle, and when in 1647 Innocent X held a competition for a new fountain in the Piazza Navona (where the Pamphili were expanding their family palazzo), Bernini was the only prominent sculptor in Rome not invited to submit a design.

But the pope had not reckoned on Bernini's ingenuity and persistence. With the help of Innocent's nephew-in-law Prince Niccolò Ludovisi (or perhaps — the stories differ — Innocent's sister-in-law Donna Olimpia), Bernini contrived to smuggle an anonymous model for the fountain into the papal presence. Pope Innocent, immediately taken with the design, studied the miniature sculpture for a rapt half hour before he caught on. "I have been tricked," he finally announced. "This design cannot be by anyone but Bernini, and the only way to resist executing his works is not to see his plans." The pope was won over, and Bernini received the commission. "Rome sometimes sees poorly," was Bernini's comment on the episode, "but it never goes blind."

Several years later, Bernini expressed his appreciation for the commission with typical panache. In mid-1651 the pope and his entourage — some fifty courtiers — scheduled a special outing to visit the almost-completed fountain. During his detailed and enthusiastic inspection, the pope was disappointed only once: when he asked if the waters could be turned on briefly, he was told, regretfully, that the conduits were not quite ready. Finally, after more than an hour, the pope reluctantly prepared to leave. His departing gesture was to bestow a benevolent and approving blessing on the fountain, and as he turned away he heard a sudden roar. When he turned back to the fountain, he saw water gushing from all sides. Bernini, knowing in advance of the pope's visit, had arranged for the fountain's inaugural flow to be triggered by the papal blessing. "In giving us this great unexpected joy," the pope told Bernini, "you have added ten years to our life."

The fountain itself is a marvel of engineering. Pope Innocent's concept — to furnish the piazza with a new fountain centerpiece by raising an ancient Egyptian obelisk that lay in pieces in the ruined Circus of Maxentius to the south of the city on the Appian Way — was not a radical one. Some sixty years earlier, Pope Sixtus V had raised obelisks at important sites all over Rome. But Bernini placed this particular obelisk in a position that had never been seen before: he set it directly over a dramatic void in the supporting sculpture at its base. This void — the "Idea" that Bernini would have attributed to God's inspiration (and undoubtedly the feature that so entranced the pope when he saw the original model) — probably caused concern among skeptics during construction, but in fact the general plan is capable of supporting far larger structures, as the similarly shaped Eiffel Tower in Paris was to prove two centuries later.

Iconographically, the fountain's program is typical of the Baroque era, representing the spread of Christianity throughout the four continents of the then known world. The crowning feature atop the obelisk is the Pamphili dove, symbolizing both peace and the triumph of Christianity over paganism. The obelisk itself is an ancient symbol of sunlight, here transfigured by the dove to represent the light of religious revelation. The four figures on the rocks at the obelisk's base are river gods, representing what was at the time thought to be the earth's four most important rivers: the Danube in Europe (closest to S. Agnese, reaching out to straighten the papal arms), the Ganges in Asia (holding an oar, perhaps representing the river's navigability across the length of India), the Nile in Africa (with its head covered to indicate that the river's source was unknown), and the Rio de la Plata in America (with its arms raised, and with coins on the rocks alongside symbolizing the wealth of the New World). All the figures were designed by Bernini, but they were executed by his assistants. Bernini himself is said to have carved (or at least finished) the rock, the palm tree, the lion, and the horse, all of which needed to be carved on-site; he was also presumably responsible for the entertainingly unrealistic armadillo — an exotic animal he had clearly never seen — in the basin below and behind the figure representing the Rio de la Plata.

As the central element of the square, the fountain is a true sculptural showpiece — a towering, forceful vertical that seems, because of the void below, almost to float above its elaborately carved base. It would be hard to imagine a more effective foil for the architecture around the perimeter. Visually enticing as the surrounding buildings are — a fine and typical Roman motley called to order by the church of S. Agnese — it is the fountain, with its bravura sculpture and refreshing rushing waters, that gives the square its incomparable aura of permanent holiday.

3-12 SANT' AGNESE IN AGONE
Girolamo Rainaldi (1652–1653), Francesco Borromini (1653–1655), Carlo Rainaldi (1657–1666), Gianlorenzo Bernini (1666–1668), Carlo Rainaldi or perhaps Pietro da Cortona (1668–1672)
(Piazza Navona)

According to legend — actually a number of legends — St. Agnes was a beautiful young girl who was born in the late third century shortly before Rome converted to Christianity. When she was about thirteen years old, she renounced marriage in favor of Christ, and her frustrated suitors betrayed her Christianity to the authorities. She was consigned to a brothel, but when she was stripped of her clothes, her nakedness was hidden from view by the sudden and spontaneous growth of her hair. Continuing to resist the threats of her persecutors, she was condemned to be burned at the stake, but the flames refused to touch her. Ultimately she was beheaded, and was buried on the Via Nomentana, where one of Rome's oldest churches (dating from around 350 C.E. and still intact) was built in her honor.

Though there is no evidence to document the story of St. Agnes beyond the fact of her martyrdom, the Piazza Navona was traditionally thought to be the location of the brothel in which she was confined. A church was constructed on the site as early as the eighth century, but when Pope Innocent X renovated the piazza in the mid-1600s, he decided to replace the existing structure entirely, in part because it was oriented away from the piazza, with its entrance facing the Via dell' Anima and its choir abutting the square's central space. The new church was to be a far larger structure, intended to complement the size and scale of the enlarged Pamphili family palazzo next door and the magnificent new fountain in the center of the square.

The project did not go well. The initial design was completed by Girolamo Rainaldi (with the help of his son, Carlo) in 1652; within a year, both the façade and the interior had progressed to a height of at least ten feet. The design was much criticized, however, and by June of 1653, Rainaldi was replaced by Borromini, who preserved Rainaldi's layout for the interior but began anew on the façade, pulling Rainaldi's work down. By 1655, when Pope Innocent X died, the undecorated dome (except for the lantern) was in place, the interior was finished up to the level of the column capitals, and the façade had reached the level of the cornice. But Innocent's heirs lost interest and Borromini lost heart, and in 1657 Carlo Rainaldi returned under the auspices of Innocent's nephew Carlo Pamphili. Rainaldi was in turn dismissed in 1666, when Pamphili died and the project was taken over by his widow, who effectively put Bernini in charge by adding him to the commission overseeing completion. Bernini moved on in 1668, and the finishing touches were carried out by either Carlo Rainaldi (returning yet again) or Pietro da Cortona.

Given such a history — too many cooks with a vengeance — the façade of S. Agnese has no business being as good as it is. The basic plan is Girolamo Rainaldi's, the basic design is Borromini's, the twin towers are Carlo Rainaldi's (Borromini's design called for towers that possessed less height but more invention), and the attic is Bernini's (Borromini's design called for a more prominent balustrade and a higher, more complex pediment over the main entrance). But somehow all the disparate elements manage to cohere beautifully, and only Bernini's plain triangular entrance pediment fizzles — an unexpectedly pedestrian detail that looks distinctly halfhearted, given the boldness of the architecture around it.*

Inside, the building's split-personality origins are far more visible. On the lower level (up to the cornice), the decoration is limited to carving, reflecting Borromini's preference for pure architecture accented only by sculpture; on the upper level (above the cornice), painting and gilding predominate, reflecting Bernini's propensity to combine all the arts into one grand, comprehensive scheme. This artificial segregation sets off an unseemly decorative contest, with marble sculpture squaring off against gilded painting. To make matters worse, the whole interior is so profuse in its decoration that the overall effect verges on cacophony, as each level tries to outshout the other.

---

*Bernini is sometimes said to have expressed his view of Borromini's façade in his design for the Fountain of the Four Rivers, where he — so the story goes — arranged the postures of the fountain's four river gods to show unanimous disapproval: the Danube turns away in protest, the Ganges *rows* away in protest, the Nile covers his head rather than look, and the Rio de la Plata throws up his arm to protect himself from falling masonry. Entertaining as this rumor may be, it cannot be true, since the design of the fountain predates the design of the church by several years.

In the end, it is probably best to try to ignore the visual noise and concentrate on the space itself, which is far more successful than the decoration. The ground plan is unusual for Rome, being based on a centralized Greek cross, a plan that eliminates the usual nave and lends the dome special prominence and drama. Both Bramante and Michelangelo favored this type of plan for St. Peter's, but ultimately the idea was rejected in favor of the traditional cross shape with long nave. Had the Greek cross plan been carried out at St. Peter's, the church of S. Agnese gives a fair idea — on both the inside and the outside — of what the result would have looked like.

3-13 PALAZZO MADAMA
Façade: Paolo Maruscelli, 1642
(Corso del Rinascimento, opposite the Corsia Agonale entrance into the
Piazza Navona)

Like most Roman palazzi, the Palazzo Madama possesses a façade that is straightforward and unadventurous in its architectural organization: three rows of windows (four if the attic is included) exhibited in prosaic array, with the ground-floor entrance portal fitting in a bit awkwardly, as if it had barged its way into the composition at the last minute. The individual window-surrounds, however, are neither prosaic nor awkward. They are richly and crisply carved, and their air of elegant High Baroque fancy dress makes the more conventional windows on the neighboring palazzi look embarrassingly naked. The row of smaller attic windows, especially, is deftly and imaginatively handled, with the window-surrounds growing logically out of the architrave, which detours around the windows both to hang from and merge with the lively carved frieze between architrave and cornice. The façade as a whole may not be memorable as architecture, but its windows possess high style.

Nearby Museum: In the Piazza di S. Apollinare (two blocks directly north of the Piazza Navona), the sixteenth-century Palazzo Altemps has been recently restored, and is now an adjunct of the Museo Nazionale Romano. The museum is devoted entirely to ancient sculpture, and the display centers around the Ludovisi collection, begun in 1621 by Cardinal Ludovico Ludovisi, nephew of Pope Gregory XV. As was the custom at the time, many of the pieces were extensively restored by the finest sculptors of the day (among them Bernini and Algardi), but the labels and drawings accompanying the statuary do an admirable job of sorting out what is what. The high points of the extensive collection are undoubtedly the famous *Ludovisi Throne,* a Greek work dating from the fifth century B.C.E. that depicts the birth of Aphrodite from the sea, and the *Galatian Committing Suicide,* a first-century B.C.E. Roman copy of a Greek bronze (in ancient times the bronze was part of a grouping that also contained the original of the *Dying Gaul* in the Capitoline Museum).

3-14   ENTRANCE TO THE STADIUM OF DOMITIAN
Completed 86 C.E.
(Piazza di Tor Sanguigna, outside the Piazza Navona at its north end)

When Mussolini widened the Corso Rinascimento (to the east of the Piazza Navona) in the 1930s, he supplied the answer to a question that had been debated among Rome's city planners for decades: Should the Piazza Navona be opened up to accommodate traffic and to provide a boulevard view of the Palazzo di Giustizia across the river? Happily, the piazza was left intact and traffic was rerouted around it, although several of the buildings at the northern end were demolished and replaced. In the process, the ruins of the ancient northern entrance to Domitian's Stadium were excavated and then left open to street view (on the left after exiting the piazza). The display provides a powerful demonstration of how far the ground level of the city has risen over the centuries.

3-15   PALAZZO DI GIUSTIZIA
Guglielmo Calderini, 1887–1911
(Across the Tiber, but best viewed from the south side without crossing the river, from the point where the Via Zanardelli meets the Ponte Umberto)

Outside the northern end of the Piazza Navona, the vista up the Via Zanardelli from the Piazza di Tor Sanguigna ends in a fine view-stopper: the wide central bay of the enormous Palazzo di Giustizia, built to house law courts and judiciary offices. But the walk up the street for a full view ends in disappointment. The building as a whole, it turns out, possesses what is probably the most overdressed façade in the entire city. It is a perfect example of the late-nineteenth-century architectural phenomenon known as *horror vacui* — the compulsion to fill up every inch of available wall space with elaborate decoration, to slather on the Classical detailing as if it were so much cake icing. In the early 1900s, buildings such as this began to give Neoclassicism a bad name, and the backlash that followed ultimately produced a sweeping architectural revolution. After a reign of some five hundred years, Classicism was banished utterly, and the stripped-down form-follows-function look of twentieth-century Modernism took over as the ruling style.

Over the years, however, many Roman residents have come to view the Palace of Justice with affection, if not respect. Recently cleaned, restored, and reoccupied — the swampy ground next to the river was inadequately prepared when the palazzo was built, and for decades the entire building sat empty because it was in danger of collapse — the palazzo occupies a prime piece of riverfront property next to the Castel S. Angelo, and the river setting shows off the façade to great advantage. Nowadays the building appears to have settled in quite comfortably, and has come to seem an accepted member of the Roman palazzo family, like an aged and eccentric aunt who insists upon wearing all her jewelry all the time.

3-16   LARGO FEBO

SANTA MARIA DELL' ANIMA
Façade: possibly Giuliano da Sangallo, ca. 1500

SAN NICOLA DEI LORENESI
Façade: Francesco Giardini (François du Jardin), 1635–1636
(West of the Piazza Navona, at the north end of the
Via di S. Maria dell' Anima)

An unexpected oasis, tucked away in the midst of a tangle of medieval streets near the north end of the Via di S. Maria dell' Anima. The piazza (officially known as the Largo Febo) is tiny, but its burst of greenery makes it one of old Rome's most picturesque hidden corners. The two churches abutting the piazza are unprepossessing but offer a notable architectural contrast.

The larger (and older) is S. Maria dell' Anima, built around 1500. Like S. Agostino, the façade was one of the first in the city to reflect the Renaissance passion for antiquity, and like S. Agostino, the result is distinctly clumsy. The Classical vocabulary is competently spelled out — pilasters and cornices to differentiate the three stories, columns and pediments to frame the ground-floor window and door openings. But the individual elements relate to one another only in the most tentative and rudimentary fashion, and appear tacked onto the wall surface as if added at the last minute to gussy things up. The pilasters are the worst offenders; spindly as matchsticks, they are over-powered in the middle by the façade's cumbersome window openings and enfeebled at each end by an awkwardly spaced pairing. Once again, the problem of how to design an architecturally unified Classical churchfront remains unsolved.

Across the street, the little church of S. Nicola dei Lorenesi makes the solution look easy. Built long after S. Maria dell' Anima, the façade is unexpectedly reserved for its Baroque date (1635), as if purposely taking its cues from its neighbor. Exactly the same vocabulary is used, but this time the elements cohere into a unified composition, and the pilasters seem to grow naturally out of the wall surface, serving visually both to support the façade's cornices and to frame its niches and windows. It is not an especially notable façade — well-ordered prose rather than intricate poetry — but its effortless confidence makes the façade of S. Maria dell' Anima look primitive and oafish by comparison.

3-17 SANTA MARIA DELLA PACE
Façade and piazza: Pietro da Cortona, 1656
Cloister: Donato Bramante, 1500
(Piazza di S. Maria della Pace, west of the Piazza Navona; best approached from the south, along the Via della Pace)

S. Maria della Pace.

Buried in the center of chaotic old Rome and eccentrically situated at the end of what appears to be a short, insignificant cul-de-sac, S. Maria della Pace is one of the city's smallest churches. But its size and obscure placement are misleading in the extreme; as architecture, S. Maria della Pace is anything but small. The apparent cul-de-sac has some memorable Baroque tricks up its sleeve.

At first sight, it is the church's unusual semicircular entrance portico that attracts — and startles — the eye. With its paired Doric columns and gently swelling roof, the portico looks like a tiny Roman temple unexpectedly grafted onto a Christian churchfront. In part, the melding of two such disparate wholes may be read as an elaborate (and typically Baroque) symbolic gesture: the pagan entranceway precedes the church proper just as pagan religion preceded Christianity. But architecturally the portico is more than just an ingenious historical conceit. It is also the jewel-like centerpiece of a small *tour de force* of Baroque city planning that embraces the entire piazza.

The plan was conceived for a purely practical reason: to alleviate traffic jams. During the first half of the seventeenth century, S. Maria della Pace came to occupy a special place among neighborhood Roman churches. Because it was situated near the papal law courts, and because it enjoyed the unusual privilege of celebrating mass in the afternoon, the church attracted an uncommonly distinguished daily congregation that included many of the nobles, church dignitaries, judges, and lawyers who had been tied up in court all morning. Worshippers of such high social standing of course required the latest fashion in transport, and in seventeenth-century Rome, fashion dictated elaborate horse-drawn carriages, the bigger the better. But S. Maria della Pace was tucked away inside a maze of narrow medieval alleyways and afforded no easy access. So traffic jams around the church became the daily norm, along with unseemly quarrels over precedence and protocol — who outranked whom, who had the right to approach first, who had the right to park where, and so forth. By 1655, when Cardinal Fabio Chigi was elected Pope Alexander VII, the problem had become a notorious civic embarrassment.

Alexander VII had a special interest in the church — it contained a Chigi family chapel constructed by his ancestor Agostino Chigi and decorated by Raphael in the early 1500s — and he was determined to find a solution to the traffic problem. He called in Pietro da Cortona as planner and architect, and a small but ingenious urban renewal project was soon under way. Several of the houses opposite the church were purchased and torn down to create turnaround room for carriages, and Cortona integrated his façade designs for the secular buildings facing the new piazza with a bold plan for a brand-new churchfront. Alexander's pleasure in the result is evident from the decree he inscribed on the wall to the left of the church:

It is forbidden for anyone to build buildings, add stories, make any changes to the exterior or any renovations in this piazza of S. Maria della Pace, or its environs, or on the adjacent streets. If anyone dares to disobey this pronouncement they will be penalized . . . June 27, 1659.

The dramatic effect of S. Maria della Pace's bold and revolutionary portico — the first of its kind anywhere — tends to overshadow the rest of Cortona's façade. But the façade as a whole, if less radical than the portico, is no less remarkable. With typically Baroque ingenuity, Cortona has here combined two traditional but seemingly antithetical façade conventions into a single, unified whole.

As a moment's study reveals, the portico and the upper story above it constitute only the central portion of S. Maria della Pace's overall design. Despite the fact that the church's interior is only as wide as the portico, Cortona has given the façade subsidiary side wings. These wings are in fact false fronts — neither side-wing doorway leads into the church proper, and the doorway on the right does not even lead to an interior, but rather to a narrow side street — and their only purpose is to increase the church's exterior visual impact. Compared to the straightforward boldness of the portico, the design of the wings is extremely complex: on the lower story the slightly recessed wings extend the façade in a straight line from the central section, while on the upper story the dramatically recessed wings introduce a bold curve that allows the walls to step far back from the remainder of the façade. Although this complexity may at first glance appear capricious, in fact it constitutes a critical element in Cortona's larger piazza scheme.

The extra upper-story stepback is key. It allows the curved upper-story walls to be read in two ways: as part of the church façade (a vertical continuation of the lower-story wings) or as part of the piazza (a horizontal continuation of the secular buildings that abut the church). If the upper-story wings are read as part of the church, then the two-story façade reaches out to meet the encircling piazza, and the façade as a whole takes on (in variant form) the twin-bell-tower profile of the Piazza Navona's S. Agnese in Agone. If, on the other hand, the upper-story wings are read as an extension of the piazza, then the piazza walls wrap around the church's ground-floor wings, and the church façade itself echoes the wide-lower-story-narrow-upper-story profile of the Gesù. As a result of this ingenious ambiguity, the decorous bell towers (or rather bell tower, since one is unfortunately missing) possess a dual character, and Cortona, with characteristic skill, has shaped them accordingly: large enough to add the necessary vertical emphasis when read as part of the church façade but small enough to be unobtrusive when read as part of the piazza.

S. Maria della Pace's side wings, then, purposely blur the demarcation line between churchfront and piazza wall. But no matter how the overall façade composition is read, piazza and church walls meld to form a unified whole — a 360-degree panorama that envelopes the visitor and transforms the piazza into an outdoor anteroom to the church. Despite the piazza's small size, secular and sacred architecture do not jostle each other for pride of place. Instead, they actively complement one another, endowing Cortona's little temple front with a sympathetic setting that enhances its gemlike qualities to maximum advantage.

In so successfully combining an antique temple with a modern church façade, Cortona invented a synthesis that was to prove extraordinarily influential. Architects all over Europe took up his basic idea, reshaping it for their own purposes and in their own styles. The most famous variation of all, however, can be found a mere twenty blocks away: the twin churches of the Piazza del Popolo, which serve to give the walled inner city one of the most dramatic and satisfying urban entranceways of the entire Baroque era.

One final feature of the Piazza della S. Maria in Pace deserves special note: its skewed street layout. The near symmetry of Cortona's overall design unites the piazza's separate buildings into a single coherent composition, but this symmetry is hidden from distant view by the Via della Pace, which approaches the church at a quirky oblique angle. Happily, this accident of medieval street layout serves the piazza well. A more formal perpendicular approach would no doubt have increased the composition's power, allowing the new façade to broadcast its increased architectural importance out to the surrounding streets. But (as Cortona no doubt understood) the eccentric informal approach ultimately produces a more exhilarating effect: a feeling of sudden surprise and unexpected discovery. As a result, the Piazza di S. Maria della Pace possesses a special modesty all its own — an air of hidden cityscape treasure.

S. Maria della Pace's interior (entrance to the left of the portico, or through the opening to the left at 5 Via Arco della Pace) is the work of an unknown fifteenth-century architect, and Cortona's only revision of consequence involves the octagonal dome. The original dome was undecorated; Cortona applied to it an elegant Baroque decorative motif — possibly of his own invention — that combined Gothic ribs with Classical coffering. The most notable architectural feature of the interior, however, is not in the church proper at all, and predates Cortona by more than a century: the tiny cloister.

The cloister was begun around 1500 and completed in 1504. It was the first Roman project of the great Donato Bramante, who in his midfifties abandoned an established architectural practice in Milan and moved to Rome, where he quickly superseded Giuliano da Sangallo as the favored papal architect and went on to design both the original plan for St. Peter's (much modified by later architects) and the seminal Tempietto at S. Pietro in Montorio on the Janiculum Hill. His work here contrasts sharply with Cortona's façade and piazza outside, and with good reason: to walk from the piazza into the cloister is to step back in architectural time some 150 years, from High Baroque to High Renaissance. Compared to Cortona's virtuosic complexities of shape and space, Bramante's little courtyard looks quite simple and straightforward, its overall effect grave and perhaps even a little severe.

Despite its apparent simplicity, however, Bramante's design is not without its oddities, and adverse criticism began soon after Bramante's death with the art history chronicles of Giorgio Vasari ("not a work of perfect beauty," was his cryptic comment). Vasari's censure is thought to stem in part from disapproval of the columns on the upper story, which are centered over the open arches below and thereby violate the convention of "void over void, solid over solid" established by such Roman antiquities as the Colosseum and the Theater of Marcellus. Moreover (and more shockingly), Bramante's upper-story employment of alternating Corinthian columns and Composite pilasters runs counter to an even more important antique precedent. As the surviving ruins throughout Italy make abundantly clear, ancient architects *never* intermingled the orders within a single colonnade. In Classical times (as Bramante well knew), Doric, Ionic, Corinthian, and Composite columns were seen as distinct and mutually exclusive inventions, each with its own individual parts, proportions, and personality. To mingle them would have been to pervert them, and an ancient architect would have viewed a mixed-order colonnade as visually confused and conceptually wrongheaded.

Bramante's reasons for violating the "void-over-void" convention were probably practical: the height of each cloister story was dictated by pre-existing buildings, and given this constraint it would have been impossible to construct upper-story archways identical (or even proportionate) to those on the ground floor. Practical considerations, however, cannot account for Bramante's decision to employ elements from the Corinthian and Composite orders within a single colonnade. Here Bramante's motives must have been less mundane and more intellectually adventurous, and to understand his purpose, it is necessary to view the courtyard composition as a whole, upper and lower stories together. As a number of modern scholars have argued, *all* the ancient Classical orders then come into play.

Three of the orders are immediately apparent: Corinthian columns and Composite pilasters on the upper story, and Ionic pilasters raised onto pedestals on the lower. But the fourth order — the Doric, simplest of the four — seems at first glance to have been omitted. A closer look at the ground-floor piers, however, suggests that the Doric order may be present after all, albeit in a stripped-down, rudimentary form. It can be seen on the *sides* of the piers, where the impost blocks — the narrow projecting ledges from which the arches between the piers spring — can be read as rudimentary Doric capitals. The side surfaces of the piers can thus be viewed as embryonic Doric pilasters (a reading which may at first seem far-fetched, but which is reinforced by the true pilasters set into the back walls underneath the arches).

Bramante, then, was probably conducting a bold experiment when he designed this simple courtyard. Rather than slavishly copying the architecture of ancient Rome, he was mixing and combining all four Classical orders in a radically new way. Despite its lack of historical precedent, however, Bramante's use of the Classical vocabulary was far from arbitrary (and far from merely decorative). As the courtyard's ground plan reveals, Bramante positioned the Classical elements of his design with meticulous — even at times relentless — rigor.

Geometry supplies the template. At ground level, the four courtyard sides enclose a perfect square, and each arch of each side fronts on an area that is also a perfect square, exactly one-sixteenth the size of the central space. Thus when the ground plan of the cloister as a whole is mapped out, it fits exactly onto a thirty-six-square grid. It is this grid that dictates the positioning of all the courtyard's piers, and also the positioning of the courtyard's off-center entrance (since the grid produces an even number of bays on each side, no central entrance is possible).

For modern viewers conditioned to view geometry as a purely mathematical phenomenon, Bramante's use of the square grid may seem nothing more than sensible. But during the High Renaissance, simple and regular geometric shapes were viewed as more than just mathematically elegant. In their perfection of proportion and form, they were seen as Godlike and God-given, a reflection of the underlying scientific order that rules the natural world. For Bramante and his peers, the rigors of geometry would thus have betokened not only architectural exactitude, but aesthetic harmony and religious revelation as well.

From the Renaissance point of view, then, it was the courtyard's carefully planned geometry, not its Classical borrowings, that served to make the overall composition visually coherent and intellectually compelling. And it was the carefully planned geometry that rendered the courtyard's egregious violation of Classical precedent acceptable. If properly ordered by geometry (so the theory went), formerly incompatible Classical elements could be combined to produce an innovative architectural synthesis that embodied the aesthetic, scientific, and religious beliefs of the day. The result would be a newly flexible Classical architecture — a vital revivification of the long-lost Classical tradition that would permit a freedom of invention and would engender a beauty of form unknown to the ancients.

How successful was Bramante's experiment? A close look at any of the ground-floor corner piers suggests that even Bramante himself may have considered the outcome problematical. The piers' most peculiar architectural feature can be found attached to the bottom of the entablature in the right angle where the courtyard sides meet: a strange, tiny, carved excrescence that looks more like an invasive barnacle — hornet's nest? — than a purposeful piece of architectural decoration. This protuberance, upon closer examination, turns out to be a pair of mirror-image curlicues, and a quick glance at any of the ground-floor pilaster capitals establishes the curlicues' identity exactly: they are Ionic capital scrolls, identical to their neighbors. And they are placed exactly where the ruling geometric grid dictates, at the point where they would otherwise appear if the ground-floor arcade, rather than turning a corner, continued on in a straight line to produce more arches and more Ionic pilasters.

A similar analysis applies to the pilaster pedestals, visible in fragmentary form at the ground level of all four corners: the pedestals are placed exactly as required by the ruling grid, only to be immediately and rudely truncated by the arcade's right-angle turn. And the tapered pilaster shafts are present as well, although they are so ruthlessly diminished that they read merely as pieces of vertical molding that travel up the corner crevices and all but disappear as they rise. Thus the full pilaster ensemble — pedestal, shaft, and capital — is in fact visible at all four corner angles, albeit in brutally mutilated form.

The result, aesthetically, is far from pleasing. Visually, the pilasters are reduced to weak, reedlike slivers, and the tiny capital scrolls look shrunken and powerless, offering no support whatsoever to the entablature immediately above. In the end the courtyard's piers, which so lucidly display their Ionic pilasters along the courtyard's sides, seem to be crushing and devouring those same pilasters at the corners.

Bramante, in all probability, was perfectly aware of the uncompromising ruthlessness of his corner design. His motives for allowing such an obvious awkwardness, however, remain a matter of debate. In planning the courtyard, he may have simply opted for intellectual rigor over visual grace, choosing to abide by the intellectual dictates of his geometric grid no matter what the visual cost. But it is also possible (as a number of critics have argued) that his true purpose was more subtle than such a straightforward either/or would imply. Rather than attempting (and failing) to create a perfect architectural synthesis of Classicism and geometry, Bramante may instead have been attempting to illustrate the practical limitations that render such an idealized goal impossible to achieve in reality. He was, by this view, stating a problem rather than laying out a solution, and his corner design was meant to offer a criticism of High Renaissance architectural theory, not a vindication of it.

The problem — how to construct Classical corners for interior courtyards that are both visually and conceptually satisfying — is more aesthetic than functional, more a matter of visual appearance than physical strength. Visually, courtyard corners require emphasis; a courtyard entirely enclosed by identical columns will appear weak at the corners because the corner columns must work alone to support the courtyard's corner angles while the other columns are working together to support the courtyard's straight sides. Thus the human eye tends to seek out extra strength at the point where a courtyard's sides meet, even though that strength may not be structurally necessary.

The question of how best to achieve courtyard corner emphasis was to bedevil architects for years to come. Many solutions were tried; like the church-façade problem — how best to employ the Classical vocabulary on non-Classical churchfronts — the courtyard-corner problem became a recurring issue of Renaissance and Baroque architectural design. Bramante's solution here (if solution it was meant to be) was one of the very first, and remains one of the most famous. Awkward it may be, but its awkwardness more lucidly expresses the problem than any other solution of its era.

3-18   VIA DEI CORONARI
(North of the Piazza di S. Maria della Pace)

A street of antiques dealers, and many of the shop buildings are even older than the artifacts sold within. Laid out ramrod-straight during Imperial times, the Via dei Coronari fell to ruins and all but disappeared during the Middle Ages. It was revived in the late 1400s by Pope Sixtus IV, who offered special financial incentives for the construction of new buildings along the ancient axis in order to improve downtown access to the Vatican. Most of the Renaissance structures survive to this day. The street's unusual length and straightness give it a character unique to the area, and in recent years the welcome ban on automobile traffic has transformed it into a window-shopper's promenade — a quieter and gentler alternative to the more famous Via dei Condotti across town.

3-19   SAN SALVATORE IN LAURO
Interior: possibly Ottaviano Mascarino, 1591
(Piazza di S. Salvatore in Lauro, off the north side of the Via dei Coronari)

The façade is a ponderous nineteenth-century afterthought, but the interior dates from the 1590s; though little known, it is probably the best High Renaissance church interior in the entire city. The design is generally attributed to the little-known Ottaviano Mascarino, although Anthony Blunt — famous British art expert and Russian spy — is skeptical, and suggests in his *Guide to Baroque Rome* that the design was sent down from Venice by a follower of Palladio. The original effect was marred by renovations and superfluous decoration during the 1700s, but the architectural skeleton remains intact and strong.* To feel the true Palladian majesty, it is necessary to imagine the interior stripped of its distracting marble and paint, so that the architectural elements can speak for themselves. The Renaissance goal was to achieve power without becoming oppressive, and the columns and cornice here, despite their great size and visual weight, do not overwhelm.

3-20   PALAZZO TAVERNA
Complex of buildings dating from the fifteenth through the nineteenth centuries
(Via di Monte Giordano, south of the Via dei Coronari; main entrance
opposite the Via degli Orsini)

The sprawling Palazzo Taverna is gated and private, but its most memorable feature is public: the view through the main entrance (on the Via di Monte Giordano opposite the Via degli Orsini) into the courtyard. The steep

---

*Except in the apse, where the Baroque high altar set into the apse wall rudely interrupts the line of the bold Renaissance cornice, otherwise unbroken around the whole interior. The Baroque intrusion here is particularly regrettable, for it breaks through and obscures the architectural skeleton at the point of maximum liturgical focus.

and dark entryway tunnel supplies a splendidly dramatic frame for the (hopefully) sunlit fountain beyond.

As the canted walls to the left of the main entrance and the remains of the medieval tower on the Vicolo Domizio suggest, the palazzo traces its origins back to a medieval fortress. Strategically located on an artificial hill (the "Monte Giordano" of the street name), the complex of buildings overlooked the entire western end of the Campus Martius, including bridgehead access to the Vatican across the Ponte S. Angelo; for four hundred years it served as headquarters to the Orsini, one of the most powerful families in the city. Ingrid D. Rowland, in *The Culture of the High Renaissance*, describes the area in the year 1490:

For centuries, this flood-prone terrain had been divided among several families of feudal landholders, the infamous "barons," each of them ensconced within a sprawling palazzo in a different section of town. Most of the popes in the Middle Ages had been supplied by two such baronial families — the Colonna, with most of their feudal holdings to the south of Rome, and the Orsini, with vast lands to the north. Other families, the "black nobles," had never produced a pope, but their cardinals and warriors had managed virtually every conclave and every meeting of the city government; their gangs of liveried thugs were as dangerous as the *viri strenui*, the "strongmen," who hung about the portals of the Palazzo Orsini on Monte Giordano (a hill built up from the crumbled remains of the Palazzo Orsini's previous incarnations) or the equally imposing Palazzo Colonna. By the end of the fifteenth century, Rome had yet to complete the transition from a baronial city to a papal city, although the College of Cardinals, hoping to keep the barons in their place, had begun routinely to choose popes from non-Roman families, and often families of no previous political consequence whatsoever.

A walk through the mud and slops of a Roman street could still be a dangerous venture, when it led through baronial turf. On the most tranquil day a stroll through the city meant threading an obstacle course of soldiers, rattling carts of wine, grain, and vegetables, street vendors, prostitutes, pilgrim tourists, and endless entourages: cardinals riding to the hunt amid a retinue of yapping dogs; bankers in cavalcade on their expensive horses; popes, priests, and the faithful in solemn procession. Near Monte Giordano, Piazza Savelli, or Piazza

Colonna, however, a jacket of the wrong color, the wrong badge on a hat, a swagger too jaunty, or the wrong company could bring on an attack by the neighborhood baron's toughs, the *bravi*. The meandering Tiber always flowed close by, ready to cancel the evidence, as it had once concealed many a murder in ancient Rome and carried off the carnage from the arenas.

The Orsini family occupied the Palazzo Taverna until 1688, and (as the passage above suggests) in its heyday the palazzo functioned as the nerve center for an entire neighborhood. Like most of the great Roman palazzi, its occupancy was not limited to the owner and his immediate family; rather, the building (or, as in this case, the huge complex of buildings) served as a base of operations for a whole society-in-microcosm. The owner would of course occupy the grandest suite of rooms (usually found on the *piano nobile*, one floor above street level), but the other floors and attendant buildings would be occupied by a huge extended family of rich and poor relatives, employees, advisers, artists, musicians, servants, goons, hangers-on, and even tradespeople who rented ground-floor shop space to service both the palazzo and the more modest houses nearby. The tradition of what nowadays would be called mixed-use development — commercial and residential, grand and modest, rich and poor, all to be found in a single building or block of buildings — survives in Rome to this day, giving the city's historic center a demographically diversified character that is unique among European capitals.

3-21 SANTI CELSO E GIULIANO
Carlo de Dominicis, 1733–1735
(Via del Banco di Santo Spirito, south of the Ponte S. Angelo)

*SS. Celso e Giuliano, with the Palazzo Albirini-Cicciaporci beyond
and the Palazzo del Banco di S. Spirito in the distance.*

Designed by the little-known Carlo de Dominicis at the tail end of the Baroque era, SS. Celso e Giuliano has never attracted much attention, in part because it is overshadowed by the spectacular view of the Castel S. Angelo at the end of the street. But it ought to be better known, for it possesses one of the strongest Baroque façades and one of the loveliest Baroque interiors in the city.

The façade as a whole is quite conventional in design — there is no new architectural ground being broken here — but de Dominicis employs the traditional Baroque vocabulary with admirable proficiency and panache. The full panoply of Baroque façade conventions is confidently on display: subtly curved wall surfaces topped with sinuously curved broken pediments; bold columns, half columns, and pilasters; incisively carved capitals; inventively conceived and confidently carved decoration around the niches and windows. Especially impressive is the assured manner in which the multiple capitals of the columns and pilasters are layered in stepped-back groups of two or three. Despite their complex design, these nested capitals never get in each other's way, and the secondary capitals always retain a strongly individual character despite their subsidiary positions. Overall, the façade combines the two main visual characteristics of the Baroque — forcefulness and fluidity — with great skill and assurance.

The minor details, too, are worth searching out and lingering over. Delicately carved garlands — not all identical — link the capitals across the façade; bouquets of flowers in various stages of bloom peek out from behind the palm fronds that decorate the ground-floor oval window; an elegantly shaped keystone projects irrepressibly forward from the center of the ground-floor entablature. Even the tiniest of details can beguile: above the lettering on the ground-floor frieze, tiny pine cones nestle among the rectangular dentils to mark the entablature's changes in direction as it moves in and out across the façade. Further decorative refinements abound, but even a small sampling is enough to make the message clear. This is one of Rome's most lovingly ornamented façades.

The interior is a surprise and a pleasure. Here is no riot of multicolored marble, no clamorous slathering on of gold. For once the color scheme remains simple (gray-green paint with gilded accents) and serves to highlight rather than obscure the design's architectural elements. Spatially, the interior plan is straightforward but strong; the side chapels and apse are all large enough to possess clear identities of their own, but they are not so emphatic as to rob the interior of the feeling of unity supplied by the main oval space and its dome. The transition from wall to dome is beautifully handled, marked by an unusually unobtrusive cornice that allows the dome to grow naturally out of the walls below, a structural continuation rather than a separately conceived addition. Above the cornice, the dome's ribs reverse the decorative scheme below (grooved pilasters supported by paneled pedestals on the ground floor, paneled pilasters supported by grooved pedestals in the dome). The dome pedestals, moreover, are decorated at their tops with a flourish of capital-like ornamentation, so that the ribs as a whole can be read — a further ingenious reversal of the ground-floor plan — as upside-down pilasters.

The subsidiary ornamentation is richly applied, and may not be to everyone's taste. But it never obscures the visual strength of the pilasters, cornice, and ribs that serve as an architectural framework for the whole. Everything is beautifully carved — as on the façade, leisurely exploration is a pleasure — and the high point comes, appropriately enough, at the peak of the dome, where the oculus rim serves as a handy perch for a flock of inquisitive cherubs who peer down at the goings-on below. The cherub idea was not new (it was borrowed, along with much else in the interior, from Bernini's S.

Andrea del Quirinale, built across town some seventy-five years earlier), but it is splendidly executed. All in all, the interior possesses both delicacy of feel and unity of design,* qualities that are, alas, all too rare in Roman churches.

3-22 PALAZZO ALBERINI-CICCIAPORCI
Raphael, 1515–1521
(Via del Banco di S. Spirito, across the Vicolo del Curato
from SS. Celso e Giuliano)

Not an exceptional palazzo, but notable in that it possesses the only façade in the city known to have been the work of Raphael. The design clearly influenced Giulio Romano's façade for the Palazzo Stati-Maccarani, which was built at a slightly later date and is quite similar in general organization (Giulio was Raphael's principal pupil and assistant, and completed a number of the paintings that Raphael left unfinished at his death in 1520). Raphael's design, however, is in every way less extreme than Giulio's. The ground-floor blocks are delicate rather than massive, as if the rustication pattern were merely incised on the exterior of the wall; the middle-story pilasters are visually quite strong, and do not contrast markedly in power with blocks on the floor below. Overall, Raphael's composite design — the visual relationship of the three horizontal layers relative to one another — is much more balanced and evenly cadenced than Giulio's, and only the interrupted "arcade" on the bottom layer (where the arch openings are divided by a wide band of stone into lower rectangles and upper semicircles) suggests the era of Mannerist experimentation that is about to dawn.

The dates of the two palazzi point up a startling and often overlooked fact. Raphael's High Renaissance Palazzo Alberoni-Cicciaporci was designed (probably) in 1515; Giulio's Mannerist Palazzo Stati-Maccarani was begun in 1520. Yet the High Renaissance is often said to date only from 1499, when Bramante moved to Rome from Milan. In fact, the Italian High Renaissance in architecture lasted for only a very short period — scarcely

---

*Marred only by the decoration of the side chapel to the left of the apse, which introduces a shamefully discordant note and has not been mentioned until now in the hope that it has gone unnoticed.

more than two decades — and was limited in practice to a single generation of architects.*

3-23 PALAZZO DEL BANCO DI SANTO SPIRITO
Antonio da Sangallo the Younger, 1525
(Via del Banco di S. Spirito, at the south end, at the beginning of the
Via dei Banchi Nuovi)

Constructed a decade later than Raphael's Palazzo Alberini-Cicciaporci and at the end of the same street, Sangallo's façade for the Palazzo del Banco di S. Spirito is an experiment that does not quite come off. That is to say, it is typically Mannerist. Instead of employing the standard three-story division that Raphael had used nearby, Sangallo opted for giant pilasters that unite the upper two stories, with decorative circular openings to demarcate the division between floors. But the elements look haphazardly arrayed, and the twin sets of giant pilasters are so awkwardly spaced that they read neither as two comfortable pairs nor as one decisive line of four. It is only after concentrated inspection that the overall idea becomes clear: a triumphal arch raised on a podium. The eye is meant to read both upper floors (including the arms and statuary at the top) as a single forceful Classical entity — an almost impossible task given that the central opening of the supposed triumphal arch is filled in with wall and the composition as a whole seems suspended in midair. The giant pilaster was not to come into its own until twelve years later, when Michelangelo so magnificently employed it (in an entirely different way) in his designs for the new façades at the Campidoglio.

---

*The dates are impossible to pin down with exactitude, but the Early Renaissance is commonly said to have begun in the 1420s (in Florence), the High Renaissance to have arrived by 1500, and the Mannerist era to have begun around 1520 (and to have continued for the rest of the century). The tag "Mannerist," it should be noted, is a relatively recent development. During the nineteenth century, art historians usually characterized the period 1520–1600 as "Late Renaissance," in part because they saw its experimentation as a sign of aesthetic decline. It was only in the twentieth century, when the architecture of the period was reassessed more positively, that the term "Mannerism" as applied to architecture came into general (and nonpejorative) use, supplanting "Late Renaissance" as the preferred categorization.

TOUR 4

OLD ROME III:
THE CAMPUS MARTIUS (SOUTH)
FROM THE TIBER BEND TO THE JEWISH GHETTO

THE THIRD OF the Campus Martius tours covers the area south of the main east-west avenue, the nineteenth-century Corso Vittorio Emanuele; it completes the circuit of the Tiber Bend area, and ends at the Jewish Ghetto. Before beginning the tour, however, readers who have a special desire to see St. Peter's might wish to consider a detour across the river. The walk from the Castel S. Angelo to St. Peter's Square is not a long one (five blocks straight west down the Via della Conciliazione); the six entries that cover the detour can be found in Tour 11.

The centerpiece of the area south of the Corso Vittorio Emanuele is the Palazzo Farnese (pictured above), the most famous of Rome's Renaissance palazzi. The building is ponderously aristocratic in character, but an unpretentious counterbalance can be found just a block away: the Campo dei Fiori, a piazza that since 1869 has served as old Rome's largest daily market. The Campo dei Fiori is a working square, with produce stands that appear in the early morning and disappear in the early afternoon, and it goes about its business without any special fuss or show. Most of the streets nearby follow suit; unlike the area around the Spanish Steps (which is nowadays given over entirely to luxury shops), the Campo dei Fiori neighborhood retains an aura of ordinary commerce, of a city earning its daily bread. This no-nonsense attitude is, in its way, just as Roman as the splendors of the showplace Piazza Navona. Indeed, it is the combination of the two — the coexistence of the mundane and the flamboyant, the everyday and the unusual — that gives the Campus Martius the special character that sets it apart from the rest of the city.

4-1   TIBER EMBANKMENTS
Lungotevere and Tiber embankments: construction begun 1876
(Best viewed from the center of the Ponte Vittorio Emanuele)

Until the twentieth century, Rome's most important commercial traffic artery was the Tiber, which served as the city's shipping lifeline both to the Mediterranean downriver and the interior of Italy upriver. But the Tiber flooded regularly, and every thirty years or so the entire Campus Martius area, from the Tiber Bend to the Spanish Steps, would find itself under six feet of water. In the late nineteenth century, Rome's city planners took the situation in hand and built the steep embankments that now channel and control the river.

The construction project was huge in scale, took some thirty years to complete, and involved a succession of major and minor contractors overseen by a special council, a special planning office, the Ministry of Public Works, a commission representing the city of Rome, a commission representing the province of Lazio, and a commission representing the nation as a whole. The resulting bureaucracy was so Byzantine in its organizational complexities that in 1900, when a section of the new embankment along Trastevere collapsed, the commission formed to investigate the accident was unable to assign blame.

Critical as the need for flood control was, the embankment project produced one other major benefit: the boulevards that run along either side of the river. The sweep of the wide, tree-lined *lungotevere* — *lungo* means "along," so the name *lungotevere* means "along the Tiber" — is best experienced at the center of the Ponte Vittorio Emanuele, where the full extent of the Tiber Bend is visible. Aesthetically, the boulevards are unabashedly Parisian in inspiration, but the snakelike course of the river keeps them from becoming over-formal. Functionally, their main purpose is to replace the river itself as a traffic carrier — to allow the river traffic, permanently shifted from the waters to the banks, to cut through the city with speed and efficiency.

Today the volume of traffic along the *lungotevere* has reached levels that would have astonished the nineteenth-century city planners, but the boulevards still do their assigned job remarkably well. And their beneficial effect on the remnants of the river should not be overlooked. With their greenery and constant motion, they both soften and enliven the relentlessly brutal embankments. Without them, the modern Tiber would be nothing but an intrusive, oversized ditch.

4-2   VIA GIULIA
Laid out early sixteenth century

CORSO VITTORIO EMANUELE
Laid out late nineteenth century

Just south of the Ponte Vittorio Emanuele, two long, more-or-less parallel streets offer a study in contrast: the Via Giulia, laid out in the early 1500s, and the Corso Vittorio Emanuele, laid out in the late 1800s. The Via Giulia was named for its creator, Pope Julius II; when it was laid out, it was the most spacious and imposing street in the city. Julius's plans were ambitious: he meant for the street to connect at both ends with bridges crossing the Tiber (thus improving access to the Vatican), and he drew up designs for a huge palace near the north end that would serve as a new center for both ecclesiastical and civic government. The bridge at the street's northern end was never built, however, and Julius's successors never completed construction of the palace. A few of its gigantic travertine blocks still survive; they can be seen sticking out into the street — the locals refer to them as "street sofas" — at No. 62.

The Corso Vittorio Emanuele came much later, and finished what the Via Giulia started. Across town, the ancient Romans had laid out the Via Flaminia (now the Via del Corso), supplying the city with a thoroughfare that remains the main north-south axis to this day. But no such east-west axis was ever constructed — the Via Giulia was neither long enough nor central enough to serve — and for centuries the Campus Martius area remained a maze of short, narrow streets that seemed to lead nowhere but into each other. Traffic in the area had been a problem since the fifteenth century; in the late nineteenth century, when the city began to experience its explosive modern population growth, the need for improved east-west access became acute. So a swath was cut through the labyrinth, and the Corso Vittorio Emanuele emerged from the chaos.

As necessary evils go, it is not too bad. Demolition began in 1884, and most of the façades along the new street were constructed over the next twenty-five years. The nineteenth-century architects who designed them (in contrast to most of their twentieth-century successors) respected the long tradition of Roman palazzo design, and today the street blends with the surrounding cityscape quite unobtrusively. Originally full of grandiloquence, it is now shabby-genteel — Neoclassical pomp looking a bit frowzy around the edges.

The main weakness is the character of the street itself. It is not straight enough to possess the power of the Via del Corso, and it is not wide enough to function as a true boulevard. Neither fish nor fowl, it lacks a distinctive personality. Still, its layout preserved most of the historically important buildings along the route, so it does its job without ripping the visual fabric of the city to pieces. All in all, it could have been a lot worse, as the later Via della Conciliazione leading to St. Peter's attests.

4-3   CHIESA NUOVA ORATORY
Façade: Francesco Borromini, 1637 onward
(Piazza della Chiesa Nuova, on the Corso Vittorio Emanuele,
to the left of the Chiesa Nuova)

Borromini constrained. The fathers of the Chiesa Nuova knew what they wanted for their Oratory façade: plain brick, thank you, and plain pilasters, and not too much in the way of decorative competition for the church next door. Borromini gave them what they asked for, discarding several of his original plan's bolder elements and all of its rooftop finery. The famous Borrominian elements are still present: the curved façade, the play between convex and concave in the lower and upper central bays, the geometrically inventive crowning pediment, the exotic detail work on the pilaster capitals and window-surrounds. But the shallow wall curve is rigid and tense, and the contrasting curves of the central bays seem held in check, unable to break free of their imprisoning pilasters. Only in the decorative motifs of the central upper bay does the true Borrominian spirit — the inspired marriage of controlled geometry and inventive fantasy — manage to break out.

The rest feels reined in and overdisciplined, as if worried that too much creativity may be bad for the soul.

4-4 CHIESA NUOVA (SANTA MARIA IN VALLICELLA)
Façade: Fausto Rughesi, 1593–1606
Interior: Matteo da Città di Castello and Martino Longhi the Elder, 1575–1606
(Piazza della Chiesa Nuova, on the Corso Vittorio Emanuele)

The "Chiesa Nuova" — New Church — was the nickname given to S. Maria in Vallicella while it was being constructed in the late sixteenth century, and (like the Palazzo Nuovo on the Capitoline Hill) the name stuck. The façade is the only Roman work of the little-known Fausto Rughesi and might best be described as serviceable. Its decorative scrolls and paired pilasters derive from the church of the Gesù down the street, but here the two stories are essentially the same width, and the main doorway is flanked by paired columns.

Still, there is a new idea here, and it is an idea that signals the beginning of a new style. The columns that frame the central doorway — and the entablature and curved pediment the columns support — have stepped forward, almost detaching themselves from the façade. No longer merely decorative attachments to the wall behind, they possess a sculptural presence — a Baroque presence — all their own, giving the design as a whole a strong central focus. On the rest of the façade, however, this strength quickly dissipates; once the eye moves away from the main entranceway, the pattern of pilasters elsewhere seems a pale echo of the paired columns. Compared to more famous Baroque façades (S. Susanna on the Quirinal Hill is the preeminent example, finished three years before the Chiesa Nuova), Rughesi's overall design seems to lack the courage of its own convictions.

Indeed, even Borromini's relatively simple façade for the Oratory next door shows up the weaknesses of Rughesi's design. Borromini's single pilasters look like sentinels standing at attention, holding the brick skin of the Oratorio stretched and taut. Rughesi's paired pilasters, by comparison, appear slack and flaccid, and on the upper story they look far too weak for the bold triangular pediment they support. Subdued as the Oratory façade is (at least by Baroque standards), it still possesses far more visual power than its neighbor.

The Chiesa Nuova's spacious interior answers the Gesù's riot of marble with a riot of gilded stucco. The Baroque decoration is consistently applied throughout, but — as at the Gesù — the feast quickly becomes an argument for famine. No pilaster without its gilded capital, no painting without its gilded frame, no vault without its gilded coffering — with no place to rest, the eye quickly grows tired and the mind soon rebels. The onslaught is unrelenting, and the mental fatigue it engenders makes a close examination of the interior particularly difficult. This is a shame, for the art in the church is especially fine.

Notable Works of Art: The vaults of the nave, dome, and apse were all painted by Pietro da Cortona (architect of the little piazza outside S. Maria della Pace, the vestibule of S. Maria in Via Lata, and a number of other notable Baroque buildings) over an extended period of time during the mid-seventeenth century. The subjects include *The Vision of St. Philip* (1664–1665, in the nave, illustrating an episode during the construction of the church when the Virgin Mary was said to have interceded to keep a weak beam from collapsing the ceiling onto the workers below), *Trinity* (1647–1651, the dome), *Isaiah, Jeremiah, Daniel,* and *Ezekial* (the dome pendentives), and *Assumption of the Virgin* (1655–1660). Surrounding the high altar are three paintings by Peter Paul Rubens, all dated 1606–1608: *Gregory the Great with St. Papianus and St. Maurus* (to the left), *Virgin and Child* (center), and *St. Domitilla with St. Nereus and St. Achilleus.* In the left transept is Federico Barocci's luminous *Presentation of the Virgin in the Temple,* finished 1603; it is one of two paintings by Barocci in the church (the other is *The Visitation,* 1583–1586, in the fourth chapel to the left), and is a particularly fine illustration of his special gift for complex spatial organization and resplendent color. The *Entombment* in the second chapel to the right is a copy of the Caravaggio original (1602–1604), now in the Vatican.

4-5   VIA DEL GOVERNO VECCHIO

Like the Via dei Coronari several blocks to the north, the Via del Governo Vecchio is a street for leisurely strolling. Along its meandering five-block course, no single building stands out as especially remarkable, but most of the structures are hundreds of years old, and the ensemble offers a pleasing contrast to (and relief from) the modern Corso Vittorio Emanuele, with its insistent hustle and bustle.

The street begins in back of the Chiesa Nuova Oratory in the Piazza d'Orologio, named for Borromini's distinctive corner clock tower. Renaissance origins are evident on the façade of the modest palazzo at Nos.

14–17, with its crude but confident Classical arcade and cornice on the upper stories (compare the smaller and plainer house next door at No. 13, built a century earlier, in the 1400s). The larger palazzo at No. 39 gave the street its name: the Palazzo del Governo Vecchio (also known as the Palazzo Nardini). Constructed between 1473 and 1478 by Cardinal Stefano Nardini, governor of the city under Pope Paul IV, the building was originally called the "Palazzo del Governo"; the modifier *vecchio* — "old" — was added after the seat of the papal governors was moved to the Palazzo Madama in 1741.

Across the street from the Palazzo del Governo Vecchio, the houses at Nos. 123, 121, and 118* offer a further example of changing architectural styles, representing the fifteenth (No. 118), the sixteenth (No. 123), and seventeenth centuries (No. 121). Farther along and crossing the street once more, No. 66 is traditionally said to be the smallest house in Rome; crossing back to No. 104, the faded remains of a sixteenth-century fresco can be seen on the upper wall, showing the building's owner dictating to his secretary. Finally, at the street's end, an eighteenth-century wall plaque (on the right at the beginning of the Vicolo dell Cancelleria) serves as a reminder that some problems never go away. "By order of the District President," it says, "it is forbidden to throw any garbage whatsoever into this alley, as prescribed by public proclamation October 23, 1755."

4-6   PASQUINO
Probably third century B.C.E., installed in its current location 1501
(Piazza di S. Pantaleo, off the Corso Vittorio Emanuele
south of the Piazza Navona)

A mutilated piece of sculpture, sitting on a pedestal at the eastern end of its own little piazza. Pasquino is the first and most famous of Rome's "talking statues," which from the sixteenth century onward frustrated the official censors by sprouting — usually in the dead of night — pieces of paper on which were written barbed epigrams and satirical verses commenting on the events of the day. It was set up in 1501, and began to speak shortly thereafter.

---

*To most foreigners, the Roman street-numbering system is a model of perversity, apparently fashioned to convey as little useful information as possible. Starting at the beginning of the street (in this case the Piazza d'Orologio), the numbers run consecutively along the left side to the end of the street (in this case the Piazza di Pasquino), at which point they jump across the street and head back on the right side toward the origin, still increasing as they go. Thus, at any given point, the numbers of buildings facing each other across the street bear no consistent relation to one another, and run in opposite directions to boot. *Che confusione!*

According to legend, the talk began with a tailor named Pasquino, whose shop was nearby. His work took him behind the scenes at the Vatican, and the gossip he passed on to friends — along with caustic commentary — made him famous as a neighborhood wit. When he died, his quips were sorely missed until someone thought to christen the statue with his name and appoint it his successor. Other statues around town quickly found voices of their own,* and the irreverent public dialogue that resulted quickly became a Roman institution. The official censors were of course not pleased, and several popes are said to have wanted Pasquino thrown into the Tiber (the notoriously unpopular Adrian VI supposedly changed his mind only when told by his advisers that Pasquino, like a frog, would croak still louder in the water).

The fragment is thought to represent the torso and head of Menelaus, king of Sparta and husband of Helen of Troy. It was famously described by Bernini as the finest of all antique sculptures, a judgment that has over the years produced much head scratching among sculptors and critics. In addition to centuries of cutting commentary, the statue also gave rise to the English word *pasquinade* (a piece of satire).

4-7 PICCOLA FARNESINA (MUSEO BARRACCO)
North façade: Enrico Guj, 1898
South façade: Antonio da Sangallo the Younger, 1523–1530
(Corso Vittorio Emanuele 168, on the south side across from
the Piazza di S. Pantaleo)

With the construction of the Corso Vittorio Emanuele in the late 1800s, many of the palazzi in the area did an about-face: their unprepossessing backsides suddenly overlooked the city's main east-west traffic axis and became fronts in need of dressing up. The tiny sixteenth-century Piccola Farnesina — now known as the Museo Barracco after Senator Giovanni Barracco, the nineteenth-century senator who assembled the collection of antique sculpture displayed within — originally fronted south (and was considerably larger); the present main entrance wall, facing north, was designed by Enrico Guj in 1898. Best viewed from across the Corso Vittorio Emanuele, the later façade acquits itself quite well; in the inevitable architectural comparison

---

*Other talking statues included Marforio (a giant river god, originally at the southeastern base of the Capitoline Hill, later moved to the courtyard of the Campidoglio's Palazzo Nuovo), Madame Lucrezia (a female bust — possibly the goddess Isis — outside S. Marco), Abate Luigi (a toga-clad orator next to S. Andrea della Valle in the Piazza Vidoni), Il Facchino (a porter carrying a water barrel on the Via Lata), and Il Babuino (a statue of the god Silenus, set up on the Via del Babuino and nicknamed "the baboon" because it was so ugly).

between the sixteenth and nineteenth centuries, the nineteenth century comes off just fine.

In his façade details, Guj frankly copied Antonio da Sangallo's designs of 1523; the window-surrounds are identical to those on the palazzo's former front, and the arches of the loggia derive from the little court on the building's east side. The motifs themselves are typical of the Renaissance, but Guj employed them here in a distinctly non-Renaissance way. Instead of opting for symmetry — centering the loggia on the façade and putting the windows to either side — he chose a more subtle equilibrium, using the extra width of the left side of the façade to balance the depth of the loggia on the right. The result is an unbalanced arrangement of Renaissance motifs that looks wrong (at least historically) but feels impudently right. In a city where architecture is usually balanced to a fault, such heresy comes as a refreshing variation, and Sangallo's measured Classicism on the palazzo's other elevations looks prudishly straitlaced by comparison.

Nearby Museum: Across the Corso Vittorio Emanuele from the Piccola Farnesina is the Palazzo Braschi, constructed in the late 1700s by Pope Pius VI. It was the last of the great structures built to house papal relatives and entourages, and it now houses the *Museo di Roma,* finally reopened after fifteen years of renovation and restoration. Unhappily, there are no maps, models, or photographs, and the art and artifacts on display illustrate the history of Rome only in the most tangential way. As a city museum it is a major disappointment.

4-8 PALAZZO DELLA CANCELLERIA

Constructed 1487–1517, architect unknown (possibly Baccio Pontelli)
(Piazza della Cancelleria, off the south side of the Corso Vittorio Emanuele)

Palazzo della Cancelleria.

Of all the Renaissance palazzo façades in Rome, the façade of the Cancelleria is probably the most difficult to understand, much less to relish. But it is historically important, and the fundamental issue it raises demands attention. Like Bramante at the cloister of S. Maria della Pace a few blocks to the north, the architect of the Cancelleria meant his Classical design to serve a purpose beyond simple revivalism. He meant it to be emblematic of the scientific investigations and religious convictions of his day.

Begun in 1487 or 1488,* the Cancelleria was the first palazzo in Rome to attempt a full-blown architectural revival of the ancient Classical tradition. The owner (as the inscription on the façade immodestly announces) was Cardinal Raffaele Riario, nephew of Pope Sixtus IV. He is said to have financed construction — the cost was 60,000 scudi, an immense sum — out of a single night's gambling winnings.

---

*Unusually for Rome, no primary-source records of the palazzo's actual construction are known to exist (they were perhaps destroyed during the Sack of Rome in 1527), so the architect is unknown. The traditional attribution to Bramante cannot be correct, since Bramante did not arrive in Rome until 1499; recent research favors Baccio Pontelli, architect of the Sistine Chapel. The compressed triumphal arch around the main doorway is a later addition, added by Domenico Fontana in 1589.

At first glance — second and third glances as well — the Cancelleria's façade looks quite straightforward. Above a massive ground-floor base, the two upper floors are divided horizontally by pilasters into alternating wider and narrower bays, the wider bays containing windows. At each end of the façade, the wall steps forward to project ever so slightly into the street, creating end pavilions that highlight three bays each (a central window bay flanked by a nonwindow bay on each side). Despite the façade's forthright design, however, its overall effect is distinctly problematical. One difficulty is the awkward empty wall space created by the nonwindow bays, which turns out to be visually ambiguous — narrow enough for the eye to want to read the flanking pilasters as pairs, but not narrow enough for the eye to succeed. Another difficulty is the façade's large size — its vast expanse of looming wall — which robs the delicate pilasters of visual impact and makes the subtle forward projection of the end pavilions look timid and weak. In the end, the façade's Classical elements possess a disconcertingly tentative air, as if provisionally etched onto the massive wall surface rather than forcefully carved out of it. The façade seems to be trying a Classical costume on for size, but the costume's elegance fails to hide the monolithic stolidity of the body beneath.

Given that the Cancelleria façade was the first of its kind in Renaissance Rome, it is tempting to attribute its shortcomings to its unsophisticated simplicity. But this simplicity is deceiving. In fact, the façade's organizational principles are anything but straightforward; the apparently forthright arrangement of windows and pilasters turns out to have been generated by a dizzyingly complicated exercise in esoteric mathematical proportion. Unlike the square cloister at S. Maria della Pace (which was built a decade or so later), the façade is not organized around a simple and obvious geometric shape. Instead, it is ruled by the complex and unique geometric proportion known today as the Golden Section.

The Golden Section is a geometric oddity. It is the only ratio (as in "A is to B") that is also a proportion (as in "A is to B as C is to D"). As shown above, the Golden Section divides a given line into two parts so that the ratio of the smaller part to the larger part is identical to the ratio of the larger part to the whole (that is, section A is to section B as section B is to the whole A+B). Thus the proportion possesses two terms instead of the usual four; instead of the usual "A is to B as C is to D," the Golden Section can be expressed, "A is to B as B is to A+B." Numerically the Golden Section ratio is approximately five-eighths; but it is not *exactly* five-eighths, and the job of pinning the number down definitively turns out to be mathematically impossible because the decimal places go on forever (that is, the ratio when expressed numerically is an irrational number, in this case .6180339...).

The Golden Section fascinated Renaissance scientists. Luca Pacioli, the most famous mathematician of the day, wrote an entire book on the subject and called the book *The Divine Proportion*. The Golden Section (his book explained) lies beyond the realm of precise mathematical definition, and therefore possesses profoundly mystical qualities; being inexpressible, it is like God, "occult and secret," and its three parts — smaller segment, larger segment, and whole — should be viewed as geometrically emblematic of the Holy Trinity. Visually, Pacioli held that the proportion's special geometric status gave it special aesthetic appeal, and that its use as an organizing principle in art and architecture would produce exceptional beauties that transcended the ordinary. In short, Pacioli meant the "divine" in his title to be taken quite literally. The Golden Section, for him, was the line where the realms of art and science met and merged to reflect the mystical nature of God.

The design of the Cancelleria façade employs the Golden Section over and over again. As a general organizing principle, it can be found in the critical relationship between wider and narrower bays: the width of a nonwindow bay is to the width of a window bay as the width of a window bay is to the width of the two bays together. In the individual architectural elements, it can be found repeatedly in related vertical and horizontal dimensions: in the ratio of width to height in the windows, for instance, or the four-pilaster groupings (a window bay plus the windowless bays on either side) of the middle story.

As if all this were not abstruse enough, a further organizational complication — probably meant to point up the use of the Golden Section — arises at the façade's end pavilions. In the middle of the façade, the straightforward parade of window bays (pilaster/window/pilaster units separated by empty space) sets up a simple horizontal rhythm of PWP|PWP|PWP. But the façade's end pavilions suggest a different rhythm. Because they highlight a window flanked by four pilasters instead of two, the pavilions seem to imply that the middle of the façade should be read according to a second rhythm consisting of alternating flanked and unflanked windows (PPWPP|W|PPWPP|W|PPWPP), or perhaps even a third rhythm — most complicated of all — consisting of a series of four-pilaster units where the pairs of pilasters overlap (PPWPPWPPWPPWPPWPP).

The Cancelleria façade, then, is not so simple as it looks. Can it be more beautiful than it looks as well? Or — to put the question less flippantly — does the conceptual beauty of the Golden Section guarantee the visual beauty of the design it generates? Alas, for most twentieth-century viewers, the answer must be an emphatic no. Perhaps Renaissance eyes were different, or at least differently trained; perhaps Renaissance connoisseurs could look at the façade and see the theory, and the theory made the façade beautiful. But to most twentieth-century eyes, the consistency of proportion that rules the design of the Cancelleria façade is not in any way intuitively visible. The ruling geometry remains, like God, "occult and secret," and as a result the façade it engenders remains visually inert.

Despite the façade's shortcomings, however, it remains an important illustration of the High Renaissance obsession with theory. Contrary to popular belief, the architectural goal of that theory was not — or was not only — to revive the Classical tradition in a dignified and pleasingly evocative manner. As the Cancelleria façade attests, the aim of High Renaissance architects was far more grandiose: nothing less than to employ the old Classical vocabulary utilizing a new geometric syntax so as to embody the philosophical relationship between science and God. If the goal was achieved (so the theory went), the result would be a grand architectural synthesis — a melding of aesthetics, history, science, philosophy, and religion that to the Renaissance mind was the very definition of perfect beauty.

Not all High Renaissance buildings fell as far short of their theoretical goal as the Cancelleria. In Rome, two other structures — both designed by the great Donato Bramante — stand out as especially important. One is the aforementioned cloister at S. Maria della Pace, which succeeds in making its rigorous geometry intuitively obvious but fails to merge that geometry effectively with the ancient Classical orders. The other is the little Tempietto in the courtyard of S. Pietro in Montorio on the Janiculum Hill. There, happily, everything comes together with a cogency that is stunning in its assurance and authority.

Although Bramante had nothing to do with the Cancelleria façade, he may have had a hand in designing the Cancelleria's interior courtyard, with its forty-four antique columns (said to have been plundered from the ruins of the *Hecatostylon,* the famous hundred-column courtyard outside the meeting room where Julius Caesar was assassinated). The columns were reraised here about the same time that Bramante was working on the cloister at S. Maria della Pace; as a pair, the courtyards represent two of Rome's earliest attempts at Classical courtyard design.

The results here, like the results at S. Maria della Pace, are problematical. The columns themselves are displayed to great advantage; straightforwardly arrayed to carry two stories of arcade, they are slender, graceful, and serene. But the courtyard as a whole is less successful, for several reasons. For one thing, the corner problem — the need for extra visual emphasis at the angles where the arcades meet — is crudely addressed. The square corner piers do supply added thickness (another single column at the corners would look disturbingly weak), but their flat-surfaced pilasters introduce an entirely new and disruptive architectural idea. Compared to the simple grace of the columns, the pilastered piers look stubby, disjointed, and out of place.

A second visual problem is at once more subtle and more pervasive. The courtyard's three stories vary in height, with the tallest story at the bottom and the shortest at the top. This arrangement repeats the dimensions of the façade, where the massive rusticated ground floor supports the more delicately decorated upper stories. But visually there is a critical difference between the palazzo façade and the courtyard: the façade is fundamentally an arrangement of solids (the closed bays of the upper two stories), while the courtyard is fundamentally an arrangement of voids (the open arches of the arcades). And voids, to the human eye, read quite differently than solids.

The increased height of the ground-floor arches, for instance, does not make the ground-floor arcade as a whole look stronger. Rather the reverse: the ground-floor arches end up looking more delicate than the middle-story arches because their extra height makes them appear more slender (and makes the middle-story arches look stocky and squat by comparison). To further compound the problem, the top story — in height the shortest of the three — appears heaviest of all because it contains no voids, and the extra weight of the brick wall seems to bear down uncomfortably on the openings below. Thus the conventional upward progression of heavy/medium/light is here defeated; despite the fact that the height of the floors decreases with each story, the heaviest floor appears to be at the top and the lightest floor appears to be on the bottom. This perverse visual reversal produces a subtly discomfiting effect, as if the slender columns are not quite up to shouldering the load they are being forced to carry.

Visual anomalies such as these did not go unnoticed by sixteenth-century architects. New ideas followed quickly, and by midcentury Roman courtyard design had achieved a remarkable level of confidence and sophistication. A particularly fine example, dating from 1577 and designed by Giacomo della Porta, can be can be found just three blocks away, at the Palazzo della Sapienza.

Today the Campo dei Fiori is one of old Rome's lesser outdoor spaces, noted mainly for its thriving produce market. But during the Renaissance the piazza was the city's central square — the Piazza Venezia of its day — and after 1600 it was the site of choice for public executions. The statue in the center commemorates the piazza's first and most famous victim, the freethinking philosopher, astronomer, and mathematician Giordano Bruno, who was burned at the stake for heresy by Pope Clement VIII. The origins of the monument are typically Roman. As Christopher Hibbert explains in *Rome: The Biography of a City:*

> The statue ... in the center of the square is by Ettore Ferrari and was erected here in 1887 as a result of a political row. The mayor of that time was Duca Leopoldo Torlonia. He had been active in promoting the urban development of Rome, the street lighting of the Corso and the excavations in the Forum. But he made the mistake, from a political point of view, of paying an official visit to the Cardinal Vicar and requesting him to express the good wishes of the Roman people to Pope Leo XIII on the occasion of his Jubilee. This provoked the instant dismissal of the mayor by the anticlerical prime minister, Crispi. And, in order to scotch any notion of a closer relationship between the Roman civic authorities and the Vatican, Crispi followed up the dismissal of the mayor by the erection of the monument to Giordano Bruno and other reputed heretics whose names and likenesses are preserved in medallions around the base of the monument. Among those commemorated are Erasmus, Vanini, Pallario, Servetus, Wycliffe, Huss, Sarpi and Campanella. People standing in front of the statue on Sundays are liable to be approached by small boys with footballs who ask them to move out of the goal.

The produce market is justly famous and fills the square to overflowing. Its great virtue is its ordinariness, and the message of its daily commercial ritual — that the city's heart is still beating strong — is both reassuring and exhilarating. In the morning, when all the umbrella stalls arrive to set up shop, the Campo dei Fiori becomes old Rome's most hardworking piazza: unpretentious, industrious, highly productive, and irreplaceable.

4-10 PALAZZO FARNESE

Façade: Antonio da Sangallo the Younger, 1534–1546
and Michelangelo, 1546–1549
(Piazza Farnese, southwest of the Piazza di Campo dei Fiori)

The eight-hundred-pound gorilla of Roman palazzi. Straightforward in style and massive in scale — it occupies an entire city block, with another full city block as forecourt — the Palazzo Farnese commands immediate attention, if not immediate respect. Foursquare, monolithic, an irresistible force reified into an immovable object — no other palazzo in Rome possesses such implacable presence and power. When it was built in the mid-1500s for Pope Paul III, it caused a sensation, and for centuries to come it set the standard of grandeur against which all other Roman palazzi were judged.

The architect was Antonio da Sangallo the Younger, and his design for the façade was not exactly adventurous. Two nearby palazzi (the Palazzo della Cancelleria and the Palazzo Caffarelli-Vidoni) had already addressed the fundamental question of Roman palazzo façade design: how should Classical architectural elements be employed on the front of an aristocratic residence? The answer, in both cases, followed the same general plan: on the ground floor, a plain but rusticated base to suggest a podium; on the *piano nobile* (and sometimes the floors above), an arrangement of repetitive columns or pilasters to divide the façade into bays and to set off the windows.

Sangallo chose to ignore this precedent and instead opted for a no-nonsense formation of windows resting on horizontal cornice-like ledges running the entire length of the façade. With the exception of the cornice ledges (which do not really read as cornices because they are so unemphatic and because they support the windows above rather than topping the windows below), the Classical elements are limited to the window treatments. As might be expected, the *piano nobile* possesses the most forceful window design: a complete aedicule (that is, two columns supporting an entablature topped by a pediment) with alternating curved and triangular pediments. The other floors are given variations of the *piano nobile* surrounds, simpler on the ground floor and lighter on the top floor, where the arched windows break into the entablature.

Compared to this decorous arrangement of windows, the lavishly carved and emphatic roof cornice may come as a shock, and with good reason. Sangallo's design for the palazzo's crowning element did not appeal to the pope, and when Michelangelo took over construction upon Sangallo's death, a new and heavier cornice was substituted. There is a certain irony here, for as architects Sangallo and Michelangelo were not exactly kindred spirits. As James Ackerman describes it in *The Architecture of Michelangelo:*

> Sangallo's scheme . . . is the antithesis of Michelangelo's organic design [in buildings such as the palazzi at the Campidoglio]. . . . What differentiates Sangallo's approach from Michelangelo's is the absence of the metaphorical expression of the stresses of the structure. . . . Sangallo treated the façade as a neutral two-dimensional plane of brick upon which the stone frames of windows and doors could be set as sculptural relief. . . . The neutral plane of the wall veils any intimation of the equilibrium — or as Michelangelo would have it, the struggle — of load and support. There is nothing to suggest the ponderous downward pressures of the building, since the horizontal accents overwhelm the vertical . . . This imparts a calm and ease to the façade unknown in Michelangelo's work, and to complete the effect Sangallo envisaged a thinner and light cornice; one which would be less calculated to suggest compression than Michelangelo's.

As always with Michelangelo, however, the sense of compression is kept under control. Michelangelo's cornice may be heavier than Sangallo's, but it is also higher, since Michelangelo inserted extra wall space between the upper row of windows and the cornice. This extra space transforms the cornice; instead of reading as a topping element to the windows, it reads as an independent entity — a fourth horizontal with enough presence to stand up to the three horizontal rows of windows below. By redesigning the cornice in this manner, Michelangelo gave the upper floor room to breathe, and increased the expansive sweep and spaciousness of the façade as a whole.

Still, the extreme regimentation of the façade produces some obvious problems. The design's three enlivening elements* — the rusticated central entranceway, the central window above the entranceway (the only feature of the façade besides the cornice that was redesigned by Michelangelo), and the quoins that emphasize the façade's outer vertical edges — all seem intrusive, impinging uncomfortably on the space of the adjacent windows. And the overall effect, though admittedly powerful, is also monotonous and oppressive.

---

*Recent cleaning has uncovered a fourth enlivening element: a bizarre collection of red brick geometrical designs that decorate the façade for no apparent reason and without apparent rhyme. What are they doing there? Who was responsible? Were the sixteenth-century bricklayers encouraged to entertain themselves during construction? Was the recent cleaning overzealous, uncovering something that was never meant to be seen? Art historians are startled, and (for the moment, at least) baffled.

The Classical aedicules may lend the façade an air of elegance, but in the end they are just window dressing, and the feel of brute force remains paramount.

One well-known bit of trivia concerning the palazzo should perhaps be mentioned and is worth bearing in mind for later recall. Visitors to St. Peter's — even visitors who upon entering are particularly struck by an impression of size — often do not realize exactly how immense that vast interior really is. To drive the point home, guides often point out that Bernini's bronze canopy over the high altar is 95 feet high — as it happens, the exact same height as the Palazzo Farnese.

4-11 SANTA MARIA DELLA QUERCIA
Filippo Raguzzini, 1727–1731
(Piazza della Quercia, southeast of the Piazza Farnese)

Easily overlooked, but worth attention. The architect, Filippo Raguzzini, is best known for the little stage-set piazza outside S. Ignazio, and his great gift — there as here — was the ability to make a simple design sing. Compared to other Baroque churches, the façade of S. Maria della Quercia is pared down to an extreme: a single sinuous curve (concave-convex-concave) decorated on the lower story with four vertical pilasters that support a plain horizontal entablature running the entire width of the façade. Not much, but in this case it is more than enough.

The key element is the design of the middle pair of pilasters. Rather than allow them submissively to follow the curve of the wall surface, Raguzzini compresses them — folds them — to make them look as if they are being swallowed up by the curved wall behind. The pilasters do not merely decorate the façade, they *interact* with it.

From this simple but ingenious idea, everything else follows logically. Moving horizontally, the outer pilasters are compressed only slightly, in keeping with the curve of the wall, which is most pronounced in the center and eases away almost to flatness at the sides. Moving vertically, the angles formed by the pilasters give rise, above the lower-story capitals, to an entablature that breaks out into jaunty zigzags; the entablature's pronounced protruding cornice — the most forceful element in the whole design — all but cakewalks across the façade, strutting its stuff with a jazzy, syncopated rhythm that both transforms and enlivens the mellifluous curve below. On the upper story, simplicity returns; all the Classical details except the cornice are eliminated, and the underlying geometry of the design is left to speak for itself. And at the very top, the middle bay is crowned by a curved pediment that vertically mimics the outward swell of the façade below.

First-rate Baroque architecture is almost always visually complex, and the simplicity of Raguzzini's design here sets it apart. Rather than load up his façade with decorative intricacies, he takes a single architectural idea, explores its ramifications, and then stops. In part, this strategy reflects the fashion of his day: Raguzzini was a Late Baroque architect, and architectural taste was beginning to shift away from virtuosic complexity. But the strategy's end result — the limpid, unadorned lyricism that makes this modest façade so memorable — cannot be attributed merely to changing historical convention. It is evidence of that rarest of achievements among architects, an original vision developed into a wholly individual style.

4-12 PALAZZO SPADA
Façade: Giulio Merigi da Caravaggio, 1549; stucco work: Giulio Mazzoni
Colonnaded passage off interior courtyard: Francesco Borromini and
Giovanni Maria di Bonito, 1652–53
(Piazza Capo di Ferro, adjacent to the Piazza della Quercia)

The façade of the Palazzo Spada is so lively in its decoration that at first glance it is often taken for High Baroque. In fact, it predates the Baroque era by half a century. The lack of columns or pilasters is the giveaway; as a closer look reveals, the use of the Classical vocabulary is rudimentary, limited to the roof cornice and the triangular pediments over the statuary niches.

The overall theme is ancient history rather than ancient architecture. In the niches on the *piano nobile* stand statues of eight Roman heroes (from left to right: Trajan, Pompey, Fabius Maximus, Romulus, Numa, Marcellus, Julius Caesar, and Augustus), with written tributes inscribed on the wall plaques on the top floor. In between, stucco cherubs install a profusion of celebratory swags and medallions, which serve to disguise the mean proportions of the square windows. The vivacity of the decoration makes the palazzo one of the few Renaissance buildings in Rome that allows itself to put on a playful face, and in this sense it is the anti-Farnese, offering a welcome contrast to that vast sobersides just up the street.

The interior courtyard continues the same theme, with statues of Roman gods and an especially fine frieze depicting battling centaurs. The courtyard's main attraction, however, is the *prospettiva,* the colonnaded and barrel-vaulted passageway leading to a statue of a Roman warrior raised on a high pedestal. The passageway was constructed by Borromini in 1652–1653, and it is one of the most entertaining exercises in false perspective ever created.

Although the statue looks to the casual eye to be close to life-size, it is actually 2½ feet tall and situated far closer to the main courtyard than it appears. The illusion is created by the cunning construction of the passageway, where the paving becomes progressively narrower (and higher) and the columns progressively shrink in size.

4-13 POMPEY'S THEATER
(Via di Grotta Pinta, east of the Piazza di Campo dei Fiori)

An urban ghost. As every schoolchild used to know, it was in a room off the portico of Pompey's Theater that Julius Caesar was assassinated on March 15, 44 B.C.E. Today the merest trace of the theater remains: the curve of the Via di Grotta Pinta, which follows the line of the seats in the auditorium. Most visitors to the spot assume that the site of Caesar's murder is very close by, but the word *portico* in this context refers not to an entrance porch but to a rectangular colonnade enclosing a large courtyard to the east of the auditorium. The site of Caesar's assassination is thought to be at the portico's other end, just west of the excavated Republican temples in the Largo Argentina.

4-14 PALAZZO MASSIMO ALLE COLONNE
Baldassare Peruzzi, 1532–1538
(Corso Vittorio Emanuele, east of the Piazza di S. Pantaleo)

Palazzo Massimo alle Colonne.

Peruzzi's curved façade for the Palazzo Massimo alle Colonne is a famous example of Mannerism — that catchall term used to characterize sixteenth-century architectural experiments that left the Renaissance behind but failed to arrive at the Baroque — and his design is nothing if not adventurous. But the end result seems more than a little puzzling.

Certainly the lower floors are impressive enough. The paired pilasters march smartly along the curved ground-floor wall, turning themselves into columns to create the entrance and then back into pilasters at the other end. The no-nonsense entablature is crisp and clean, with a projecting cornice that both caps the columns below and supports the window pedestals above. In thus merging upper and lower architectural elements, Peruzzi rejects the Renaissance façade convention of clear differentiation between separate floors, and instead melds the motifs of the two lower stories into a unified and satisfying visual whole.

But what is going on with the two top stories? Renaissance tradition called for rustication on the ground floor only, and windows of progressively diminishing visual impact as the building rises. Ignoring these conventions, Peruzzi rusticated the entire façade (producing a startling netlike effect) and introduced two rows of identically sized rectangular windows that are differentiated only by their decoration. The resulting contrast between the small windows and the large undifferentiated wall surface into which they are set is odd and uncomfortable, making the windows look like cramped, secretive portholes. When combined with the strong lower stories, the overall effect is more than a little bizarre, transforming the façade as a whole into a cryptic architectural riddle.*

---

*Nikolaus Pevsner, for one, is somewhat more sympathetic to Peruzzi's conundrum. In *An Outline of European Architecture,* he writes: "In the Palazzo Massimo there is a poignant contrast between the deep darkness of the ground-floor loggia and the papery thinness and flatness of the upper parts. The first-floor windows are shallow in relief compared with what the High Renaissance regarded as appropriate, the second- and third-floor windows are small and have curious leathery surrounds. They are in no way differentiated in size or importance as they would have been in the Renaissance. Moreover, a slight curve of the whole façade gives it a swaying delicacy, whereas the squareness of the Renaissance front seemed to express powerful solidity. The Palazzo Massimo is no doubt inferior to the Palazzi Caffarelli-Vidoni and Farnese in dignity and grandeur; but it has a sophisticated elegance instead which appeals to the over-civilized and intellectual connoisseur."

4-15 PALAZZO DELLA SAPIENZA
Courtyard: Giacomo della Porta, 1577
(Corso Rinascimento, south of the Via degli Staderari)

The east end of the Palazzo della Sapienza courtyard serves as the entrance to S. Ivo della Sapienza, and Borromini's billowing dome and spiral lantern command the attention with such force that the surrounding architecture is often overlooked. But the Sapienza courtyard deserves attention in its own right. Designed by Giacomo della Porta and constructed some sixty-five years before the church, its sober and measured arcades contrast sharply (but not unhappily) with Borromini's boldly original shapes.

Elegantly understated in effect, Della Porta's courtyard employs ideas that were originated many decades earlier by other architects. Far from being copycat architecture, however, it develops and refines those ideas with consummate skill and sophistication. The result is the most beautiful Renaissance courtyard in Rome, and a high point of Renaissance design. Henry James admired it greatly; searching for the source of its beauty, he commented on the need to take "time to puzzle out, if you could, the essence of the insolent secret. It was all really, with the very swagger of simplicity, a matter of . . . the mutual relation of parts."

True enough, but which parts, and what relation? James does not say, but a comparison with the earlier and more primitive Cancelleria courtyard several blocks away may help to explain what he means. At the Cancelleria, the three stories of the courtyard decrease in height with each successive floor, in an attempt to establish a progressive diminution of visual weight. But the result turns out to be visually perverse; since the middle-story arches look squatter than the lower-story arches, and since the top story is solid wall rather than open arcade, the upper stories appear heavier than the lower, not lighter. The overall effect is distinctly discomfiting.

Apparently recognizing these problems, Della Porta took an entirely different tack at the Sapienza. For one thing, he moved the top-story windowed walls on the long sides of the courtyard back, which dramatically deemphasizes their presence and allows the three-story courtyard to read, at least in part, as a two-story arcade. More importantly, however, he made the relative proportions of the upper and lower arcades close to identical. Common sense suggests that such a design would produce a displeasingly top-heavy effect, particularly since the upper arcade must carry a more emphatic protruding cornice than the lower. But the courtyard as a whole exhibits no such top-heaviness, and the lower story does not look in the least overburdened. How did Della Porta pull off such a neat visual trick?

In part, the answer lies in the introduction of an extra architectural element on the upper arcade, an element that was unknown during antiquity: the balustrade.* Della Porta uses the balustrade to fill in the spaces between the pedestals supporting the upper-arcade pilasters, and its role in the overall composition is critical. If the balustrade were not present, the pedestals would read as vertical elements, elongating the upper-arcade pilasters into pedestal-pilaster units. But the introduction of the balustrade makes the pedestals read as horizontal units — part of the balustrade itself — and as a result the upper-arcade pilasters can be read independently of their pedestals and as all but identical (except in their capitals) to the ground-floor pilasters below. This interrelationship of balustrade, pedestals, and pilasters visually disguises an intriguing discontinuity: the pedestal-pilaster units on the upper arcade are about 10 percent taller than the pilasters on the lower arcade (if the pedestals are omitted from the measurement, the pilasters are about 10 percent shorter). These same dimensions of course apply to the archway openings: if the balustrade is read as a void, then the upper arches are taller than the lower, but if the balustrade is read as a solid, the upper arches are shorter and squatter. This ambiguity may account for the fact that it is extremely difficult for the naked eye to make out exactly how the upper archway openings are sized in relation to the lower. Against expectations, however, the end result is not in the least disturbing; the upper arcade does not seem overly heavy or oppressive, and the overall effect is admirably balanced and stable. Visual ambiguity, in this instance, serves to create visual equilibrium.

This same equilibrium can be seen in the design of the courtyard's individual bays. Here another critical element comes into play: the use of piers instead of columns. Piers, unlike columns, have flat sides, and these flat sides allow for the use of variably sized pilasters (taller primary pilasters attached to the front of the piers facing the courtyard and shorter secondary pilasters attached to the sides). It is the pilasters that generate the rest of the bay design: the primary pilasters support a simple horizontal entablature that runs around the perimeter of the entire courtyard, and the secondary pilasters support the molded arches of the arcade.

Now an arch, it should be noted, appears to the eye to be pushing up and out. But it is the special beauty of Della Porta's bay design that this push is

---

* As an elegant alternative to solid waist-high restraining panels, balustrades had been used in palazzo courtyards for some time when Della Porta designed the Sapienza; the earliest known Renaissance balustrade dates from 1484, in the choir loft of the Sistine Chapel at the Vatican.

rigorously controlled and constrained. Here, once again, James's "mutual relation of parts" is key. The curved arch moldings just touch the horizontal entablature moldings at the center of each bay, and just touch the edges of the tall primary pilasters at the sides of the bay where the arch springs from the secondary pilasters; moreover, the arch and entablature moldings echo each other in size and shape. As a result of this three-point contact and visual similarity, the upward-and-outward force of the arch appears to be held in check by the pilasters and entablature that frame and trap it, pushing back with an equal opposing power. The two separate compositions — one an entablature supported by tall pilasters and the other an arch supported by short pilasters — thus lock themselves together into a unified and balanced visual whole that is taut and trenchant. And again, the use of piers and pilasters is critical. The design would not be possible with single columns (as in the Cancelleria courtyard), because a pair of single columns could not support both entablature and arches at the same time.

The concept of using both a curved arch and a straight entablature in the same composition was not new to the Renaissance. Historically the entablature was of course Greek in origin, an integral part of the exterior colonnades that gave Greek temples their uniquely powerful presence. The origin of the arch is more obscure; contrary to popular belief, the Greeks understood and constructed arches but chose to employ them sparingly, mostly limiting their use to underground structures (such as tombs and sewers) that were subject to external pressures. It was the Romans who brought the arch into general use, and when Roman architects began to employ it regularly, they faced a fundamental question. Given the architectural traditions inherited from the Greeks, how would the arch fit in?

The question was a tricky one. To Roman architects (as to later Renaissance architects), Classicism represented a sophisticated architectural language. It possessed a vocabulary (the individual architectural elements themselves, such as columns, entablatures, pediments, and all their parts and subparts), a grammar (the ways in which the various individual elements are combined to form the Doric, Ionic, and Corinthian orders), and a syntax (the ways in which a specific order may be varied so as to give each individual building an architectural meaning — an architectural personality — all its own). Such a structure may sound limiting, but even in Greek times the canon of conventional rules was far from rigid, and Greek temples as a group were far more varied in style and character than is commonly thought. But the introduction of the arch was more than just a stylistic variation, and more than a simple expansion of the Classical vocabulary. It was a challenge to that vocabulary at its most basic level: a new way to construct an opening. The fundamental technique of trabeation — the post-and-lintel construction method that the Greeks so ennobled by shaping the post into a column and the lintel into an entablature — was to be replaced with a different method of construction altogether, an alternative to trabeation that came to be known as *arcuation*. The flat-topped openings of the Greek colonnade were to be transformed into the round-topped openings of the Roman arcade.

This fundamental shift left the Romans facing a choice: either find a way to adapt the old conventions of the Greek orders to the new shape, or invent new architectural elements to mold and define the arch on its own. As might be expected, Roman architects chose the solution that preserved the Greek architectural tradition, a solution that combined the new with the old. The paradigmatic expression of this compromise is the Roman triumphal arch, a newly conceived structure that frames a round-topped Roman opening with a square-topped Greek order. But if this solution managed to preserve the Greek conventions, it also transformed those conventions in a fundamental way. In a Greek temple, the columns and entablature play a critical structural role in holding up the temple roof. In a Roman triumphal arch, the columns and entablature hold nothing up; they are applied to the outer surface of the triumphal arch and possess no structural purpose whatsoever.

This is not to say, as some purists would have it, that the Romans reduced the Greek orders to the role of mere decoration. The arch may be doing the heavy lifting, so to speak, but it is the columns and entablature that carry the meaning, that call up all the architectural, historical, civic, and religious associations that the Romans wanted especially to preserve. The Arc de Triomphe in Paris illustrates the point. The main reason the famous arch fails to look Classical — the reason it looks so Frenchified — is that it possesses no columns, which robs its entablature of visual support and puts that entablature on an equal footing (or lack of footing) with the structure's many other decorative carved panels.

Nowadays, the Neoclassical building boom of the nineteenth century has rendered Classically framed archways so commonplace that they scarcely warrant a second glance. But second glances can be illuminating. Even within the constraints of this single motif, the range of design variation and quality turns out to be astonishingly wide, both in ancient and modern times. Among successful antique examples, the Colosseum is perhaps the most famous; its cohort of Doric, Ionic, and Corinthian half columns do not so much flank their arches as stand guard beside them, like sentries at perpetual attention.

In Della Porta's day, the Classically framed arch had been common architectural currency since the beginning of the Renaissance, more than a century earlier. Bramante, for one, had used the motif fifty years before on the ground floor of his cloister at S. Maria della Pace, and here again comparison is illuminating. Even though the architectural elements used in the two courtyards are almost identical, Bramante's courtyard looks crude and slack compared to Della Porta's. Bramante's primary pilasters are placed on pedestals, which robs them of power and diminishes their relation to the secondary pilasters on the sides of the piers; in addition, Bramante's arch is naked (it lacks moldings) and visually unrelated to the entablature above. In the end, the S. Maria della Pace cloister remains a varied collection of architectural elements that never quite coheres into a unified whole, an experiment that doesn't quite come off.

There is nothing experimental about Della Porta's courtyard. The Sapienza is an architectural recipe perfected, all the ingredients expertly calculated and expertly combined. The arches and their frames fit together so logically and coherently, and with such precision and finesse, that the overall design looks easy and inevitable.* But such a "mutual relation of parts" is far from inevitable, as many other courtyards and façades around the city will attest. Only rarely does architecture achieve such exquisite balance, and it is this balance — and the simplicity and clarity of the elements used to achieve it — that give the Sapienza its special and exquisite Renaissance character.

But what of Borromini's S. Ivo, constructed at the far end of the courtyard almost a century later in an entirely different style? Normally such a stylistic disjunction would produce aesthetic dysfunction — a jarring clash between surroundings and centerpiece. Happily, Borromini addresses the problem directly: he pays homage to Della Porta's design by retaining the courtyard's archway motifs on the two lower floors of the church façade.

---

*If the design has a flaw, it can be found — where else? — at the corners, where that old bugbear of Renaissance architecture, the "corner problem," crops up yet again, just as it did at S. Maria della Pace and the Palazzo della Cancelleria. Della Porta addresses the issue — how to pump up the courtyard corners so that they function visually as strong full-stops for the arcades they terminate — with great cleverness, but he does not so much solve the problem as finesse it. He introduces an extraneous element at the ends of the courtyard's long sides: an extra, narrower bay with a shorter, rectangular opening. It might be expected that such an anomalous intrusion would stick out like a sore thumb, but in fact the extra bays are quite unobtrusive, and can even be viewed as buttressing the arcades, serving as compressive architectural bookends to the serried ranks of arches. It looks fine, and it is supremely ingenious, but as an answer to the corner problem it was conceptually too inelegant ever to become a canonical solution.

And by using the curve of that façade to mediate between the correctitude of Della Porta's arcades and the iconoclasm of his own dome and lantern, he builds a visual bridge that connects the Renaissance and the Baroque. The stylistic contrast thus becomes a journey rather than a conflict, and the opposition is pure exhilaration. Superior quality rules, and rules supreme, for nowhere else in Rome — perhaps nowhere else in Europe — is the difference between the two architectural eras illustrated so clearly, so concisely, and so dramatically.

4-16   SANT' ANDREA DELLA VALLE
Church: Giacomo della Porta, Fabrizio Grimaldi, Francesco da Volterra, Carlo Maderno, 1591–1621
Façade: begun by Carlo Maderno, ca. 1620; finished by Carlo Rainaldi and Carlo Fontana, 1662–1666
(Piazza di S. Andrea della Valle, facing the south end of the Corso Rinascimento)

Like S. Ignazio and the Chiesa Nuova, S. Andrea della Valle is a stylistic descendant of that most influential of all Roman churches, the Gesù. Its construction history is singularly complicated, stretching over some thirty years and involving a confusing succession of architects that included Giacomo della Porta, Fabrizio Grimaldi, Francesco da Volterra, and Carlo Maderno. The stately dome — known with certainty to be the work of Maderno — is the second largest in Rome after St. Peter's.

The façade history is no less complex, starting with Maderno in the 1620s and ending (after a long hiatus) with Carlo Rainaldi and possibly Carlo Fontana in the 1660s. The final result, as Baroque façades go, is rather tame: forcefully carved columns that are tempered by being set back into the wall surface, a modest stepback progression (from center door to paired columns to side-end pilasters) that emphasizes the central entranceway only slightly, and conventional carved decoration around niches and windows. It is all competently done, but visual excitement is decidedly lacking, and in the end the façade's most intriguing feature is the absence of the expected scrolls to either side of the upper story. Instead, there is a sculpted angel on the left, with no matching figure on the right. The right-hand angel, it turns out, was never even started; Pope Alexander VII criticized the left-hand angel shortly after it was finished, and the enraged sculptor (Ercole Ferrata) refused to continue with the job, proclaiming, "If he wants another, let him make it himself."

The interior offers an illuminating contrast with both the Gesù (several blocks to the east) and the Chiesa Nuova (several blocks to the west). The comparison with the Gesù is succinctly summarized by architectural historian John Varriano in his survey *Italian Baroque and Rococo Architecture*:

S. Andrea was begun in 1591 as the Mother Church of the newly founded Theatine Order. . . . Its original architects, Padre Francesco Grimaldi and Giacomo della Porta, attempted a revision of Il Gesù with an eye toward achieving a less ponderous and more engaging interior. Using a ground plan similar to that of the Jesuit church, they altered the proportions of the interior, increasing the height of the elevation by about one fourth. The architects also emphasized vertical movement through the use of bundled pilasters that thrust upward into the entablature to meet the ribs of the vault. The tempo of movement down the nave is thereby quickened and the entire architectural system is unified and tightened. The lazy horizontal sprawl of Il Gesù with its paired pilasters becomes a tense equilibrium of horizontals and verticals, and what at Il Gesù are flat areas of wall surface, ripple and vibrate at S. Andrea della Valle. Without violating tradition, S. Andrea achieved a certain animation and individuality that usually was so lacking in other works of its period.

In its decorative scheme (as opposed to its architectural design), S. Andrea resembles the Chiesa Nuova more than the Gesù. The two churches share a predilection — a passion, even — for gilding; unlike the Gesù, neither uses colored marble to achieve richness of effect. But there is a critical difference in decorative strategies, a difference that makes the S. Andrea interior read as sumptuous where the Chiesa Nuova interior reads as gaudy. At the Chiesa Nuova, the gilded-stucco decoration in the vaults forms a complicated pattern of interlocking geometric shapes; as a consequence, the eye is constantly drawn away from the ceiling frescoes, which end up looking like mere fill-in. Here, the balance between painting and gilded stucco is far more successful. The decoration overhead serves to frame and set off the art, not to smother it, and as a result the paintings in the vaults attract the eye far more powerfully than in the Chiesa Nuova. Interestingly, both the art and its gilded framework on the nave ceiling are modern. They date from the early 1900s, when the nave pilasters were both fluted and gilded and a new floor was installed during a major renovation.

4-17   PALAZZO CAFFARELLI-VIDONI
Rear façade: possibly Raphael or Lorenzetto, 1524
(Via del Sudario, east of S. Maria della Valle)

Like the nearby Piccola Farnesina, the Palazzo Caffarelli-Vidoni is a nineteenth-century turnabout: the construction of the Corso Vittorio Emanuele in the late 1800s reversed the palazzo's orientation, and the undistinguished rear façade was given a face-lift to bring it up to snuff. Nevertheless, the original front façade remains the more important, its present back-alley orientation notwithstanding. The design has traditionally been ascribed to Raphael, who is said to have based it on Bramante's design for Raphael's own house (since destroyed), but the attribution is suspect because Raphael died in 1520, four years before construction began. Vasari, writing some decades after Raphael's death, attributes the design to Raphael's pupil Lorenzetto.

Whoever the architect may have been, he clearly knew what he was about. The top story and the façade's inordinate length should be ignored; both are the result of later expansion. The core idea is the contrast between the ground floor and the *piano nobile* above, between horizontal and vertical architectural elements. Visually, the ground floor serves as a horizontal supporting podium, with the alternating wide and narrow bands of rustication producing a look of compression that adds to the ground-hugging feel. The paired Tuscan (Roman Doric) half columns of the *piano nobile,* on the other hand, stand crisply forth from the wall surface, offering strong vertical support for the entablature that runs the full length of the façade. The overall design of the upper story is not complicated, but its arrangement of alternating column-pedestal and window-balustrade units is compact without being crowded. Such tightness was unusual in its day and imparts to the façade an air of boldness that prefigures the Baroque. The design might have served as a model for other Renaissance palazzi, had the Palazzo Farnese not claimed preeminence with such unchallengeable authority.

4-18   LARGO ARGENTINA RUINS
First to fourth centuries B.C.E.

An unexpected sunken island of ruins, besieged but not overwhelmed by traffic. The four Republican temples — actually three and a third, since the southernmost temple remains mostly buried under the Via Florida — are among the oldest excavated ruins in the city; they are best viewed from the southeast corner (next to the medieval Torre del Papito), where the layout becomes clear. The rectangular temple next to the partially excavated temple is the oldest, probably dating from the early third century B.C.E.; the other structures date from the late second or early first century B.C.E. (the partially excavated temple), the early first century B.C.E. (the circular temple), and the mid-to-late first century B.C.E. (the northernmost temple, which replaced earlier temples on the site dating back to the third century). While the structures were being excavated in the late 1920s, Mussolini ordered the site enclosed within high walls; his purpose, according to a famous joke around town, was to keep the public from seeing that he was having the ruins built from scratch.

Today the Largo Argentina ruins are home to a large number of cats — there is a cat sanctuary, and the cats can be adopted — and Eleanor Clark, in *Rome and a Villa,* gives a memorable description of the mad feline dash for shelter at the beginning of a cloudburst:

> The lines they trace are … all in a criss-cross as of night projectiles over a battlefield. It is each not to the nearest cover but the predetermined one, which may be halfway round the ruin or all the way across the lawn … so for a few seconds the whole ground is a contradiction of flying cat-furs, which resolves itself in a moment without collision or argument or even a swerve of line unless a particular place were taken, when the late-comer shoots off by the same mystic geometry to the nearest alternative. Then there is no further move.

4-19 FONTANA DELLE TARTARUGHE (TURTLE FOUNTAIN)
Giacomo della Porta (design) and Taddeo Landini (sculpture), 1584
(Piazza Mattei, south of the Largo Argentina)

A treasure, hidden away in a drab little side-street piazza where only the dedicated explorer will find it. Compared to the boisterous, full-throated chorus of Rome's grander fountains — the Trevi, say, or the Fontana dei Quattro Fiumi in the Piazza Navona — the voice of the Fontana delle Tartarughe is the gentlest of murmurs. But it is no less a masterpiece for its lack of pretension.

The fountain's ruling conceit is simple: four nude youths, astride four tame dolphins, offer helping hands to four thirsty turtles (the *tartarughe* for which the fountain is named). The youths, with their artfully similar poses, are typically Mannerist in their self-consciously twisted and off-balance poses. But contorted as those poses are, they are never for a moment awkward or strained. The sculptor, Taddeo Landini, was trained in Florence, and he gave the figures a sinuous charm worthy of Botticelli himself. Unexpectedly for Rome, the four youths are the epitome of Florentine sculptural grace.

Still, it is the turtles for which the fountain is named, and with good reason. Their presence here is extraordinarily enlivening. Unflinchingly realistic in their inelegant turtleness, they have been lifted to the upper basin by the youths below, and are scrabbling for purchase on the rim. The momentary precariousness of their situation — will they find the footholds they seek without further assistance? — brings an electric touch of drama to the entire composition, transforming the youths' elegant Mannerist poses into moving gestures of concern and compassion. During World War II, the Romans themselves were similarly concerned: when the Nazis marched into Rome, the turtles were carefully removed and hidden away for safekeeping, and they were lovingly returned to their traditional positions only after the Allies had liberated the city. Among Rome's outdoor sculpted animals, these four humble and endearingly graceless creatures have long occupied a special place.

Given the fountain's idiosyncratic theme, one historical fact must come as a shock: the turtles are not original to the work. They were added seventy years later, during a restoration of the fountain in 1658, replacing more conventional dolphins (a common symbol of resurrection and salvation in Christian iconography). Local residents will announce with great confidence that Bernini was responsible for the change — who but the greatest of all Baroque sculptors could have conceived such a brilliant conceptual fillip? But tempting as this hypothesis may be, there is no documentary evidence whatsoever to support it. In fact, the author of this audaciously eccentric stroke of genius is entirely unknown.

4-20 PALAZZO MATTEI DI GIOVE
Courtyard and exterior façades facing the Via dei Funari and the Via
Michelangelo Caetani: Carlo Maderno, 1598–1617
(Piazza Mattei, northeast corner; entrances on the Via dei Funari and the Via
Michelangelo Caetani)

The late-sixteenth-century wing of the Palazzo Mattei is large and imposing, but its unexceptional architectural features are completely overshadowed by the collection of sculpture exhibited around (and built into the walls of) the building's courtyards, main staircase, and loggia. The sometimes arbitrary placement of the pieces gives the overall display a misleadingly haphazard look; in fact the collection's originator, Duke Astrubale

Mattei, was one of the first "collectors" in the modern sense, rigorously documenting his purchases and restorations. The collection varies in quality — some of the items on display are mere curiosities — but when it is good, it is very good indeed. Of particular note are two deeply carved and magnificently preserved bas-reliefs (originally front panels on marble sarcophagi), one located at the bottom and the other on the landing of the staircase leading up to the loggia.

Not everything, it should be noted, is antique. A good many of the busts are reproductions purchased or commissioned by Mattei, and in 1634 he commissioned a series of round bas-relief medallions of Holy Roman Emperors through the centuries and down to his own day, which he inserted in the courtyard walls between the antique bas-reliefs. The purpose of these visually intrusive additions was apparently to flatter the existing emperor, Ferdinand II, to whom Mattei claimed to be related and whose ambassador Mattei regularly entertained.

4-21   SANTA MARIA IN CAMPITELLI
Carlo Rainaldi, 1662–1675
(Piazza Campitelli, between the Piazza Mattei and the Via del Teatro di Marcello)

S. Maria in Campitelli.

Carlo Rainaldi's façade for S. Maria in Campitelli was constructed at the height of the Baroque era, and it displays more columns and pilasters — thirty-two in all — than any other church façade in Rome. The effect is more than a little overpowering, particularly given the narrowness of the church's piazza. But the overall design is carefully worked out and skillfully assembled.

The ruling motif is the aedicule, employed in three progressive sizes. The smallest can be found at the center of each story, where the aedicule's columns, entablature, and crowning pediment serve to frame the entrance door and the upper–floor window. These central elements are surrounded by larger aedicules that rise the full height of the story; the larger aedicules are in turn surrounded by a single giant aedicule (two columns high, with a broken pediment at the roofline) that frames the entire façade (except for the two narrow ground-floor outer wings). Viewed in this manner, the façade's main emphasis is vertical, a complex arrangement of five concentric and interconnected Classical frames. But the frames' forward-and-back alignment — the full-story aedicules protrude farther forward than the door and window aedicules, while the giant outer aedicule pulls back — creates a strong secondary horizontal emphasis. When the façade is read across rather than up-and-down, the columns predominate, stepping in and out in a complicated but lively rhythm that contrasts dramatically with the foursquare aedicules.

The façade, then, is one of Rome's most ambitious architectural compositions. But how successful is it? The basic problem, of course, underlies all Baroque façade design: how to manipulate, how to juggle, how to balance a set of differently scaled but similarly shaped Classical elements into a unified interlocking whole. Answers can be seen all over the city, but few are as ambitious as this.

Rainaldi almost, but not quite, pulls it off. The aedicules nest themselves logically and comfortably, and the thirty-two columns and pilasters never get in each other's way. Particularly impressive is the rounded pediment of the larger upper-story aedicule, which doubles without strain as a portion of the full-façade pediment that surrounds and encompasses it. But the weak point — visually a serious flaw — is not the composition's inner interlock, but rather its outer framing. At the very top of the façade, the break in the full-width pediment makes the peak look like a circumflex, an afterthought topping to the stronger rounded pediment immediately below; at the sides of the façade, the outer columns are identical to their peers and thus lack the power to emphasize the façade's vertical edges. As a result, the outer aedicule fails to enclose the overall composition with finality, frittering away the force of the inner full-story aedicules, which in the end dominate uncomfortably. Still, Rainaldi's achievement is not to be dismissed lightly. He has bid a Baroque grand slam, and he almost makes the contract.

The interior is one of Rome's most monumental spaces, and as complicated in its plan as the façade. William L. MacDonald gives a detailed description in his *Architecture of the Roman Empire:*

The design is a study in harmonics whose tonic is the main axis (about 50 meters long). Chords are repeatedly struck by subordinated spaces of different sizes and shapes paired symmetrically along the progress of this central line. The building's enclosing wall narrows progressively overall from entrance to apse, but in measured steps of expansion and contraction that come to a halt at the narrowest, furthest part of the building. The result is a series of right-angled sequences unifying rather than unsettling the building's configuration, which is superlatively scenic. From the entranceway, ranges of coulisses [side scenes as on a stage set] are seen left and right. Without column files [columns set out in straight rows], volumes predominate. Triads thrive, and various shapes are played off against each other with great success. As in most Baroque churches, the whole repertory of ancient architecture is used: monumental and lesser orders, barrel vaults, a dome and a half-dome, niches, aediculas, and so on, all unified in a design whose final purpose is to focus attention on a venerated icon centered in the apse wall.

All very true. But why, then, is the overall effect so dispiriting? Perhaps it is a matter of size; bigger is not necessarily better, and in sacrificing human scale the interior seems to have sacrificed its heart as well. Perhaps it is the exaggerated style: the massive clustered "triad chords" of columns and pilasters support one of the mightiest interior entablatures in Rome, and the combination of the two pumps up the Corinthian order — traditionally considered the most elegant of the Classical orders — almost to the point of caricature. Or perhaps it is the lack of curves in the ground plan: the placement of the clustered columns and the in-and-out movement of the entablature feels almost threatening in its blocky angularity. But whatever the cause, the immense space in the end feels cold and overcalculated, and even the sunlight flooding through the windows under the dome seems deprived of all warmth.[*]

---

[*]This is a harsh judgment, and perhaps a benighted one. William L. MacDonald's endorsement of Rainaldi's interior is seconded by John Varriano in his survey *Italian Baroque and Rococo Architecture;* after several pages of detailed (and enthusiastic) analysis, Varriano concludes: "Rainaldi's interior is a perfect expression of the sensibility of the High Baroque. . . . Spatial boundaries no longer are rigidly fixed, masses are broken and constantly shifting, and light is . . . carefully controlled. To enter the building is to have one of the most splendid and solemn architectural experiences possible in Rome."

In the spring of 1562, workers digging in a private garden next to the church of SS. Cosma e Damiano at the edge of the long-abandoned Forum made an intriguing discovery: a jumbled pile of antique marble fragments that, unlike most such finds, did not appear to be remnants of an ancient building or statue. The fragments were uniformly thin and flat — apparently part of a large panel or slab — and were covered with incised markings.

The markings were cryptic, and it was not until the relics reached the hands of Cardinal Alessandro Farnese and were turned over to his Director of Antiquities that their true significance was recognized. These were pieces of the Marble Plan, mentioned by historians of late antiquity: a huge marble map (42½ feet high and 59½ feet wide) of the city of Rome, produced during the reign of the emperor Septimius Severus (193–211 C.E.) and hung in a special room next to the Forum of Peace known as the Hall of the Marble Plan. Since the initial find in 1562, about 10 percent of the map has been recovered, and the excavated fragments — numbering more than a thousand — have enabled historians to establish with certainty the identity of many of the ancient ruins scattered around the city.

One such ruin is located at the east end of the Via del Portico d'Ottavia, on the edge of the old Jewish Ghetto. The two ancient rows of columns carrying entablature and pediment — one with a medieval arch inserted in place of the two right-hand columns, the other built into the wall of the medieval church of S. Angelo in Pescheria — are battered and bruised; as the picturesquely jumbled collection of antique odds and ends on the back side of the front pediment attest, they have over the centuries been much damaged and reconstructed. During the Middle Ages, they were thought to be the front and back of a small temple, but — as the Marble Plan makes clear — they did not originally stand alone. In antiquity, they were part of a far larger structure: the grand and imposing Porticus of Octavia, a covered rectangular walkway built around 25 B.C.E. by Augustus and dedicated to his sister Octavia. The walkway stretched for several city blocks and enclosed a whole complex of public buildings, including two sizable temples dedicated to Jupiter and Juno, Greek and Roman libraries, schoolrooms, meeting rooms, and exhibition space for a large collection of bronze and marble statuary (including the famous Medici Venus, now in the Uffizi in Florence). Today nothing is left of the complex but these two fragments, which were originally roofed over to serve as the main entrance porch and gateway of the Porticus.

4-23 SYNAGOGUE AND JEWISH GHETTO

Synagogue: Osvaldo Armanni and Vincenzo Costa, 1901–1908
Ghetto walls constructed 1555 and demolished 1848;
buildings demolished 1880–1887
(Lungotevere de' Cenci, between the Porticus of Octavia and the Tiber)

In the architecture of Europe and America, the nineteenth-century enthusiasm for the backward historical glance usually took one of two forms: Neoclassical or Neo-Gothic. Both styles had their fanatical devotees. Thomas Jefferson designed the campus of the University of Virginia around an elegant Classical porticus, and Henry Adams quoted Gibbon on the subject of the great Gothic cathedrals: "I darted a contemptuous look on the stately monuments of superstition." The impassioned English critic and essayist John Ruskin spoke for the opposing camp. His treatise *The Seven Lamps of Architecture* stood Gibbon's argument on its head, championing the Gothic style (when properly executed) as "pleasing to God" and characterizing the architecture of the Renaissance as a "foul torrent."

Most of the time, however, more moderate views prevailed, and the choice of style often depended upon the nature of the building. The Classical style (either Renaissance Revival or the purer Greek Revival) was considered especially appropriate for government buildings and public institutions such as museums; the Gothic style was especially suited to churches. The choice was by no means automatic — London's Houses of Parliament are a famous example of government Gothic — but most important buildings of the day looked back to one style or the other.

Occasionally, however, more esoteric historical sources were invoked. Rome's main Synagogue — a large but mannerly building constructed in 1901 on the site of the razed Jewish Ghetto — is a case in point. Recognizing that the strong Christian and pagan connotations of the Gothic and Classical styles rendered them unsuitable for a Jewish temple, the Synagogue's architects adopted instead an eclectic program that combined the very old and the very new. On the building's four façades — each façade a different composition — they employed decorative motifs drawn from ancient Assyrian and Babylonian sources, meant to invoke the events and times of the Old Testament. Above the façades, the unusual four-sided dome (set on a square drum) was frankly modern, sheathed in what was then a brand-new light-weight nonrusting metal alloy: aluminum. As an element of the Roman skyline (particularly as seen from the surrounding hills), the distinctive shape of the dome serves a double visual purpose: it sets the Synagogue apart from Rome's other religious structures, and it marks the site of the Jewish Ghetto with an architectural memorial that is instantly recognizable.

The history of the Jewish community in Rome is not a happy one. The humiliations and intermittent persecutions of the Middle Ages were followed, in 1555, by a papal edict establishing the Ghetto. The streets of Rome's main Jewish community were closed off with walls and gates, and its citizens were confined within a small area that stretched from the Tiber to the Via del Portico d'Ottavia.

The Ghetto covered some seven acres — essentially the four city blocks on either side of the modern Via Catalana, one of which is now occupied by the Synagogue. The gates were closed inexorably every evening at sundown, imprisoning some 3,500 inhabitants within 130 buildings, many of them mere hovels. Being adjacent to the Tiber, the area was prone to flooding, and sanitary conditions, even by the poor standards of the day, were abominable. The inhabitants were forbidden to engage in most professions, and what revenue they did manage to generate was heavily taxed. And for more than two hundred years, Christian religious services were compulsory every Sunday (the façade of S. Giorgio della Divina Pietà — situated opposite the eastern gate of the Ghetto at the Ponte Fabricio — still retains its propagandizing inscriptions in Hebrew and Latin, displayed beneath a fresco of the crucifixion).

The quarantine ended in 1848, when the gates of the Ghetto were torn down by order of Pope Piux IX; the last remaining Ghetto houses were demolished in 1887 when the Tiber embankments were constructed. But the transformation of the Ghetto into a Jewish quarter did not save its residents from the fascist persecution of World War II. On October 16, 1943, the city's German occupiers raided the quarter's new buildings and rounded up their occupants; ultimately, more than 2,000 Jews were deported to Nazi concentration camps. Very few of them ever returned.

TOURS

5 - 6

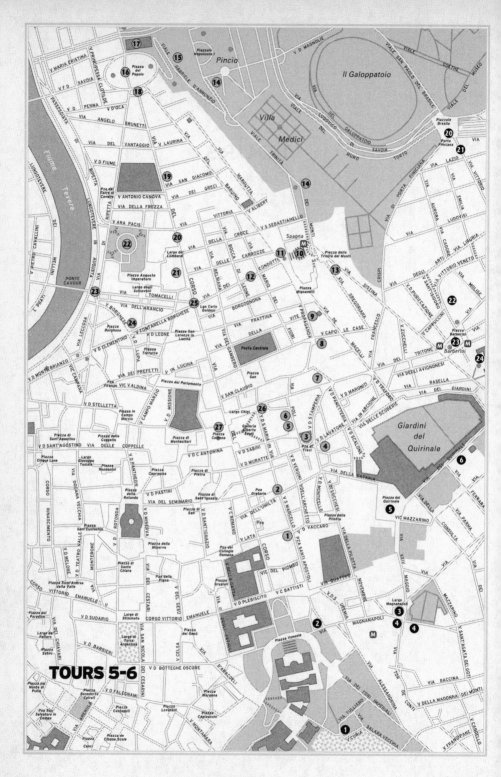

TOURS 5-6

MAP #2
TOURS 5 — 6

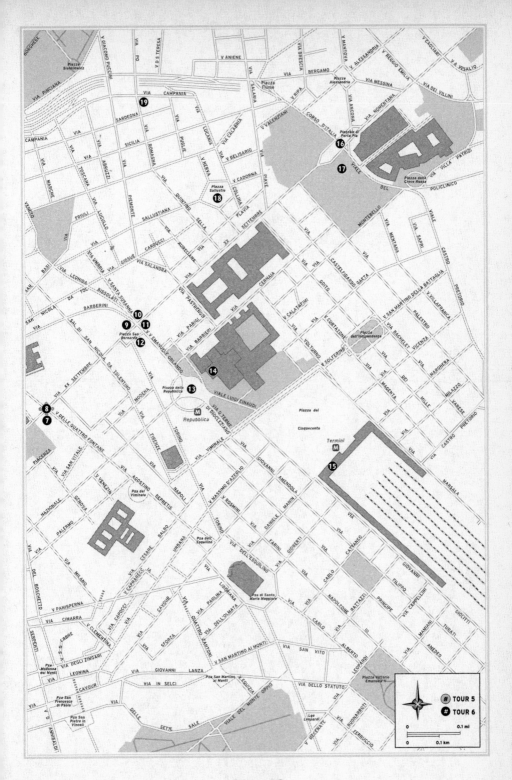

MAP #2
TOURS 5 — 6

TOUR 5

—•—

BAROQUE ROME I:
AROUND THE CORSO
FROM THE PIAZZA VENEZIA
TO THE PIAZZA DEL POPOLO

ROME'S LONG THOUSAND-year decline came to an end with the Renaissance, but the real building boom did not arrive until the Baroque era — the seventeenth and eighteenth centuries — when the city was virtually transformed. Rome at last began to expand again, and the natural course of development was to the east of the Campus Martius, beyond the ancient Via Flaminia (today the Via del Corso, or just "the Corso"). The area between the Corso and the Pincian Hill became a new center of activity, appealing particularly to foreign visitors; by the beginning of the nineteenth century, when the young English poet John Keats died of tuberculosis in rented rooms on the Piazza di Spagna, it was completely built up. The star attractions — perhaps the most famous in the entire city — are those two extravagant and incomparable set pieces, the Trevi Fountain (pictured above) and the

Spanish Steps. They are the very quintessence of Roman panache and pride, and (along with the Piazza Navona) stand today as the preeminent emblems of the city's Baroque revival, when Rome was at long last reborn as a great European capital.

5-1 PALAZZO ODESCALCHI (REAR)
Façade: Gianlorenzo Bernini, 1664
(Piazza dei Santi Apostoli 80, northeast of the Piazza Venezia)

The road not taken. At the Campidoglio, Michelangelo employed the independent giant pilaster — more than one story in height and not part of an overall triumphal arch design — to add vertical power to façades that would otherwise be weighed down by excessive horizontality. Michelangelo's motif went uncopied in Rome for more than a hundred years, until the mid-1600s, when Bernini used it here and at the nearby Palazzo di Montecitorio. Despite Bernini's stamp of approval, however, the idea failed to catch on, and even during the Baroque era, very few palace façades departed from the windows-lined-up-like-ducks-in-a-row model supplied by the Palazzo Farnese. The resulting lack of variety is a shame, for the relentless repetition of similar palazzo exteriors throughout the city turns what would otherwise be an unexceptionable architectural convention into a wearying architectural cliché.

The façade here, incidentally, is not quite as Bernini intended. The palazzo's most unappealing feature — its excessive and lopsided length — is due to an eighteenth-century expansion. Bernini's original façade comprised only thirteen bays (as opposed to the current twenty-four), with seven pilastered bays in the middle, three unpilastered bays at each end, and a single entrance in the center. The overall effect would have been much more compact, and the façade's focal point — the entranceway bay, turned into a single vertical composition by the addition of an aedicule door-surround and upper-story decorative arms — would have been much more effective.

5-2 GALLERIA SCIARRA
Giulio de Angelis, 1885; frescoes: Giuseppe Cellini
(Piazza dell' Oratorio, north of the Piazza dei SS. Apostoli,
facing the north end of the Via di S. Marcello)

Little noticed today, but revolutionary in its time. The Galleria Sciarra dates from the 1880s, and its skylighted courtyard is generally recognized as the first building in Rome to employ modern skyscraper technology, which replaced traditional masonry walls made of stone or brick with much lighter-weight walls supported by a gridded metal framework. When the courtyard was built, however, the twentieth-century rebellion against Classical decoration was still several decades off, so the metal support structure here is mostly encased in a conventional collection of vertical pilasters and horizontal cornices. The true support system is visible only at the ground-floor entryways, where the plaster veneer is stripped away and four thin cast-iron columns are allowed to stand forth on their own.

Nowadays, of course, metal frame construction is ubiquitous, and what sets the Galleria Sciarra apart is not the underlying metal skeleton but the skin that covers it: the opulent frescoes that decorate every square inch of the available wall surface. The program is elaborate. Enthroned female figures personify exemplary virtues on the upper part of the middle story, scenes of bourgeois domestic life illustrate the virtues' practical applications on the lower part, hortatory Latin maxims decorate the pilasters on the lower story ("little boy, learn to greet your mother with a smile," advises one, quoting from Virgil's fourth *Eclogue*), and the whole is ornamented with a profusion of pseudo-antique patterned decoration that fills every inch of leftover wall space. To present-day viewers who do not share the nineteenth century's love of fancy dress and decoration, the juxtaposition of lavish Belle Epoque costumes and straitlaced Victorian moral sentiments (not to mention the gratuitous neo-Pompeian embellishments) may seem at best jarring, at worst hypocritical. But given such ingenuously enthusiastic excess (moral no less than visual), it seems peevish to take offense. In a city crammed to bursting with pious religious art, a bit of purely secular sermonizing can feel almost refreshing.

5-3 TREVI FOUNTAIN (FONTANA DI TREVI)
Nicola Salvi, 1732–1740
(Piazza della Fontana di Trevi)

So famous it has become a cliché, and a tourist trap to boot. But even the professional tour guides with their flagged umbrellas and canned speeches cannot kill it. Like Rome itself, the Trevi Fountain is indomitable: a big-hearted, boisterous, rumbumptious *tour de force* of inundated rocks, trees, gods, horses, and tritons, all bursting forth from a Baroque triumphal arch that does double duty as backdrop for the fountain and centerpiece for the palazzo façade behind. The whole thing teeters precariously on the edge of pomposity — an eighteenth-century warm-up for the nineteenth-century Victor Emmanuel Monument nearby. But it is rescued by its tiny piazza. Paris would have given it a grand (and deadening) boulevard approach,* but Rome leaves it tucked away in a maze of streets as if it were just another neighborhood civility. The tour groups may be swooning, but the city takes it in stride, and that saves the day.

Stylistically, the Trevi's vitality springs from its confident synthesis — its enthusiastic embrace — of opposites. At one extreme are the side wings of the palazzo façade, whose giant pilasters and aedicular window-surrounds — based upon Michelangelo's unexecuted plan for the Palazzo del Senatore on the Campidoglio — are pure architecture. At the other extreme are the intricately stepped levels of the fountain, whose carved rocks are pure sculpture. Taken together, the palazzo wings and the fountain rocks embody a whole series of artistic contrasts: symmetrical vs. asymmetrical, geometric vs. geomorphic, formal vs. informal, urban and urbane vs. rustic and rough. Between these extremes is the triumphal arch, out of which both façade and fountain seem to grow, and it is the arch that is the key to the whole composition. Its bold columns and niches stand forth from the echoing pilasters and windows of the palazzo wings, but its heavy architectural mass is softened and enlivened by its abundant statuary, and particularly by the central figure of Oceanus, who rides forth out of his niche to command the waters below. Because of the arch's mediating presence, the overall progression from abstract architectural form to naturalistic sculptural display — from aedicule-encased windows to niche-enclosed statues to freestanding rocks and figures — is fluid and seamless. As architectural historian John A. Pinto puts it in *The Trevi Fountain*:

> So perfectly fused are the three component elements of Salvi's fountain — architecture, sculpture, and water — that they can never completely be separated. The smooth masonry and elegant decoration of the architecture are made to appear the logical refinement of the irregular *scogli* [rocks] below; the eye moves from water and reefs to shell, niche, and pilaster in a progression of increasingly formal definition. … The architecture of the Fontana di Trevi appears to grow organically from the living rock.

---

* And almost did. In 1811, architect and town planner Giuseppe Valadier, under the auspices and thumb of Napoleon, drew up plans to demolish the entire block to the south of the fountain. Luckily the plans were never carried out.

The fountain's iconography, as might be expected, relates entirely to water. The central figure of Oceanus — the god of water in all its forms — rides an oyster-shell chariot drawn by two unruly winged and fish-tailed horses; the horses are attended by two tritons — mermen — one of whom announces Oceanus's arrival through a conch-shell trumpet. In the niches to either side of Oceanus, female figures personify Fertility (on the left, holding a cornucopia) and Health (on the right, offering a libation to a snake, symbol of the god of medicine, Aesculapius). The bas-reliefs above these two figures illustrate the antique history of the Trevi waters: on the right, the discovery of the source (springs at Salone, some ten miles east of Rome); on the left, the construction of the aqueduct arcades that carry the waters through the city. Across the attic of the triumphal arch, four more figures symbolize the benefits of water by displaying fruit, grain, grapes, and flowers, and at the very top two winged Trumpeters of Fame install the escutcheon of Clement XII.

All this is straightforward enough, and quite conventional. Less expected — and far more engaging — are the small, easily overlooked sculptural touches that amplify the iconographical theme. Scattered among the fountain rocks (and occasionally elsewhere as well) is a wealth of sculpted plant life, sometimes readily visible and sometimes tucked away in hidden nooks and crannies. Oak tree, fig tree, grapevine, acanthus plant, leek, marigold, prickly pear — over thirty species of flora are represented, along with the occasional snail or lizard out for a feed or a sun bath. The power of water to destroy is acknowledged as well, and with considerable wit: on the right-hand palazzo wing, the base of the outermost pilaster is cracking and crumbling, splitting into pieces as it returns to its natural state and falls away onto the rocks below.

The reputed origin of one particular detail perhaps deserves special (if skeptical) mention. On the right-hand edge of the basin, above the retaining wall running along the Via della Stamperia, there rises a small subsidiary set piece: an outcropping of rock that turns on the street side into a colossal urn, repository for the waters that drip into a drinking trough beneath the outcrop on the fountain side. The urn (so the story goes) was not part of architect Nicola Salvi's original plan. But during the fountain's construction, Salvi's visits to the site — he was often seen climbing around the rocks to inspect the progress of the carving — were regularly interrupted by patrons of a barbershop on the Via della Stamperia, who would emerge half-shaven to criticize his work. Salvi, in a fit of pique, added the urn to his design and placed it so as to block completely the barbershop view.

The fountain's history dates back some two thousand years. It was on June 9, 19 B.C.E. that Rome celebrated the opening of the aqueduct known as the

Aqua Virgo, constructed by consul Marcus Agrippa to supply water to the newly completed complex of buildings on the Campus Martius. In those days the Aqua Virgo probably continued almost to the Tiber, but in medieval times maintenance of the final section of the aboveground arcade carrying the water conduit was discontinued, and the functioning Aqua Virgo — the only aqueduct to be repaired after the barbarian invasions — ended here. The Piazza di Trevi thus became an important site, and for more than a thousand years it remained the principal gathering spot of Rome's water-carriers, who transported and sold the aqueduct's waters throughout the entire city. (The origin of the name "Trevi," incidentally, is not known with certainty. But there is archaeological evidence suggesting that three of the seven streets that currently converge on the fountain adhere closely to the Roman street layout of ancient times. Such a convergence was known in Latin as a *trivium,* and the fountain's name may derive from the Italian equivalent *tre vie,* or "three streets.")

The fountain that exists today dates from 1730, when the newly elected Pope Clement XII decided to rebuild the fountain already in place. An elaborate architectural competition ensued — at one point some thirty different models were exhibited in the nearby Quirinal Palace — and the complicated judging process dragged on for two years. In the end the winner was Nicola Salvi, and his ambitious design was probably chosen because it addressed, with particular skill, a very specific problem. In the 1720s, the owners of the nearby Palazzo Poli had purchased and demolished the buildings to either side of the existing fountain, and had replaced them with a new and distinctly undistinguished addition to their palazzo that flanked the fountain with identical wings. Salvi's proposal for the fountain included a complete redesign of this façade — ultimately he ended up constructing a second and false front, as can be seen at either corner of the palazzo — and he thereby incorporated the preexisting building into the composition in a way that the other proposals did not.

Salvi was thirty-five years old when he won the competition for the new Trevi, and it was his first major commission. Unfortunately it was also his last, for he spent the rest of his life supervising the Trevi's construction, turning down other work in order to see the job through. Although he was present to see the waters begin to flow at the partially completed fountain's inauguration in 1743, he did not live to see the finishing touches put in place (in 1744 he was stricken with partial paralysis, and he died in 1751, eleven years before the final pieces of sculpture — the two horses with their attendant tritons — were finally installed). As a legacy, however, Salvi's lone major commission is more than enough to keep his name alive, for the Trevi's exemplary fusion of architecture, sculpture, and water probably captures the abiding spirit of Baroque Rome — its self-confidence, its panache, its willingness to risk excess — better than any other monument of its era.

5-4   SANTI VINCENZO ED ANASTASIO
Façade: Martino Longhi the Younger, 1646–1650
(Piazza della Fontana di Trevi, southeast corner)

Given the stentorian thunder of the Trevi Fountain, who could possibly want to turn around to consider yet another church? Located at the southeast corner of the Piazza di Trevi, SS. Vincenzo ed Anastasio finds itself in a tough spot, all but overwhelmed by the virtuosity of the fountain it overlooks. But the church deserves attention, for it possesses one of the boldest and (in subtle ways) one of the oddest of Roman Baroque façades.

Sponsored by Cardinal Giulio Mazarin and designed by Martino Longhi the Younger, the SS. Vincenzo ed Anastasio façade was the first in Rome to allow its columns to step completely away from the wall surface, and the first to sport multiple nested pediments at its crown. The structural boldness of the end result is remarkable even for Rome. The façade seems barely to possess a wall surface at all; it is almost as if the façade's basic building blocks had miraculously disappeared, allowing the columns and entablatures and pediments to stand alone and to speak entirely for themselves. Only the large, blank vertical stone panels on the ground floor read as flat wall, and even these were meant to be disguised (Longhi wanted them carved with bas-reliefs, but the carvings were never executed).

The upper story, especially, is a compositional *tour de force*. Twin sets of triple columns support a triple-stepped entablature crowned by a triple pediment, while above the central window, sculpted angels and cherubs set various sponsor-celebrating insignia and paraphernalia in place (the cherub-flanked cardinal's hat near the peak is a particularly fine touch). The whole, meanwhile, is buttressed at the sides by voluptuous *caryatids* — columns brought to life — lifting the façade's final set of capitals into their assigned positions. The composition's various architectural and decorative elements interlock with parade-ground precision, and stand forth with an assured confidence that is strong and bold and proud. The Baroque style, militant and triumphant, has clearly come into its own.

The lower story echoes the upper in its triplets of columns, but expands the composition both horizontally and vertically. The sides push out to create the wall panels, with extra columns to mark and turn the corners; the base extends downward to become a set of seven steps that accentuates the façade's three-dimensionality.* The recessed central doorway allows the column triplets to be read horizontally as well as vertically, almost as if a curtain of columns has been drawn apart in the center to reveal the door behind; as frame for the doorway, the columns support an entablature topped by two curved pediments, the smaller of which contains a memorably quirky piece of decoration: a carved shell that somehow manages to look gracefully squashed. At the pediments' peak, the upper- and lower-story compositions merge into one as the larger pediment breaks open to make room for the decorative sculpture hanging down from the upper-story window.

The forceful Baroque qualities of the façade — its bold three-dimensionality, its adventurous complexity, its celebratory sculptural decoration — are unmistakable, even if their effect is dampened by the waters of the Trevi close by. The façade's oddities, however, are less obvious. Unexpectedly, a more detailed comparison of the upper and lower stories uncovers some marked eccentricities.

The upper story, for all its complexity, is a model of structural clarity: each column clearly supports its own section of entablature and its own section of pediment. But on the lower story, the architectural relationships are far more ambiguous. Here the column triplets support not three but two nested pediments, and the relationship between pediments and columns is far less stable. The smaller pediment is barely wide enough to connect comfortably with the inner pair of columns below; the larger pediment appears too wide for the middle columns but not wide enough for the outer. Why would Longhi employ such an equivocal design?

The most likely explanation is a technical one, for in choosing to flank both his lower-story doorway and his upper-story window with triple columns, Longhi faced a problem. The upper-story columns must be spaced far enough apart to allow room for the three pediments above, but if the lower-story columns are spaced the same distance apart — if the lower-story columns are to align vertically with their counterparts above — there will not

---

*Oddly, the steps seem to be a critical element in Longhi's overall design. If, in the mind's eye, the steps are excluded from the lower-story composition, then the lower story's outer parts — the end columns and the double pediment — seem almost to disconnect themselves and float away from the center. When the steps are included, however, they act visually to hold all the parts together, reaching out to the outer columns and providing extra weight at the composition's base to counterbalance and anchor the double pediment above. This phenomenon, which is easy to see in photographs, can be difficult to make out on-site, in part because the Trevi Fountain (constructed long after the church) interrupts the requisite sightlines and in part because the steps are often rendered all but invisible by sightseers who have come to see the fountain.

be enough room for the doorway. Longhi solves this problem — daringly — by sacrificing vertical column alignment. He spaces the lower-story columns more tightly than the upper and then uses the double pediment to disguise the fact that the upper- and lower-story column groupings do not line up.

The double pediment, in effect, discourages the eye from reading the vertical elements of the façade in a conventional straight-up-and-down fashion. When focusing on the innermost columns of the lower-story triplets — the two columns that flank the doorway — the eye tends to travel up the left-hand column, across the curve of the small pediment above the door, and back down the right-hand column to the ground; when focusing on the middle or outermost columns of the lower-story triplets, the eye travels up to the larger pediment, along the pediment's curve to the point where it breaks off, and then continues on up along the *innermost* columns of the upper story to the façade's peak, where it finds a curved pediment (the smallest of the three) that echoes the smaller curved pediment below. By interrupting the vertical lines of the façade in this manner, the lower-story pediment prevents the upper-story columns from being read as vertical extensions of the columns below. As a result, the misalignment of the columns becomes extremely difficult to make out. Longhi is tricking the eye, with remarkable success.

Was such trickery necessary? Could Longhi have given the entire façade (upper *and* lower stories) the extra width necessary to allow for "proper" column alignment? Did he deliberately choose visual trickery over structural clarity? At a distance of 350 years, the answers to these questions can only be a matter of conjecture, but whatever the answers may be, one fact remains: the façade of SS. Vincenzo ed Anastasio is not so completely and typically Baroque as is generally thought. The ambiguities inherent in the design of the lower story suggest an intentional stylistic throwback to the Mannerist era — a return to a time when architects were self-consciously flouting the "rules" of the High Renaissance and replacing stable visual order with unstable visual experiment. Thus Longhi seems, in his overall design, to be traveling in two directions at once; on the upper story he forges boldly ahead into new Baroque territory, while on the lower he turns back to the Mannered style of his sixteenth-century predecessors. The end result is a most unusual stylistic hybrid indeed. It is a difficult trick to pull off, but it is a measure of Longhi's great skill as a designer that the façade's stylistic eccentricities, so pronounced once noticed, are all but invisible to the casual eye.

5-5 SANTA MARIA IN TRIVIO
Façade: Giacomo del Duca, 1573–1575
(Piazza dei Crociferi, just to the northwest
of the Trevi Fountain)

One of two small façades, a block apart, that together illustrate with great vividness and clarity the jump from Mannerist to Baroque. S. Maria in Trivio is the earlier of the two, designed around 1573 by Giacomo del Duca; the façade is perhaps his most successful experiment in Mannerist rule-breaking.

The overall gridlike organization of the three stories is straightforward and respectful of precedent: the lower stories, with their giant pilasters, recall Michelangelo's palazzi on the Campidoglio, while the upper story takes its shape from Della Porta's design for the Gesù. The façade's carved decoration, however, is anything but traditional. The scrolls that might be expected to buttress the central section of the upper story are missing; they have migrated, and can be found, shrunken and standing wrong end up, on either side of the front door. More scrolls turn up — or rather turn down — above the door, where they break through the conventional triangular pediment to drape an unexpected garland down into the pediment's center opening. Other anomalies (among many) include the capitals of the upper-story pilasters, which correspond to no known antique order, and the odd porthole-like windows that interrupt the entablature's carved frieze. Perhaps most unusual of all are the upper story's miniature obelisks, a reference to the city's ancient past — no less than forty-eight obelisks dotted the city in Imperial times — that brings to the façade an unexpected suggestion of Gothic steeple.

Clearly, the values so prized by the High Renaissance are being ignored. The stately solemnity of the Pantheon — the visual gravity and decorum that was the Holy Grail of High Renaissance architectural theory — is no longer the goal. Del Duca is instead following the lead of Michelangelo, who valued originality and invention far more than his predecessors. Del Duca's inventive details here are executed with unusual skill: despite the overall flatness of the façade, its architectural motifs possess a look of crisp authority, at once sharp and delicate. As with all Mannerist architecture, the feeling is of conscious, sophisticated play with architectural tradition — the purposeful breaking of rules to see if anything interesting will result. What eventually resulted, of course, was full-blown Baroque, an example of which, similar in shape and scale, can be seen one block to the north along the Via Poli.

5-6 SANTISSIMO SACRAMENTO ORATORY
Domenico Gregorini, 1727–1730
(Piazza Poli, north of the Piazza dei Crociferi)

Del Duca's Mannerist façade for S. Maria in Trivio and Gregorini's Baroque façade for the Oratorio SS. Sacramento share some obvious structural characteristics: both are three bays wide, and both top their extra-wide central bays with a crowning upper-story pediment. Beyond the basic organization, however, the dissimilarities are far more prominent than the similarities. Except for its protruding cornice at the base of the top story, Del Duca's façade is rigidly two-dimensional in effect; its decoration is almost free of curves, and each decorative element occupies its own isolated space, as if drawn on an artist's grid. By contrast, the three-dimensional ins and outs of Gregorini's façade — its bulging wall surfaces, canted columns, receding side windows, fluid pediment — look molded by a sculptor's hand, and the various parts seem to be flowing into and over one another in a way that is almost organic. The wall surface possesses a plasticity — almost a rubbery elasticity — that is quite different in effect from Del Duca's right-angled rigidity. Three main design factors account for the change, and they are the factors that separate all High Baroque churchfronts from their Mannerist predecessors: the step forward into the third dimension, the integration of independent parts into a united whole, and the love of supple, flowing, voluptuous curves.

As Baroque façades go, Gregorini's work here is fairly restrained, and not entirely successful. Its most interesting feature, in fact, may be the way its central device — the broken pediment on which the two statues sit — fails to do its assigned job. The overall purpose seems clear enough: the upper and lower stories are meant to be unified by the broken pediment, which reads as both a cap to the lower-story entranceway and (in the vacated middle) a base for the central upper-story window. As at SS. Vincenzo ed Anastasio nearby, the eye is thus meant to see the upper-story window-surround — columns and pilasters supporting an elaborate pediment — as a visual continuation of the broken pediment, with the window-surround perched atop the pediment pieces so as to straddle the gap below and connect the pediment pieces together. It should be a fine Baroque balancing act, unifying the two separate stories into a seamless whole. But the trick never quite comes off: the lower-story entranceway elements seem uncomfortably far apart to read as a single unit, and the upper-story window-surround, beautiful as it is, lacks sufficient power to serve as a visual continuation of the much heavier broken pediment below. As a result, the façade lacks the overall unity of its more accomplished Baroque peers — S. Marcello, say, or Borromini's famous S. Carlino — and must regrettably be characterized as a near miss.

5-7 AQUA VIRGO FRAGMENT
Constructed 46 C.E.
(Via del Nazareno 14, across the Via del Tritone from the Piazza Poli and to the east)

When it was constructed in the nineteenth century to connect the Corso with the Piazza Barberini, the Via del Tritone must have been a model street: straight, wide, and welcoming. Today it is heartily disliked by almost everyone, and with good reason. Raucous and overcrowded, relentlessly commercial, it assaults the senses with such a noxious conglomeration of visual, aural, and olfactory pollutants that even the Romans complain.

Who would guess, then, that a few yards away down the Via del Nazareno a large chunk of ancient aqueduct remains intact? Constructed in 46 C.E. by the emperor Claudius (who was repairing damage caused by his predecessor, Caligula), the imposing travertine arches once carried the water conduit of the Aqua Virgo, which emerged from the Pincian Hill a short distance away and traveled aboveground to the Baths of Agrippa near the Pantheon. In ancient times the structure towered over the traffic that passed through its arches; since then the ground has risen so far that today the entire arcade is below street level.

5-8 SANT' ANDREA DELLE FRATTE
Dome and campanile: Francesco Borromini, ca. 1653–1665
(Via di S. Andrea delle Fratte, north of the Via del Nazareno)

Architecturally, S. Andrea delle Fratte is not important or distinguished, but it possesses a fine ancillary appendage — a Baroque campanile — that is often overlooked (and that is best viewed from Via di Capo le Case, which runs along the church's northern flank). Given the humdrum architectural character of the rest of the church, the slim, fanciful bell tower and the heavier drum behind it (which encloses and buttresses the interior dome) come as something of a shock. In fact, neither was part of the initial design. The church's original architect — the obscure and unadventurous Gaspare Guerra — died in 1622 with only the nave completed; the dome, transepts, chancel, and campanile were not begun until 1653, when Francesco Borromini was called in to finish construction.*

Borromini is thought to have followed Guerra's plans for the interior, but on the exterior the stamp of his very personal style is unmistakable. The campanile, especially, shows him at his most inventive. The open cylindrical bell chamber is conventional enough — Anthony Blunt calls it "the most Classical structure that Borromini ever produced" — but as the tower rises, its forms become at once smaller and more fantastical. In the upper section, an elongated and buttressed pedestal supports a flamelike quartet of scrolls carrying a spiky metal crown; at the very top, a delicate, open-work cross all but disappears into the sky. Despite its ever-increasing complexity of design, the campanile as a whole seems to grow more and more attenuated as it climbs higher and higher, until it finally vanishes in a wispy architectural puff of smoke.

In his day (and for a long time afterward), Borromini was often accused of utilizing arbitrary and capricious forms. But the logic underlying his choice of motifs here is clear enough, and beyond reproach. Taken together, the three sections of his tower embody a symbolic journey through history, beginning with the ancient past and ending with the present. The severely Classical lower section straightforwardly reflects the architectural traditions of pagan antiquity; the far more animated middle section — where the columns of the lower section are transformed into elegant sculpted angels — celebrates the advent of the Christian era; the evanescent upper section honors the patron who financed the church's completion, the Marchese Paolo del Bufalo (the crown is a marchese's coronet, and the quirky faces that peer out between the scrolls belong, appropriately enough, to four head of buffalo). For Borromini himself, the upward progression may have had a more personal meaning as well. As the forms become more complex and more inventive, the campanile — and by extension the architect — throws off the time-honored conventions of both antique and Renaissance Classicism in favor of a freer and more individual architectural vision.

In explicitly and respectfully acknowledging the importance of its Classical forebears, S. Andrea's campanile gracefully resolves a fundamental Baroque dilemma: how to move beyond the past without condemning it. But Borromini's architecture was not always so conciliatory. Although he

---

*The church's interior was completed by 1665, but the exterior drum and the lower portion of the campanile remain unfinished to this day. Both were meant to be stuccoed, and the drum was meant to carry a lantern that would have complemented and dominated the campanile.

designed relatively few buildings, he became famous (and infamous) for his willful departures from architectural tradition. More than any other architect of his era, he was ruled by the desire to explore, to invent, to break free of established convention. Just how radical this break could on occasion become can be seen a few steps away, at his extraordinarily idiosyncratic façade for the Collegio di Propaganda Fide.

Notable Works of Art: Inside the church, the two large sculpted angels flanking the entrance to the chancel were originally carved by Bernini for the Ponte S. Angelo, but Pope Clement IX declared them too beautiful to stand outdoors in the wind and the rain. Replicas were made, and the originals were placed here in 1729.

5-9 COLLEGIO DI PROPAGANDA FIDE
West façade: Francesco Borromini, 1646–1666
(Via di Propaganda, north of the Via di S. Andrea delle Fratte)

Borromini's most perplexing façade, at once daring and disquieting. The middle story is the clear focus of attention; the pronounced setback of the windows makes their wall spaces read as niches, and Borromini has filled them with variations on the standard aedicular window-surround, which are so boldly conceived and carved that they possess the presence and force of sculpture. Setting off these window niches are emphatic pilasters, rising from the ground floor to support a dramatic overhanging cornice. The façade's most critical point — the middle-story central bay, with its extra width dictated by the carriage entranceway below — is bolstered by ingenious special treatment: the pilasters on either side are canted toward each other, and the window is topped by an entablature that turns unexpectedly convex in the center, thrusting forward where the other window-surrounds shrink back. With his usual assurance, Borromini here molds the wall surface into three dimensions, giving the middle story's decoration an extraordinary plasticity and power. Moreover, that power is purely architectural; there are no Baroque angels or cherubs hovering about. Unlike his great rival Bernini, who loved the theatricality that sculpture can bring to architecture, Borromini was an architectural purist.

Forceful and inventive as these details are, the façade as a whole is more problematical and raises many questions. Why is the ground floor so aggressively plain, with only a few Barberini bees to lighten the general blankness? Why is the overhanging cornice — normally an architectural full stop — topped by a tall attic that fritters away the façade's rising crescendo of power with an additional layer of lesser detail?* And what of the overall effect? Most of the façade's decoration is so crisply carved as to look almost razorlike, going beyond vigor to achieve a sharpness that borders on threat. The minatory aspect is further heightened by the narrow street, which disallows all but close-up views that accentuate the façade's looming, assertive architectural details. What is going on here?

Clearly a part of the answer lies in Borromini's relentless drive to experiment. Like Michelangelo, he was determined to invent the future rather than copy the past (in his writings he approvingly cited Michelangelo's remark that "one who follows others never gets ahead of them"). And like Michelangelo, the precedents of antiquity were for him merely a starting point. Creativity, for Borromini, was not the slave of rule and convention, but its master.

Beyond the desire to experiment, Borromini's goal here is open to conjecture. Perhaps he is setting out to prove that power is not a function of size — to show that an ordinary façade on an ordinary street, possessing no special benefit of scale or location, can be given exceptional force of personality through pure design. The simplicity of the building's ground floor (and the utter dreariness of the side wings) would seem to support this view, for they set off the virtuosity of the rest of the façade by their very plainness.

An alternative interpretation (and an unusually enthusiastic endorsement) is offered by Christian Norberg-Schulz in his survey *Baroque Architecture:*

> The main façade on the Via di Propaganda is an extraordinary work. Immense pilasters unify the austere wall. In the middle and on the ends they are obliquely placed, as if the system was changing under the pressure of slow but irresistible forces. Between the pilasters large plastic aediculae break through. The whole façade is a study in compression and dilation, and expresses better than any other work of the epoch the role of the wall as the meeting-point of outer and inner forces.

The effect of simultaneous compression and dilation is most pronounced on the middle story: the wide pilasters seem to be squeezing the window-surrounds into deformed, compressed shapes, and the window-surrounds

---

*The attic is a later addition, but it is thought to have been constructed from Borromini's designs.

seem to be pushing back in an attempt to straighten themselves out and avoid being crushed. In the central bay, the opposing forces achieve an even more remarkable balance, bringing the entire façade into play. The bay's extra width seems to be pushing both side wings apart, while at the same time the canted pilasters and the convex cornice above suggest that the central bay has buckled from the pressure on either side. The overall effect is almost nightmarishly surreal: a putatively Classical façade that has come alive to do battle with itself.

Whatever Borromini's ultimate goal may have been, he has broken many traditional rules and defied many established conventions along the way. The giant pilasters are heretically wide, the modillions hanging from the underside of the cornice are heretically heavy (and irregularly spaced to boot), and the grooved vertical elements that flank the front door — piers? columns? pilasters? there is no architectural term that will describe them — are heretically shaped, far narrower at the base than at the top. To Borromini's contemporaries, however, the most jarring offense was probably the middle-story jump directly from giant pilaster to cornice. By long-accepted tradition, a cornice was the climactic feature of a three-part entablature (architrave, frieze, and cornice) that rested on columns or pilasters topped by more or less conventional capitals. Here, Borromini has not only failed to give his pilasters recognizably Classical capitals, he has also completely eliminated the expected architrave and frieze, setting the heavy cornice directly atop the pilasters. To many of his Roman compatriots, such license represented the willful destruction of a venerable and honorable tradition.

Borromini's contemporaries were not the only ones to object. After the Baroque era ended, Borromini's architecture was roundly condemned by the reigning Neoclassicists, and for two centuries he was viewed mostly as a perverse, idiosyncratic rebel. "Borromini observed precisely all the rules for displeasing the eyes," says one famous eighteenth-century denunciation. "He was completely insensitive to that part of architecture which concerns beauty . . . unhappily, evil is followed and good rejected." It was not until the twentieth century, when the overthrow of tradition became a tradition in its own right, that Borromini's reputation began first to revive and then to soar. Today he is generally considered the most original genius of his day, if not the entire Baroque era. But the question of whether he went too far with this particular façade is still being debated.

5-10 SPANISH STEPS
Francesco de Sanctis, 1723–1726
(Piazza di Spagna)

View of the Piazza di Spagna looking south; the Palazzo di Spagna is to the right (the large building with chimney stacks) and the bottom of the Spanish Steps is on the left.

Pure bravura. Cascading down the Pincian Hill in a torrential rush, the Spanish Steps epitomize that most fundamental of Baroque principles: form is more than just function. The exuberant Baroque design — which is craftily skewed to adjust for the fact that SS. Trinità dei Monti above and the Piazza di Spagna below do not line up on the same axis — turns what might have been an ordinary staircase into much, much more. Inspired form here *expands* function, so that the steps serve not only as a land bridge between two levels of the city, but also as a breathtaking set-piece focus for the Piazza di Spagna, an elegant formal approach for SS. Trinità dei Monti, a beloved neighborhood promenade for residents, an irresistible meeting place for tourists, a world-famous gathering spot for students, and an incomparable showcase for masses of azaleas in the spring. Now *that* is function.

The nickname "Spanish Steps" is something of a misnomer. The tag derives from the Piazza di Spagna at the steps' base, so called because one of the palazzi off its southern end — the Palazzo di Spagna — has since 1622 been the residence of the Spanish ambassador to the Vatican. But the steps' design and construction had nothing whatsoever to do with Spain. In fact, the staircase is entirely French in origin.

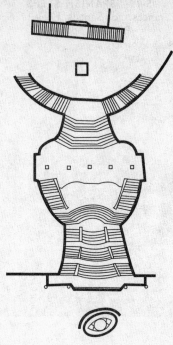

Plan of the Spanish Steps showing its skewed alignment.

The French presence in the area began in the late fifteenth century, when a group of Minims — a new order of friars from France — took over the existing villa at the top of the Pincian Hill and began construction (in 1502) of SS. Trinità dei Monti. Talk of linking the church with the piazza below began soon after the façade of the church was completed in 1570, but nothing was done until 1661, when a *chargé d'affaires* at the French Embassy died and left a bequest of 10,000 scudi for construction of a staircase. Cardinal Mazarin, then prime minister of France, called in Bernini, who designed an elaborate ramped project centered around a life-size equestrian statue of Louis XIV. But the proposed statue's inflammatory implications — a challenge not only to the political supremacy of the pope but also to the aesthetic supremacy of the ancient statue of Marcus Aurelius on the Capitoline Hill — doomed the project from the start. Some fifty years of inconclusive negotiation and bureaucratic red tape followed, until the monks at last adopted (and Pope Innocent XIII approved) a new plan by the little-known Francesco de Sanctis that incorporated elements suggested by the favored papal architect of the day, Alessandro Specchi.

Construction began in 1723; upon completion in 1726, the staircase immediately became one of the acknowledged sights of Rome. For De

Sanctis, however, the project ended unhappily. In 1728, the steps were badly damaged by a rainstorm, and he found himself the defendant in a messy, protracted lawsuit. He never received another commission, and the staircase was not repaired until 1737, six years after his death.

Today, more than 250 years later, the Spanish Steps remain in excellent repair, and still serve to energize the entire neighborhood, now the city's most expensive and fashionable shopping quarter. And the recent ban on automobile traffic in the area has expanded the steps' function still further: they are now the best spot in Europe for measuring the pulse of a great capital city. To sit at the top in the late afternoon on a sunny summer day is to be given a God's-eye view of Rome awakening from its daily siesta. During the midday heat, the square and street below are all but deserted, populated only by stragglers sticking close to the buildings in search of shade. But as the sun begins to set, the pace of life perceptibly quickens, shoppers and tourists and students begin to appear, pedestrian patterns become more varied and complex, small groups coalesce into clusters, clusters grow to become crowds, and the crescendo of activity swells until the entire square is filled with a single teeming throng. The scene comprises thousands of mundane individual routines, but it is the time-honored role of the Italian piazza to transform individual routine into group ritual, and the Spanish Steps here make that transformation visible — palpable — to anyone who cares to look.

5-11   FONTANA DELLA BARCACCIA
Gianlorenzo (or possibly his father Pietro) Bernini, 1627–1629
(Piazza di Spagna)

Swamped in its own little pond at the base of the Spanish Steps, the Barcaccia Fountain is Bernini's most congenial piece of outdoor sculpture. The metaphorical significance of the leaky boat is open to question. Scholars suggest it commemorates either the sham sea battles held by the ancient Romans on the spot (which was the site of Domitian's naumachia) or the ship of the Catholic Church, whose cannons (according to a poem written by Urban VIII) ease the world's troubles with calming water. Local legend, on the other hand, says it commemorates the Christmas Day flood of 1598, when the area was under some 20 feet of water and a real barge washed ashore here. But the iconography is secondary; what matters most is the humane civic gesture. Set into the pavement below ground level — the available water pressure was low — the Barcaccia is more than just a witty centerpiece for the piazza. It is an irresistible invitation to pause, to sit, to relax, to bathe tired feet, to admire the surroundings. In its own quiet and understated way, it is the perfect foil for the trumpet-blast of the Spanish Steps, and the contrast makes this one of the most civilized spots in Rome.

5-12 VIA DEI CONDOTTI
(Running west from the Spanish Steps)

The most famous shopping street in Rome consists, architecturally, of a series of May-December marriages: up-to-the-minute shops that follow the whim of fashion married to Renaissance and Baroque palazzi that have changed hardly at all for hundreds of years. Happily, the marriages work, and the new and the old cohabit comfortably and prosperously.

The Via dei Condotti's most venerable attraction is the Caffè Greco (No. 86), founded in 1760 and famous during the nineteenth century as a gathering place for foreign artists and writers visiting the city. Despite modernization, the café's interior still retains something of its nineteenth-century feel, and its walls are hung with mementos of famous patrons. Byron, Baudelaire, Stendhal, Goethe, Gogol, Berlioz, Lizst, and Wagner were all devotees; Hans Christian Andersen lived for a time upstairs, Tennyson and Thackeray stayed across the street, and a nearby palazzo on the Via Bocca di Leone (No. 43) harbored one of England's most celebrated married couples, the eloped poets Elizabeth Barrett and Robert Browning. During the nineteenth century, the English presence in the area was particularly pronounced, and traces of what the Romans came to call "the English ghetto" remain even today, most notably at the Spanish Steps, which are flanked at their base by twin monuments to English culture: Babington's Tea Shop, which has been serving afternoon tea since 1896, and the Keats and Shelley Memorial Museum, located in the apartment where the English Romantic poet John Keats lived, and where he died of tuberculosis at the age of twenty-five.[*]

---

[*]Keats's modest rooms are among the most lovingly tended in the city, filled with literary memorabilia and maintained much as they were when he died on February 23, 1821. His burial site — in the small Protestant Cemetery next to the pyramid of Gaius Cestius at the Porta S. Paolo — is beautifully preserved as well (Tour 9), and for poetry lovers a leisurely afternoon visit to his grave is highly recommended as an antidote to sightseeing overload.

5-13 PALAZZO ZUCCARI
Entrance portico: possibly Filippo Juvarra, 1711
Side entrance: Federico Zuccaro, 1590–1603
(Piazza della Trinità dei Monti, atop the Spanish Steps to the right)

At the top of the Spanish Steps on the right, occupying the little promontory where the Via Sistina and the Via Gregoriana meet at an acute angle. The Palazzo Zuccari was built by the artist Federico Zuccaro in the late 1500s; the entrance portico was added much later, in 1711. From a purist point of view, such after-the-fact modifications are to be deplored, but when the addition is as elegant and well mannered as this, it is surely churlish to complain. The wide opening and deep overhang of the ground-floor minicolonnade offer accommodating shelter to visitors arriving in bad weather; the balustraded belvedere above promises a splendid view when the weather is fine. The gently swelling roof is supported by miniature Ionic piers so delicate they look borrowed from a doll's house, and at the top sits a pine cone, in ancient times an attribute of the wine god, Bacchus. What more enticing welcome could a visitor want?

The portico's gracious architectural gesture contrasts sharply with the side entrance to the palazzo (originally the entrance to the garden), several doors down the Via Gregoriana. Designed by Zuccaro himself, the Mannerist doorway and window-surrounds break with Rome's decorous Classical tradition more violently than any before — or since.

5-14 VILLA MEDICI
Begun by Nanni di Baccio Bigio and Annibale Lippi, 1564, and completed by
Bartolomeo Ammanati, 1576 onward
(Viale della Trinità dei Monti, northwest of the obelisk atop the Spanish Steps)

CASINA VALADIER
Giuseppe Valadier, 1813
(Viale Adamo Mickievics — the continuation of the Viale della Trinità dei
Monti — northwest of the obelisk atop the Spanish Steps)

From the top of the Spanish Steps overlooking the Piazza di Spagna to the Piazzale Napoleone overlooking the Piazza del Popolo, the Viale della Trinità dei Monti follows the ridge of the Pincian Hill. Along the way, two buildings offer a notable architectural contrast, one private and forbidding, the other public and welcoming.

The first is the Villa Medici (on the right down the road from SS. Trinità dei Monti), a hilltop retreat completed in the late 1500s by Cardinal Ferdinando dei Medici, who later succeeded his brother as Grand Duke of

Tuscany. The fortress-like exterior makes few concessions to civility; with its noncommittal, blank-faced façade and canted ground-floor walls, it seems determined to repel casual visitors and to make even the most determined sightseer think twice before entering. This singular hauteur is not the whole story, however, for the façade on the building's other side — facing the extensive gardens — is one of the most ingratiating in the city. It was built for private and aristocratic enjoyment, however, and today is accessible only for guided tours on weekend mornings during certain months of the year, or sometimes when the French Academy (which has owned and occupied the building since 1801) mounts exhibitions in the interior.

Farther along the Viale della Trinità dei Monti, a ramp angles off the road on the right, leading up to the Casina Valadier. The structure is a tight little cube wrapped in pilasters and topped with building blocks. With its elegant portico and graceful double staircase (on the front) and its stumpy Doric ground-floor columns (on the sides and back), it looks for all the world like a bit of Regency London — of John Nash — transported magically to Rome. The architect was Giuseppe Valadier, and his purpose (in 1813) was to give Rome its first public-garden cafe, the gracious centerpiece of the new park laid out atop the Pincian Hill. Both the cafe and the park were a great and enduring success,* but eventually (in the twentieth century) the park fell out of favor and the cafe into neglect. Happily, fashion may now have returned: the building was recently restored to its original beauty and purpose, and in summer it once again bursts into resplendent architectural flower, blossoming with festive umbrellas and awnings. Long may they bloom.

5-15 PIAZZALE NAPOLEONE
Giuseppe Valadier, 1809–1814
(Along the western side of the Viale del Belvedere, the continuation of the Viale Adam Mickievicz)

The Piazzale Napoleone is actually a terrace atop the Pincian Hill overlooking the Piazza del Popolo. Laid out in the early nineteenth century (along with public gardens behind that have been recently and beautifully restored), it quickly became the most fashionable promenade in Rome,

---

*A recent edition of the Blue Guide, in describing the cafe's fashionable clientele over the years, offers up a splendidly bizarre list of representative devotees: Richard Strauss, Benito Mussolini, King Farouk, Mahatma Gandhi, and Chiang Kai-shek. Imagine them all there at the same table.

famous for its sunset views. Henry James loved the spot, and gives a detailed description of it in his notebook from 1873:

> The last three days I have regularly spent a couple of hours from noon baking myself in the sun of the Pincio to get rid of a cold. The weather perfect and the crowd (especially today) amazing. Such a staring, lounging, dandified, amiable crowd! Who does the vulgar stay-at-home work of Rome? All the grandees and half the foreigners are there in their carriages, the *bourgeoisie* on foot staring at them and the beggars lining all the approaches. The great difference between public places in America and Europe is in the number of unoccupied people of every age and condition sitting about early and late on benches and gazing at you, from your hat to your boots, as you pass. Europe is certainly the continent of the practiced stare. The ladies on the Pincio have to run the gauntlet; but they seem to do so complacently enough. The European woman is brought up to the sense of having a definite part in the way of manners or manner to play in public. To lie back in a barouche alone, balancing a parasol and seeming to ignore the extremely immediate gaze of two serried ranks of male creatures on each side of her path, save here and there to recognize one of them with an imperceptible nod, is one of her daily duties. The number of young men here who, like the coenobites of old, lead the purely contemplative life is enormous. They muster in especial force on the Pincio. . . . Sometimes I lose patience with its parade of eternal idleness, but at others this very idleness is balm to one's conscience. Life on these terms seems so easy, so monotonously sweet, that you feel it would be unwise, would be really unsafe, to change. The Roman air is charged with an elixir, the Roman cup seasoned with some insidious drop, of which the action is fatally, yet none the less agreeably, "lowering."

Today fashion has moved on — the Piazza di Spagna and the Corso are now the preferred venues for self-display — but the view remains. Its centerpiece is the distant St. Peter's, with the Vatican Palace, the Vatican walls, and the Vatican Hill all to be seen just to the right of the great dome.

Piazza del Popolo.

Nowadays, most first-time visitors approach Rome from the south — from the airport at Fiumicino — and they usually pass through the ancient city walls at the Porta S. Paolo. That gate has its charms (mainly the Pyramid of Gaius Cestius, which signals the presence of antiquity in no uncertain terms) but it is nevertheless one of the walled city's many back doors. The front door is all the way across town on the north side, at the Porta del Popolo.

To appreciate the Porta del Popolo's key placement, an act of historical imagination is necessary. Until the twentieth century, when the modern city finally outgrew the ancient walls, the gate marked the boundary between urban and rural. Inside lay the Piazza del Popolo; outside lay fields and vineyards. The contrast would have been extreme, and it supplied the climax to an approach sequence that must have been thrilling to the eighteenth- and nineteenth-century travelers who experienced it.

The journey was by coach, and at a certain point in the middle of the countryside the driver would unexpectedly draw his horses to a halt. The passengers would clamber out to see what had caused the interruption, and they would find themselves on a hilltop looking south. *"Ecco Roma!"* the driver would cry, throwing out his arms toward the distant city, in view at last. As the coach approached the ancient walls, the road — the Via Flaminia, some two thousand years old — would become straight as an arrow. Then, upon arriving at the Porta del Popolo, the travelers would once again disembark, and as they walked through the gate from country to city, they would confront the Piazza del Popolo — and Rome — head-on: on the left the church of S. Maria del Popolo, straight ahead the Egyptian obelisk of Ramses II, and beyond the twin temple-front churches at the head of the famous trident, three long straight streets that plunged deep into the urban core, one leading to the Spanish Steps, one leading to the Capitoline Hill, and one leading to the Tiber riverfront. No other city in Europe announced — *proclaimed* — its presence with such a dramatic architectural set piece. Today the exhilarating contrast between urban and rural has disappeared, but the Piazza del Popolo remains, and will still make its grand proclamation to anyone willing to walk through the gate and take the necessary imaginative leap.

It was Sixtus V, that most forceful and farseeing of Rome's city-planning popes, who brought the modern Piazza del Popolo into being. Sixtus's papacy lasted only five years — from 1585 to 1590 — but in that short space of time he transformed the city. Under earlier popes, Rome's rudimentary city planning had been mostly a matter of single, isolated streets. Pope Sixtus IV (1471–1484) had restored the Via dei Coronari, in the middle of medieval Rome, to its ancient and straight course; Pope Julius II (1503–1513) had laid out the Via Giulia and its twin the Via Lungara, the two long, straight streets that parallel each other on either side of the Tiber just beyond the river's bend; Pope Leo X (1513–1521) and Pope Paul III (1534–1549) had built the Via Ripetta and the Via del Babuino, the right and left tines of the Piazza del Popolo trident, to either side of the ancient Via del Corso; Pope Pius IV (1559–1565) had built the Strada Pia (now the Via del Quirinale and its continuation, the Via XX Settembre) along the mostly unoccupied crest of the Quirinal Hill. Other lesser projects — clearing a piazza here or building a fountain there — were similarly isolated in scope and limited in effect.

Sixtus V had grander ideas, for he sensed what was coming. In medieval times the city had shrunk drastically, occupying only the Campus Martius area, from the Via del Corso to the Tiber Bend. The rest of the ancient city was mostly abandoned, with a few isolated settlements surviving around the major outlying basilicas such as St. Peter's, S. Giovanni in Laterano, and S. Maria Maggiore. With the advent of the Renaissance, however, the city had begun to revive, and its derelict areas east of the Campus Martius began to attract inhabitants. The population, which had sunk to astonishingly low levels during the late Middle Ages (around 15,000 inhabitants, down from a possible peak of 1,500,000 in antiquity, a 99 percent decline), began to increase at a steady rate, reaching 54,000 in the census of 1526–27. In addition, the city's transient population — mainly religious pilgrims, but also diplomatic retinues and affluent tourists — began to grow as well, furnishing a welcome stimulus to the local economy. Rome, moribund after more than a thousand years of decline, was at long last on the rise.

Sixtus could see the city's potential for growth, and he understood that orderly expansion required a master plan. So he raised four ancient obelisks in the center of four conspicuous empty spaces — spaces that are now the Piazza del Popolo, the Piazza di S. Pietro, the Piazza di S. Giovanni in Laterano, and the Piazza dell' Esquilino (in back of S. Maria Maggiore) — and he laid out a network of long, straight streets around and between them, streets that connected the city's major outlying monuments both with each other and with the streets that his predecessors had laid out before him. These new thoroughfares gave the burgeoning settlements around the outlying basilicas easy access to the existing downtown, and (more importantly) they formed a skeleton around which the city could expand and grow. As Sixtus's favorite architect, Domenico Fontana, described it at the time:

> Our lord [has] opened many most commodious and straight streets in many places.... At a truly incredible cost, and in conformity with the spirit of so great a prince, [he] has extended these streets from one end of the city to the other, without concern for either the hills or the valleys which they crossed; but, causing the former to be leveled and the latter filled, has reduced them to most gentle plains, and charming sites, revealing ... various and diverse perspectives.... The most celebrated is the street called Felice, which originates at the church of Santa Croce in Gerusalemme, passes the church of Santa Maria Maggiore, and then continues on to the Trinità dei Monti from where one descends to the Porta di Popolo: which in all comprises a distance of two miles and a half, and throughout straight as a plumb line and wide enough to allow five carriages to ride abreast.

The obelisks that Sixtus raised were important as well. As landmarks, they served a multiple purpose: they transformed unfocused empty space into focused city space, they made the important nodal points of the new street plan visible from great distances, they kept new nearby construction at bay, and — not incidentally — they established once and for all the Roman tradition of the prominent piazza centerpiece. These were important city-planning innovations, and the pride that Sixtus and his followers took in their visionary improvements is evidenced in the Vatican Palace, where the Sistine Hall of the Vatican Library is frescoed with views of the city, one of which pictures the entire length of the Strada Felice. That pride was entirely justified, for Sixtus V's ability to see the city whole meant that when the Baroque era began around 1600 (ten years after Sixtus's death) the underlying organizational plan that would so effectively support and enhance Rome's great Baroque set pieces — the Spanish Steps, St. Peter's Square, the Trevi Fountain, the Piazza Navona — was ready and waiting.

The Piazza del Popolo as it exists today is not quite the equal of the four famous Baroque *tours de force,* but it comes close. The twin Baroque churches (built 1658–1679) add immeasurably to the overall effect, serving as a second and inner gateway to the urban core, and the hemicycle terminations to right and left (planned and constructed by Giuseppe Valadier in the early 1800s) round off the space with unobtrusive authority.

What's missing is life. Until recently the piazza was *too* full of life — endless streams of traffic from every direction continually hemmed in by improvised car parks on the periphery and in the center. The restrictions on nonessential automobiles in the area have alleviated the traffic problem, which is all to the good. But the absence of cars has left the piazza looking curiously listless; the large open space seems to be in limbo, cleared and expectant but waiting for a party that never starts. In this instance, too little activity is almost as discomfiting as too much.

5-17 SANTA MARIA DEL POPOLO
Possibly Andrea Bregno, 1472–1477, with embellishments
by Gianlorenzo Bernini, 1655–1657
Chigi Chapel: Raphael, 1513–1516
Cybò Chapel: Carlo Fontana, 1682–1686
(Piazza del Popolo, north end)

Like S. Maria sopra Minerva, S. Maria del Popolo is one of Rome's museum churches, better known for its art than its architecture. When the church was built in the 1470s, it was very plain, both outside and in (the only striking features of the façade — the chopped-off pieces of curved pediment at either end — are a later Baroque addition). In the 1650s, Bernini was called in to decorate the nave, and his embellishments are unusual in their restraint. Eschewing colored marble and gilding, he took his cue from the fragments of entablature that already existed above the nave half columns: he expanded the fragments to form a continuous entablature that follows the line of the arches to run the entire length of the nave, with graceful life-size stucco figures perched on top. For a Baroque "improvement," the result is unexpectedly consistent with the plain travertine half columns below.

Two of the church's side chapels are of special architectural interest. The earlier — the second chapel on the left — was designed by Raphael in 1513 as a burial site for the immensely wealthy banker Agostino Chigi. Chigi is said to have spent 22,000 ducats on the chapel (outspending even the pope, Julius II, who a few years earlier had allotted Michelangelo a mere 16,000 ducats for his proposed tomb in St. Peter's). What Chigi got for his money fairly stunned the city. Rather than settle for the usual adjunct space subsidiary to the nave, Raphael created an independent room with a High Renaissance personality all its own, a miniature and modernized Pantheon that provided a foretaste of the new St. Peter's across town, just beginning construction. At ground level the plan is octagonal, with the corner segments shortened to give extra space for the entrance, altarpiece, and tombs. But beginning at the level of the semicircular arches, the sides of the octagon disappear, and the architecture becomes an essay in ascending circles, rising upward to culminate in the mosaic of God on high looking down at the viewer looking up. The profusion of circles is typical of the High Renaissance, and they dominate the space below so powerfully that the introduction of an unrelated shape — the triangles of the two pyramid-shaped tombs set into the side arches — feels almost painful in its angular intrusiveness.

The Cybò Chapel (second on the right) was constructed more than 150 years after the Chigi Chapel; funded by Cardinal Alderamo Cybò and designed by Carlo Fontana, it was a conscious attempt to outdo in splendor and grandeur Raphael's work across the nave. Wisely, however, Fontana chose not to compete with Raphael on his own terms. Rather than employ a wide-ranging decorative scheme that combined sculpture, mosaic, and painting, Fontana banished sculpture and mosaic, and allowed painting (and a single band of gilding) only in the dome and at the altar. Otherwise he opted for pure architecture, constructed out of a single material: marble, always and everywhere. The result is one of the most unusual small spaces in Rome: a cool, dark, cavelike room that feels as if it has been burrowed out of a small mountain of richly variegated marble.

Beyond its art and architecture, S. Maria del Popolo possesses one other notable claim to fame. In the winter of 1510–1511, the church and its attached convent played host to an unknown twenty-seven-year-old visitor from northern Europe named Martin Luther. When Luther arrived in Rome, he was full of pious anticipation and enthusiasm. But the reception he received was less than friendly, and his attitude soon changed. As Ingrid D. Rowland describes it in *The Culture of the High Renaissance:*

It was not always easy . . . to be a German in Italy; the Italians made it plain to one and all that they were the most civilized people in Europe, if not the whole world. The Germans who came there to study found that their own Latin accent was considered peculiar and that among Latin speakers, especially those of Ciceronian persuasion, they themselves were liable to be called "barbarians." What enraged Luther in particular, however, was the power of money to command the Vatican's version of the Kingdom of God. He knew that the new buildings he could see all around him in Rome owed their proliferation to the sale of indulgences among his own people. To his mind, the Church had long since crossed the line between dignified pageantry and senseless luxury; he could see overelaboration everywhere, in embroidered vestments, polyphonic music, dinner parties with courtesans, and all of it carefully insulated from the ordinary people the Church was supposedly created to serve. The hermetic culture of the humanists and the insular Latin jargon put him off — as, in fact, it was supposed to do — but he understood it well enough to understand the nature of the snubs he received.

When Luther left Rome, he was full of rage, and ultimately his ringing denunciation of the papacy — "the whore of Babylon," he called it — became the rallying cry of the Protestant Reformation.

Notable Works of Art: Of the four statues of prophets in the corner niches in the Chigi Chapel, Bernini's *Habakkuk and the Angel* (1655–1661, on the far right) stands out as a Baroque *tour de force*, bursting out of its assigned space; the other prophets are *Daniel* (near left, also by Bernini), *Jonah* (by Lorenzetto from a design by Raphael, far left), and *Elijah* (also by Lorenzetto and Raphael, near right). The revolutionary character of Caravaggio's work at the beginning of the Baroque era is dramatically illustrated in the Cerasi Chapel (to the left of the high altar), where Caravaggio's two paintings (*The Conversion of St. Paul*, on the left, and *The Crucifixion of St. Peter*, on the right) can be compared with a much more restrained altarpiece by Annibale Carraci (*Assumption of the Virgin*) that was painted at exactly the same time (1601). Also more restrained, but memorably gentle and delicate, are the Renaissance frescoes by Pinturicchio in the Della Rovere Chapel (first to the right), especially the altarpiece *Adoration* (1485–1489). The completely unrestrained late-Baroque funerary monument to Maria Flaminio Chigi (on the pier to the left of the Chigi Chapel) was designed by Paolo Posi in 1771.

The history of renovation that transformed the area just inside the Porta del Popolo from a small, shapeless open space into a spacious and dramatic piazza is long and complicated, stretching over some four hundred years from the fifteenth to the nineteenth centuries. The raising of the obelisk by Pope Sixtus V in 1589 was the seminal act, giving the space a centerpiece and marking it as important. But it was Pope Alexander VII (1655–1667) who was responsible for the masterly architectural gesture that definitively established the piazza's character. When Alexander heard in 1658 that the Order of the Discalced [Unshod] Carmelites was planning to build a new church at the beginning of the Via del Corso, he intervened — not to prohibit construction, but to insist that a second and identical church be built across the street, and that both churches should face the piazza rather than the Corso.

The job was more complicated than it might seem, for the plots of land involved were of different sizes (the plot on the left longer and narrower than the one on the right), and space was not to be wasted. Architect Carlo Rainaldi (assisted by Carlo Fontana, who may have taken over the project at a later date) therefore planned the churches using different shapes: an oval for S. Maria di Montesanto (on the left) and a circle for S. Maria dei Miracoli (on the right). During the later stages of construction, Bernini was called in to make sure the differing dome shapes were disguised as effectively as possible; it was he who made the final adjustments to the design of S. Maria di Montesanto, thickening the masonry of the dome on the long sides and making the ribbed sections of the two domes facing the square identical in shape and size (the domes differ otherwise, the one on the left having twelve ribbed sections and the one on the right only eight). The optical illusion is remarkably successful — the glancing eye reads the domes as identical even though the concentrating eye can see their differences.

Carlo Rainaldi is something of a forgotten man among Roman Baroque architects; his work is inevitably overshadowed by his slightly older contemporaries Borromini, Bernini, and Cortona, the three leading lights of the Roman Baroque era. The twin churches are not flashy — Rainaldi's façade and interior at S. Maria in Campitelli are far more complex in design — and they obviously owe a great debt to the temple-front precedent set by Cortona at S. Maria della Pace. But they possess an aptness of placement that renders them instantly memorable. As Esther Janowitz puts it in *The Architecture of Rome:* "The churches do not merely monumentalize the entrance into the city, they also make it sacred: they are the first harbingers of St. Peter's, the destination of pilgrims arriving from all over the world."

5-19   GESÙ E MARIA

Church body: Carlo Milanesi, 1633, and Carlo Rainaldi, 1674
Façade and interior decoration: Carlo Rainaldi, 1674
Interior tomb statuary: Francesco Cavallini, Francesco Aprile,
Michele Maglia, 1675–1687
(Via del Corso, on the east side, south of the Via di Gesù e Maria)

The church itself is undistinguished — an underdone façade and an overdone interior — but inside, the statuary set into the wide nave piers separating the side chapels is instantly memorable. Sitting in upper-level galleries, a small band of urbane seventeenth-century aristocrats are frozen in mid-gesture (sometimes, it seems, in mid-speech) as they look toward the altar in attitudes varying from pious to garrulous. The figures are splendidly enlivening, breathing life into an interior that is in every other way completely conventional.

The entire scheme was commissioned around 1675 by Cardinal Giorgio Bolognetti, Bishop of Rieti; his plan in effect turned the nave of the newly constructed church into a family burial chapel. He is entombed in the second pier to the left, beneath the depiction of himself at prayer, and the other sculpted figures all represent members of his family entombed in the other piers. The sculptors are far from well known (Francesco Cavallini on the two piers toward the altar, Francesco Aprile on the first pier on the right, Michele Maglia on the first pier to the left), but they have captured the spirit of the day — the spirit of Bernini, the presiding genius of Baroque freeze-frame sculpture — with skill and panache.

5-20   VIA DEL CORSO

The city's spine, and ramrod straight. Plunged like a driven sword from the Porta del Popolo to the Piazza Venezia — from what was until recently the edge of the city to its very heart — the Corso's unyielding rigidity produces a bracing sense of order and strength amid the chaos of the surrounding street plan. As its detractors constantly point out, its flaws are all too evident: it is too narrow, too crowded, too noisy, and too dirty. But it is also vibrantly, electrically alive — the nerve center for a full quarter of the inner city. And now that its automobile traffic has been brought under some semblance of control, it has come into its own (along with the neighboring Via Condotti) as the city's proudest promenade. During the day it bustles with shoppers and tourists; in the evening it is thronged with the youth of Rome on self-confident parade.

The Corso's origins are antique, and in ancient times it was the city's main route north to Europe and the rest of the Roman Empire. As the empire declined and the city shrank, the street lost its status as a central thoroughfare, and its buildings fell to ruins. Its revival began with the Renaissance, and its name derives from the wild carnival horse races inaugurated by Pope Paul II in the fifteenth century. Today it is once again one of Europe's great streets, and tangible proof of Rome's indestructibility.

5-21 SANTI AMBROGIO E CARLO AL CORSO
Dome: Pietro da Cortona, 1668
Façade: Luigi Omodei, 1682–1684
(Via del Corso, on the west side, south of the Largo dei Lombardi)

Everything here is oppressive except the dome. The designer of the façade, Cardinal Luigi Omodei, was a churchman who thought himself a talented amateur architect, but he fell into a common design trap: he assumed that an increase in size would automatically produce an equivalent increase in power. But problems of scale can be extremely tricky, as the results here show. The heavy-handed columns and pilasters, with their coarsely carved capitals, generate an equally heavy-handed pediment; the spaces in between are filled catch-as-catch-can by a haphazard jumble of doors and windows. The end result is an overdeveloped muscularity that verges on parody — Classicism pumped up on steroids.

Pietro da Cortona, however, was far from an amateur, and his dome is one of Rome's finest (best appreciated from the back of the church rather than the front). At the time he designed it, Cortona is thought to have been toning down his High Baroque style, for architectural fashion had temporarily turned against the creative freedom of the previous fifty years. Accordingly, the drum and upper part of the dome are as sober and correct as any purist could wish. But compressed in between — peeking out, as it were — is an attic of playfully decorated oval windows determined to show its Baroque stuff, no matter how solemn the surroundings. The lantern on top sympathizes, and the resulting interplay between decorum and exuberance is beautifully balanced. The whole composition is a stylistic marriage of

Renaissance and Baroque that ought, at least in theory, to produce disastrous irreconcilable differences. But Cortona makes the marriage work.

5-22   PIAZZA AUGUSTO IMPERATORE
Tomb of Augustus, 32–28 B.C.E.
(West of SS. Ambrogio e Carlo al Corso)

Compared to Hadrian's fortress-like mausoleum across the river, the ruined tomb of the emperor Augustus possesses a forlorn and neglected look, as if the city had temporarily parked it to one side and then forgotten about it. The structure has had a checkered history. Built by Augustus during his lifetime, it was — and is — the largest tomb in the Roman world (Hadrian was careful not to exceed its dimensions), and it served as a burial site for all the emperors until Trajan, whose ashes were placed under his column near the Forum. Originally, the circular base was faced with travertine and surmounted by a huge mound of earth almost 150 feet high, planted with cypresses. In its ruined state it has been built upon many times; over the centuries it has served variously as a fortress, a vineyard, a formal garden, a beast-baiting arena, a bull ring, a circus ring, a theater, and a concert hall.

The concert hall was torn down in 1937, when Mussolini decided to return the tomb to its ruined state as a centerpiece for a new, modern square. The results were uniformly bleak.* In laying out the square, Mussolini's planners faced a difficult problem: the three churches around the perimeter all face in the wrong direction. Two of the churches ended up hidden behind modern buildings (the seemingly pointless double arch at the square's southwest corner makes more sense from the other side, where it links the two church façades). The third church — S. Carlo al Corso, at the southeast corner — possesses a magnificent dome and a superb massing of rounded volumes at its apse end. But a backside is still a backside, no matter how shapely.

Nor does the architecture of the new buildings help in any way. The architects were attempting to achieve a stylistic synthesis of Classical and

---

*Some of the bleakness will perhaps be alleviated shortly, when the construction scaffolding comes off Richard Meier's new building on the piazza's west side (built to house the Ara Pacis, a large and magnificently carved sacrificial altar dating from the time of Augustus that was unearthed nearby in 1938). The design of the new building — unabashedly Modernist — has caused considerable controversy, but the preliminary indications are distinctly promising. Since the rest of the square's perimeter is proto-Modernist already, Meier's Modernist structure will probably not look out of place, and it may supply an illuminating stylistic contrast with the buildings constructed by Mussolini and his architects. In any case, the new structure should give the perimeter of the square a much-needed primary focus.

Modern that would reflect the glory of Mussolini's fascist regime, and the massive buildings with their stripped-down columns do achieve a certain muscularity. But it is a brutal and brainless sort of power that does nothing to show off the square's ancient ruined centerpiece. Given such surroundings, the inscription on the face of the building on the east side seems a sad boast: "The Italian people are an immortal people who forever discover a season of spring in their hopes, their passions, their greatness."

5-23   PORTO DI RIPETTA
(Piazza del Porto di Ripetta, southwest of the Piazza Augusto Imperatore at the east end of the Ponte Cavour)

Porto di Ripetta (destroyed by the construction of the Lungotevere during the late 1800s).

Not "porta," which means "gate," but "porto," which means "port." For centuries, the Piazza del Porto di Ripetta was the terminus for all river commerce coming down the Tiber from the interior. In 1707, papal architect Alessandro Specchi designed a gracefully curved staircase for the site leading from the piazza down to the river. But the Tiber flooded regularly, and at the end of the nineteenth century, the steps were removed and replaced with the current embankment; all that remains is Specchi's centerpiece fountain, moved slightly to the south from its original position. Given the need to tame the Tiber, the loss was probably inevitable, but it is no less sad for being necessary.

5-24 PALAZZO BORGHESE
Courtyard: Martino Longhi the Elder or Flaminio Ponzio, ca. 1585
(Largo della Fontanella di Borghese)

One of the most tantalizing — and frustrating — entranceways in the city. The front door of the Palazzo Borghese (on the Largo della Fontanella di Borghese) is usually open, but access to the courtyard beyond is almost always barred by an electronic iron gate and a discreetly placed sign reminding visitors that the palazzo is private property. The courtyard and the garden behind it cry out for exploration, but the sightseer must make do with the view.

The courtyard dates from the late 1500s — the Mannerist era — but the quirky, experimental feel of Mannerist architecture is nowhere to be seen. This is architecture of great boldness and sophistication, and the confidence with which it solves the visual problems that bedeviled earlier Renaissance courtyards (the Cancelleria, say, or the cloister at S. Maria della Pace) anticipates the Baroque era to come.

The key idea is the paired column. When used as a repetitive architectural motif, double columns often manage to eat their cake and have it, too: they possess the presence and elegance of single columns but at the same time supply the extra stabilizing width and mass of thicker piers. As a result of the increased pier-width space between arches, the visual rhythm of the courtyard arcades is significantly stretched (this: ⌒⌒⌒ rather than this: ⌒⌒⌒) and the arches do not seem to bounce along in the boing-boing-boing manner so prevalent among single-column arcades.

The paired columns also supply an elegant solution to the corner problem: one column per courtyard side, with an intervening pier (mostly but not entirely hidden by the columns) at the corner angle to supply the desired extra mass and visual emphasis. The corner supports thus read as triple rather than double units, but since two of the three units are columns, the ruling paired-column motif of the arcades is cunningly preserved.

Finally, the paired columns allow for a new solution to the problem of vertical hierarchy. Early Renaissance courtyards had repeated the dimensions of their palazzo façades, with each story of arcade decreasing in height so that the most massive arcade would be on the bottom. But this system produced a perverse visual effect — tall archway openings below and squat archway openings above — that undermined the desired vertical progression. Here, the two main stories of arcade are essentially identical in height, and hierarchy is achieved by other means. First, the decreased height of the upper-story Ionic columns (because they are placed on pedestals) makes them appear far more delicate than the Doric columns below; second, the decreased diameter of the upper-story columns allows for wider spacing of the column pairs, which imparts an airier feel to the upper arcade; and third, the introduction of a balustrade to connect the pedestals on the upper story diminishes the total area of the upper archway openings relative to the openings below. All of these features serve to emphasize the mass of the lower story — to give it extra strength and presence — so that it appears weightier than the upper even though the dimensions of the two arcades are virtually identical.

Today the overall effect of the courtyard is somewhat marred by modern intrusions — parked cars and downspouts at the corners — and the over-sized antique statuary on the ground floor (installed shortly after the court-yard was finished) is wincingly out of scale with the arches and the statuary atop the upper arcade. But these defects are easily ignored. As architecture, the Palazzo Borghese courtyard remains today what it has always been: one of the first completely realized and fully mature courtyard compositions in Rome, and one of the most beautiful.

5-25 LARGO CARLO GOLDONI
(Via del Corso, at the beginning of the Via dei Condotti)

With rare exceptions, the streets in the Campus Martius area are a sur-veyor's nightmare, laid out higgledy-piggledy and helter-skelter to no appar-ent purpose. Amid all the confusion, the Largo Goldoni offers a rare glimpse of order. Five straight streets converge here (the Via dei Condotti to the east, the Via della Fontana di Borghese and the Via Tomacelli to the west, and the Via del Corso to the north and south), and at a certain unmarked spot near the center, three far-off view-stoppers unexpectedly click into place: the Spanish Steps (to the east), the Victor Emmanuel Monument (to the south), and the obelisk in the center of the Piazza del Popolo (to the north). The sur-prise is bracing, clarifying, and reassuring. Suddenly, the Roman street maze seems not quite so complicated, and for once the city seems to be offering a well-ordered choice among palpable destinations. The impression of cityscape order quickly passes — turn toward the west and the two remain-ing streets peter away to nothing, step away from the center and the view-stoppers immediately disappear. But in a neighborhood where most streets seem to lead only to more streets, even a fleeting glimpse of intelligible order is welcome.

5-26 SANTA MARIA IN VIA
Façade: Giacomo della Porta, 1579 (lower story);
Carlo Rainaldi, 1681 (upper story)
(Via di S. Maria in Via, off the Via del Corso to the east at the Largo Chigi)

S. Maria in Via possesses a façade at war with itself: a lower story designed by a sixteenth-century Mannerist architect and an upper story designed by a much later Baroque architect who failed to recapture the old spirit. Della Porta's lower story is straightforward and understated, its most interesting (and typically Mannerist) feature being the way the extra carved frieze at the same level as the pilaster capitals robs those capitals of all their architectural force, turning them into decorative wall elements almost indistinguishable from the wall itself. Rainaldi's upper story, while continuing the simplicity of the lower, possesses a pronounced verticality — narrow pilasters, almost upright scrolls — that is entirely opposed to the restrained horizontality below it. As a result, the top story weighs heavily on the bottom, the bottom story looks too weak to support the top, and neither looks very happy. An object lesson in failed proportion.

5-27 PIAZZA COLONNA
Column of Marcus Aurelius: 180–193 C.E.
Palazzo Chigi: Giacomo della Porta, 1588 (Corso façade);
Felice della Greca, 1658 (piazza façade)
SS. Bartolomeo ed Alessandro di Bergamaschi façade:
probably Carlo de Dominicis, ca. 1735
Palazzo Wedekind: Giuseppe Valadier, 1815 (not constructed until 1838)
Galleria Colonna (Galleria Alberto Sordi): Dario Carbone, 1916–1922

One of Rome's few underperforming piazzas. The raw materials are quite promising: a famous antique centerpiece, three imposing palazzi from three different centuries on three sides, and a miscellany of buildings (including a tiny Baroque church) on the fourth. But the modern ban on traffic has had an oddly enervating effect, robbing the space of life, and on the east side the traffic seems to flow up and down the Corso without taking much notice. Like the Piazza del Popolo, the Piazza Colonna seems to be waiting for something to happen, and the whole feels distinctly less than the sum of its parts.

The Column of Marcus Aurelius was constructed shortly after Marcus Aurelius's death in 180 C.E. by his son Commodus, in frank imitation of the Column of Trajan, erected near the Forum some seventy years earlier. Like its predecessor, the column celebrates military victories — it depicts Marcus Aurelius's campaigns against the German tribes north of the Danube — and it survived the Middle Ages because for many centuries it was owned by the monks of the nearby church of S. Silvestro in Capite, who collected an entrance fee from pilgrims and tourists wishing to climb to the top. In its carvings, the column is bolder and easier to read than the Column of Trajan because the reliefs are more deeply incised, but the narrative program — almost nothing but battle — lacks the variety of anecdotal detail that gives the earlier column its greater fame. The statue of St. Peter at the top dates from Sixtus V's renovation of 1589, when Domenico Fontana encased the old base in a new cladding bearing an inscription that erroneously identifies the monument as the Column of Antoninus Pius, which in ancient times stood nearby.

The Palazzo Chigi on the north side (opposite the church) is the oldest palazzo on the square, dating from the late Renaissance. The façade facing the Corso (around the corner from the square) was constructed first, and is notable mainly for the positioning of its windows, which cluster toward the façade's center and thus depart from the precedent of absolute regularity established by the Palazzo Farnese. Oddly, the piazza façade — which was constructed seventy years later — returns to the Farnese model and is considerably less interesting as a result.

The palazzi facing each other on the square's east-west axis were designed almost exactly one hundred years apart (1815 for the Palazzo Wedekind on the west side, 1916 for the Galleria Colonna on the east side), and are far more interesting taken as a pair than individually. The façades are quite similar in overall organization, and the later design is surely a respectful tip of the hat to the earlier. But an entire architectural era intervened, and it shows. The Palazzo Wedekind follows the standard Farnese pattern in the regularity of its window arrangement and the plainness of its wall surface, but it marks the beginning of nineteenth-century Neoclassicism by introducing a new and (for Rome) unprecedented feature on the ground floor: a sheltering colonnade constructed of salvaged antique columns. A century later, the Galleria Colonna echoes that colonnade but adds to it a full bag of Neoclassical decorative tricks spread over the rest of the façade, including rough-hewn pillars, paired columns, single half columns, decorative carvings, and crowning statuary. Compared to some of the other structures built at the same time (the Victor Emmanuel Monument, say, or the Palazzo della Giustizia), the Galleria's façade is notably restrained. But the restraint of the Palazzo Wedekind is of a different order entirely — it seems a product of quiet inner dignity rather than showy outer dress — and by comparison the Galleria Colonna looks just a bit vulgar. Gentlemanly decorum has given way to lordly pomp: the history of nineteenth-century Neoclassical architecture in a nutshell.

TOUR 6

⸙

BAROQUE ROME II:
THE QUIRINAL AND VIMINAL HILLS
FROM THE PIAZZA VENEZIA TO THE PORTA PIA

Monastero, e Chiesa di S. Susanna delle Monache Cistercienesi
1. Chiesa, e Monastero detto, 2. Chiesa di S. Maria della Vittoria, e Conv. dei PP. Carmelitani Scalzi, 3. Strada Pia, 4. Fontana dell'acqua felice a piedi di Termini

$\mathcal{D}$URING ROME'S BAROQUE heyday, the expansion of the city from the Corso to the east ended at the Piazza Barberini, and it was not until the late 1800s — essentially modern times — that the area between the Piazza Barberini and the ancient city gate at the Porta Pia was fully built up. Rome underwent a tremendous growth spurt in 1870, when it was declared the capital of a newly united Italy, and development in the area centered around two expansive new avenues: the long, straight Via Nazionale, which functioned as the main approach to the new railroad station constructed just south of the ancient Baths of Diocletian, and the curved Via Veneto, which snaked its way up the Pincian Hill from the Piazza Barberini to the Porta Pinciana.

Even in ancient times the area was sparsely populated (it was the site of the parklike Gardens of Sallust), and during the Renaissance and Baroque eras its character was predominantly suburban — open country-side dotted with a few aristocratic villas that overlooked vineyards and gardens. Only the narrow east-west thoroughfare that ran along the crest of the Quirinal Hill (from the Piazza del Quirinale to the Porta Pia) attracted concentrated construction, in the form of four Baroque churches in the space of four blocks. Today that sequence of churches — S. Andrea al Quirinale, S. Carlo alle Quattro Fontane, S. Susanna, and S. Maria della Vittoria (the latter two are pictured previously) — is little visited by ordinary tourists, but it is a place of pilgrimage among architects and students of architecture. Individually, each of the churches possesses a remarkable wealth of artistic invention given its modest size (S. Carlo — nicknamed "San Carlino" — is famous for being small enough to fit *inside* any one of the four piers that support the dome over the crossing in St. Peter's). Collectively, the four churches represent the finest Baroque ecclesiastical ensemble in the entire city.

6-1 SANTI LUCA E MARTINA
Pietro da Cortona, 1634–1650
(Via del Tulliano, off the Via dei Fori Imperiali on the back side of the Victor Emmanuel Monument)

The façade of SS. Luca e Martina was designed by Pietro da Cortona, the third member of the sixteenth-century architectural triumvirate — the other members were Bernini and Borromini — that brought the Baroque style into full flower. His design here would be unexceptional except for one small but critical feature: the wall surface begins to curve. Cortona has introduced, for the first time in Rome, a slight but definite convexity into the façade's central section. As a result, the paired pilasters at the ends serve to frame a wall that is no longer flat but is being molded into three dimensions, like a piece of clay sculpture. The columns on the ground floor heighten the effect; instead of merely framing the doorway, they seem to be emerging from the wall surface with the full force of a colonnade.

Despite the strength of the columns, however, the effect of the façade as a whole is oddly disturbing in its isolation, looking as if it were intended to be the centerpiece of a suite of buildings attached to either side. In fact, the structure was not completed as originally planned. Cortona intended the façade to possess short side wings that angle back at either end. These wings would have added significantly to the façade's power: they would have diminished the stolidity of the paired pilasters that flank the central curve, they would have considerably increased the sculptural plasticity and three-dimensionality of the façade as a whole, and they would (probably) have given the façade the necessary breadth and strength to act as an effective complement to the beautiful dome. In the end, the absence of the side wings is a small loss, but a telling one, since it keeps the façade from achieving the kind of bold Baroque effect that Cortona later realized with such mastery at S. Maria della Pace.

CHIESA DEDICATA A S·LVCA EVANGELISTA ET A S·MARTINA V·M·DOVE FV L ANTICO TEMPIO DI MARTE IN CAMPO VACCINO.
Architettura del Cavalier Pietro Berrettini da Cortona.
1 Arco di Settimio Seuero. 2 Chiesa di S·Gioseppe e S·Pietro in carcere 3 Chiesa di S·Adriano

Engraving of SS. Luca e Martina showing the short angled flanking wings that were never built.

The interior of the church mirrors the exterior in its use of columns and curves, but here there is no holding back, and the end result is confidently and completely Baroque. The Greek-cross shape is marked out by a profusion of columns and pilasters, all arranged so that the columns step forward into prominence at the four crossing piers and step back into recesses within the arms of the cross. As John Varriano describes it in his survey *Italian Baroque and Rococo Architecture*, "24 columns and 16 piers faced with pilasters interact to keep the eye constantly in motion ... and [to] create a varied and free-moving surface that comes to rest only at the three principal altars." Visually, the walls all but completely disappear, transformed into a complicated array of columns and pilasters, all supporting the arches that support the dome, with the whole extravagant display held together by a single unifiying architectural element — the entablature that rings the entire space.

In the vaults and dome above, the complex decoration continues the architectural spectacle; the decoration is of special historical note because it combines, for the first time anywhere, Gothic ribs and Classical coffering. Indeed, the coffering in the dome goes beyond Classical — it is highly original and highly stylized in design — and was perhaps considered extreme even by Cortona's contemporaries (it was not until Bernini simplified Cortona's supple and sumptuous coffer shapes into more traditional straight-sided polygons that the combination of ribs and coffering became an accepted Baroque convention).

Finally, one further feature of the interior should perhaps be stressed: the lack of marble and gilding. To quote John Varriano again, "the interior of SS. Luca e Martina is richly textured, even painterly, but makes little use of color. Except for three altar paintings, framed in marble, the limestone masonry unifies the space in a silvery monochrome that becomes more luminous as the height increases." Thus the overall design, which is otherwise open to the charge of excess, is in at least one critical way quite restrained.

6-2 SANTA MARIA DI LORETO
Ground floor: Antonio da Sangallo, 1522–1552
Upper floor and dome: Giacomo del Duca, 1573–1583

SANTISSIMO NOME DI MARIA
Antoine Dérizet, 1736–1741
(Off the southeast corner of the Piazza Venezia; best viewed from a distance on the pedestrian islands to the south, where the two churches' façades can be seen together and compared)

A fraternal pair of churches, similar in overall shape and size but not in detail, one from the sixteenth century and the other from the eighteenth. The modern clearing and landscaping of the area has left the churches more or less isolated, and has given them a visual prominence they on no account deserve. Still, the view of the twin structures from the planted pedestrian island to the south makes for an illuminating architectural comparison.

The older is S. Maria di Loreto, nearer the Piazza Venezia. The ground-floor façade — a plain-vanilla Renaissance arrangement of paired pilasters that frame niches and doorway — was probably designed by Antonio da Sangallo and constructed beginning in 1522. Five decades later, Giacomo del Duca added the drum and dome in a new and very different style. In sharp contrast to the straightforward Classicism of the ground floor, Del Duca's upper stories are full of Mannerist oddity and experiment. The pedestal and balustrade of the drum's front window break through into Sangallo's triangular pediment; eight odd little buttresses protrude from the base of the dome; on top the intricate lantern audaciously thrusts its tiny columns beyond the supporting base, holding them in suspension from the sides rather than supporting them from below. "In the lantern," says Anthony Blunt, "Del Duca created a brilliant but fantastic structure which deeply shocked his successors and was never imitated."

The shock, presumably, was of excessive license: Del Duca was a pupil of Michelangelo, and was one of the few architects willing to follow the master's example of adventurous experimentation wherever it might lead. But Del Duca lacked Michelangelo's genius for integrating his experimental motifs into a coherent whole. The drum window, for instance, seems to take a savagely destructive bite out of the pediment below; the dome base imparts to both the dome and drum an uncomfortable look of squat compression; the lantern all but overpowers the dome on which it rests. In the end, Del Duca's experiments fail to add up, and remain a quirky collection of unrelated idiosyncracies.

More than a century later, Antoine Dérizet — a Frenchman who spent most of his adult life in Rome — put up a deliberate variation, smoother, stricter, and better. Unlike its neighbor, SS. Nome di Maria rises from an octagonal foundation, so the transitions from floor to floor — from base to drum to dome to lantern — seem less abrupt and less gawky. Here the paired half columns that set off the front door are allowed to carry an uninterrupted pediment, the drum above is given enough height to make it stand tall as it supports the dome, and the lantern is toned down so as to sit comfortably on its dome cushion. The details, too, are more consistent: as the eye sweeps up from ground floor to lantern, the successive curves of pediment top, drum-window top, dome-window top, and dome profile seem all of a piece, while next door the miscellany of similarly placed angles and curves and circles fight each other to an uneasy draw. Dérizet's Baroque refinement makes Del Duca's Mannerist experiments look clumsy and crude.

Still, Del Duca's failure is in some ways more memorable than Dérizet's success. Dérizet's design was far from innovative; working at the tail end of the Baroque era, he employed conventional motifs that had been in use for more than a century. Del Duca, on the other hand, was willing to go out on a limb — to take risks by experimenting with the conventions of his day — and it was out of such experiments that the Baroque style eventually evolved. And when Dérizet's urbanity and polish have been absorbed and appreciated and forgotten, it is Del Duca's lantern that sticks in the mind — a brilliant architectural carousel waiting for the music that will start it rotating splendidly round and round.

Rome is famous for its cityscape juxtapositions: ancient ruins cropping up amid modern palazzi, medieval campanili towering over Baroque churchfronts. Such enlivening contrasts can be seen all over the city, but the grouping in the Largo Magnanapoli — a noisy little traffic roundabout constructed by the nineteenth-century city planners who laid out the Via Nazionale to the east — is worth special attention. The place to stand is on the northern sidewalk, between numbers 158 and 159, at the point where the tall palm tree in the center of the roundabout falls exactly between the church and the tower beyond. To the far right, the top of the Victor Emmanuel Monument (1884) rises above the ancient ruins of Trajan's Market (second century C.E.); to the far left, the fancy Baroque pediment of SS. Domenico e Sisto (1628) peeks over the plain wall enclosing the Villa Aldobrandini gardens. In the middle, flanking the palm tree, stands the odd-couple pairing of the church of S. Caterina da Siena (c. 1640) and the leaning Torre delle Milizie, a fortified tower built as a stronghold by Pope Gregory IX in the thirteenth century. And in the center, sharing the roundabout with a fine display of greenery, is the most venerable relic of all: a fragment of the Servian Wall, built to protect the growing city in the early fourth century B.C.E. and uncovered in 1876 when the street level in the area was lowered. It was an exceptional find, for it places at the heart of the overall composition a powerful symbol of the past that is almost twenty-five hundred years old.

6-4 SANTA CATERINA DA SIENA A MAGNANAPOLI
Façade: Giovanni Battista Soria, ca. 1641
(Largo Magnanapoli, east of the Piazza Venezia)

SANTI DOMENICO E SISTO
Façade: Nicolo Torriani, 1632
Staircase: Vincenzo della Greca, 1654
(A few yards up the Via Panisperna from the Largo Magnanapoli)

Largo Magnanapoli before the nineteenth-century lowering of the ground level, showing the churches of S. Caterina da Siena (extreme right) and SS. Domenico e Sisto (center left in distance).

Another similarly shaped pair of church façades — this time both Baroque — within a few yards of each other. Neither is especially distinguished on its own, but together they make a most engaging couple indeed.

The first, S. Caterina, faces directly on the Largo Magnanapoli traffic roundabout; it was designed by Giovanni Battista Soria around 1638. As Baroque architects go, Soria was far from adventurous, but the straightforward simplicity of his best designs can be very satisfying. His façade here is an essay in triplets: three open arches below to form an entrance portico and three closed arches above for niches and window, all separated by triple nested pilasters and topped by a no-nonsense triangular pediment. The façade's few stylistic flourishes — the carved decoration within the pediment and the top portion of the upper-story window-surround — acknowledge the reigning style of the day but hardly revel in it. All in all, it is a quietly dignified performance that makes its simple, cogent statement and then, with exemplary modesty, stops.

Nearby to the left (a few yards up the Via Panisperna), the finely etched façade of SS. Domenico e Sisto is far less diffident. As architecture — the architect is unknown — it is no more adventurous than S. Caterina. But its fluid approaching staircase and abundance of crisp decorative detail make an instant impression. Particularly inventive are the vertical carved panels between the upper-story pilasters, which fill the space caused by the reduction in pilaster size without too much fussiness, and the window-surround within the top pediment, which transforms traditional decorative scrolls into curled tentacles. (The staircase that adds so much to the façade's pleasing verticality was originally some ten steps shorter; it was extended in the late nineteenth century when the ground level in the area was lowered due to the construction of the Largo Magnanapoli.)

Together, the two façades — so similar in shape and overall organization, so different in effect — offer a fine contrast in architectural personality. Both are elegantly decked out, but they wear very different clothes, S. Caterina's sober and restrained, SS. Domenico e Sisto's opulent and showy. The contrast is not in any way profound — a matter of outer guise, not inner essence — but it is flattering to both buildings, allowing each to complement the other.

6-5 PIAZZA DEL QUIRINALE
PALAZZO DELLA CONSULTA
Fernando Fuga, 1732–1737
(North of the Largo Magnanapoli)

A quirky, awkward, uncomfortable space created by three hundred years of haphazard architectural accretion. The sprawling Presidential Palace to the north — originally the summer residence of the popes — was begun in 1574; the ancient Roman horse tamers (the Dioscuri) in the center were set up in 1588; the obelisk was added in 1786; the Palazzo della Consulta to the east dates from 1732; the balustrade overlooking the city to the west was constructed in 1866. The piazza that resulted ought to be memorable: the view of St. Peter's towering over a sea of Roman rooftops is exceptional, and the theatrical fountain has all the makings of a fine centerpiece. But around the piazza's perimeter, only the Palazzo della Consulta seems to be paying attention. As a result, the space feels diffuse and unfocused, lacking the coherence and drama that bring most Roman piazzas alive. Still, the Palazzo della Consulta façade is admirably dignified, with an extra (and entertainingly undignified) fillip — a row of tiny attic windows that peep out from under the crowning cornice like spying children.

6-6 SANT' ANDREA AL QUIRINALE
Gianlorenzo Bernini, 1658–1670
(Via del Quirinale, south side, opposite the long wing of the Presidential Palace)

S. Andrea is perhaps the most elegant neighborhood church in Rome, with a façade that is one of Bernini's most accomplished inventions. The aedicule motif — an entranceway framed by columns or pilasters and crowned by a pediment — was not new; Della Porta, for one, had employed it at S. Nicola in Carcere. But Bernini's treatment is quintessentially Baroque. With tremendous assurance, he introduces a round portico atop a cascade of steps; he extends the overhang of the pediment to balance the projecting portico; he makes the plain giant pilasters turn the corners and gives them boldly clustered capitals. And then, with irresistible showmanship, he sets a rakishly tilted Pamphili coat of arms atop the portico. Like the plume in a cavalier's hat, it gives the façade a crowning touch of inimitable panache.

Inside, the walls are decorated with a richness of material and color that makes the simple oval space all but glow. Moreover (and unlike so many other Roman Baroque interiors), this is no superficial show of glitter. As always with Bernini at his best, the opulence serves a larger vision, and the architectural elements here are a subordinate consideration — the setting for the performance rather than the performance itself. That performance — the ascension of St. Andrew, to whom the church is dedicated — begins in the shallow apse and then expands to include the whole dome. There are three key points: first, the altar painting depicting St. Andrew's crucifixion (by Guglielmo Cortese); second, the pediment sculpture of St. Andrew rising toward the dome of heaven (by Antonio Raggi); and third, the dove — symbol of the Holy Spirit — stuccoed in the lantern, toward which the sculpted St. Andrew looks. Around this rising axis, Bernini has set the whole church aswarm with sculpted angels and cherubs, watching and participating in the miracle. In the apse, a flight of angels sets the altar painting in place;* around the bottom of the dome, cherubs alight to deck the windows with garlands; in the lantern, more cherubs have just arrived and peer nosily over the rim of the dome to see what all the commotion is about. The effect of all this activity is tremendously enlivening, turning the whole church into a celebration of both religion and art. Of all Bernini's works, this was his favorite, and no wonder, for it is probably the grandest

---

*The effect of angelic installation is heightened by the fact that the painting frame is tilted slightly forward, not yet quite in place.

synthesis of architecture, sculpture, and painting that the seventeenth century ever achieved.

Such a synthesis was typical of Bernini, who was beyond question the most versatile artist of his era. Although he was best known as a sculptor, he was also a skillful painter, and on occasion a writer, composer, and set designer. His artistic vision was broad and multifaceted, encompassing all the art forms of his day. As a result, he did not prize or privilege architecture over the other arts, and his buildings were usually quite conventional in conception. The interior of S. Andrea is a case in point: the overall oval shape is straightforward and uncomplicated, easily read and accepted by the eye. Its only unorthodox architectural feature is to be found at the ends of the cross-axis (at either end of the oval), where the eye is not — as might be expected — invited into a subsidiary chapel space but is instead stopped by a pier separating two chapels to either side of the cross-axis. At the axis terminations, the eye is thus deflected by a solid rather than enticed by a void — a deflection that encourages a return to the point of maximum focus, the high altar. As an artist, Bernini was here purposely playing down the visual potential of the architecture so that the architectural parts do not detract from the seamless combination of architecture, sculpture, and painting that is the church as a whole.

6-7 SAN CARLO ALLE QUATTRO FONTANE (SAN CARLINO)
Francesco Borromini, 1634–1641 (church interior and cloister)
and 1665–1667 (façade)
(Via del Quirinale, at the intersection with the Via delle Quattro Fontane)

Extreme greatness in art has two faces. One takes the usage of the time and transfigures it with humanity and intensity. The other leaps forward not only in style but into what appears to be a higher organization of humanity altogether. Rubens vs. Rembrandt, Handel vs. Bach — and Wren vs. Soane.
— IAN NAIRN, writing about the Soane Museum in *Nairn's London*

And Bernini vs. Borromini. The two were exact contemporaries (born nine months apart), but as personalities they could hardly have been more different. Bernini was astute, charming, worldly, socially adept, and ended his life acclaimed throughout Europe as the most accomplished artist of his era. Borromini was obsessive, moody, suspicious (particularly of Bernini), antisocial, and ended his life by suicide. As architects they were in important ways diametrically opposed as well, and nowhere in Rome is the contrast between their individual styles — and the brilliance of both — more evident than in the two small churches of S. Andrea al Quirinale and S. Carlo alle Quattro Fontane, just a block apart on the Via del Quirinale.

Bold as Bernini's façade for S. Andrea is, it seems quite simple when compared with Borromini's intricate work at S. Carlino. As Borromini would have been the first to admit, the inspiration for the overall design of the S. Carlino façade comes from Michelangelo. The general organization of each of the façade's two stories — full-story columns, with the wall behind divided horizontally to allow for smaller subsidiary columns on the lower portion — derives from the Palazzo dei Conservatori on the Campidoglio. There, Michelangelo invented a variably scaled arrangement of Classical elements that combined giant two-story pilasters with smaller single-story columns, and the result was a composition in which the pilasters and columns do not so much seem to hold things up as hold things together, creating a harmonious balance between the vertical and the horizontal.

Borromini felt a deep affinity for Michelangelo's architecture, and at S. Carlino he repeated the Campidoglio façade's basic design on both stories. But he took that design a critical step further — a step into the third dimension. The façade of S. Carlino not only balances up, down, and across, it balances in and out as well. Where Michelangelo's design deemphasizes the façade's wall surface (even to the point of eliminating it entirely on the ground floor), Borromini's design reinstates the wall and brings it alive with sinuous curves.

Unexpectedly, those curves are not identical on the façade's two stories. Instead of overall regularity, Borromini opts for a more complicated design, molding the walls of the upper and lower stories so that they are in part mirror images of each other, both vertically and horizontally. The ground-floor wall follows a concave-convex-concave curve (with the doorway giving the central bay just a suggestion of concave), while the upper-floor wall follows a concave-concave-concave curve (with the inserted oval sentry-box window-surround giving the central bay more than a suggestion of convex). Additionally, the side bays reverse the hierarchy of shallow wall panel and deep niche, with the lower-story side-bay niches on top and the upper-story side-bay niches on the bottom.

Against this complexity, Borromini sets a simple framework of columns. As with Michelangelo's giant pilasters, Borromini's columns are uniformly lined up across the façade surface so as to supply horizontal and vertical stability. But unlike Michelangelo's pilasters, the columns also function as a counterpoint to the wall surface. Their strength and simplicity contrast sharply with the wall's rolling curves and elaborate carved decoration; they supply a steady foursquare beat that anchors the rest of the façade and keeps its varying contours under control.

As always with Borromini, the decoration is worth examining in detail. Small touches are as inventively conceived as the larger overall design, blurring the traditional Renaissance distinction between architectural elements and decorative accents. Above the central doorway, for instance, the statue of St. Charles Borromeo is set within a semicircular niche, but the upper part of the niche is transformed into a pointed arch by the carved angel wings that frame the niche in its turn. Around each of the oval windows on either side of the doorway, flamelike palm fronds — no two are exactly alike — envelope the window frame, forming a tentlike canopy as they meet within a flaming crown above. The flame motif is repeated in the column capitals, and a similarly creative attention to detail can be found across the whole façade. In Borromini's hands, the line between architecture and decoration all but disappears.

Small as the S. Carlino façade is, its dynamic design and wealth of decorative invention give it a *brio* that puts many a larger Baroque façade to shame. The composition as a whole combines extremes of fluidity and stability — a liquid undulating wave of wall controlled by a solid unbending framework of columns — with consummate assurance and ingenuity. The result may not be so startling as the dome and spiral lantern of Borromini's other great Roman masterpiece, S. Ivo della Sapienza, but the curves of the S. Carlino façade are no less inventive than the billowing shapes of the S. Ivo dome, and the S. Carlino façade (unlike the S. Ivo dome) displays those curves within a strong Classical framework. It is this combination of old and new — the columns and entablature combined with the undulating walls — that gives the S. Carlino exterior its special status among Roman churchfronts. For many architectural historians, S. Carlino possesses the quintessential Baroque façade.

After the intricacies of the façade, S. Carlino's cloister (entrance to the right of the façade or through the church proper, depending on which door is open) comes as a shock. The tiny courtyard is simplicity itself. The ruling motif is the Serlian arch — a columned three-opening unit containing a central archway that is flanked by unarched (flat-topped) side openings — but with an unexpected twist. On the cloister's long axis, Borromini has bent the side sections of the arch forward. In doing so, he has successfully — and brilliantly — finessed the courtyard corner emphasis problems that so bedeviled earlier Renaissance architects. "The corner is the enemy of all architecture," Borromini once stated, and this simple but powerful insight can be seen everywhere in his buildings.

FONTANA DI MERCVRIO NEL GIARDINO DEL GRAN DVCA DI TOSCANA ALLA TRINITA DE MONTI ADORNATA DI STATVE DI METALLO AVANTI IL PORTICO DELLA FACCIATA INTERIORE DEL PALAZZO. *Architettura di Annibale Lippi 9.*

A typical Serlian arch, named after Sebastiano Serlio (1475–1554), the Renaissance architect and theorist who first illustrated it in his book L'Architettura.

As architecture, the courtyard is the most restrained interior space Borromini ever created. But modest and pared down as the design is, there is no lack of Borrominian invention. Above the ground-floor columns, for instance, the corner panels (and the balustrade above) are given a slightly convex bulge, mirroring the pronounced entasis (swelling) of the columns. The effect of this small adjustment is considerable, as can be seen by comparing the lower story with the upper. Around the upper perimeter, the entablature atop the columns is uniformly straight — there is no convex bulge at the canted corners — and the lessening of tension can be clearly felt. This decrease in power is not inappropriate, however, since the upper-story elements are clearly meant to be subsidiary to the lower.

The balustrade is worth examining as well. "The most ingenious feature of the whole cloister," Anthony Blunt calls it in his monograph *Borromini*, "where Borromini breaks with every Renaissance convention and introduces the maximum effect of movement and variety into a small detail." Renaissance architects, Blunt goes on to explain, always designed their balustrades so that the bulge of each individual baluster came in the middle. Michelangelo was the first to break with this tradition, moving the bulge downward so as to increase the appearance of stability. Borromini goes even further, turning every other baluster upside down so that the bulges alternate between low and high. He justified this innovation in terms of improved sight lines, explaining that it allows anyone sitting behind the balustrade to get the best possible view of activity below. But (as Blunt notes) it is legitimate to wonder if he did not invent the form as much for its aesthetic appeal as for its practicality.

Inside the church proper, the theme established by the courtyard — the basic eight-sided lozenge shape — is repeated, but now it is given full, symphonic orchestration. And just as the upper floor of the exterior was a reverse image of the lower, the general plan of the church interior is a reverse image of the courtyard. Here it is the corner segments of the lozenge that are straight, and the sides and ends that are curved. Moreover, convex is replaced with concave: whereas in the courtyard the corner segments bulge inward toward the center of the courtyard, inside the church the sides and ends curve outward to create spaces for subsidiary chapels.

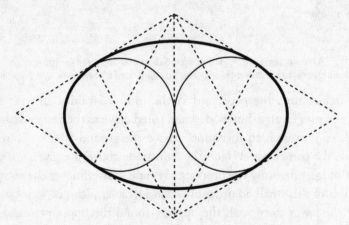

Diagram showing geometric genesis of S. Carlino ground plan.

As at S. Ivo, the overall design is geometrical in its genesis: an oval — clearly seen outlined around the bottom of the dome — derived from two circles inscribed within two equilateral triangles. The oval itself is ordinary enough (and reminiscent of Bernini's interior at S. Andrea down the street), but what Borromini does with it is extraordinary. He creates a spatial play that is even more daring than on the façade outside, for now in addition to up, down, across, in, and out, Borromini adds *around,* and the overall effect is almost dizzying in its complexity.

Once again, however, that complexity is firmly controlled. As on the façade, the composition is anchored by strong, plain columns. The columns are arrayed around the perimeter in groups of four, but this time — unlike the façade — the groups are spaced so as to create a visual ambiguity. The four-column groupings can be read in two ways: either as centered on the interior's sides and ends (in which case each set of four columns delineates a chapel and frames a chapel altar), or as centered on the interior's corners (in which case each set of four columns frames the statuary niches over the doorways between the chapels). But whichever way the columns are read, their march around the perimeter of the interior constitutes the steady beat around which the music of the curved walls swoops and swirls.

The possibilities for double reading are not limited to the ground-floor columns. In fact, the *entire* interior can be read in two different ways. The first reading — probably the most common, given the text-trained human eye — is a horizontal one. Viewed in this manner, the S. Carlino interior consists of three stacked but separate zones: the ground floor, with chapels and niches framed and defined by the vertical columns; an intermediate zone, with alternating arches and pendentives (the latter filled with oval medallions that recall the medallion at the peak of the façade); and the dome, with a complicated coffering pattern copied from the fourth-century ceiling mosaics at S. Costanza, outside the city walls on the Via Nomentana. This reading spotlights the distorted character of the architectural elements in the intermediate zone — the way in which the ends of the arches twist themselves about as they meet the entablature below, and the way in which the peaked pediments within the arches curve and flatten. These distortions impart to the zone as a whole a look of severe compression, a rubbery sort of give which seems to imply that the dome above is extremely heavy, pressing down to distort what were once semicircular arches and straight-sided pediments into deformed shapes that are skewed, flattened out, and distinctly non-Classical. By this view, the interior as a whole embodies the Baroque at its most extreme — the antithesis of Renaissance balance, regularity, and order.

But another reading is possible, and equally plausible. A shift in focus is required, however — a shift from the horizontal to the vertical. When examining, say, the shallow chapel flanked by columns that contains the high altar, the eye must travel up the left-hand column, up through the entablature, along the squashed pediment, and back down to the floor along the right-hand column. Similarly, if the focus is shifted to the chapel's outer columns, the eye must travel up the left-hand column, through the entablature, along the curved arch to the edge of the dome above, and back down to the right-hand column. Read in this way, the ground floor and the intermediate zone above it unite into a single composition, and the ground-floor columns support not only the entablature but also the flattened pediments and twisted arches above. Moreover, if the eye reads all of these elements at one time — all four columns and arch and pediment together as a single visual unit — an extraordinarily powerful composition emerges. It is almost as if Borromini took a conventional two-dimensional composition — outer columns supporting a curved arch and inner columns supporting a triangular pediment — and gave the center a push backward into the third dimension. The result is a potent yet supple molding of conventional two-dimensional architectural elements within a three-dimensional space. And it is the apparent distortions of the intermediate zone — those twisted arches and flattened pediments — that give the composition its special sinewy intensity, as if at any moment the pushed-out center could spring back into its two-dimensional configuration.

The dome, too, is transformed. When the arches of the intermediate zone are seen as supported by the columns below them — as a continuation of the vertical forces on the lower floor — they gain substantially in visual power. As a result, the feel of support for the dome is dramatically increased; far from weighing down heavily on the arches, the dome now seems balanced atop them, lightly placed and almost weightless. A different visual order is established, and the tensions inherent in the horizontal reading of the interior are resolved. Both readings are equally possible, however, and once both are seen and understood, the eye can shift back and forth between them at will.

As with so much in Borromini's architecture, this extraordinary play between tension and balance derives from Michelangelo, whose layout for the Campidoglio — part oval and part trapezoid — evinces a similar duality. But such willful ambiguity is not a typically Baroque characteristic, and from the very beginning, opinion about Borromini's buildings was divided. On the one hand, the monks who commissioned S. Carlino — the Spanish Order of the Discalced [Unshod] Trinitarians — were immensely pleased with their new church, and boasted that they received requests for drawings of the building from all over Europe. "With regard to artistic merit, fantasy, excellence, and singularity," one of them wrote, "nothing similar can be found anywhere in the world. . . . Everything is arranged in such a manner that one part supplements the other and the spectator is stimulated to let his eye wander about ceaselessly." But Giovanni Pietro Bellori, a prominent seventeenth-century critic and biographer who championed a more traditional Classicism, called Borromini "a complete ignoramus, the corrupter of architecture, the shame of our century," and in a lecture delivered while Borromini was still alive, he widened the condemnation to include Baroque architects in general: "Everyone imagines in his head a new idea or phantom of architecture. . . . They use, almost deliriously, angles and broken and distorted lines, they tear apart bases, capitals and columns with crowded stucco decoration and trivial ornaments and with faulty proportions, in spite of the fact that Vitruvius condemns such novelties."

Even the great Bernini failed to discern the rigorous geometry that generates the tensions and ambiguities in Borromini's designs. "A painter or sculptor in their architecture take as their guide to proportion the human body," he said, "but Borromini must have based his on chimeras." Bernini's incomprehension was perhaps understandable, however, given the fact that his own ideas about architecture differed markedly from Borromini's. For Bernini (as for most Baroque architects) the paradigmatic artistic goal of the day was aesthetic synthesis: the fusion of all the visual arts — architecture, sculpture, painting — into a seamless whole that would overwhelm the viewer with its intensity. When Bernini achieved this goal, as at S. Andrea al Quirinale just down the street, the result is highly theatrical in effect, and the interior architecture of S. Andrea functions almost in the manner of a stage set — the constructed environment in which the painted and sculpted drama of St. Andrew's ascension to heaven takes place.

But at S. Carlino (as with all Borromini's buildings), the drama is purely architectural. Whereas Bernini relied on sculpture, painting, and decoration to bring his architecture alive, Borromini remained an architectural purist. He eschewed painting and sculpture, and though he used carved decoration brilliantly, its role was always subsidiary. In a Borromini building, it is the architecture alone — the complex shaping of interior space and the supple molding of exterior mass — that rules. This emphasis on pure form sets him apart from the other architects of his generation, and makes him one of the great loners of architectural history. But he was a loner of the highest genius: an iconoclastic Classicist who used the Classical vocabulary to create an architectural language that was deeply personal, uniquely individual, instantly recognizable, and in its special way incomparably beautiful.

6-8 QUATTRO FONTANE
1588 onward
(At the intersection of the Via del Quirinale and the Via delle Quattro Fontane)

A small urban amenity, courtesy of that ferocious town planner Sixtus V: four building-corner fountains, planned in 1588 to mark the crossroads of the newly laid-out Strada Pia and Strada Felice (now the Via del Quirinale /

Via XX Settembre and the Via delle Quattro Fontane, respectively). Over the years, the fountains have survived much rebuilding of the attached structures (only the Palazzo Albani on the southeast corner is as old as its fountain, and the office block on the northeast dates from the 1920s). The grouping's overall theme is esoteric in the extreme — even Baroque scholars have had trouble deciphering its symbols — with the fountains at the southwest and the southeast corners representing the Tiber and the Nile, respectively, and those at the northwest and northeast corners representing the goddesses Juno and Diana. Eleanor Clark, in *Rome and a Villa*, calls the scenes "jaded allegories"; Anthony Blunt, in his *Guide to Baroque Rome*, describes the reigning symbolical confusion as follows:

> The iconographical scheme is curious, with two rivers and two goddesses and it may have been originally planned with four rivers and changed later — perhaps in order not to compete with the Four Rivers Fountain in Piazza Navona. It is even possible that the generally accepted identification of the goddess at the northwest corner as Juno may not be correct as she is shown with a swan instead of her usual peacock and leaning on a crowned lion, no doubt a heraldic allusion which has not so far been clarified. Further, the figure in the [northeast] fountain may be Night rather than Diana, since she holds poppies in her left hand.

Pope Sixtus no doubt meant the grouping to focus attention on the center of the crossroads, with its ramrod-straight vistas shooting off to Michelangelo's Porta Pia to the east and the obelisks of the Esquiline, Quirinal, and Pincian hills to the south, west, and north. The available space, however, was too small to allow for a crossroad centerpiece, so today there is no place to stand amid the ever-present traffic. Still, the splendid views are well worth a foray to the center if there is a momentary lull.

6-9 SANTA SUSANNA
Façade: Carlo Maderno, 1597–1603
(Via XX Settembre — the continuation of the Via del Quirinale — facing the Piazza di S. Bernardo)

Renaissance and Mannerist architects had been experimenting with antique architectural motifs on their church façades since the 1400s, but the persistent problems they encountered in attempting to fashion a new

Classical churchfront grammar were not authoritatively solved until the beginning of the seventeenth century. It was then, in 1603, that Carlo Maderno completed the rebuilding of S. Susanna. His façade was epoch-making, for its synthesis of antique elements is at once bold and controlled, and possesses a look of easy confidence that the more tentative solutions of the Mannerist era utterly lack. After more than a century of inconclusive experimentation, the Age of the Baroque was at hand.

The façade for Il Gesù (left), designed by Giacomo della Porta some thirty years before Carlo Maderno's façade for S. Susanna.

Maderno's achievement looks especially compelling when his façade is compared to two others, one across town and one across the street. First: Il Gesù, with a façade designed by Giacomo della Porta around 1571. Della Porta's façade was enormously influential, and Maderno clearly used it as the prototype for S. Susanna. The general shape and organization are almost identical, but Maderno (possibly harking back to an unused plan for the Gesù by Vignola) rejects Della Porta's use of paired pilasters as the ruling motif. Instead, he employs a mixture of columns and pilasters, ordering them in a visual hierarchy that strengthens the basic Gesù design on three counts: greater stability (the increased use of columns anchors the ground story and gives it extra muscle to support the upper story); greater centrality (the center-outward progression from double columns to single columns to pilasters on the ground floor and from double to single pilasters on the upper floor dramatically accentuates the façades's receding planes); and greater verticality (the outer bays become progressively narrower, increasing the façade's overall ratio of height to width). The result is a tremendous jump in assurance and intensity, the jump that separates sixteenth-century Mannerism from seventeenth-century Baroque. The two sets of scrolls embody the change: Della Porta's are mere curlicues, sprawling and flaccid; Maderno's are coiled springs, lean and taut. It is as if Maderno took the Gesù façade and gave it a sharp prod in the back, springing it to attention.

Second comparison: S. Maria della Vittoria, to the right of S. Susanna across the Largo di S. Susanna (the Via Leonida Bissolati). Built more than twenty years after S. Susanna, G.B. Soria's façade is clearly based on Maderno's. But Soria lacked Maderno's skill at balancing architectural motifs, and the result is distinctly awkward. The most conspicuously discordant element is the curved pediment between the upper and lower stories. Whereas Maderno's corresponding pediment harmonizes with the roof pediment above (it is identical in shape yet clearly subordinate in size), Soria's pediment sounds a wrong note (different in shape yet uncomfortably close in size). Moreover, Maderno's pediment is firmly supported by the bold columns below it; the pilasters supporting Soria's pediment look far too weak for the job. As a result, Soria's pediment looks tacked on and top-heavy, as if about to drop off the façade onto the steps below.

The contrast holds for the façades' other motifs as well. Maderno's columns and pilasters serve as strong focusing frames for the niches between them; Soria's pilasters — particularly on the upper story — look like mere space fillers, and tend to disappear into the wall surface. Maderno's scrolls are strong and sinewy; Soria's scrolls are soft and doughy — and then made to do extra work by supporting statuary. Maderno's decoration enhances; Soria's decoration dominates. In the end, S. Maria's façade looks diffuse and halfhearted, as if cowed by its confident predecessor across the street.

At bottom, it is the strong sculptural quality of Maderno's façade that sets it apart from its Mannerist predecessors and makes it the first of the great Baroque façades. During the Mannerist era, architects viewed the church-front problem primarily as one of wall decoration; here the wall all but disappears, and the architectural elements seem to stand forth on their own, possessing the same strong presence as the sculptured figures in the façade niches. Maderno never sacrifices logic for boldness, however, and despite the strength of its individual parts, the façade as a whole reads as a coherent, unified architectural statement. Order, balance, and hierarchy are all triumphantly preserved. The new rhetorical power that resulted was to become a defining characteristic of great Baroque architecture, and — with the addition of the famous Baroque curves — was to find its ultimate expression in the churches of Bernini and Borromini, just down the street.

An added note: Maderno's design for the S. Susanna façade was also the first in Rome to incorporate the satellite buildings on either side. Quite plain in design, the side buildings echo the church façade's details only at top and bottom (balustrade and steps), thereby framing the church façade without competing with it. In addition, they effectively double the size of the composition, and to take in the integrated building complex after concentrating on the church façade alone is to experience yet another Mannerist-Baroque jump — from isolated single building to unified multiple ensemble.

6-10 SANTA MARIA DELLA VITTORIA
Façade: Giovanni Battista Soria, 1625–1627
Cornaro Chapel: Gianlorenzo Bernini, 1644–1652
(Via XX Settembre, across the Largo di S. Susanna from S. Susanna)

The interior of S. Maria della Vittoria was entirely redecorated during the Baroque era, and the result is so extreme in its gilded luxury that the space all but groans under its weight of decorative overload. One of the side chapels, however, must be separated out from the surrounding overabundance of marble, for it is an extraordinarily powerful synthesis of sculpture, painting, and architecture. The Cornaro Chapel (the last on the left, in the short transept) contains as its centerpiece Bernini's most famous piece of sculpture, *The Ecstasy of St. Theresa;* Bernini himself designed the surrounding architecture and decoration, down to the smallest detail of exquisitely veined marble.

During the Victorian era (and earlier), the uninhibited extravagance of Bernini's statue was considered to be in extremely poor taste, and even obscene. ("If *that* is divine love," said one eighteenth-century wag, "I know it well.") But the charge of prurience is not supported by the historical evidence, for Bernini — who was extremely devout — has depicted St. Theresa's ecstasy exactly as she described it:

> Beside me, on the left hand, appeared an angel in bodily form.... In his hands I saw a great golden spear, and at the iron tip there appeared to be a point of fire. This he plunged into my heart several times so that it penetrated to my entrails. When he pulled it out, I felt that he took them with it, and left me utterly consumed by the great love of God.

The pain was so severe that it made me utter several moans. The sweetness caused by this intense pain is so extreme that one cannot possibly wish it to cease, nor is one's soul then content with anything but God.

Bernini considered the *Ecstasy* to be his finest work, and he took the greatest possible pains in designing its setting. He placed the sculpture within an architectural frame of double columns, entablature, and pediment that merges with the chapel's altar below; the columns are canted, the pediment is broken and curved, and the entablature design is repeated on the walls of the chapel, all of which give the impression that the back wall has suddenly opened like a parted curtain to reveal the sculpture behind. The theatrical effect is further heightened by the light that streams down on the scene from a window concealed behind the pediment. More light enters through the chapel's upper window, illuminating the ceiling, on which sculpted and painted angels push aside clouds to reveal the radiant Holy Dove. On the chapel floor, sinister marble skeletons — intimations of earthly death answering the Dove's promise of heavenly life — are inlaid into the pavement. And on the side walls, occupying architectural niches carved to look like opera boxes, sit sculpted members of the sponsoring Cornaro family who — like us — observe and discuss the miracle before them.

As many a critic has pointed out, Bernini has here fashioned a Baroque *concetto* of prodigious virtuosity. Through a seamless fusion of sculpture, painting, and architecture he depicts and explores both the three levels of Christian reality (heaven, earth, purgatory) and the three levels of Christian spirituality — God (the painted angels above), the saint (the central sculpture), and ordinary man (the galleries of Cornaro onlookers on the sides). And by giving the members of the Cornaro family positions and postures effectively identical to us, the viewers, he invests the *concetto* with an immediacy that reaches out to envelop the onlooker with unprecedented power.

Ultimately, Bernini's aim with *The Ecstasy of St. Theresa* was to create not so much a spotlit religious sculpture as a complete and engulfing religious vision; he was attempting to merge sculpture, painting, and architecture so dramatically that the work is transformed from religious art into religious theater. He never surpassed the intensity of his achievement here, and he surpassed the scale only once, when he enlarged the conception to include an entire building — the church of S. Andrea al Quirinale, three blocks down the street.

6-11 FONTANA DELL' ACQUA FELICE
Domenico Fontana, 1585–1587
Moses Statue: Leonardo Sormanno
(Piazza di S. Bernardo, across the Via XX Settembre from
S. Maria della Vittoria)

The Renaissance rediscovered more than just Roman Classicism; it also rediscovered how to build self-congratulatory civic monuments. This was the first, built by Sixtus V to commemorate the construction of the aqueduct that restored running water to the Quirinal after a thousand-year drought. The designer, Domenico Fontana, was Sixtus's court architect; by giving such exaggerated pride of place to the dedicatory inscription, he turned what might have been an elegant trio of arches into a boxy lump. The central statue of Moses achieved instant notoriety when it was unveiled. Tradition holds that its supposed creator, Prospero Antichi, boasted that it would surpass Michelangelo and then committed suicide because of the storm of jeering criticism it evoked (the story is a later fabrication, and the sculptor is now known to have been Leonardo Sormanno, with Prospero da Brescia working as his assistant).

6-12 SAN BERNARDO ALLE TERME
Early fourth century and early seventeenth century
(Piazza di S. Bernardo alle Terme, opposite S. Susanna)

An undistinguished church with a distinguished origin. The building was consecrated and given a Baroque overhaul (both inside and out) around 1600. But beneath the Baroque costume, the original structure is much older, dating from around 300 C.E.: a round pavilion attached to the western corner of the Baths of Diocletian, which covered some 32 acres to the northeast and southeast. The original interior coffered vault — about half the size of the Pantheon — has survived intact.

6-13 FONTANA DELLE NAIADI
Mario Rutelli, 1911

PALAZZI DELL' ESEDRA
Gaetano Koch, 1886–1913
(Piazza della Repubblica)

Rome's silliest piazza centerpiece. There is some good sculpture in the Piazza della Repubblica, but it is not to be found at the fountain, whose voluptuous naiads caused a scandal when they were unveiled in 1911. The collection of water-spouting statues — marine monsters being wrestled into submission? — borders on parody, satirizing the whole idea of uniting myth, sculpture, and water. The naiad models are said to have been two sisters, both actresses from the musical theater of the day; in their old age they supposedly enjoyed daily walks to the fountain to admire their former selves, and the sculptor, a Sicilian, is said to have traveled to Rome once a year just to take them out to dinner.

When the piazza was constructed in the late nineteenth century, it constituted a critical element in a larger plan that affected growth within the city walls for decades to come. The overriding problem, of course, was traffic. In 1870, Rome was declared the capital of a newly united Italy, and the city's increased national importance produced a major growth spurt (from 1870 to 1900, the population more than doubled, from 200,000 to 460,000). A primary concern was access to the railroad station, which had been constructed in the 1860s just south of the ancient ruined Baths of Diocletian. The land around the station was mostly undeveloped, but at the point where urban buildup began — at the Largo Magnanapoli, several blocks east of the Piazza Venezia — the street plan was chaotic. Some sort of control was clearly needed to keep the chaos from spreading east, as the open area between the occupied city and the railroad station was gradually built up.

The solution was the first of Rome's modern traffic arteries: the Via Nazionale, a broad, straight avenue that stretched from the eastern edge of the existing city core to the Baths of Diocletian. The new thoroughfare provided access to the railroad station, created a spine around which development could logically grow, and took the pressure off the area's existing main road, the narrow Via del Quirinale atop the Quirinal Hill. More than a decade later, beginning in 1884, a similar avenue (the Corso Vittorio Emanuele) was cut on a more crooked path through the Campus Martius from the Gesù to the Tiber Bend, and these two new major arteries — approaching the central Piazza Venezia from opposite sides — at long last supplied the city with an east-west traffic axis comparable to the Via del Corso, the long, straight street that had provided north-south access since ancient times.

The circular Piazza della Repubblica serves as the eastern termination of the Via Nazionale, and takes its shape from the exterior walls of the ancient baths, which once formed a semicircular exedra where the square's curved palazzi now stand. The arcaded palazzi — designed in 1886 by the Neoclassicist Gaetano Koch, who also built the Palazzo Margherita (now the

American Embassy) on the Via Veneto — are massive in size, but their understated detail gives them an appealing air of gentlemanly restraint. Only at the buildings' ends, where pavilions step slightly forward to give a sense of emphasis and closure, is decoration allowed to enliven the design, and it is here, high up on the top floor, that the piazza's good sculpture can be found — strong, wide-hipped caryatids stand proudly forth, complemented by toga-draped male companions whose legs dangle casually over the edge of the pediment on which they so nonchalantly sit. The women stare straight ahead, as if standing military watch; the men survey the activity in the piazza below, and seem far more alive than the fountain's hyperactive naiads.

6-14 SANTA MARIA DEGLI ANGELI AND THE BATHS OF DIOCLETIAN

Baths: constructed 298–306 C.E.
Church: constructed by Michelangelo out of the intact remains of the tepidarium and frigidarium, 1561; renovated and decorated by Luigi Vanvitelli, 1749
(Piazza della Repubblica, northeast corner)

The ruins of the Baths of Caracalla are better known and attract more visitors, but the Baths of Diocletian possess something that their more famous rival lacks: a major structure that is still intact. During the Renaissance, the main hall of the complex was converted into a church, a transformation that protected the structure from destruction during later building booms. Though redecorated during the eighteenth century, the church is still the best place in Rome to get a feel for the scope and scale of the ancient baths.

Constructed atop a spur of the Viminal Hill, the Baths of Diocletian faced northeast, away from the hectic bustle of downtown; the rear wall of the complex faced the ancient city down what is now the Via Nazionale. The complex was the largest in the city, covering more than 32 acres. It occupied the area that today is bounded roughly by the Via Torino, the Via del Viminale, the Via Volturno, and the Via XX Settembre. (Remnants of the circular corner pavilions that terminated the baths' rear wall can still be seen on the Via del Viminale, where the remains of the pavilion wall protrude into the sidewalk, and on the Piazza di S. Bernardo, where the interior of the pavilion remains intact within the church of S. Bernardo alle Terme.) Capable of accommodating many thousands of bathers — estimates run as high as 9,000 — the baths offered changing rooms, steam rooms, hot baths, tepid baths, cold baths, an outdoor swimming pool, outdoor exercise areas, and (for the less energetic) gardens and libraries. Inside the central bath block, the most impressive space was the great hall of the frigidarium, with plunge pools at its four corners and an elaborate exterior façade to the north-east fronting on the swimming pool. It is this hall (along with the much smaller circular tepidarium to the southwest) that survived into the Renaissance.

In 1561, Pope Pius IV, overseeing the construction of the nearby Via Pia (now the Via XX Settembre), commissioned Michelangelo to transform the building into the church of S. Maria degli Angeli. Since the shell of the structure was intact, the main problem Michelangelo faced was the question of church orientation. Should the long axis of the hall serve as the church's nave and chancel, or as its transepts? The nave/chancel solution might seem the obvious answer, but Michelangelo rejected this option, and chose to use the hall as transepts. This choice required the addition of a new space to accommodate a high altar and choir; this new chancel space was created by breaking through the northeast façade and building on the land once occupied by the swimming pool.

The reasons behind Michelangelo's unorthodox ground plan were not recorded, and the matter has given rise to much speculation. As James Ackerman notes in *The Architecture of Michelangelo,* Michelangelo's considerations may have been practical (his plan made the chancel accessible from the cloister that was being constructed at the same time) or they may have been aesthetic (given the presence of the circular tepidarium, the only way to achieve bilateral symmetry in the overall design was to use the tepidarium space as a highly unorthodox vestibule/nave). "If the great hall had been used as a nave," says Ackerman, "the plan would have been grossly unbalanced by the large rotonda [the tepidarium] on one side. In making the rotonda the vestibule, every part of the church became symmetrical about the entrance-to-altar axis."

Whatever Michelangelo's motivations may have been, the resulting layout is distinctly odd. The church ground plan in effect reverses the usual Latin-cross spatial hierarchy; instead of the expected long nave with short transepts and chancel, it produces a short nave with a narrow chancel and extra-wide transepts. Visually, the transepts dominate the entire space, and the overall effect is more than a little disorienting.

When viewed as a Roman bath rather than a Christian church, however, S. Maria degli Angeli is not in the least disorienting, and its immense interior remains to this day one of the most exhilarating spaces in the entire city. The vast hall dwarfs all who enter; standing at its center, it is easy to see why so many medieval Romans thought that the ancient city had been built by a race of giants. In antiquity the effect of immense size would have been even more dramatic, for renovations to the interior raised the floor level some five feet.* But even at its reduced height the space is awe inspiring, and among surviving Roman interiors only the Pantheon is more redolent of the city's illustrious ancient past.

One final oddity should perhaps be noted in passing. American visitors entering S. Maria degli Angeli may be startled to feel themselves gripped by the unexpected conviction that the ancient Romans invented the railroad station. This reaction, though disconcerting, is entirely appropriate. The architects who designed the great American railroad terminals of the late nineteenth and early twentieth centuries — Grand Central Terminal in New York City, Union Station in Washington, D.C., and dozens of other structures — were passionate admirers of Classical architecture. They loved the huge scale and steamrolling power of Roman public architecture, and they consciously modeled their railroad stations on the great Roman baths of antiquity.

Nearby Museums: The vast and famous collection of Classical antiquities owned by the *Museo Nazionale Romano*, which was formerly housed in the remains of the Baths of Diocletian, is now on display in four separate locations, three of which are nearby (the fourth is the Palazzo Altemps, north of the Piazza Navona). The major part of the collection is in the nineteenth-century Palazzo Massimo alle Terme, a block southeast of the Piazza della Repubblica (at the end of the Via delle Terme di Diocleziano). A smaller display can be found in the *Aula Ottagonale* (Octagonal Hall), one block north of the Piazza della Repubblica (on the short Via Giuseppe Romita between the Via Cernaia and the Via Parigi). The epigraphic collection — written inscriptions and plaques — is housed in a modern building on the site of the baths, around the corner from S. Maria degli Angeli toward the Stazione Termini (entrance off the northwest side of the Piazza dei Cinquecento). If time is limited, the Octagonal Hall presents the most attractive option.

---

*During the Middle Ages, the hall was entirely stripped of its ancient decoration; when Michelangelo began the transformation of the building into a church, the space was an all but empty shell, and the only vestige of Classical antiquity remaining was the set of eight monolithic columns with Corinthian capitals that supported the naked vaults. All the rest of the current decoration — including the columns in the nave and chancel and the entablature that runs around the perimeter of the entire interior — was added during the eighteenth century. The eighteenth-century renovation did *not* (as so many guidebooks state) reorient the church; the much-repeated claim that Michelangelo's plan used the main hall as a nave is erroneous.

6-15 STAZIONE TERMINI
Entrance façade: Eugenio Montuori and associates, 1950
(Piazza dei Cinquecento, southeast side)

The modernization of Rome's nineteenth-century railway station began in 1938, but construction was halted by World War II, and the new front entrance — the last element to be completed — was not unveiled until 1950. At the time, the design was extravagantly praised for its clean lines and dramatic form, and the station quickly gained a widespread reputation as one of Modern architecture's greatest successes.

Today, opinion is more divided, if no less passionate. "The city of Rome could not have a more exciting entrance," says Renzo Salvadori in his *Architect's Guide to Rome* (1990). "The solution of the projecting roof is brilliant . . . the curved roof connects the concourse and the platforms in a functional way, creating fluid, well-lit spaces; glass walls, recourse to metal structures, well-defined details all help to make up 'the finest train station in Europe,' as it has been acclaimed by architectural critics." But Dennis and Elizabeth De Witt, in their *Modern Architecture in Europe* (1987), compare the building to Brasilia, Oscar Niemeyer's famously ill-fated Utopian attempt to obtrude a new Modernist capital city into the midst of the Brazilian jungle. "Like Niemeyer's Brasilia," they say, "this naive vision of the future is rapidly becoming an anachronistic image of the past."

Nothing looks up-to-the-minute once its minute has passed, and in part the negative judgment simply reflects the station's inevitably advancing age. But it also reflects a development that would probably have shocked the original architects: buildings like this, so thrillingly new and forward-looking in 1950, have today become so common as to look downright ordinary. Fashions change in architecture as in every form of art, and in the late twentieth century the Modernist movement — like so many architectural movements before it — has become the victim of its own success.

Whatever verdicts the future may bring, one particular design oddity is worthy of special note. For all its apparent simplicity, the monolithic office building that looms over the entrance concourse has a trick up its sleeve. From the station's piazza, the building's façade reads to the casual eye as ten stories tall — ten horizontal expanses of marble separated by nine bands of normal-sized windows. In fact, the building is only five stories tall, and its windows are half normal size. Thus the entire structure appears, at first glance, to be far more massive and much farther away than it actually is. Contrary to appearances (and received Modernist dogma), form is in this case quite divorced from function.

Designed by the eighty-six-year-old Michelangelo for Pope Pius IV, the Porta Pia is one of Rome's most distinctive architectural oddities. The gate's historical significance is described by James Ackerman in *The Architecture of Michelangelo:*

> The Porta Pia, erected on the inner face of an ancient fortified gate enclosure just north of the original Porta Nomentana, differed in function and form from any city gate of the Renaissance or earlier times. Though set into a defensive system, it was an indefensible thin brick screen barely strong enough to sustain its own weight — a record of the moment when the Romans abandoned hope of using their ancient walls as an effective defense against modern artillery. Furthermore, it faced inward, towards Rome, evading for the first time a tradition which from prehistoric times had turned gates toward the highway and countryside as an introduction to the city behind. Michelangelo's gate belongs more to the street than to the walls; it was pure urban scenography — a masonry memento of the temporary arches erected in the Renaissance to celebrate the arrival of princes, though without their triumphal connotations. The street, too [which was newly constructed], was more theatrical than utilitarian, since it crossed one of the least populated and congested quarters of Rome, where no important buildings were raised before the end of the century.

> Stylistically, the gate is a mixed bag. Its most powerful feature is the central portal, where Michelangelo appears not so much to have given his imagination free reign as to have let it run riot. The standard Renaissance aedicule — a doorway or window-surround consisting of a pair of flanking columns supporting an entablature topped by a pediment — is here utterly transformed. Heavily grooved pilasters, capitals that consist of blank spaces topped by single corbels supporting rows of wedge-shaped *guttae* (normally part of a Doric architrave), a curved arch sitting atop a rusticated flat-topped arch framing the opening, a curved pediment consisting of scroll fragments connected by a garland hanging beneath a dedicatory inscription, a secondary triangular pediment framing the primary curved pediment, slivers of secondary (and even tertiary) pilasters outside the primary grooved pilasters — all these are unorthodox in the extreme, and there is not a conventional

Classical element in sight. The end result looks almost as if Michelangelo had combined two (or perhaps even three) separate portal designs into a single composition, commingling their various parts with anarchic abandon.

From a High Renaissance viewpoint — a viewpoint that prized both historical correctitude and clarity of form — none of this makes any sense whatsoever. And the rest of the gate does not help matters. The blind windows and the bizarre ornaments above them* appear adrift in a sea of blank wall surface, the battlements sticking up to either side of the upper story look disconcertingly like toy angels, and the central crowning full-story tower — probably meant to be framed by obelisks on the empty pedestals at either end of the gate — looks isolated, exposed, and out of proportion with the composition below. Some experts (Ackerman among them) have suggested that Michelangelo's interest in the Porta Pia was limited to the central portal, and that the tower and some of the wall decorations were designed by others. Certainly the contrast between the central portal and the tower (which is actually a nineteenth-century reconstruction, the original having collapsed soon after it was built) suggests as much. Unconventional as the elements of the central portal may be, they interlock with each other in a way that creates a tense visual equilibrium, like a three-dimensional jigsaw puzzle that would collapse in a heap if any single piece were removed. The tower, by contrast, is merely applied decoration, similar in style but not in effect to the portal below.

Among Roman gates the Porta Pia is unusually idiosyncratic, but in its day the composition may not have looked quite so willful as it does today. As Ackerman explains:

> There are so few surviving Renaissance city gates that it is tempting to overemphasize the eccentric character of the Porta Pia. In old engravings and in illustrations to theoretical works we find that a certain fantasy was *de rigueur* in sixteenth-century gate design that would not have been admissible in other civic structures. Together with villas and garden architecture, gates were classified in the genre called Rustic. . . . The Rustic genre not only favored roughly finished masonry but encouraged unorthodox motifs, combinations of orders and materials. Serlio, in the preface to his book [*Libro estraordinario* of

---

*The eccentric upper ornaments are probably ecclesiastical in significance: patens (Eucharist plates) hung with lappets (priestly stoles).

1551], explained the fashion on the grounds first, that the public liked new things, and second, that the taste for inscriptions, arms, symbols, sculptural relief and statuary could be better accommodated by cautiously breaking the rules.

Michelangelo's breaking of the rules, of course, was anything but cautious, and the frank iconoclasm of the Porta Pia central portal exhibits his willingness to experiment at its most extreme. Modern art historians eventually came to view such eccentric experiments as a separate style — Mannerism — and its advent in the sixteenth century spelled the end of the High Renaissance in architecture.

Today the Porta Pia is the only important Mannerist gateway left on the Quirinal Hill, but — as contemporary engravings show — in the late sixteenth century the hill was covered with them (they mostly served as entrances to the gardens and vineyards of the aristocratic villas that dotted the area). Two of those engravings are reproduced below, and the designs illustrate with great clarity the eccentricities of the Mannerist style. The more conservative of the two appears at first glance to be quite straightforward, with plain Tuscan (Roman Doric) columns set against rusticated piers that flank a rusticated archway. But one feature of the overall design is distinctly odd: the way in which the upper seven voussoirs of the archway impinge upon the horizontal entablature, obscuring the central portion of the entablature entirely. Such an intrusion would never have been countenanced by the High Renaissance, with its emphasis on order and clarity. But the effect is distinctly enlivening; the rustication, which on the side piers is content to serve as background for the columns, seems to muscle its way forward above the arch, demanding and achieving front-and-center pride of place. The Escher-like visual ambiguity that results — how can rustication that is behind the columns end up in front of the entablature that the columns support? — is quintessentially Mannerist.

In the other engraving, the columns undergo a remarkable transformation, and seem to emerge from the background rustication as stacks of boulders, with only the fifth and seventh sections of the boulder-columns chiseled down to conventional column shape. Here (as with Michelangelo's Porta Pia), the overall design seems to combine and interlock two entirely separate compositions: a foreground composition consisting of the boulder-columns and the entablature they support (topped by a double-scrolled pediment) and a background composition consisting of the piers and arch behind the columns, which rise up behind the foreground pediment to support a second and higher entablature (with a second scrolled pediment) topped by grotesque disembodied heads on pedestals.

Sixteenth-century Mannerist gateways (since destroyed) on the Quirinal Hill near the Porta Pia: Villa Grimani (left); and Villa Sermoneta (right). (Engravings taken from the later editions of Vignola's book on the Classical orders, first published in 1562.)

These gateway designs are architecturally "mannered" in the sense that they abandon all pretense of historical correctitude; invention and ingenuity have taken over, and fantasy is favored over decorum. To the purists of the sixteenth century, such departures from the accepted canons of the day must have seemed at best wrongheaded, and at worst artificial, precious, and self-indulgent. But some of Michelangelo's contemporaries and immediate followers — in Rome the architects Giulio Romano, Giacomo della Porta, Giacomo da Vignola, and Giacomo del Duca — reveled in the freedom that Mannerism allowed, and their experiments were to lead, at the beginning of the seventeenth century, to a full-blown new style: the Baroque.

6-17 BRITISH EMBASSY
Sir Basil Spence, 1971
(Via XX Settembre, south side, just inside the Porta Pia)

Given the fact that its enclosing front fence/wall pulls off the depressingly perverse trick of making finished travertine look like rough concrete, it is tempting to dismiss Sir Basil Spence's 1971 British Embassy as just another overbearing example of 1960s Brutalism. But another view is possible, for Spence's building is brutal in a very Roman way. It shares many characteristics with the Roman palazzi of old: a visually unimportant ground floor, an emphatic *piano nobile* immediately above, an upper story that echoes the *piano nobile* in a diminished way, relentlessly repetitive window design, a heavy overhanging cornice at the top. As with all Modernist architecture, the vocabulary is rigorously non-Classical, but the façade's emphatic horizontality pays clear homage to the Palazzo Farnese and its many Roman imitations.

The result is not without irony. The Brutalist movement faded in part because a new generation of Contextualist architects hated the way in which the Brutalist buildings so often refused to acknowledge their surroundings — refused to merge comfortably with the existing (usually nineteenth-century) cityscape. But here Rome's longstanding tradition of ponderous palazzo design comes to the rescue, and the aggressively assertive look of the British Embassy seems, in its own twentieth-century way, to fit right in.

6-18   VILLA OF THE GARDENS OF SALLUST
40 B.C.E.
(Piazza Sallustio, north of the Via XX Settembre)

Another of Rome's majestic belowground ruins, particularly unexpected in the midst of this very nineteenth-century section of town. Best seen through the iron fence at the Via Sallustiano end of the Piazza Sallustio, the excavated (and now reused) remains here are part of one of ancient Rome's earliest and most famous suburban villas. The original structure dates from around 40 B.C.E., when Caius Sallustius Crispus retired as governor of Africa to write history, and to spend his vast fortune — plundered during his governorship — building the famous gardens that bore his name. Surrounding his villa, he created the most luxurious private park in Rome, covering the entire east end of the Pincian Hill and the valley below it, from the present-day Piazza Barberini north to the Porta Pinciana and east to the Piazzale di Porta Pia. The entire complex was later appropriated by the government for Imperial use (the emperor Nerva died here). The villa — much rebuilt — survived until 410 C.E., when it was burned by Alaric the Goth.

Vincenzo, Fausto, and Lucio Passarelli, 1963–1965
(Via Campania and Via Romagna intersection, northwest of the Villa of the
Gardens of Sallust; best approached up the Via Romagna and best viewed
from the sidewalk next to the Aurelian wall where the Via Campania
and the Via Romagna meet)

Like a great deal of Modern architecture at its best, Studio Passarelli's 1963 office-apartment complex functions as sculpture as well as architecture. The recessed ground floor serves as an all-but-invisible base for the two grandly massive objects that seem to float above it: three stories of glass cube and four stories of concrete crisscross. The two contrasting compositions are brilliantly combined, synergistically forming a whole that is far greater than the sum of its parts.

The building pays respectful homage to two giants of Modern architecture: Mies van der Rohe, who first conceived of the glass curtain wall in his architectural drawings of 1919–1920 (and who went on to design some of America's most influential glass skyscrapers in the 1950s), and Frank Lloyd Wright, who made the concrete cantilever famous in 1936 when he built Fallingwater, perhaps the most celebrated private residence of the twentieth century. The two conventions are usually felt to be antithetical in both appearance and spirit, the one hiding its structural skeleton beneath an outer skin of glass, the other stripping itself down to its bare structural bones. But opposites can sometimes attract, and their marriage here brings a whole host of basic architectural issues into vivid focus: office vs. home, work vs. play, simplicity vs. complexity, discipline vs. freedom.

The lower block presents the street with a face of controlled, dispassionate professionalism: sleek, urbane, strictly ordered, even-tempered. Surely the work inside must progress like clockwork, smoothly and efficiently. The upper block rejects these virtues utterly, exploding into a complicated, syncopated architectural rhythm full of spontaneity and surprise. Its jazzy jumble of verticals and horizontals, artfully bedecked with softening greenery, seems to promise interiors full of idiosyncrasy and invention. Each block sets off and comments on the other, yet they do not seem to intrude on one another, maintaining their strong separate existences through a skillful exploitation of the surrounding street layout (the lower block is situated parallel to the section of ancient city wall running along the Via Campania, while the upper block is given a twist and oriented parallel to the buildings behind, along the Via Sardegna).

As if all this were not enough, the building is graced with wit to boot. On the attic of the lower cube, the glass panels are occasionally popped out and replaced by unexpected concrete flower boxes, as if the upper stories were sending out feelers to explore the viability of the potentially hostile environment below. And on the Via Romagna side, the curtain wall commits heresy: a number of the glass panels have been omitted to frankly expose the structural element beneath, which turns out (logically enough) to be one of the vertical columns that emerges into the open air above.

It is a virtuoso performance, rigorous in its intelligence and dazzling in its skill. Modern architecture today is much decried for its all-too-evident failures — too many city streets turned bleak and inhuman by too much glass and concrete. But here glass and concrete are used with imagination and daring. The result is a triumph: a building that contrasts two famous Modern dogmas — *less is more* and *form follows function* — in a way that rescues the overused ideological catchphrases from sterile cliché and invests them with real meaning.

6-20 PORTA PINCIANA
Constructed ca. 400 C.E. as an improvement to the original Aurelian Wall
begun 271 C.E.
(At the north end of the Via Veneto)

Today metropolitan Rome extends far beyond the boundaries marked out by the ancient Aurelian city wall, and most of the wall's eighteen original gates now merely serve as incidental passageways between the bustle within and the bustle without. The Porta Pinciana is a rare exception. Topographically and visually, it still means something, despite its patched-up state. It interrupts the cityscape just where an interruption is needed: at the top of the Via Veneto, where the edge of the Ludovisi quarter abuts the southern boundary of the Villa Borghese, the city's most important public park. Like the Piazza Barberini at the Via Veneto's opposite end, the gate brings the street to an emphatic full stop; at the same time its archways offer tantalizing glimpses of unexpected greenery beyond. The result is antiquity redeemed — a perfectly placed ruin that stands proud amid the traffic, at once a resonant reminder of the city's past and an integral part of its present. The nineteenth-century city planners who laid out the Via Veneto area swept much away, but here they preserved, and preserved well.

Porta Pinciana.

6-21   VIA VITTORIO VENETO
Opened 1886

Poor Via Veneto. In the 1950s and 1960s, the stretch just below the Porta Pinciana was the most fashionable spot in the city. Celebrities and paparazzi turned the street into a boisterous sidewalk playground where café society reveled at night and nursed hangovers during the day, and for a decade the street overflowed with the trendsetters and trend followers so memorably satirized by Federico Fellini in his famously decadent 1960 film *La Dolce Vita.* But by the 1970s, fashion had moved elsewhere, leaving in its wake today's slightly forlorn collection of half-filled cafés and venerable old hotels. The street's reputation lingers on, but the magic, sadly, is long gone.

Still, the late-nineteenth-century hotel architecture looks better every year, and the street itself is a beauty — a long, wide, expansive, tree-lined double curve that sweeps down its hill with languid ease and style. In the 1980s, there were rumors of a trendy Postmodern face-lift, but thankfully nothing was done. Let the Via Veneto age gracefully in her own nineteenth-century way, and if fashion returns — the impeccably modish interior of the new Hotel Aleph on the nearby Via di S. Basilio is worth a look — she will be all the more impressive for having kept her dignity intact.

6-22 SANTA MARIA DELLA CONCEZIONE (CAPPUCCINI)
Felice Antonio Casone, 1626
(Near the bottom of the Via Veneto, north of the Piazza Barberini; the entrance to the crypt is halfway up the right-hand flight of stairs, the entrance to the church proper is at the top of the stairs)

The church, both inside and out, is plain and unprepossessing. But the crypt is the creepiest place in Rome. Laid with earth imported from the Holy Land, it originally served as the burial ground for the attendant monastery's Capuchin friars. Eventually the crowding problem became acute, and some 4,000 skeletons were dug up to make room for new graves. The five basement chapels were then covered from floor to vault with the disinterred bones, arranged into intricate patterns and formed into ornate niches, some large enough to contain the full skeletons of brethren known to have been particularly pious. No doubt the impulse to preserve the remains was natural enough, but the result is visually macabre and aesthetically grotesque — death as interior decoration. Appropriately, the whole grisly display is specially lit on All Saints' Day, the day after Halloween.

A different kind of *frisson* can be found upstairs: the tombstone of Antonio Barberini, set into the floor in front of the main altar. Barberini was the older brother of Pope Urban VIII, a cardinal, and the church's founder. His tombstone — undoubtedly at his instruction — commemorates none of these facts. It is a simple marker without name or date, bearing only the inscription *hic jacet pulvis cinis et nihil:* "here lies dust, ashes, and nothing."

6-23 PIAZZA BARBERINI
Fontana del Tritone: Gianlorenzo Bernini, 1643
Fontana delle Api: Gianlorenzo Bernini, 1644; new base, 1915

What a mess. The piazza's raw materials suggest another of Rome's great cityspaces: a pleasingly irregular shape, a famous fountain, a trident of narrow streets at the east end, all fed by two major and nicely contrasting traffic arteries — the dramatic, tree-lined Via Veneto, with its fine sweeping curves, and the straightforward, no-nonsense Via del Tritone, all big-city bustle. But nothing works. The architecture around the perimeter is relentlessly undistinguished, the amorphous traffic island in the center has no purpose other than to fend off the cars and buses that threaten Bernini's Triton Fountain, and the Triton Fountain itself is far too small to command the space it inhabits, looking lost and forsaken amid all the traffic.

Bernini deserves better. His fountain was commissioned by Urban VIII in

1642; stylistically, it may represent an artistic tribute to Michelangelo, for the triton's massive torso and heavy, workingman's hands recall the special power of Michelangelo's sculpture that his contemporaries aptly named *terribilità*. Thematically, the fountain is one of Bernini's typically elaborate literary conceits. It illustrates a passage from Ovid's *Metamorphoses* that describes the end of the Great Flood: Neptune's son emerges from a giant scallop shell supported by four dolphins to blow on his conch-shell trumpet and announce the receding of the waters. At the same time, the composition as a whole suggests a subsidiary and more specialized meaning. In the elaborate symbolic language of the day, the triton stood for literary immortality and the dolphin stood for princely benefaction; when linked with bees from the Barberini coat of arms, the symbols combine into a fancy piece of papal flattery: the triton is trumpeting the virtues of Urban VIII's Latin verse.

The smaller Fontana delle Api (Fountain of the Bees) is less elaborate, but no less badly displayed: it stands forlornly in the middle of the sidewalk at the bottom of the Via Veneto. Originally — and much more sensibly — it was set into the corner of a palazzo at the Via Sistina end of the piazza; in 1865, it was removed and the pieces put into storage, and in 1915, the upper portion was given a new base and installed at its current location. When it was originally constructed, the fountain scandalized the neighborhood, for its inscription stated that it had been erected in the twenty-second year of Urban VIII's pontificate, when in fact the twenty-first year still had several weeks to run. The superstitious populace tried to head off disaster by chiseling out the final "I" in "XXII," but to no avail — Urban died eight days before the year was out.

6-24 PALAZZO BARBERINI (GALLERIA NAZIONALE D'ARTE)
Carlo Maderno, 1625, with some features designed by Gianlorenzo Bernini and Francesco Borromini during construction after Maderno's death in 1629
(Via delle Quattro Fontane, south of the Piazza Barberini)

At long last, an important seventeenth-century palazzo that emphatically rejects the Roman tradition of monotonous regularity established by the Palazzo Farnese. With its arcaded entrance façade set between embracing wings, the Palazzo Barberini offers a more civilized and enticing welcome than any other palazzo of its era, and its expansive feel — it sprawls rather than looms — comes as a refreshing change.

The innovative design was probably due to the building's location. When it was first constructed, the palazzo stood at the edge of the inhabited city, and the nearby hedged gardens and open fields made the site more suitable for a suburban villa than an urban palazzo. So architect Carlo Maderno took as his model the garden façade of the Villa Farnesina, built by Agostino Chigi in 1508 (it was later purchased by the Farnese family) at the edge of Trastevere. But the Villa Farnesina was a relatively small structure, used only for afternoon retreats and the occasional evening *soirée;* the Palazzo Barberini is a full-blown palace — more than 150 rooms as originally constructed — designed to reflect the status and power of the Barberini family during the papacy of the Barberini pope Urban VIII. Maderno probably meant his design to offer the best of both worlds, and the result was the most individual of Rome's great papal palazzi. The building was never copied, however, and it remains to this day the city's only significant departure from the long tradition of monolithic palazzo design.

The façade's three tiers of arches with their varying Classical orders derive, of course, from that most famous of Classical models, the Colosseum. Such stacked arcades were not unknown in Renaissance palazzo design, but they were always employed in the interior courtyards, and never on an exterior façade. Here the variations in the orders — Doric on the bottom, Ionic on the middle, Corinthian on the top — give rise to parallel variations in the arches, which get progressively narrower and are given more elaborate frames as they rise. The effect is to draw attention away from the palace's two main blocks (the building is more or less H-shaped, and the cross-piece main façade is functionally its least important section), which makes the building seem a great deal smaller than it actually is.

On the palazzo's south side (around the corner on the right when facing the entrance façade), one architectural feature is worthy of special note: a pair of antique columns that help support a pair of semiruined archways that serve as a bridge from the palace to the gardens. The condition and design of the archways — half of one of the arches has fallen away and been replaced by a wooden drawbridge, the central voussoir of the other arch is noticeably misplaced, and the column capitals are slightly too small for their columns — suggest the remnants of a medieval structure built with antique spoils. In fact, the entire bridge was built during an extensive remodeling in the 1670s, and it constitutes the first architectural folly — a "ruin" constructed from scratch to look old and dilapidated — ever constructed in Rome. The supervising architect was the little-known Angelo Torrone, but the idea and design may have come from the seventy-nine-year-old Bernini, long a favorite of the Barberini family.

Today the palazzo is home to the *Galleria Nazionale di Arte Antica,* a national museum of mostly Baroque painting. The collection is large, and a portion of it is also on display at the Palazzo Corsini in Trastevere; on display here are works by (among others) Fra Filippo Lippi, Piero di Cosimo, Raphael, Bronzino, Tintoretto, El Greco, Caravaggio, Poussin, and Bernini. The most dramatic painting, however, is original to the palace and can be found in the grand salon: Pietro da Cortona's *The Triumph of Divine Providence and the Accomplishment of Its End through the Pontificate of Urban VIII Barberini,* one of the most elaborate (and pompously named) ceiling frescoes of the Baroque era. The museum is entered through the northern wing, up an elegant square staircase constructed by Bernini from an initial design by Maderno (the staircase's counterpart in the southern wing — oval rather than square, and even more elegant in its sinuous curves — was constructed by Borromini, probably in conscious competition with Bernini).

TOURS

7 – 9

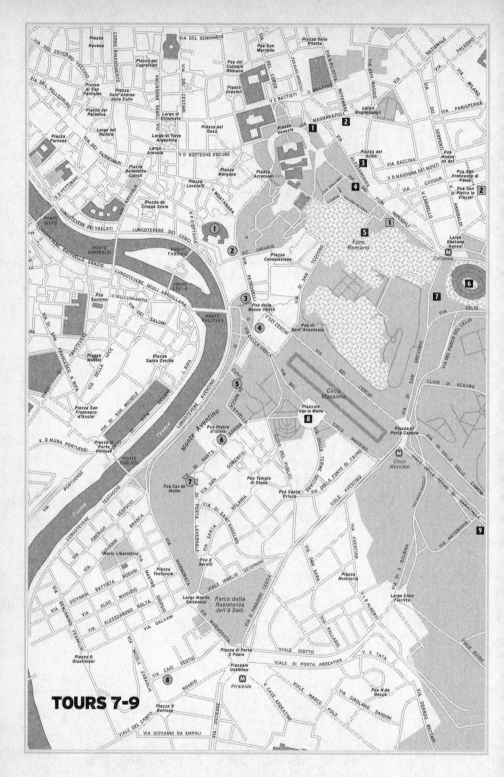

TOURS 7-9

MAP #3

TOURS 7 — 9

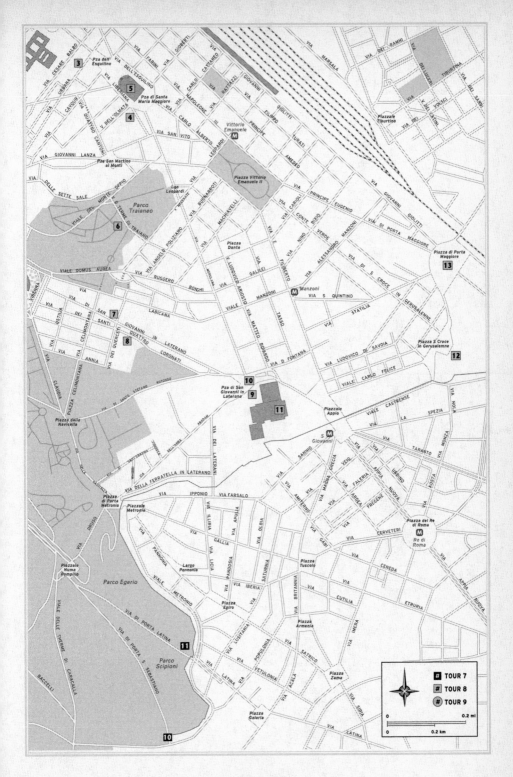

MAP #3

TOURS 7 — 9

TOUR 7

◆

ANCIENT ROME:
THE FORUMS, THE COLOSSEUM, AND BEYOND
FROM THE PIAZZA VENEZIA TO THE APPIAN WAY

Veduta del Colosseo
1 Anfiteatro Flavio, oggi detto Colosseo u Arco di Costantino Imp. 3 Fontana antica che fioriva nell'Orto di S. Maria la Nuova 9 Chiesa e Convento di S. Bonaventura

*T*ODAY THE MOST important squares of downtown Rome — the Piazza Venezia, the Piazza Colonna, the Piazza Navona, the Piazza di Spagna — are to be found to the north of the city's geographical center at the Capitoline Hill. But in ancient times it was the southern half of the walled city that was more important. The nerve center was the complex of forums on the south side of the Capitoline, bordered by the Colosseum (pictured above) and the Palatine Hill (the home of the emperors, and the source of the English word *palace*); beyond this hub lay the Circus Maximus and the Baths of Caracalla — both famous attractions — and the Appian Way. After the decline that came with the Middle Ages, the succession of downtown building booms that began in the Renaissance and ended with Mussolini's fascist projects of the 1930s destroyed most of the Classical remains in the northern half of the city. But a number of the ancient structures to the south, though ruthlessly plundered for building materials, did not entirely disappear. As a result, the southern half of the walled city is particularly rich in ruins, and the walk from the Piazza Venezia to the ancient city gate at the Porta San Sebastiano focuses almost exclusively on antiquities. The ruins are mostly of historical rather than architectural interest — unhappily, there is not much architecture left to be seen — but they are an integral part of Rome's past, and at times poignantly evocative of Rome's long-lost ancient glory.

7-1 COLUMN OF TRAJAN
Constructed 110–113 C.E.
(Off the southeast corner of the Piazza Venezia)

Usually constructed to celebrate military victories, freestanding columns were a tradition in ancient Rome. The Column of Trajan is the most famous, and with good reason. It is an artistic and engineering marvel: 125 feet high, consisting of 19 marble drums laid on top of one another with a spiral staircase hollowed out inside, the exterior carved with 155 scenes containing over 2,600 figures, all illustrating Trajan's two campaigns against the Dacians (inhabitants of modern-day Romania) at the beginning of the second century. Unlike the later Column of Marcus Aurelius, which is mostly given over to generic battle scenes, the Column of Trajan depicts specific historical episodes in almost cinematic detail, and their remarkable variety of incident makes the carvings one of the best historical records of Roman warfare techniques in existence. The column is also Trajan's burial site; by special dispensation of the Senate (since interment within the city walls was illegal), his ashes were placed inside the column's base after he died in 117 C.E.

The modern redevelopment of the area has isolated the column in an awkward space at the southeast corner of the Piazza Venezia, where it shares a site with the equally isolated churches of S. Maria di Loreto and SS. Nome di Maria. In its day, however, the column was a focal point in a much larger complex, all built at the same time: the roofed Basilica Ulpia and the open-air Forum of Trajan to the south, and two small multistory libraries closely flanking the column to the east and west (the emperor Hadrian added the final building of the complex — the Temple of the Deified Trajan — after Trajan's death, but its exact location, presumably to the north, has never been uncovered). An inscription at the column's base boasts about the new buildings and suggests that the height of the column was purposely calculated *ad declarandum quantae altitudinis mons et locus tantis operibus sit egestus:*

"to show how high a mountain at the site of such great works had been cleared away" (the site had been occupied by a saddle ridge connecting the Capitoline and Quirinal Hills, and apparently the entire ridge was carted away prior to construction).

Two of Trajan's successors were honored with similar commemorative columns. The Column of Antoninus Pius — constructed after the emperor's death in 161 C.E. — is now lost, although its elaborately carved base can be seen in the Vatican Museum; the Column of Marcus Aurelius, erected 180–193 C.E., survives intact in the center of its eponymous modern square, the Piazza Colonna. All three columns were erected at the height of Rome's power, but the tradition continued well into Rome's decline, as evidenced by the very last antique monument to be dedicated in the Republican Forum, a freestanding column commemorating the visit of the Byzantine emperor Phocas. Amanda Claridge's description of the monument in the *Oxford Archaeological Guide to Rome* suggests how far things had fallen since the glory days of empire:

> On the north side of the marble pedestal is an inscription: "To our best, most gracious, most pious lord Phocas, supreme commander in perpetuity, crowned by God, triumphant, emperor forever. Smaragdus, previously praepositor at the Palatium, patrician and exarch of Italy, devoted to his Grace because of the innumerable benefactions of his piety, the peace brought to Italy and liberty preserved, placed this shining statue of his Majesty on top of this sublime column to his perennial glory, on 1 August C.E. 608." Phocas was actually a brutal centurion in the Byzantine army who had usurped the throne in 602 by assassinating the emperor Maurice and his five sons, and was himself deposed and tortured to death in 610. As the careful wording indicates, Smaragdus only placed Phocas' statue on top, he did not claim to have built the column monument itself, which belongs to the fourth century, in its turn recycling an earlier monument taken from elsewhere.

Rome's best-known modern commemorative column is to be found at the south end of the Piazza di Spagna: the Column of the Immaculate Conception, constructed by Pope Pius IX in 1857 to celebrate the acceptance of the doctrine of the Immaculate Conception as official Church dogma (the doctrine refers not, as many non-Catholics assume, to the Virgin Mary's conception of Jesus, but rather to St. Anne's conception of Mary).

7-2 TRAJAN'S MARKET
Constructed 107–110 C.E.
(East of the Column of Trajan)

A remarkable urban set piece containing some 150 shops, constructed at the same time as the adjacent forum. Trajan's "market" was not a single unified building, but rather two separate market buildings enveloped by a terraced hillside neighborhood served by upper and lower streets connected by staircases. The overall plan is complex, but the basic shape of the exterior (lower) market was generated by the rounded exedra of the forum, which forced the narrow street outside the forum wall to take a semicircular detour around the forum's eastern end. Above and behind the two semicircular levels of shops — the roof of the first level constitutes the promenade of the second level — a second street serves the neighborhood's upper buildings, which include apartment houses and a second rectangular multistory market building containing still more shops. The whole is best viewed from the east side of the Via dei Fori Imperiali, but the neighborhood feel is best experienced by exploring the various parts at close hand (the entrance is on Via IV Novembre, up the steps a block east of Trajan's Column).

7-3 IMPERIAL FORUMS
Constructed 54 B.C.E. to 113 C.E.
(Via dei Fori Imperiali, stretching from the Piazza Venezia to the Via Cavour, with a visitors' center containing a model of the forums in antiquity south of the Via Cavour on the left)

As the Via dei Fori Imperiali makes its way from the Piazza Venezia to the Colosseum, it traverses — and partly covers over — the ruins of what was once the nerve center of Imperial Rome. During Republican times (the fifth to the mid-first centuries B.C.E.), the nucleus around which the city grew was the Republican Forum, at the base of the Palatine and Capitoline Hills. But as Rome's power and influence increased, the Republican Forum became more and more crowded, and by the last half of the first century B.C.E. it was bursting at the seams with both monuments and people. Additional civic space was clearly needed, and in 54 B.C.E. Julius Caesar began construction of the Forum of Caesar, a large open rectangle that was flanked on its long sides by covered colonnades and that served both as a public space and as a forecourt for a new temple dedicated to Venus. As the city and its empire continued to grow, Caesar's Forum became the model for four adjacent Imperial Forums, constructed over the next 150 years by the emperors Augustus, Vespasian, Nerva, and Trajan. It is these forums — civic centers used for both private and public business — that were located where the Via dei Fori Imperiali now stands.

Walking from the Piazza Venezia toward the Colosseum, it is still possible to map out the locations of the Forums from their ghostly remains. On the left side of the Via dei Fori Imperiali next to the Column of Trajan, four rows of reerected granite columns mark the location of the roofed Basilica Ulpia, constructed by Trajan and in its day the largest basilica in the city; next to it lies the open-air Forum of Trajan, the last forum to be constructed (106–113 C.E.). Beyond the Forum of Trajan lies the Forum of Augustus (chronologically the second forum, built fifty years after the Forum of Caesar), with its high, stepped platform supporting the Temple of Mars Ultor and its pair of curved exedrae flanking the temple. Next comes the Forum of Nerva (chronologically the fourth forum, and actually built by Nerva's predecessor Domitian but dedicated by Nerva in 97 C.E.); it was sometimes called the Forum Transitorum because it was in part a reclaimed street separating the Forum of Augustus from the Temple of Peace. The latter, often called the Forum of Vespasian and chronologically the third to be built, was a large open court with an outdoor altar constructed by Vespasian 71–75 A.D; nothing of it remains except a hall off one corner, which has been preserved as the church of SS. Cosma e Damiano. The Forum of Caesar has also disappeared completely, but its site (on the right side of the Via dei Fori Imperiali opposite the Forum of Trajan and the Forum of Augustus) is currently being excavated.

As civic improvements, the Imperial Forums were hugely expensive, in part because the land involved was already occupied by valuable houses and commercial properties that needed to be purchased prior to construction (the uneven far wall of the Forum of Augustus suggests that some properties were not available at any price). In addition to tax revenues, funds sometimes came from the sale of war plunder — the Temple of Peace and the Forum of Trajan were financed by the sale of spoils from the Jewish War and the conquest of Dacia, respectively — and sometimes (as was the case with Trajan's Basilica Ulpia) from the emperor himself out of his own personal funds. No expense was spared, and the scale of construction and opulence of materials was such that it could still impress the emperor Constantius when he visited the city from Constantinople in 357 C.E. Eventually, however, destructive earthquakes and even more destructive scavengers — not to mention Renaissance and Baroque architects — took their toll, reducing the remains to the ruin it is today.

Plans to improve the traffic connection between the Piazza Venezia and the Colosseum were first drawn up by Napoleon's city planners in the early nineteenth century, and were revised regularly during the next hundred years. Nothing was done, however, until 1932, when Mussolini ordered the recent excavations of the Imperial Forums filled in to make way for a wide, straight boulevard that (so the story goes) would enable him to see the Colosseum from his office balcony in the center of the Palazzo Venezia. The resulting Via dei Fori Imperiali is rigid and formal in feel — more Parisian than Roman, and utterly antithetical to Rome's ruling spirit, which is quintessentially un-Parisian in its exuberant preference for panache over pomp. Plans to shut down and reexcavate the stretch nearest the Piazza Venezia surface periodically, but so far they have come to nothing.

The Via dei Fori Imperiali was Mussolini's most notorious cityscape intervention, but prior to World War II, his city planners effected a number of other changes, mostly meant to improve traffic flow. These are usually identifiable by the modern buildings that were constructed along the widened avenues and open piazzas; they include the Via del Teatro di Marcello (on the opposite side of the Victor Emmanuel Monument, running south from the Piazza Venezia to the Piazza Bocca della Verità), the Viale Aventino (running south from the Colosseum to the Porta S. Paolo), the Piazza Augusto Imperatore (around the ruins of the tomb of Augustus), the Corso Rinascimento (running parallel to the Piazza Navona on its eastern side), and — most disastrous of all — the Via della Conciliazione (running from Hadrian's Tomb to St. Peter's Square). The unnecessary ruthlessness of some of these modernizations was not lost on subsequent generations, and since World War II the city within the walls has remained basically unchanged.

7-5   ROMAN FORUM AND PALATINE HILL
(Via dei Fori Imperiali opposite the Via Cavour; other entrances off the Via di S. Gregorio, the Via di S. Teodoro, the Via dei Monte Tarpeo, and the Via di S. Pietro in Carcere; admission to the Roman Forum is free, while the Palatine Hill shares an admission charge with the Colosseum)

FRAGMENT OF THE BASILICA OF MAXENTIUS
Construction begun 308 C.E. (also called the Basilica of Constantine)
(Inside the Forum, at the southeast corner, close to the Via dei Fori Imperiali)

What to say? There are no buildings to speak of here, only the odd ruin and the memory of buildings long vanished. But the memory is so strong — the feeling of historical past so poignant — that architecture is beside the point. It is the *place* that matters. And the place, for all its ghostly trappings, remains very much alive.

In part, the source of the site's special power lies in its terrain — a combination of hill and valley, abruptly abutting each other, that would make the landscape memorable even if the ruins did not exist. Centrality plays a role, too, both geographical and historical. The Palatine was the earliest of the Seven Hills of Rome to be inhabited, the spot where a small group of Iron Age settlers first put down permanent roots in the eighth or ninth century B.C.E. Over the centuries, as the settlement slowly expanded, it spread to the protective ring of hills nearby: the Capitoline to the northwest, the Quirinal, Viminal,* and Esquiline to the northeast, the Caelian to the southeast, and the Aventine to the southwest. But the Palatine remained the main settlement, and its importance was emphasized around 600 B.C.E. when the valley abutting the hill on the north — originally a marshy burial ground — was drained and put to civic use as a public forum. As the valley was gradually transformed, the settlement on the Palatine changed as well, becoming first a wealthy residential enclave and then the site of the Imperial Palace, home of the Caesars for three hundred years.

As the city and then the empire grew, the Forum became the nerve center of all things Roman, its buildings and commemorative structures serving every conceivable public purpose. Religious temples, assembly halls (most notably the Curia, meeting place of the Roman Senate), law courts, business exchanges — these were just the most important structures in what eventually became a densely packed complex of buildings, everywhere interspersed with an ever-increasing collection of monuments celebrating the spread of Roman control and influence throughout the entire Mediterranean world. By Imperial times, the crush in the Forum had become a significant problem, and the adjacent Forums of Caesar, Augustus, Vespasian, Nerva, and Trajan were all constructed to relieve the overcrowding. The new forums competed successfully with the old, but they never

---

*Today the Viminal Hill is barely noticeable — a slight rise in elevation between the Via Nazionale and the Via Cavour that is dominated by the Quirinal and Esquiline Hills on either side. Considerable confusion exists as to the extent of the Viminal in ancient times, since the mass of dirt and rock that was carted away to construct Trajan's Forum and its adjacent market is sometimes characterized (probably erroneously) as the westernmost slope of the original Viminal.

matched it in symbolic importance, and the ancient Via Sacra — the road that led from the Colosseum through the heart of the Roman Forum and then wound its way up the steep slope of the Capitoline to the most important building in the city, the Temple of Jupiter — remained the time-honored processional route until the end of the empire, and after.

During the Middle Ages, both the Forum and the Palatine were essentially abandoned; the Forum's last monument was dedicated in 608, a single freestanding column dedicated to Phocas, Emperor of Byzantium, perhaps in gratitude for his gift of the Pantheon to Pope Boniface IV. As the city declined, the center of the shrunken metropolis shifted to the Campus Martius (around the Campo dei Fiori), and the Forum became a backwater. By the twelfth century, the most famous public space in antiquity had become mostly private, taken over by Rome's factious noble families, who built so many crude defensive towers (*torri* in Italian) atop the ruins of the ancient buildings that the area became known as the *Campo Torrecchiano*. These towers, too, eventually fell, and by the eighteenth century, the Forum had changed its name again, becoming known as the *Campo Vaccino* for the cows that grazed in the grassy fields covering the ruins.

Today the Forum remains, at heart, an open field; despite extensive modern excavations, almost nothing of the ancient civic center survives. But the clamorous modern city has kept itself at bay, and by doing so it has, in its secular way, marked the empty site as sacred. More than anything else, it is this gesture of separation and sanctification that gives the site its special power, creating a zone of quiet that allows the ruins to cast their unique spell.

One recent change deserves special mention. In the late nineteenth century, when the Forum was systematically excavated down to its Imperial level, both the Forum and the Palatine became the special preserve of archaeologists and antiquarian sightseers (the astonishing depth of the excavation can be appreciated by noting the midair entrance door to the church of S. Lorenzo in Miranda, built into the Temple of Antoninus and Faustina next to the Forum's main entrance). In recent decades, the Romans themselves rarely visited, understandably disinclined to pay the hefty entrance fee. But in 1999, in anticipation of the deluge of pilgrims expected for the Jubilee year 2000, the city fathers did themselves proud. They opened up the Forum to all and sundry, free of charge, and turned the site into a city park (the Palatine shares an admission charge with the Colosseum). The native populace responded with enthusiasm, and the Forum quickly became a fair-weather promenade. The combination of native strollers, foreign tourists, and archeological explorers is altogether enlivening, and turns the site into a huge free-form piazza. After fifteen hundred years, the valley is once again a public forum.

Lovers of ancient history will want to assess the ruins in detail. Guidebooks may be purchased in the souvenir shop at the entrance; non-specialists, in exploring the ruins less systematically, should be sure to seek out the views from the Palatine. And everyone should seek out one ruin in particular: the Basilica of Maxentius (at the southeast corner, next to the enclosing fence and close to the Via dei Fori Imperiali). Only a portion of the side wall remains, but it is enough to give some idea of the original structure's vast size and steamrolling power. Its massive arches, towering high above, are magisterial and more than a little brutal, as if punched out by some giant Imperial fist. A further shock comes when the rest of the building's ground plan is puzzled out from the surrounding ruins. The three surviving arches, it turns out, are merely side and subsidiary spaces off the central longitudinal nave; the roof of the basilica's main space would have been half again as high. Even by today's standards, the space enclosed would be immense.

7-6 THE COLOSSEUM
Constructed 72–80 C.E.
(Piazza del Colosseo)

The most celebrated ruin in the world, and Rome's signature monument. Paris and London possess iconic architectural emblems as well — the Eiffel Tower and Big Ben — but these are nineteenth-century structures. Will they still be standing, even as ruins, in two thousand years? Lord Byron, writing in 1818 (and paraphrasing Gibbon, who was himself quoting from the writings of the Venerable Bede, a full thousand years earlier), declaimed the famous old prophecy:

> *While stands the Colosseum, Rome shall stand;*
> *When falls the Colosseum, Rome shall fall;*
> *And when Rome falls — the world.*

The ancient Greeks possessed semicircular theaters built into the sides of hills, but the amphitheater — a freestanding structure consisting of a central arena completely surrounded by tiers of seats — was a Roman invention.

According to the historian Pliny the Elder, its origins date back to an attention-grabbing architectural gimmick. In 53 or 52 B.C.E., one Scribonius Curio Iunior sponsored a series of theatrical shows and gladiatorial contests to honor his deceased father. To attract the public, he constructed two gigantic semicircular wooden theaters that were mounted on wheels and pivots. For the theatrical shows, the theaters were positioned either side by side or back to back; for the gladiatorial contests, the theaters were rotated on their pivots and pushed together to form an amphitheater. The story is apparently true — it occurs in Cicero as well as Pliny — but the twin movable theaters cannot have been the source of the amphitheater concept, since the stone amphitheater in Pompeii is known to date from 80 B.C.E. Still, Curio's idea was a clever one, and the spectators were apparently wowed: toward the end of the games they insisted on staying in their seats while the theaters were moved. Pliny comments, with astonishment, on the sight:

> What is most amazing is the madness of a mob bold enough to take its place in such treacherous, rickety seats. Here we have a populace that has conquered the earth, subdued the whole world, governed tribes and kingdoms, dispatched its dictates to foreign peoples, heaven's representative — so to speak — among mankind . . . all swaying on a gigantic moving contraption . . . supported by a couple of pivots, doomed to perish at any moment if the framework were wrenched out of place.

The Colosseum, of course, does not pivot; it is one of the most massively immovable stone structures ever built. But it is not as massive as it might be, and for one reason: the arch. The ancient Greeks knew about the arch, but for some reason they never exploited its architectural possibilities. The Romans were far more sophisticated in their engineering, and they recognized the special physical properties that an arch possesses. They understood that a round-topped opening is much stronger than a horizontal-topped opening, because forces pressing down on the stones of an arched opening are pressing the stones together, while forces pressing down on a rectangular opening are pulling the stones apart (stone, it turns out, is much stronger under *compression* — stress that pushes — than it is under *tension* — stress that pulls). So an arch can do much more architectural work than a normal doorway. Moreover, when arches are used extensively in the construction of a wall or a building, they create empty spaces that make the structure much lighter than it would otherwise be. The Colosseum has 240 arches on its exterior, and the interior — beneath the higher seats — is honeycombed with vaulted passageways. If those arches and passageways did not exist, the weight of the structure would be hugely and dangerously increased.

The Colosseum was begun by Vespasian in 72 C.E. and inaugurated by his son Titus in 80 C.E.; known in antiquity as the *amphitheatrum Caesareum*, it did not receive its current name until the Middle Ages (the term *colossus* originally referred to a colossal bronze statue of Nero that stood nearby). Oval in shape, it held some 50,000 spectators — ancient sources say 87,000, but this a doubtful number — who gathered to watch gladiatorial contests, wild-animal hunts, and public executions, sometimes all in one day. The arena in the center possessed a sand-covered wooden floor with trapdoors, beneath which ran a network of tunnels capable of accommodating several hundred noncombatant workers and backstage (really understage) technicians; high above and set into the amphitheater's outer walls, tall wooden masts supported the removable awning that shaded the tiers of seats from the sun. On the exterior at ground level, each of the 80 entrance arches was numbered — spectators were given passes telling them where to enter — with the central arches on the two long sides reserved for dignitaries and the end arches giving access to the arena in the center. Seating was rigorously controlled, with the emperor and the Vestal Virgins facing each other in central boxes on the long sides just above the arena. Senators sat at the same level, and above them the rest of the citizenry was placed according to rank, starting with the equestrian class (the rich) and ending with working-class plebeians, slaves, and women, who were segregated into separate sections at the very top. Most of the seating was plain stone, although senators were allowed to supply their own more comfortable chairs and the highest level contained tiered wooden benches supported by scaffolding. Amenities included interior fountains and lavatories; decoration included statues on pedestals in the exterior arch openings that faced the surrounding city.

Even during the Imperial era, the structure was prone to fire damage. August 23, 217 C.E. — the feast of Vulcan — was the date of the worst catastrophe, which began when the upper tier was struck by lightning. The strike was widely considered an omen of the impending death of the emperor Macrinus, who had (so the story goes) made the mistake of abolishing the horse races traditionally held in Vulcan's honor. Rossella Rea, in *The Colosseum,* gives a description of the disaster that followed:

The fire broke out in the balcony, the *portico in summa cavea*, where wood was used extensively for the plebs' seats and posts to support the awning. With these structures as fuel, the flames calcined [heated] the stone surfaces, and when cold water [from the rainstorm that followed the lightning] met the red-hot travertine, the cracking process accelerated. Metal clamps that anchored the blocks exploded, and the structures started to give out. As things began to collapse, the colonnaded portico fell into and devastated the *cavea* [the tiers of stone seats], and from there it sank into the arena, dragging everything along with it like an avalanche. Here the fire was refueled by the innumerable pieces of wood in the underground chambers. Before long, the amphitheater was transformed into an enormous brazier that kept burning until all combustible material was gone. For five years the monument was unfit for use, and it was during this time that it was largely reconstructed.

The last recorded gladiatorial contests took place in 434 or 435 C.E., but animal hunts continued until at least 523 C.E. By the later sixth century, however, a small church had been installed, and housing began to appear in the deteriorating archways. Around 1200, the Frangipane family occupied and fortified the structure; by the mid-1300s, the exterior wall of the south side had collapsed, and for the next four centuries the ruin was used as a quarry, supplying stone for new construction during the Renaissance and Baroque eras. Pope Sixtus V (1585–1590) wanted to turn the entire structure into a wool factory, but his plans were abandoned by his successors.

By the early nineteenth century, the stone plundering had stopped, and the Colosseum became famous as one of Rome's most luxuriously overgrown ruins. In 1855, the English botanist Richard Deakin published *Flora of the Colosseum,* in which he catalogued and illustrated some 420 different species of trees, grasses, flowers, and weeds to be found on the site (some of the species were so exotic that their seeds can only have been brought to the arena in the intestines of the wild animals imported from Africa and Asia in antiquity). All this wondrous mass of vegetation was cleared away in the 1870s, in the interest of archaeological preservation.

Architecturally, the Colosseum's influence was widespread. On the exterior, the sensible arrangement of the orders (Doric — actually Tuscan, since the columns possess pedestals — on the bottom, Ionic in the middle, Corinthian on the top, with Corinthian pilasters on the solid wall at the highest level) was widely copied, both during antiquity and during the Renaissance, when it became a favorite method of organizing multistory courtyards.* The interior design was even more influential. The eighty arched openings did not, as might be expected, merely conduct spectators to an oval aisle surrounding the arena from which they climbed to their seats. Rather, the arches led to a complicated system of interior passages and staircases that allowed access to the various seating levels from within the structure itself. This arrangement allowed for speedy and convenient exit through those same exterior arches — they were called *vomitoria* — at the end of the day, when most of the spectators needed to leave at the same time. The interior structure of the Colosseum was thus designed with a double purpose: not only did it support the tiers of seats, it also served as the primary means of traffic control, conveying spectators to and from their seats as directly as possible. It was a brilliant concept — the Modernist injunction *form follows function* inevitably springs to mind — and it is used in the construction of stadiums to this day.

7-7 ARCH OF CONSTANTINE
Dedicated 315 C.E.
(North end of the Via di S. Gregorio, between the Colosseum and the Forum)

The triumphal arch was a Roman invention, and its adoption in later times by later cultures has made it a familiar architectural convention. The Arc de Triomphe in Paris, Marble Arch in London, Washington Square Arch in New York — most large Western cities possess at least one such monument, and many possess several. Familiarity, in this instance, has bred acceptance, and few people nowadays give triumphal arches a second glance, much less a second thought. But a second thought will quickly lead to a third: architecturally speaking, the triumphal arch is a very strange beast indeed.

As William L. MacDonald describes it in *The Architecture of the Roman Empire*, the arched opening in a wall is a fundamental architectural form:

---

* One of the most famous variations is to be found in the English town of Bath. There, in 1754, the architect John Wood the Elder designed a magnificent set piece: a collection of three-story town houses whose connected identical façades faced each other around an open circle. Because Wood based the uniform façade design on the exterior of the Colosseum, he called his circle of houses "the Circus" (the modern distinction between *circus* and *amphitheater* not yet being in common use). The term *circus* caught on, and by extension came to mean (at least in England) any circular urban open space or roundabout ringed by buildings. Thus the center of London's West End — Piccadilly Circus — traces its name back to the Roman Colosseum.

Above all an arch is a mechanism of transit and transition. It sharply marks a division between two areas or places without sealing off either . . . [It] invites passage and suggests the presence beyond of a place different from that before it, of an experience in contrast to that of the present, near side.

This is all perfectly straightforward, and beyond dispute. But the effect of a *freestanding* arch is far from straightforward. As MacDonald goes on to observe, Roman triumphal arches were "in a pragmatic sense . . . paradoxical because they were openings one could walk around." Their voids do not signal transit (since the archways can be easily circumnavigated) and their solids do not signal transition (since the space on one side is no different from the space on the other). Moreover, the Classical columns, which in Greek buildings always functioned as vertical posts to hold up horizontal lintels, here serve no functional purpose whatsoever, and are merely applied to the surface of the structure as exterior decoration. In a triumphal arch, the Modernist doctrine that form follows function is entirely subverted.

Physical function, that is. Metaphorical function is another matter altogether. In fact, the purpose of the freestanding Roman triumphal arch was *entirely* metaphorical. Like the giant freestanding column, it was meant only to celebrate, commemorate, and memorialize. But the freestanding column at least retained some semblance of functional purpose, if only to support a statue of the individual whose life it honored. The triumphal arch abandoned functional purpose altogether. In inventing it, the Romans took a conventional architectural element with a useful function — a monumental portal used to mark an important entrance into a walled city or building — and isolated it for purely symbolic reasons, turning it into a passageway to nowhere. It is a very strange thing to have done, and where the original idea came from is anybody's guess.

The Arch of Constantine was dedicated on July 25, 315 C.E., and its large size and prominent location next to the Colosseum have made it the most famous antique arch in Rome, if not the entire world. The main inscription, carved into the attic on both sides of the arch and originally bronzed, makes the honorary purpose of the monument clear: "To the emperor Flavius Constantine the Great, pious and fortunate, who by divine inspiration and his own great spirit with his army avenged the state in rightful battle against the tyrant and all his faction, the Senate and the People of Rome dedicate this arch as a mark of triumph" (the "tyrant" was the emperor Maxentius, whose six-year rule ended when he was defeated by Constantine in 312 C.E. at the Battle of the Milvian Bridge on the northern outskirts of the city). Historically, the inscription is notable because it marks the beginning of a new kind of trouble for Rome: it commemorates, for the first time, a battle between factions within the empire, as opposed to a conquest of foreign peoples outside it.

Architecturally, the arch seems at first glance unexceptional. In its basic structure — a main archway flanked by a pair of subsidiary archways — it mimics the Arch of Septimius Severus, which had been constructed in the Forum more than a hundred years earlier (the other basic type of triumphal arch — with a single opening — is considerably less imposing, as witness the first-century Arch of Titus nearby, visible up the road leading into the Forum). But if the overall form of the arch is straightforward, its decoration is not. As Imperial monuments go, the carvings on the Arch of Constantine are downright bizarre.

As might be expected, the story of Constantine's campaign against Maxentius is depicted in detail, and can be followed in sequence on a six-part frieze that moves counterclockwise around the structure below the roundels and (on the long sides) above the subsidiary arches. Starting on the short side farthest away from the Colosseum, the six scenes depict: 1) The Departure from Milan; 2) The Siege of Verona; 3) The Battle of the Milvian Bridge; 4) The Entry into Rome; 5) The Address to the Roman People in the Republican Forum; 6) Distributing Largesse to the Roman People in the Forum of Caesar. Artistically, the frieze's most obvious feature is its lack of conventional realism. In the last panel, for instance, the scene is carved so that the size and stance of each figure reflects the figure's importance (the emperor in the center — he has lost his head — is largest of all and is shown in full frontal view). In this the panel foreshadows the religious mosaics of the medieval era, in which figures were routinely sized according to the prevailing ecclesiastical hierarchy.

Many other carvings on the surface of the arch celebrate Constantine's victory in a style similar to the frieze: winged victories (on the front of the column pedestals and in the spandrels of the central arch), soldiers and prisoners (on the sides of the pedestals), river gods (on the spandrels of the side arches), and allegorical depictions of the sun and the moon (in the roundels on the short sides). But the remaining carvings — and visually they are by far the most prominent — look quite different. The long-side roundels, the attic and archway panels, the freestanding attic statues — these are all carved with a realism and an attention to specific detail (and, some would say, a competence) that the six-part frieze depicting Constantine's campaign entirely lacks. One of the first documented references to this strange stylistic discrepancy was made by the little-known Mannerist sculptor Flaminio Vacca, who wrote in

1594: "I inspected [the attic statues] carefully, and am certain that they are by the same hand and the same master who fashioned the column [of Trajan]. It is certain that they were transported to the Arch of Constantine because on the base I saw clumsy carving done in Constantine's day, when the art of sculpture had been lost."

Vacca's hunch was correct: the most prominent carvings on the Arch of Constantine are *spolia,* removed from other monuments and reused. The best known is the Great Trajanic Frieze, a single continuous bas-relief of superbly carved battle scenes that was cut up into four panels and placed in the main-arch passageway and on the attic of the short sides of the arch; the bas-relief dates either from the reign of Domitian (81–96 C.E.) or Trajan (98–117 C.E.). On the long sides of the arch, the roundels above the subsidiary arches are thought to be slightly later in origin, probably dating from the reign of Hadrian (117–138 C.E.), while the eight rectangular attic panels are later still, from the reign of Marcus Aurelius (161–180 C.E.) or Commodus (180–193 C.E.). The roundels depict scenes of hunting (bear, boar, and lion) and scenes of religious sacrifice to various deities, while the rectangular panels depict scenes of the emperor at war (on the side away from the Colosseum) and at peace; exact dating is difficult because in every instance where an emperor is depicted, his head has been recut into a portrait of Constantine (or of Licinius, Constantine's coemperor for the first half of his reign). Last but most certainly not least are the freestanding attic statues, dating from the reign of Trajan and known to represent prisoners taken during Trajan's conquest of Dacia (modern Romania) in 102–106 C.E. Despite their militaristic origins the statues are not at all triumphalist in feel; against all expectations, the figures possess an air of quiet dignity — of nobility, even — that is genuinely moving.

The Arch of Constantine, then, is a composite Imperial monument of very strange pedigree indeed, and it has had connoisseurs and art historians scratching their heads for centuries. Why would Constantine — the most powerful man in the Western world — condone a large and prominent memorial to himself that was patched together out of bits and pieces taken from earlier monuments? Was he trying to associate himself in the public mind with the earlier emperors whose monuments he recycled? But if that was the case, why is his victory against Maxentius — the *raison d'être* of the entire monument — depicted in a frieze that constitutes a minor element in the overall scheme? Moreover, was the "primitive" style of the Constantinian carving (as opposed to the earlier carvings) a matter of choice or a matter of necessity? If it was a matter of choice, was the change in style meant to reflect the decline of paganism and the increasing power of Christianity? If it was a matter of necessity, what sort of crisis — aesthetic or economic or political — produced the "decline" in carving skills? Or was the "decline" merely a change in the aesthetic zeitgeist, a shift that favored legible symbolic meaning over naturalistic effect? And what, in the end, does the arch add up to? Is it a halfhearted aesthetic pastiche, the sign of a civilization in decline? Or was it a grand composite, a conscious attempt to combine the artistic style of the past with the new and more symbolic style of the present? The answers to these questions remain very much a matter of conjecture, rendering the Arch of Constantine not only the most famous of triumphal arches, but also the most puzzling.

7-8   PALATINE VIEW AND CIRCUS MAXIMUS
Circus Maximus: Sixth century B.C.E. and onward
(Piazzale Ugo la Malfa, at the midpoint of the Via del Circo Massimo)

The Palatine Hill is normally approached through the valley of the Roman Forum, but the most imposing view of the hill is on the opposite side. From the Piazzale Ugo la Malfa on the northern slope of the Aventine, the commanding height of the Palatine can be seen in its full force and power, with the remnants of the Imperial Palace complex overlooking the valley of the ancient Circus Maximus. Most of the palace proper is gone, but the substructure (a set of huge arches that served to extend the complex out from the hilltop) remains intact — a massive, hulking specter that seems to be watching still, waiting for the famous chariot races to resume.

The Palatine was the site of the original settlement traditionally said to have been founded by Romulus in 753 B.C.E., and it is Rome's central hill. Immediately to the west lies the easy Tiber river-crossing that gave rise to Romulus's village; to the north, east, and south stand the other six hills that were enclosed by the fourth-century B.C.E. city wall: the Capitoline, the Quirinal, the Viminal, the Esquiline, the Caelian, and the Aventine. This topography defined the character of the ancient city to a much greater extent than it does today. Early on, the hills attracted the rich — views and breezes — and *hoi polloi* were forced to make do with the lowlands, which were in many places flood prone. With the exception of several large baths, the great public buildings occupied the lowlands as well, mostly in two separate areas: on the far side of the Palatine, where the public forums and the Colosseum were ringed by all the hills except the Aventine, and outside the circle of hills to the northwest, where the Tiber bends to form the area

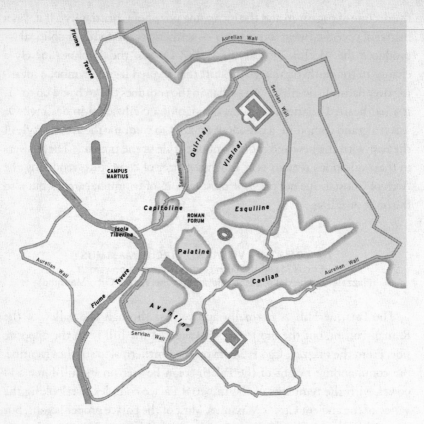

Map showing the Seven Hills and ancient walls of Rome.

known as the Campus Martius ("Field of Mars," named after the Roman god of war because it was originally used for military exercises). As the city grew, however, the geographical and topographical demarcations between rich and poor began gradually to disappear, and by the height of the Imperial era, most city neighborhoods had become decidedly mixed in character. As Richard Krautheimer describes it in *Rome: Profile of a City, 312–1308*:

> The only parts of the town given over exclusively to monumental structures were the Palatine, the Roman Forum, and the Imperial Fora, the latter segregated from the mundane world outside by huge walls. Elsewhere, the tenement houses pushed their way in between the great showpieces wherever there was space. They crowded around the fora and the Capitol, where one of the best-preserved rises as a ruin; they were at the foot of the Palatine facing the Circus Maximus, and oppo-

site the Column of Marcus Aurelius. They invaded the Campus Martius near the Mausoleum of Augustus and in the area between the temples on the Largo Argentina and the Pantheon; and they rose among the wealthy mansions on the Celian and elsewhere. True, parts of the town consisted almost wholly of tenement houses, primarily in the valleys between the hills, on the slopes, on the Tiber Island and the riverbanks, always threatened by floods. But by and large, tenements, mansions, and public monumental buildings were inextricably intermingled. Ground was expensive, and . . . public splendor, private wealth, and squalid poverty lived close together.

This heterogeneous mixture produced a metropolis that was noisy, crowded, and (at least to outsiders) verging on chaos. "Bread and circuses" is the famous formula summarizing Imperial policy for promoting stability within the city, and though glib, it is not without truth. "Bread" — in reality the grain from which bread is made — was imported in huge amounts and stored along with other goods in warehouses by the river, where at the peak of empire the docks are thought to have handled an average 2,700 tons of goods per day. As for "circuses," the most popular attractions were of course the chariot races held at the Circus Maximus and the gladiatorial contests held at the Colosseum. Buildings devoted to more elevated entertainments were located mostly on the Campus Martius: three theaters (the Theater of Marcellus, the Theater of Pompey, and the Theater of Balbus), a stadium for athletic contests (the Stadium of Domitian, now the Piazza Navona), an odeon for concerts (also built by Domitian), and two major baths (the Baths of Agrippa and the Baths of Nero). Beyond this, four more huge bath complexes served other sections of the city: the Baths of Trajan (on the Esquiline Hill overlooking the Colosseum), the Baths of Caracalla (in the valley between the Caelian Hill and the lesser peak of the Aventine), the Baths of Diocletian (on the Viminal Hill), and the Baths of Constantine (on the Quirinal Hill). At the center of it all rose the aristocratic Palatine, flanked by those two famous symbols of Roman business and pleasure, the Roman Forum and the Circus Maximus.

The Circus Maximus was probably established in the sixth century B.C.E., when Rome was ruled by kings. During Republican and Imperial times it was famous as the site of the *Ludi Romani* (Roman Games), a fifteen-day festival of chariot races, games, and military displays held every September. It could hold some 250,000 spectators, and it remained in use until the fifth century. During the Middle Ages it was ruthlessly plundered, and the site gradually reverted to open fields; in the nineteenth century, as the city expanded, the fields gradually filled up with industrial buildings, including a gasworks. These were cleared away in the 1930s, leaving only the tiniest of ruins — a small portion of an upper seating tier at the eastern end of the valley.

Today the circuit of the original racetrack is buried some thirty feet underground, and there is almost nothing to see beyond a grassy field and a ghostly shape. But the shape is enough. Size and situation impart to the site a sense of absence that is almost palpable, and in the end that sense of absence becomes — paradoxically — a powerful presence. Despite its emptiness, the Circus Maximus is one of the most evocative ruins in the entire city.

One final feature of the Piazzale Ugo la Malfa should be noted in passing: the *Roseto di Roma* — the Rose Garden of Rome — which abuts the piazza to the south and east, on both sides of the Via di Valle Murcia. As a commemorative plaque in the lower section explains, the *Roseto* was laid out on the site of what had been the city's main Jewish cemetery since 1645. In 1934, the burial grounds were peremptorily appropriated by Mussolini (for reasons of "public utility"), and most of the graves were moved to the Campo Verano cemetery, where a Jewish section had been established in 1895. The garden was established in 1950 to keep the site free of invasive buildings, and to atone, in some small measure, for the fascist desecration. Some two hundred varieties of roses are on display, and the lower section is the site of an annual beauty contest in which new varieties imported from all over the world vie for the top prize. Happily, winners are labeled, so it is possible to assess the outcome even after the competition is over. In May and June, when the garden is open all day, the *Roseto* is not to be missed.

7-9 BATHS OF CARACALLA
Constructed 211–216 C.E. with later additions
(Via delle Terme di Caracalla, near the Piazzale Numa Pompilio)

Once stupendous in scope and scale, the Baths of Caracalla were abandoned in the sixth century, and over the centuries the remains have suffered a double indignity. First, the complex was ruthlessly plundered for building materials during the Renaissance and Baroque eras (identifiable fragments are to be found as far away as the Duomo in Pisa). But these depredations produced an unexpected effect: in the eighteenth century the ravaged complex of buildings gained an entirely new fame as the most romantic ruin in Rome. In 1819, Shelley wrote most of *Prometheus Unbound* here, and he described the site in his preface:

This poem was chiefly written upon the mountainous ruins of the Baths of Caracalla, among the flowery glades and thickets of odoriferous blossoming trees which are extended in ever-winding labyrinths upon its immense platforms and dizzy arches suspended in the air. The bright blue sky of Rome, and the effect of the vigorous awakening spring in that divinest climate, and the new life with which it drenches the spirits even to intoxication, were the inspiration of this drama.

The second indignity — perhaps a necessary evil, but an evil nonetheless — came some fifty years later, when Shelley's glades and thickets were removed in order to preserve what remained of the ancient walls. Protest was immediate. Augustus Hare, the most respected of the nineteenth-century guidebook writers, grumbled that "one of the most beautiful spots in the world" had been transformed into a pile of archaeological relics "scarcely more attractive than the ruins of a London warehouse." More than a century later, in 2001, architectural historian Christopher Woodward seconded the complaint in his study *In Ruins:*

> You can uproot that alder tree, *superintendente,* erect more fences, spray more weed-killer, excavate and polish. You will preserve every single brick for posterity, and analyze the very occasional discovery of a more ornamental fragment in a learned publication. You will have a great many bricks, but nothing more. If archaeologists had arrived before Shelley there would be no *Prometheus Unbound.*

The remains today are indeed bleak in their naked isolation, but in Imperial times the Baths of Caracalla must have been one of Rome's mightiest structures. Constructed between 211 and 216 C.E. on an entirely new street behind the buildings that lined the Appian Way, the exterior walls enclosed gardens and were constructed to contain large curved exedras with central halls on two sides and tiers of stadium seats flanked by libraries on a third side. Bathers entered the main building through vestibules leading to dressing rooms, which in turn led to the most important spaces, including open courtyards for exercise, a circular and domed *caldarium* or hot bath, a smaller *tepidarium* or warm bath, a large vaulted main hall, and an open-air *natatorium* or swimming pool; subsidiary spaces and smaller suites of rooms probably contained cold plunges and steam baths.

Entry to the baths was free to Roman citizens, and the complex was capable of accommodating up to 10,000 visitors at one time. Such a huge number may seem almost inconceivable today, but in ancient times public bathing was far more than just a hygienic civility. The daily visit to the baths was a deep-rooted institution, a social and cultural custom so ingrained in the life of the city that it came to be considered an absolute necessity. Moreover, the great Roman bath complexes were symbolically important as architecture. Towering above the more ordinary buildings around them, they represented civic order in the midst of urban chaos. As William L. MacDonald describes it in *The Architecture of the Roman Empire*:

> That the bath was a vital theme of Roman urbanism, central to every-day existence, is certain. . . . Furthermore, baths reflected their urban context. Passing slowly through the varied chambers of a large munic-ipal bath, pursuing its lengthy route in stretches measured out by plunges, tubs, and pools, one negotiated a compacted, reductive ana-logue of the town itself. . . . For baths too had public halls, latrines, fountains, archways, and exedras, and sometimes peristyles as well, all set at different intervals along ritual armatures. . . . In this sense, baths were like abridged towns, with some of the chief sights of outdoor life provided indoors in sometimes sensational and luxurious form: town models free of the less desirable realities found outside. They were extremely popular, and the largest, with many amenities, provided splendid settings for leisure within nearly everyone's reach. Rising from ample, level concrete platforms honeycombed with cavities for heating and hydraulic installations, the bulky volumes and vaulted chambers of civic baths matched and perhaps surpassed official tem-ples as symbols of *romanitas*.

7-10 APPIAN WAY
MUSEUM OF THE WALLS
(Via di Porta S. Sebastiano, between the Piazzale Numa Pompilio and the Porta S. Sebastiano)

Strictly speaking, the Appian Way — the most famous of the ancient Roman roads — begins at the city walls. It still exists, but in a thoroughly modernized form; only the ancient ruins and tombs along the stretch close to the city mark it as especially old. Inside the city walls, however, a short stretch of the road's continuation (the Via di Porta S. Sebastiano) still retains something of its ancient character. Rarely visited by sightseers, it offers a unique sense of time travel.

The Porta di S. Sebastiano, now containing the Museum of the Walls.

The ten-minute walk down the Via di Porta S. Sebastiano from the Baths of Caracalla possesses two regularly alternating rhythms, one new and one old. The change in tempo is governed by the traffic light on the Piazzale Numa Pompillo, which controls the flow of automobiles entering the narrow, walled street. When traffic is flying by, the walls produce an echo-chamber effect, and the din is fairly thunderous. But as soon as the cars have passed, the urban clamor disappears completely, and the years seem to drop away. Amid the greenery and silence, the modern city seems to have vanished utterly. In ancient times, the land behind the walls on either side of the road was private gardens; after centuries of neglect, it is mostly private gardens again today, and it seems almost possible to hear, in the distance, the clatter of approaching chariot wheels.

And then, at the end of the walk, comes a perfectly placed surprise: a historical museum, one of Rome's smallest, set within the gate of St. Sebastian and devoted entirely to the subject of the ancient defensive walls that once surrounded the entire city. The walls' location, construction, and history are all explained in detail; maps, models, and labels in English as well as Italian (they talk of "engines of war") make the experience accessible even to the casual visitor. Some three hundred yards of ramparts are also open to exploration, as is the lookout post atop the tower over the gate. It is all admirably done, and deserves to be far better known.

7-11 SAN GIOVANNI A PORTA LATINA
Founded sixth century, reconstructed twelfth century
(Via di Porta Latina, just inside the city walls; from the Porta di S. Sebastiano,
either walk through the Parco degli Scipioni — there is a door on the right side
of Via di Porta S. Sebastiano about two hundred yards back toward the city
from the gate — or walk outside the walls along the Viale delle Mura Latine)

During the late eleventh and the early twelfth century, Rome saw something of a church-building boom. Several large and imposing new churches were constructed, some centuries-old smaller churches were rebuilt, and a number of brand-new parish churches were raised to serve localized congregations or monastic communities. None of these churches emerged from the Baroque era unchanged — the rage for modernization touched virtually every church in Rome — but in recent decades a number of the smaller churches have been restored to something approaching their medieval condition. The results vary, but at S. Giovanni a Porta Latina the medieval spirit has been wholly and happily revived.

Stripped of its Baroque "improvements," the church is simplicity itself. An arcaded narthex supports five stories of bell tower, and leads to a plain interior divided into nave and side aisles by two rows of antique columns, all scavenged from ancient buildings. Around the nave windows and in the chancel, ghostly, faded twelfth-century frescoes depict scenes from the Old and New Testaments (the nave), scenes from the life of St. Anne (the entrance wall), the Last Judgment (the chancel), and the symbols of the Four Evangelists, with the Twenty-Four Elders of the Apocalypse (the chancel walls).

This is humble architecture, but no less successful for its lack of aesthetic ambition. Given a few minutes' contemplation, the church and its setting create an aura of stillness and serenity that is limpidly pure, and that makes the glitter of most Roman Baroque churches seem mannered and overblown. Small touches, inside and out, contribute greatly to the overall effect of venerable sanctity: the trio of chancel windows filled with selenite instead of glass, the medieval wellhead in the entrance courtyard incised with the formula for baptism, the great towering cedar that seems to keep the bell tower company (at more than a century in age, it is the youngest thing in sight). The temptation to linger is irresistible. This is the most tranquil church in Rome, and its powerful subliminal message — that great age brings great peace — makes it one of the most memorable.

Under the shelter of the narthex, a special curiosity seems to have found a permanent home: a large and magnificent stone finial, beautifully carved.

It was designed by Borromini to sit atop the nearby Oratory of S. Giovanni in Oleo, still to be found a few yards to the south along the main road outside the church. The little octagonal building was constructed during the Renaissance — some say by Bramante — to commemorate the spot where St. John was supposedly boiled in oil, only to emerge as refreshed as from a bath. When Borromini restored the building some 150 years later, he added a frieze of roses and acanthus leaves around the exterior and the finial at the peak (now replaced by a copy).

TOUR 8

•

MEDIEVAL ROME:
THE ESQUILINE AND CAELIAN HILLS
FROM THE PIAZZA VENEZIA
TO THE PORTA MAGGIORE

Piazza di S. Giovanni in Laterano.
Obelisco, Fontana e Campanile, e portico laterale della Basilica di S. Gio. Laterano g Palaz Pontif. oggi Conservat. di povere Zitelle g Le Scale Sante g Sito g dell Obelisco A.

LIKE THE QUIRINAL Hill to the north, the Esquiline and Caelian hills (to the east and south of the ancient forums) were not heavily developed until the nineteenth century. But even at the city's lowest ebb during the Middle Ages, the area was not entirely abandoned, mostly because it was home to the pope (the medieval papal palace was located next to the first Christian church constructed within the walls, S. Giovanni in Laterano, pictured above). The well-traveled road from the papal complex to the Campus Martius ran through the valley between the two hills, and as a result the area contains the highest concentration of medieval churches in the city. It also contains — not incidentally — the most beautiful of Rome's medieval mosaics. Just as architectural historians search out the Baroque churches on the

Quirinal, art historians search out the mosaics of the medieval churches of the Esquiline, where the stylistic changes from late Classical to Byzantine to proto-Renaissance can be so clearly traced (the mosaics can usually be illuminated by coin-operated light boxes that are always worth some spare change). The churches themselves vary in size and pretension, but most of them possess a simplicity and venerability that contrasts sharply with their more modern surroundings and that may come as a welcome counterbalance to the Baroque profusions of the Campus Martius and the Quirinal.

8-1   SANTI COSMA E DAMIANO

Adapted in 527 C.E. from a hall in the first-century Temple of Peace
(Via dei Fori Imperiali, south side, between the Forum entrance and the ruins
of the Basilica of Maxentius; inside the church complex entrance, the church
proper is down the passageway at the far left corner of the courtyard)

The interior of SS. Cosma e Damiano possesses the expected nave, apse, and side chapels, but they all exhibit proportions that feel more than a little disconcerting. The nave seems far too short and the apse seems far too wide; the side chapels feel extraneous and superfluous, unintegrated into the overall space. The features of a normal longitudinal neighborhood church are all present, but in a form that looks visually off-key.

As so often in Rome, the explanation lies in the structure's origins. The room actually predates the Christian city by several centuries; it was originally constructed around 71–75 C.E. by the emperor Vespasian to serve as a corner hall — possibly a library — in his forum surrounding the Temple of Peace (the hall's circular vestibule, visible through the newly-installed window at the back of the church, is a later addition, dating from the fourth century C.E.). The hall did not become a church until the sixth century — the first of the ancient Forum buildings to be so transformed — and the side chapels were not added until the seventeenth century. Despite the religious transformation, however, the space still retains a good deal of its original secular feel — one of the few surviving examples of Roman public architecture in its more modest aspect, meant to serve rather than impress.

Today, SS. Cosma e Damiano's most prominent feature is of course the powerful mosaic that covers the upper part of the apse. It commemorates Pope Felix IV's transformation of the pagan building into a church dedicated to two Arab Christian martyrs, St. Cosmas and St. Damian, and dates (mostly) from the church's founding in 527 C.E.* As one of Rome's earliest major religious mosaics, it serves as a fitting introduction — almost an overture — to the famous collection of mosaics contained in the medieval churches that dot the Esquiline Hill. Taken as a group, the mosaics of SS. Cosma e Damiano, S. Pudenziana, S. Prassede, S. Maria Maggiore, and S. Clemente span the entire thousand-year era of the Middle Ages, and they demonstrate with great clarity the changes in artistic style during the period.

Appropriately enough for an introduction, the SS. Cosma e Damiano apse contains the most straightforward and forthright of all the medieval Roman religious mosaics. In the central area decoration is kept to a minimum. With the exception of the framing palm trees and the band of sheep representing Christ and the twelve apostles, the focus is all but exclusively on the seven figures: Christ in the center, flanked on the left by St. Paul; St. Cosmas (carrying a martyr's crown); and Pope Felix (carrying a model of the church), and on the right by St. Peter, St. Damian (with the satchel), and St. Theodore. The goal here is *theophany* (the visible manifestation of the deity), and the figures of Christ and his holy followers dominate the apse — indeed, the entire church — with great force. Stylistically, however, the Classical influence is still strong: the faces, postures, and drapery retain an individuality and a three-dimensionality that was later to disappear, as the stylized symbolic portraiture favored by the Byzantines came to replace the more naturalistic conventions of the pagan Romans. Because of this fundamental change in style, some experts consider the SS. Cosma e Damiano apse mosaic to be the last Classical work of art in Rome.

8-2 SAN PIETRO IN VINCOLI
Fifth century and later
(Piazza di S. Pietro in Vincoli, south of the Via Cavour; if the pedestrian tunnel at
the top of the steps off the Via Cavour at the Via dei S. Francesco di Paola is closed,
it is necessary to use the steps located farther east along the Via Cavour, at the
point where the Via Cavour, the Via Giovanni Lanza, and the Via dei Selci converge)

Famously disappointing. San Pietro in Vincoli ("St. Peter in Chains") is one of the acknowledged sights of Rome, and it probably attracts more visitors

---

*In the sixteenth century, Pope Gregory XIII replaced the figure of Pope Felix on the far left with a figure of his namesake Pope Gregory the Great; in the seventeenth century, the figure of Pope Felix was restored by Pope Alexander VII. The line marking the edge of the seventeenth-century restoration can be seen clearly in the row of sheep below the figures; although the restorers probably attempted to match the figure of Pope Felix (and the body of St. Cosmas, which had also been damaged by Pope Gregory) to the original design, they made no similar attempt with the replacement sheep, which are noticeably different in style from their much older compatriots.

than any other church in the city except St. Peter's. Art lovers know it as the site of Michelangelo's monumental statue of Moses, pilgrims know it as the repository for the iron chains that bound St. Peter, and tour guides know it as the only church in downtown Rome with an accessible parking lot big enough to hold ten buses at a time. The result is an endless stream of sight-seers. Throughout most of the day, whole busloads of visitors wait their turn to view the statue and the chains, and the drone of the tour guides lecturing their captive audiences never lets up.

The church itself offers no relief. Outside, the simple and dignified Renaissance portico (dating from 1475) extends an appealing low-key welcome, tour buses and souvenir stands notwithstanding. But the interior turns out to be inhospitable in the extreme. Gray floors, gray walls, gray columns, gray vault — the overall effect is cold, sterile, and bleak, with only the chancel and nave ceiling painting (early eighteenth-century Baroque) to relieve the prevailing air of drab and dismal gloom. Of all the benumbing architectural elements, the worst offender is probably the polished traver-tine floor; laid in the 1950s, it seems to suck all the life out of the beautiful-ly preserved antique nave columns, and its bland characterlessness infects the entire interior. By comparison, even the most overdecorated of Roman churches — the Gesù, say, or S. Maria della Vittoria — begins to look like a reasonable alternative.

The church was originally built in the fifth century, rebuilt in the eighth century (retaining the nave columns), and extensively restored in the 1470s. Its main purpose, however, has remained unchanged for the entire fifteen hun-dred years of its existence: to house the chains of St. Peter. By tradition there were originally two sets of chains (one from St. Peter's imprisonment in Jerusalem, the other from his imprisonment in Rome), but when the two sets were brought together to be deposited under the high altar — where they can still be seen — they miraculously linked themselves together into one.

The famous statue of Moses was originally meant for an entirely different setting — St. Peter's — and to Michelangelo its unveiling here in 1547 rep-resented a sad end to an ill-starred project that had dragged itself along through three decades of frustration and disappointment. The story begins hopefully in early 1505, when the imperious Pope Julius II summoned the thirty-year-old Michelangelo to Rome and presented him with a contract for the most highly prized commission of the day: the pope's tomb. A monument of unprecedented scale and complexity, the tomb was to be a huge freestanding four-sided structure, twenty-three feet by thirty-six feet at the base, with more than forty separate figures (Moses among them) set on three different levels. The pope approved preliminary drawings quickly, and in April of 1505, an ebullient Michelangelo set off for the quarries at Carrara to procure marble.

When he returned to Rome eight months later, Michelangelo found the pope preoccupied with an entirely different project. Discussions about where in St. Peter's to place the tomb had focused Julius's attention on the church itself — more than a thousand years old and badly in need of repair — and he had resolved, with characteristic audacity, to tear down the entire structure and build a new one. The immense new church was infinitely more grandiose in plan than the tomb, and Donato Bramante, the architect in charge, soon usurped Julius's attention (at least in Michelangelo's mind) to the point where the pope became completely inaccessible. When the foundation stone for the new St. Peter's was laid on April 18, 1506, Michelangelo had left Rome for Florence the day before, frustrated and disgusted.

A second papal summons brought Michelangelo back to Rome two years later, in the spring of 1508. But any hope of resuming work on the tomb was dashed when he was greeted by Julius's demand that he paint the ceiling of the Sistine Chapel in the Vatican Palace. Working virtually alone, Michelangelo spent the next four years creating the vast fresco cycle that was to become his most famous work.

Julius died in February 1513, and by May, Michelangelo had signed a new tomb contract with Julius's heirs. The partially redesigned tomb was now to be three-sided and set against a wall (the two lower levels, as shown on the drawing on the next page, are thought to be similar to one side of the original 1505 plan, for which no drawings survive). By 1516, only the figures of Moses and two bound slaves for the tomb's lowest level (now in the Louvre) were complete, and the project was hopelessly behind schedule. A third contract was drawn up, severely reducing the tomb in size: half as large as the previous design, with the number of figures reduced to twenty-two.

But even this scaled-down monument proved too ambitious. Other commitments intervened — the Medici pope Leo X put Michelangelo to work in Florence, the Farnese pope Paul III demanded a Last Judgment for the Sistine Chapel's altar wall — and Julius's heirs became so frustrated that at one point they threatened to sue. In 1532, a fourth contract was drawn up, calling for a wall tomb not at St. Peter's but at S. Pietro in Vincoli (Julius's titular church when he was a cardinal); in 1542, a fifth and final contract was signed, requiring Michelangelo to supply only three figures (the already completed Moses plus the smaller figures of Rachel and Leah to either side), with

Drawing for the Julius tomb project of 1513, showing the Moses figure seated and holding tablets at the middle level on the right.

the rest of the tomb to be completed by others. In 1542 — some thirty-five years after it had been so enthusiastically begun — the tomb was finally unveiled.

It is difficult to see it as a success. The tomb's various statues, all viewed head-on, are noticeably out of scale with one another, and even Michelangelo's own figures of Rachel and Leah seem dwarfed by the imposing Moses between them. And the placement of the figure of Moses is itself highly problematical. Howard Hibbard, in his biographical study *Michelangelo*, describes the statue's predicament:

As we see the imposing figure today, at eye level on the sadly reduced tomb, we get a theatrical and distorted impression — very different from seeing the statue from below, foreshortened and more distant. The *Moses* is now most effective from the front, with a clear opening of interest to our right since he turns his head, juts out his left arm, and tucks back his left leg. Michelangelo conceived the figure, however, for a position many feet above our heads that would have changed its entire proportion — the long face would have been foreshortened, the torso telescoped, the feet and left hand partially hidden. . . . Michelangelo understood the problems of perspective diminution, and apparent distortions in the figure of *Moses* chiefly derive from his desire to accommodate the statue to the position of the viewer below.

Three other sculptural peculiarities — one highly visible, the other two less so — should perhaps be noted. The pair of short, stubby horns growing out of Moses's head was a symbolic archaism consciously adopted by Michelangelo; the horns became an accepted attribute of Moses in medieval times, and they derived (as was known in Michelangelo's day) from a mistranslation of the Hebrew word for "rays of light" — halo — used to describe Moses's head. Less visible are the profiles of both himself and Julius II that Michelangelo is said to have hidden away in Moses's beard. The former is located on the chin just under the lower lip, the latter — larger but visible only in certain lights — farther down in the beard's trailing locks.

8-3   SANTA PUDENZIANA
Founded ca. 390 C.E. in baths constructed ca. 150 C.E.; much altered in the
sixteenth and nineteenth centuries
Façade: Antonio Manno, 1870
(Via Urbana, northwest of S. Maria Maggiore)

As its dramatically sunken location off the modern Via Urbana implies, S. Pudenziana is one of Rome's oldest churches.* The façade, however, is misleading; it dates only from 1870, when the outer courtyard and staircase were constructed and an undistinguished single-windowed sixteenth-century

---

*Legend has it that the church was founded in 145 C.E. by Pope Pius I on the site of the house of the Roman senator Quintus Cornelius Pudens; he and his daughters, Pudentiana and Praxede, are said to have been among St. Peter's first converts. Excavations suggest that the church actually dates from the end of the fourth century, when the hall of a small second-century Roman bath was renovated and consecrated.

façade was completely replaced. Only the columns flanking the entrance door and the carved frieze above it are genuinely medieval.

Given the nineteenth century's tendency toward bombast, the façade is unexpectedly (and refreshingly) understated. Its use of the Classical vocabulary is distinctly unorthodox, paying modest but sincere homage to the church's medieval origins and evoking a time when building a neighborhood church was more a matter of scavenging usable materials than creating an acceptable Classical design. The geometric marble frieze of the ground-floor entablature, for instance, rests not on a conventional architrave but on a simple carved ropelike coil; on the upper-story entablature, egg-and-dart moldings are pressed into similar unconventional service. All in all, it is a quietly effective evocation of the distant past, accomplished without too much show or too much Victorian fantasizing about the Middle Ages.

Most of the interior was thoroughly renovated during the Renaissance, but some of the older underlying structure can be seen where the walls remain in (or have been returned to) their original unplastered state. The strongest reminder of the church's founding, however, can be found in the apse: the oldest pictorial church mosaic in Rome, dating from around 390. The theme is *Jerusalem the Golden*. Enthroned in the center is Christ, sitting beneath a bejeweled cross and carrying a book bearing the inscription "The Lord preserves Pudentiana's church." To either side are the apostles, dominated by St. Paul (left) and St. Peter (right) about to be crowned with laurel wreaths by two women (possibly St. Pudentiana and her sister, St. Praxede). Enclosing the figures is the church of the Holy Sepulchre, with its gold-tiled roof; in the background rises the cityscape of Jerusalem. Above it all, looming through the clouds in the sky, are the mythological beasts that symbolize the four evangelists: the winged lion of St. Mark, the winged bull of St. Luke, the angel of St. Matthew, and the eagle of St. John (the latter two brutally truncated when the church was renovated in the sixteenth century).

The mosaic has been much patched over the centuries, culminating in a major restoration in the nineteenth century; the contrast between original and restored can easily be seen on the two sides of Christ's throne (the left original, the right modern), or in the heads of St. Peter and the apostle sitting next to him (the former original, the latter modern). The history of the mutilation that cut off the mosaic's outer sections is unclear. As Walter Oakeshott explains in *The Mosaics of Rome:*

> It would be of the greatest interest if we could know what was remaining of the mosaic of S. Pudenziana when it was restored by Renaissance

craftsmen. The scale and placement of the evangelist symbols ... shows that the original work was far larger than the existing remains at first sight suggest, and these huge symbols, showing against the deep blue sky, must have been an extraordinarily impressive feature. Not only was the vault of heaven represented far more grandly than the existing mosaic suggests, but also, no doubt, all twelve apostles were seated below. If the restorers cut down the size of the mosaic unnecessarily, they have much to answer for. But it is more likely that damage along all the edges was already too extensive to make full restoration possible.

Despite its problematical condition, however, the work remains unique among Roman mosaics. Though its theme is wholly Christian, its composition and detail remain thoroughly Classical. In the folds of the togas and the portraitlike features of the faces, the Rome of the Senate and the Caesars can still be felt very strongly; while Christ is shown in a formal, frontal pose that suggests symbolic manifestation, the other figures remain remarkably individualized, depicted in naturalistic postures that suggest a type of compositional realism — the Renaissance Last Supper paintings — that would not be seen again in art for a thousand years. Christian and pagan here coexist to a remarkable degree — in effect, the pagan laurel wreath has not yet been entirely supplanted by its successor, the Christian halo. These dual characteristics place the mosaic at a pivotal point in the history of art, on the very cusp between the ancient and the medieval.

8-4 SANTA PRASSEDE
Ca. 820 C.E.; extensively renovated in the thirteenth and sixteenth centuries
(Via di S. Prassede or Via di S. Martino ai Monti, south of S. Maria Maggiore)

The usual entrance is through the transept on the Via di S. Prassede, but the front entrance (through the courtyard off the Via di S. Martino ai Monti, but not always open) is far more impressive. S. Prassede was a product of the flurry of church-building that accompanied the Carolingian renaissance of the early ninth century, following the crowning of Charlemagne as Holy Roman Emperor in 800. The building was modeled on the original St. Peter's; though much smaller than Constantine's great church on the Vatican Hill, it followed a similar plan: a colonnaded courtyard leading to the church proper, which contained a nave with side aisles — in this case one aisle on each side rather than two — and a chancel with short transepts. As with so many medieval Roman churches, the interior has been much altered over the centuries. The piers that encase every third column and the nave-spanning arches above them were added for structural reasons during the 1200s; in the late 1500s, a major renovation and redecoration took place, completely transforming the nave (the column capitals were recarved, a cycle of wall frescoes depicting the Passion of Christ was installed, and the twenty-four small clerestory openings were replaced with the current large windows). Still, some traces of the original construction remain visible. In the nave, the "regularized" columns still support the original architrave, a collection of cobbled-together fragments taken from earlier Classical buildings, and in the chancel (on both sides between the crossing and the curved apse), the original scavenged columns are still intact. These latter may well be the most unusual Classical columns in the entire city: grooved shafts decorated with four rings of acanthus leaves, topped by capitals made of bunched laurel leaves held together with knotted string.

Happily, the renovations left most of the church's ninth-century mosaics intact. In the chancel, three separate compositions cover three separate surfaces (the outer surfaces of the two triumphal arches and the semidome of the apse), and the influence of the much earlier mosaics in S. Cosma e Damiano and S. Pudenziana is clear. At the peak of the arch facing the nave, Jesus and the twelve apostles (with a few additional figures) are enclosed by the golden Heavenly City, just as they were at S. Pudenziana; here, however, they are flanked by crowds of martyrs seeking admission to the holy enclosure, the doors of which are guarded by angels. On the arch attached to the chancel, the mythological beasts symbolizing the four evangelists again repeat a motif from S. Pudenziana; they are flanked by angels and two groups of elder confessors carrying gold crowns (in place of S. Pudenziana's laurel wreaths). In the semidome of the apse, the general composition is identical to the apse mosaic at SS. Cosma e Damiano, although the identity of some of the figures has changed (St. Peter and St. Paul on the right and left are now paired with St. Pudentiana and St. Praxede, respectively, and flanked by St. Zeno and Pope Paschal I, the builder of the church, whose square halo indicates that he was still alive when the mosaic was created).

Though the thematic content of the compositions is all but identical to the earlier mosaics at S. Pudenziana and SS. Cosma e Damiano, the artistic style is quite different. The informal naturalism of the figures in S. Pudenziana and the dominating force of the figures in SS. Cosma e Damiano are nowhere to be seen. Instead, it is the overall composition that gives the mosaic its power. The figures within the composition tend to be less individual, less detailed, and more two-dimensional than in the earlier mosaics, but this decrease in realism is mitigated by an increased emphasis on pattern, color, and design. The alternating use of rows and groupings of figures and the alternating use of background colors (both blue and gold for the outer arch, gold for the inner arch, and blue for the apse vault) are especially effective design devices; the treatment of clothing drapery — particularly in the two groups of elders carrying gold crowns on the inner arch — becomes almost abstract in its reductive but elegant simplicity.

This change in style is sometimes viewed as a decline, and linked with the city's own decline from a center of empire to a provincial capital with papal pretensions. But another explanation is possible. When S. Prassede was built, artistic influence from the east — Byzantium (modern Istanbul), where Constantine had moved the Imperial capital in 330 C.E. — had been growing for centuries, and the Iconoclastic Controversy of the eighth century (the bitter dispute over whether religious art and imagery should be banned because it violated the "graven images" prohibition contained in the Ten Commandments) had deeply divided the church. In the end the iconic imagery was allowed, but the need to separate the symbolic from the real remained a continuing concern. Thus, mosaic images of Christ and the saints may have become less naturalistic not so much from a decline in talent among artists as from the artists' desire to make it clear that the images were religious symbols meant for instruction rather than miraculous portraits meant for veneration. The result of this changed emphasis was a growing bias toward the abstract and the decorative that produced an entirely new style — a style that was to culminate, several centuries later, in the magnificent apse mosaics of S. Maria Maggiore and S. Clemente.

One other medieval work in S. Prassede should not be missed: the Chapel of S. Zeno, off the right aisle. Built by Pope Paschal as a mausoleum for his mother, the tiny room was conceived and constructed as a single three-dimensional mosaic. The design is crude compared to later work, but the effect — a space that wholly envelops the viewer in glittering mosaic — is unique.

8-5 SANTA MARIA MAGGIORE
Main structure ca. 435 C.E., bell tower 1377
Façade: Ferdinando Fuga, 1740
Nave mosaics: Fifth century
Apse mosaics: Giacomo Toriti, ca. 1300
(Piazza di S. Maria Maggiore)

S. Maria Maggiore.

As its name suggests, S. Maria Maggiore is one of Rome's major churches, notable for its large size, its great age, and its special ecclesiastical status as a patriarchal basilica.* Architecturally, however, S. Maria Maggiore is less important, and more than a little deceptive. Although the original building is still mostly intact, over the centuries it has been so elaborately dressed up — redecorated on the inside and augmented on the outside — that its origins are all but impossible to discern.

According to legend, the church was founded on August 5, 358 C.E. The day before, a childless Roman couple decided that they would bequeath their considerable wealth to the Church in honor of the Virgin Mary. During the night they were both visited by visions of the Virgin, who instructed them to

---

*The four patriarchal basilicas — large churches assigned to the patriarchs of the great medieval ecclesiastical provinces — are St. Peter's (assigned not, as might be expected, to the pope, but instead to the Patriarch of Constantinople), St. Giovanni in Laterano (the medieval home of the pope, and assigned to him as Patriarch of the West and Bishop of Rome), S. Paolo fuori le Mura (assigned to the Patriarch of Alexandria), and S. Maria Maggiore (assigned to the Patriarch of Antioch); St. Lorenzo fuori le Mura is sometimes granted equivalent status because it is assigned to the Patriarch of Jerusalem. These five churches plus two more — S. Croce in Gerusalemme and S. Sebastiano — make up the famous "Seven Churches of Rome," the traditional itinerary of pilgrims seeking plenary indulgence (exemption from Purgatory).

use their fortune to build a church at a location that would be marked by God atop the Esquiline Hill. The next morning, when they approached Pope Liberius to tell him of their vision, they discovered that he had experienced an identical dream. Climbing the Esquiline Hill, they found a patch of unmelted snow that had mysteriously fallen the night before, marking the spot where the church was to be built. (Historical evidence, it should be noted, suggests that the church of the legend cannot be the same building as the existing church, which is known to date from the fifth-century papacy of Sixtus III; the earlier Liberian church did in fact exist, but it has now vanished utterly and its location has never been established.)

From the outside, only the fourteenth-century bell tower — the tallest in Rome — suggests S. Maria Maggiore's venerable origins. The rest of the medieval structure is entirely obscured by a thick encrustation of later building that began during the Renaissance and culminated in Ferdinando Fuga's entrance façade of 1740. The challenge facing Fuga was a difficult one. When he received the commission to replace the existing Renaissance portico with a new façade, the Baroque buildings flanking the church entrance were already in place, and were not to be disturbed; in addition, the thirteenth-century mosaics on the upper portion of the old façade had to be preserved and (if possible) remain visible from the piazza below.

Fuga's solution was daring: he created what amounts to a façade without walls. Starting with a conventionally shaped Roman churchfront of the Gesù type (wide lower story and narrower upper), he reduced the design to bare essentials, stripping it down to the point where it became a decorated architectural skeleton. The result is not entirely successful; the façade's eight openings tend to dominate the composition — in most lights they read as gaping holes — and the eye is too much drawn to negative space rather than positive mass. The Baroque detailing, however, is unfailingly first-rate. The four pediments are boldly carved and crisply decorated; the statuary and the balustrades (which Fuga continued on the side palaces at roof level to unite the overall composition) enliven without obtruding. The Ionic capitals of the ground-floor columns are particularly fine, with cushions and unusual diagonally placed scrolls that look as if they are being compressed — almost deformed — by the pressure of the entablature above them.

The interior, among Roman churches, is second only to St. Peter's in its combination of size and splendor. Most of the splendor dates from the Renaissance and later — the ceiling is said to be gilded with the first gold brought by the Spanish from the New World — but the church's medieval mosaics remain mostly intact. They fall into two broad categories: the mosaics along the upper nave and on the arch facing the nave above the high altar, which date from the fifth century, and the mosaics of the apse and apse arch, which date from around 1300. The earlier mosaics — along the nave a series of forty-four small panels, seventeen of which were destroyed in later renovations — represent scenes from the Old and (on the nave arch) New Testament. The later mosaics incorporate some individual scenes as well (illustrating the life of the Virgin Mary), but these scenes are clearly secondary to the main mosaic on the vault of the apse, showing the Virgin Mary enthroned and crowned by Christ in heaven.

The contrast in style is marked. The individual panels of the earlier mosaics are clearly didactic in purpose, and run along the nave and across the nave arch almost as if they were lines of text spelling out their religious lessons in pictures rather than words. In the later mosaic, however, the dependence on storybook linearity has all but disappeared. As Walter Oakeshott describes it in *The Mosaics of Rome*:

> What is new in the [apse] mosaic is its magnificent composition. . . . In the twelfth-century mosaic of the Enthronement of the Virgin in S. Maria in Trastevere, the contrast with this later version of the same theme is remarkable. The two figures in the center of that Enthronement mosaic [in S. Maria in Trastevere] are an uneasy pair because they are eccentrically placed. Christ had to occupy the central position, and so the Virgin was placed to one side. Here, however, the pattern is balanced, and composed in a roundel that is precisely central and is superbly supported by groups of angels, whose sweeping wings reach out into the field, the dark, spreading pinions forming a striking contrast with the gold. They press forward in eager worship, and the two groups, built up high on either side, give formal significance to the central roundel, as if they were holding it up as a mirror or window which made it possible to see into the depths of heaven. Behind them [to the left and right], the standing figures . . . are composed on a scale that blends well with the huge arabesque [of the Tree of Life], leaving the predominance of the central figures unchallenged, and providing an excellent foil to the intricacies of the miniature Classical detail [in the horizontal band below their feet representing the four rivers of Paradise].

The subsidiary elements of the design — the bejeweled fan at the vault peak (representing the vault of heaven), the diverse collection of birds and small animals inhabiting the spiral branches of the Tree of Life, the crowds of elders on the arch that frames the apse vault — are no less impressive. Clearly, aesthetic effect was an important consideration, and the skill with which the mosaic's various design elements are combined into a single unified composition makes this the most artistically satisfying of all the Roman mosaics.

Aside from the mosaics, almost nothing of the original medieval structure is visible. Even the columns of the nave are not as they once were (originally an unmatched miscellany scavenged from other buildings, the columns were "regularized" by Fuga in the eighteenth century to give the nave a uniform appearance). Surprisingly, all this renovation and modernization has had a perverse but not unpleasing effect: to the casual eye the interior now looks *older* than it really is. Mosaics apart, S. Maria Maggiore today could almost pass as an ancient Roman basilica of the Imperial era, restored to its original glory. It stands as an architectural reminder that the basilican form — today so firmly religious in connotation that the names of some of its basic parts (nave, apse) apply only to churches — was not religious in its origin at all. The first basilicas that rose in the Roman Forum were entirely civic in function, used for business and legal proceedings rather than religious services, and the "basilica" as a building type was invented by the pagans of ancient Rome, not the Christians who followed them. The standard antique form was rectangular, with a high central nave, lower side aisles, and a curved apse appended at the center of one side (sometimes the short side, as in later Christian churches, but also sometimes on the long side).

It was the first Christian emperor, Constantine the Great, who adopted the basilican form for Rome's earliest churches, thereby insuring that Christian religious architecture would for the next millennium — until the revival of Classicism that was the Renaissance — reject the example of the pagan religious architecture that preceded it. It was also Constantine who added to the basic basilican form (at the original St. Peter's) the one feature that set Christian basilicas apart: the transept, which in most churches crosses the nave near the apse end, thereby transforming the basic shape from rectangular to cruciform. S. Maria Maggiore repeated this transformation in its own history: the fifth-century basilica was rectangular in shape, and the transept was inserted in the late thirteenth century (and later rebuilt, around 1600, into the pair of large and elaborate Baroque side chapels that form the transept today).

Notable Works of Art: Considerable treasure is buried beneath the church, in the form of a new and exemplary museum; entry is off the right aisle, through the baptistry and then through the gift shop (where a ticket is purchased), and then outside and down the stairs just to the right. The exhibits include engravings illustrating the history of the church and paintings by Sodoma and Beccafumi (among others), but the top prize must certainly go to the extensive and beautifully displayed collection of liturgical objects and papal vestments. The minute, meticulous workmanship — particularly the sewing — on many of the objects is extraordinary, with the Barberini bees putting in a fine appearance on a set of red-and-gold parati worn by Pope Urban VIII in the seventeenth century.

8-6 FROM S. MARIA MAGGIORE TO SAN CLEMENTE
Arch of Gallienus: ca. 10 B.C.E.
Auditorium of Maecenas: ca. 25 B,C.E.
Baths of Trajan: 104–109 C.E.
(South of S. Maria Maggiore, along the Via Merulana and the Via Mecenate)

The walk down the Esquiline Hill from S. Maria Maggiore south to S. Clemente is a relatively long one, made to seem even longer by the surroundings — an area of town that is for the most part homogeneously and anonymously modern. Still, there are a few antique surprises along the way that can be searched out to alleviate the monotony. One block down the Via Merulana, the Via di S. Vita leads off to the left toward the Arch of Gallienus, a well-preserved city gate — it afforded passage through the early Servian wall, not the later Aurelian wall — that dates from the time of Augustus. Farther along the Via Merulana (at the Largo Leopardi) is the so-called Auditorium of Maecenas. The building (which possesses a modern roof) originally stood in the gardens surrounding the residence of Maecenas, a wealthy friend of Augustus and neighbor of Pompey; it probably served as a summer dining room or banquet hall, with water cascading down the seven curved steps that form the most unusual feature of the interior. Down the Via Mecenate, the Via del Terme di Traiano (on the right) leads to the pavilion-flanked gates of the modern Parco Traiano. Inside (and spread around the park to the right) are the remains of the Baths of Trajan, which were constructed on top of the *Domus Aurea*, or Golden House, a palace complex built by Nero after the great fire of 64 C.E. The *Domus Aurea* complex was immense — it covered some 20 acres, and included an artificial lake where the Colosseum now stands — but most of it was either built over or destroyed soon after Nero's assassination.

8-7 SAN CLEMENTE
Twelfth century, with remains dating back to the first through fourth centuries
(Via di S. Giovanni in Laterano, east of the Colosseum and west of
the Via dei Normanni)

Since 1677, the church of S. Clemente has been in the care of the Irish Dominicans, and it was one of their number, Father Joseph Mullooly, who in the mid-nineteenth century made a stunning discovery. At the time, S. Clemente was thought to be one of the oldest churches in the city; a reference in the writings of St. Jerome dated its founding back to at least the fourth century. But Father Mullooly, who was Prior (second in command to the Abbot) of the attached monastery, became convinced for architectural reasons that the existing church could not be the original one, and in 1857, he began to excavate and explore the ground beneath. What he found was astonishing: three separate layers of buildings, comprising the ruins of a fourth-century church that had been built atop a complex of pre-Christian buildings that had in turn been built upon the rubble of buildings destroyed in the Great Fire of 64 C.E. Excavations continue to this day.

As its splendid apse mosaics suggest, the upper church is medieval in origin. It dates from the twelfth century, and was built directly atop the ruins of the earlier church, which was probably seriously damaged or destroyed when Rome was sacked in 1084 by the Norman soldiers of Robert Guiscard. At the time, the city was caught in the armed struggle between Emperor Henry IV, who had occupied both St. Peter's and the papal quarters at S. Giovanni in Laterano, and Pope Gregory VII, who had fled to the protection of the Castel S. Angelo. Ironically, it was the rescuing Normans — defenders of the pope against the emperor — who pillaged the city, which had mostly been given over to the control of the emperor by a war-weary populace.

The mosaic on the flat outer surface of the apse arch presents a conventional miscellany of images, with the holy cities of Bethlehem and Jerusalem at the bottom, figures representing prophets and apostles at the sides, and symbols of the four Evangelists flanking a roundel showing Christ the Pantocrator (all-ruling judge) at the top. The mosaic on the curved vault of the apse, however, is more unusual, given over almost entirely to a single design conceit: the Tree of Life. With its fifty swirling coils of vines — each vine bursting at its end into a light-giving blossom that is half flower and half lamp — the mosaic possesses a decorative quality that is almost abstract. Some of the subsidiary details are distinctly odd as well. Given the medieval artistic tendency to size religious figures according to their importance, the central motif of Christ on the cross is not nearly so dominant as might be expected (the figure of Christ is here no larger than the flanking figures of the Virgin Mary and St. John). And the cross itself grows out of an unexpectedly prominent acanthus plant — a pagan rather than a Christian motif, familiar from Corinthian capitals all over the city. Finally, the images interspersed among the vines (which include scenes of everyday life above the band at the base, church fathers preaching the Word higher up, and birds symbolizing souls ascending to heaven at the top) include a row of celebratory *putti* that recall pagan Cupids as much as Christian cherubs. Given the mosaic's twelfth-century origin, where did these anomalous Classical elements come from?

They came, in all probability, from the apse of the earlier church. The Tree of Life mosaic is most likely a replica of a mosaic dating from late Classical times that was destroyed in the sack. In the twelfth century, when the later church was constructed, the new mosaic was probably created as a conscious throwback to a much earlier time — a reverent replacement for a lost work that was contemporary with the apse mosaic in S. Pudenziana (ca. 400), the oldest surviving pictorial church mosaic in Rome. Compositionally, it may not be as original or as sophisticated as the apse mosaic in S. Maria Maggiore (which dates from the same period), but its intricacies — the oddities of detail buried in and around the swirling branches — set it apart, and make prolonged exploration a particular pleasure.

The earlier church (reached down the stairs in the sacristy off the right aisle) was somewhat wider than the later church, and in its current configuration seems to possess two right aisles. In fact, the wall between these two aisles supports the outer wall of the upper church (the wall was originally a row of columns separating the nave of the lower church from its single right aisle); the second interior wall was later intruded into the ruined nave of the lower church to support the right-hand arcade of the upper nave. The current brick piers and squat brick arches in the lower nave are of course modern, constructed to replace the 130,000 cartloads of supporting rubble that were so laboriously removed by Father Mullooly and his successors.

Excavations on the third level of building (reached downstairs at the far end of the left aisle of the lower church) uncovered yet another church, but of a very different sort: a Mithraic* temple complex of the late second or early third century, built into a converted Roman house dating from the late first century. Three separate rooms have been excavated; they are thought to be the temple pronaos (the entrance-room, now partially filled by the supports for the lower church apse above), the triclinium (the dining room, containing a Mithraic altar that originally would have stood in the entrance-room), and the "schoolroom," (probably used for instructing prospective initiates). The unexcavated portion of the temple complex extends to the west, away from the church; the structure to the east (directly underneath the church, and separated from the temple complex by a narrow alleyway) is a "palazzo" that could well be the original "titular" church — a plain domestic residence in which Christian worship was illegally practiced during the first century.

Both the lower and upper churches possess some notable art, but one set of paintings perhaps deserves special mention: the frescoes in the Chapel of St. Catherine (at the beginning of the left aisle of the upper church, by the side entrance door), which include a crucifixion above the altar, scenes from the life of St. Catherine of Alexandria on the left wall, and scenes from the life of St. Ambrose on the right wall. The frescoes date from the first years of the Renaissance (ca. 1430), and are the work of Masolino da Panicale, probably assisted (and outdone) by his brilliant pupil Masaccio.

Masaccio was a revolutionary artist who died young (at age twenty-seven), but not before he had become famous. His best-known work is the cycle of frescoes in the Brancusi Chapel at S. Maria del Carmine in Florence, but the technique that so stunned the artistic community of his day is visible here as well. Compare, for instance, the figure of St. Christopher (on the left entrance pier) with most of the other figures in the chapel. St. Christopher's body — and particularly his face and bare left leg — possess a sculptural presence that most of the other painted figures in the chapel distinctly lack. That presence is due, primarily, to the fact that Masaccio has chosen to paint light as well as mass. He has painted (and shaded) the figure of St. Christopher so as to suggest — and to suggest emphatically and dramatically — a single, strong source of light within the world of the painting but beyond its frame. This was a new idea, and the skill with which Masaccio could carry it off

---

*In the Roman world, the worship of Mithras — originally the Persian god Mithra — sprang up in the second century C.E., and for a time paralleled Christianity in its growth and importance. Mithraism was especially popular among Roman soldiers (it emphasized loyalty to the emperor, and its rites rigorously excluded women); it flourished particularly during the period 180–217 C.E., when it was encouraged by the emperors Commodus, Septimius Severus, and Caracalla. After the emperor Constantine (306–337) adopted Christianity as the official state religion, Mithraism quickly declined.

astonished his contemporaries. They flocked to see his work, and his successors built on his achievement for centuries to come.

8-8   SANTI QUATTRO CORONATI
Church: Ninth century, rebuilt late eleventh century
Cloister: Early thirteenth century
Oratory of Saint Sylvester: 1246
(Via dei SS. Quattro Coronati, south of S. Clemente)

Architecturally, Quattro Coronati is something of a puzzle. If approached from the west (along the Via Capo d'Africa or the Via dei Querceti), its protruding apse looks impregnable — more like a fortress than a church — and offers no admittance. If approached from the north or east (the proper entrance, off the Via dei SS. Quattro Coronati), its sequence of spaces is highly unusual: an outer courtyard followed by an inner courtyard followed by the church proper, which consists of a short nave leading to a wide and deep apse that is markedly out of scale with the rest of the building. What is going on here?

The original ninth-century church, it turns out, covered the inner courtyard. But that structure was devastated in 1084 by the Norman soldiers of Robert Guiscard (who at the same time destroyed or seriously damaged S. Clemente, several blocks away). When the church was later rebuilt, the old apse was repaired, but the rest of the church was reconstructed on a much smaller scale, leaving part of the old nave open to the sky.

The church's thirteenth-century cloister, on the other hand, is entirely intact (off the apse to the left; ring the bell if the door is shut). As Roman cloisters go, it is simple and unpretentious, with a primitive cornice running around the garden walls above the arcade, antique fragments set into the interior walls (the architectural fragments inside the cloister's subsidiary chapel of S. Barbara are especially picturesque), and a medieval fountain primitively carved with the faces of two disconcertingly cuddly lions. What is most memorable about the cloister, however, is an intangible: the deep meditative calm that reigns over the entire space. Ten minutes here can refresh the spirit as effectively as the ice-cold waters of the street fountains outside refresh the body.

Memorable as its cloister is, Quattro Coronati has a further and even greater treasure in store: the Oratory of St. Sylvester. The Oratory is located off the church's inner-entrance courtyard; after exiting the church proper, enter the door in the center of the wall to the left. The entrance to the Oratory is then on the right; if the door is locked, the key may (usually) be obtained by ringing the bell next to the turntable set into the wall on the left and leaving a small donation. The key should be returned to the turntable.

As architecture, the Oratory is not in the least distinguished: a chapel-sized room that is primitive in design and crude in construction. But the medieval frescoes painted on the walls are extraordinary.

Beginning above the entrance door and moving from left to right, the frescoes illustrate the legend of the conversion of Constantine, the first Christian emperor. Constantine, so the story goes, had been stricken with leprosy, and his pagan advisers, desperate for a cure, had instructed him to bathe in the warm blood of children newly executed outside the city gates. But — as the frescoes show — when Constantine arrived at the site of the planned sacrifice, he was confronted by the children's mothers, and he was so moved by their anguished pleas that he refused to carry out the slaughter. That night, in a dream, he was visited by two unknown men, who told him that the Christian bishop Sylvester possessed the power to effect a cure with water rather than with blood. The next day Constantine dispatched three messengers to go in search of Sylvester, who had fled Rome in the face of Constantine's persecution. The messengers found Sylvester on Mount Saratte and implored him to return to the city. Upon his return, Sylvester listened to the emperor's story, and then called for portraits of the apostles to be brought forth; Constantine, recognizing the two strangers in his dream as St. Peter and St. Paul, knelt down in acknowledgment of Sylvester's authority. Constantine then offered himself to Sylvester for instruction and was cured of his leprosy by the holy water used in his rite of baptism. After his cure, Constantine, in gratitude, accompanied Sylvester to the site of the children's reprieve, where he knelt and presented the enthroned Sylvester with the papal tiara. Then Constantine, on foot, led Sylvester, on horseback, back through the gates of Rome, which was from that day forth the seat of Imperially sanctioned papal power.*

The frescoes date from the mid-thirteenth century, some nine hundred years after the events they relate supposedly took place. The story they tell contrasts sharply with the other (and better-known) conversion legend, in which Constantine was granted a vision of a cross of light in the sky just before his victory over his rival Maxentius at the Battle of the Milvian Bridge in 312 C.E. Both legends center on bloodshed, but they could hardly be more

---

*The fragments of frescoes remaining on the opposite wall illustrate two related legends: Pope Sylvester demonstrating the power of the Christian God to a group of rabbis by bringing a dead bull back to life, and St. Helena, mother of Constantine, identifying the true cross at the excavations at Golgotha, where Christ was crucified.

different in their underlying messages: war in the name of God on the one hand, refusal to shed innocent blood on the other. In the Sylvester story, the moral message is far more powerful, for the events that lead to Constantine's conversion are triggered not by military prowess but rather by compassion in face of human suffering — Constantine's refusal to slaughter the children.

The frescoes contain a political message as well, for the source of the story they describe is a famous written historical relic: the so-called "Donation of Constantine," an ancient document that discusses as historical fact Constantine's abdication of power in favor of Pope Sylvester. The earliest known papal citation of the document dates from 1054; thereafter the document became increasingly important as a political weapon, and was cited over and over again to support papal claims of temporal power over the emperor and the feudal nobility in the late Middle Ages. But in a famous exercise of scholarship that heralded the Renaissance in historical studies, the Donation was assailed as a forgery by Lorenzo Valla in 1440. His attack set off a heated controversy, and the issue remained under dispute for some two hundred fifty years. Today the document is universally regarded as false, and is thought to date from the eighth century, around the time that Pope Leo III and the Frankish king Charlemagne joined forces to establish the so-called Holy Roman Empire.

For anyone viewing these frescoes today, however, the political message will be secondary. It is the narrative itself that dominates the painted images, a narrative that is all the more moving because it centers not (as is usual in Christian art) on a religious act performed by a saint, but instead on a humane act performed by a pagan. By conventional aesthetic standards the drawing is far from sophisticated; the "realism" of Renaissance painting is still a very long way off. But the cycle's emotional message is no less powerful for being primitively expressed. The passionate desire to impart knowledge, and the conviction that the knowledge imparted will lead to faith and grace, can be felt very strongly here. As a result, this little room is the best place in Rome to experience the long Italian tradition of religious fresco storytelling.

8-9 SAN GIOVANNI IN LATERANO BAPTISTRY
Fifth century C.E.
(Piazza di S. Giovanni in Laterano, southwest corner)

The freestanding octagonal Baptistry of S. Giovanni in Laterano is often said to be the site of the baptism of Constantine, the first Christian emperor, but the claim is doubly erroneous: Constantine was most probably baptized on his deathbed, close by his new capital of Constantinople (modern Istanbul in Turkey), and the existing Lateran Baptistry is not Constantine's original structure. It is a replacement structure built by Pope Sixtus III (432–440) that rests on the circular foundations of the earlier Constantinian building.

The interior's most striking feature is the octagonal column screen that surrounds the green basalt font. Eight columns with varied capitals (Ionic on the four columns aligned with the entrance door, Corinthian on the two columns to the left, and Composite on the two columns to the right) support a pseudo-entablature — really a collection of carved moldings — that runs around the entire central space, and that in turn supports a second set of smaller columns below the dome. The screen does double duty; not only does it support the dome, it also focuses attention on — and creates a comfortingly protective spatial shell around — the central font. It is a simple architectural gesture, but a remarkably effective one. The rest of the interior decoration is predominantly Baroque, although some fine medieval mosaics survive (most notably in the apse of the Chapel of SS. Seconda and Rustina, out the far door opposite the entrance and to the left, which contains an elaborate fifth-century vine scroll that may have been the inspiration for the Tree of Life mosaic in S. Clemente).

8-10   PIAZZA DI SAN GIOVANNI IN LATERANO
Obelisk: Fifteenth century B.C.E.
Palazzo del Laterano: Domenico Fontana, 1586–1589
Tribune of Benedict XIV: Constructed 1743

As Roman piazzas go, the Piazza di San Giovanni in Laterano is far from memorable, in part because its most important structure — the patriarchal basilica of S. Giovanni in Laterano — is hidden away in plain view. The huge church is oriented sideways to the square, and its presence is doubly concealed, first by the placement of its front façade at right angles to (and facing away from) the piazza, and second by the sixteenth-century Palazzo del Laterano, which is attached to the side of the church and which protrudes into the square, effectively splitting it into two unequal parts. The obelisk in the middle of the piazza functions as an effective view-stopper on the approach along the Via Merulana, but its strength as a central focal point is all but completely undermined by the haphazard organization of the piazza perimeter.

Still, the square itself is of considerable historical interest. For more than a thousand years, the Piazza di S. Giovanni in Laterano was home to the pope, and the Basilica of S. Giovanni in Laterano was (and still is) the pope's official church. This special status dates all the way back to the reign of Constantine, who is traditionally considered the last emperor of the Classical era. The immediate area had been Imperial property ever since it was confiscated from the family of the patrician Plautius Lateranus by Nero in 65 C.E., and when the Christian sympathizer Constantine wrested control of the city from his brother-in-law Maxentius in 312 C.E., he donated the buildings around the square — a residential complex and a barracks housing the Imperial horseguards — to the church. The residential buildings became the first papal palace, and the barracks were torn down and replaced by a basilica, which rose as the first Christian church to be built within the city walls and the first Imperially sanctioned church of the See of Rome. Today, despite being overshadowed in the public mind by St. Peter's, S. Giovanni in Laterano remains the city's official cathedral — the Latin description is "Cathedral of Rome and the world" — and the site of the pope's seat as the Bishop of Rome.

With the government-sanctioned installation of the pope and his retinue, the Piazza di S. Giovanni in Laterano gained in importance, despite its location at the edge of the walled city. But while the piazza took on a new role, the city as a whole was facing the most serious crisis of its entire history: in 330 C.E., Constantine decided to move the Imperial government — and all the bureaucratic apparatus that went along with it — to the newly founded city of Constantinople, far to the east on the border between Europe and Asia. Constantine's removal was a devastating blow, for it reduced Rome to the status of a provincial capital. The decline that followed was inexorable and was to last a full millennium. The population figures paint a grim picture: from a probable peak of around 1,500,000 at the height of the empire (the second century C.E.), the city shrank to around 800,000 at the end of the fourth century, less than 100,000 in the sixth century, and around 35,000 in the twelfth century. The low point came in 1308, when Pope Clement V — in an action oddly reminiscent of Constantine — removed the papacy from Rome to Avignon in France; some authorities suggest that as few as 15,000 people were left behind. By any standard of measure, this was a stunning decline. Rome, once the greatest city of the Western world, had lost 99 percent of its population and was perilously close to becoming a ghost town.*

---

*The year 1300 saw a short-lived recovery from the decline, due to an innovation instituted by Pope Boniface VIII. He declared 1300 a special Holy Year (or Jubilee Year), and announced that pilgrims visiting Rome could earn plenary indulgences — exemption from Purgatory after death — by following a prescribed devotional regimen while in the city. The gambit succeeded beyond all expectations: some two million pilgrims made their way to Rome, overwhelming the city's decrepit infrastructure. Pope Boniface originally conceived of the Holy Year as a centenary dispensation, but in 1342, Pope Clement VI reduced the interval to fifty years, and in 1470, Pope Paul II further reduced it to twenty-five years. Vast numbers of pilgrims have been journeying to Rome at twenty-five-year intervals ever since.

When the papacy returned to Rome in 1377, the ancient Lateran Palace was found to be in an extreme state of disrepair, and ultimately the papal residence was moved to St. Peter's on the Vatican Hill, where it has remained ever since. The piazza lost its preeminent status as an administrative center, and languished until the Renaissance, when Pope Sixtus V commissioned architect Domenico Fontana to make major renovations. Fontana tore down most of the medieval palace remnants, raised the obelisk in the center of the piazza, and constructed two new palazzi, including the obtrusive and uninspired Palazzo del Laterano. This last is worth a look, however, if only to see what the Palazzo Farnese might have looked like if Michelangelo had not modified the original design by raising and enlarging the roofline cornice. Michelangelo's changes allowed the top-story windows of the Palazzo Farnese room to breathe, and gave the façade as a whole an emphatic crown. Fontana's façade possesses no such breathing room, and the lack of plain wall space above the upper-story windows (as compared to the floors below) makes the entire façade look chopped off by the roof cornice.

At the far end of the square on the other side of the palazzo, two medieval survivals and a medieval reproduction serve as reminders of the square's former prestige: the Scala Santa, the Chapel of St. Lawrence, and the Tribune of Benedict XIV (the first two are located inside and the last is located outside — but attached to — the second of Fontana's palazzi). The Scala Santa is a steep set of steps traditionally climbed by pilgrims on their knees, said to be the staircase that Christ descended after being condemned by Pontius Pilate; it was (according to legend) imported from Jerusalem by Constantine's mother, St. Helena, and it now leads to the much-venerated chapel of St. Lawrence, which houses a famous icon supposedly painted by St. Luke.

The exterior tribune — another word for apse — appears to contain a medieval mosaic, but the work is in fact a modern copy dating from 1743. The original was located in the medieval palace dining hall constructed by Pope Leo III (795–816); it survived the Renaissance renovations (along with the staircase and the chapel), only to be accidentally destroyed during an expansion of Fontana's palazzo in the mid-eighteenth century. Pope Benedict XIV was so appalled by the loss that he commissioned a copy made from earlier drawings, and constructed an imposing aedicule (with explanatory marble plaques) to frame and display it. His motives were in large part political. The original mosaic was an important piece of papal propaganda — a visual correlative to the Donation of Constantine, the forged medieval document that was for centuries cited by the papacy to support its claims of temporal (that is to say, earthly political) power. The mosaic in the apse proper shows Christ sending forth the apostles to preach the gospel, but it is the two trios of figures on either side of the apse that contain the political message. On the left, Christ gives the keys to St. Peter (or perhaps Pope Sylvester) and the standard of the cross to Constantine; on the right, St. Peter gives the papal stole to Pope Leo and the banner of Christianity to Charlemagne. The two groupings reflect the uneasy (and sometimes bloodily antagonistic) alliance between pope and emperor that was the Holy Roman Empire; they assert the pope's superior position by equating St. Peter (the first pope) with Christ and Pope Leo (the pope who joined forces with Charlemagne to establish the empire) with St. Peter. The issue of the pope's temporal power — his status as ruler of the Papal States in central Italy — was still an important one in 1743 when Pope Benedict constructed the tribune; Benedict's desire to broadcast the political message to the outside world explains why the new copy of the old mosaic was so oddly exposed to view from the square.

8-11   SAN GIOVANNI IN LATERANO
Main structure: Fourth century; rebuilt in the fifth, ninth, and fourteenth
centuries; interior remodeled by Francesco Borromini, 1647–1649
Façade: Alessandro Galilei, 1732–1736
Cloister: Iacopo and Pietro Vassalletto, thirteenth century
(Front entrance facing the Piazza di Porta S. Giovanni, immediately east
of the Piazza di S. Giovanni in Laterano)

S. Giovanni in Laterano.

In 1732, Pope Clement XII announced an architectural competition: after a delay of fourteen centuries, the basilica of S. Giovanni in Laterano was finally to be given a façade that would reflect its size and importance as the Cathedral of Rome, the seat of the pope, and the first church of Christendom. All the leading architects in Rome took part in the competition, and the jury deliberations were by all accounts protracted and fraught with intrigue. The architect who ultimately emerged as the winner was a dark horse: he was not a Roman and (even more shocking) his design was not conventionally Baroque. Alessandro Galilei was a Florentine, and his façade was remarkably understated, even severe, in style: a giant central aedicule — double columns supporting a plain entablature and a plain triangular pediment — flanked by giant pilasters topped by a balustrade with statues. Only the central curve-sided pedestal above the pediment and the subsidiary one-story columns within the central aedicule suggest the motion and intricacy of the Baroque; the rest is frankly straightforward, aiming at monumentality rather than complexity. The result is not exactly exciting, but neither is it embarrassing, and it marks the beginning of a new era in Roman architecture. The Baroque style had ruled the city for more than a century, but from now on, with a few notable exceptions (such as the church of S. Croce in Gerusalemme, just down the street), the Neoclassical style was to dominate. While still employing the ancient architectural vocabulary, it favored simplicity over complexity, dignity over panache, and monumentality over everything. It would last even longer than the Baroque, surviving until the beginning of the twentieth century and culminating in that huge marble pile, the Victor Emmanuel Monument.

The interior of S. Giovanni is large and demoralizing — an unhappy mixture of styles that fails to cohere into any sort of unified whole. The Gothic baldacchino over the high altar, the Baroque nave, the Renaissance ceiling, and the medieval-style floor and apse (the mosaics are predominantly modern reproductions) are unexceptionable in themselves, but the stylistic dividing lines are so abrupt that the interior as a whole looks as if it has been carved up by architectural treaty, each area coexisting in uneasy truce with its neighbor. The dominant power is the nave, which — surprisingly — is the work of Francesco Borromini, whose smaller churches of S. Carlino and S. Ivo are among Rome's most dazzling architectural glories.

Borromini was called in by Pope Innocent X because the entire church was in danger of collapse. Over the centuries, the original Constantinian building had been much damaged by periodic sack, fire, and earthquake, but it was repeatedly restored and rebuilt. By 1647, however, the nave columns and upper walls were dangerously out of the vertical, and serious renovation was required. Borromini reinforced the walls and replaced the nave supports with piers, deemphasizing the piers' unusual width by inserting aedicules (later filled with statues of the apostles) and flanking the aedicules with giant pilasters reaching all the way to the ceiling. His overall plan called for a transformation of the entire church: the ceiling was to be replaced by a vault of crisscrossed ribs springing from the pilasters, and the nave design was to be extended to the transepts and chancel. But lack of funds — and perhaps lack of enthusiasm on the part of Innocent's successor, Alexander VII, who favored Bernini over Borromini — kept these additional renovations from being carried out. Whether a complete renovation would have produced a pleasing architectural effect is an open question (most successful Roman Baroque churches are small, and bigger is not necessarily better, even when the architect is Borromini).

Relief from this stylistic cold war can be found in two places: the cloister and the Lancellotti Chapel (the fourth on the left). The architect of the chapel was Giovanni Antonio de' Rossi, designer of the unusually reserved façade of the Palazzo Altieri across the street from the Gesù, but his work here is not in the least constrained, and in the frame for the altar he has created a High Baroque *tour de force* that is not only elaborate but architecturally sophisticated as well. The chapel's central space is circular, but the circularity is disguised by the bold columns beneath the dome ribs, which are pushed four steps forward by the scrunched pilasters that flank them and that help focus attention (at the chapel's far end) on the altar niche. Within the niche, additional columns step forward from the wall behind, allowing the entablature above to serve as square statuary pedestals for a pair of life-size sculpted angels. Further altar emphasis is supplied by the pilasters that are half hidden behind the columns, which imply a subsidiary space — a second curved wall behind the curved wall of the altar painting — and which create a convincing effect of triple layering: an altar framed by an aedicule framed by a deep-set and arched niche. The composition as a whole is bold and inventive and unified, and quite a contrast to the stripped-down severities of the Palazzo Altieri façade.

The cloister (off the left aisle just before the transept) is all of a piece as well, with a garden court arcade that possesses some of the finest medieval carving in the city. It was created and decorated in the thirteenth century by the Vassalletti, a father-and-son team who were two of the most famous artists of the Cosmati school. The columns and (especially) the capitals are remarkably varied, and the cornice above them on the garden side is carved with a collection of faces — both human and animal — that border on the surreal.

8-12   SANTA CROCE IN GERUSALEMME
Main structure and interior: fourth century, renovated twelfth century,
redecorated 1741–1744
Façade and vestibule: Domenico Gregorini & Pietro Passalacqua, 1741–1744
(Piazza di S. Croce in Gerusalemme, east of S. Giovanni in Laterano
down the Viale Carlo Felice)

Like the nearby S. Giovanni in Laterano, S. Croce in Gerusalemme is very large and very old. It is traditionally said to have been founded by Constantine's mother, St. Helena, who incorporated the original church into her favorite residence, the Sessorian Palace (originally constructed by the third-century emperor Heliogabalus); it takes its name from its most famous relic, a fragment of the True Cross that Helena supposedly brought back from Jerusalem. The current façade — again like S. Giovanni in Laterano — was added during the eighteenth century, when the existing church (which mostly dated from a rebuilding of the original in the twelfth century) was extensively renovated and redecorated. Surprisingly, the wholly Baroque façade of S. Croce was designed nine years *after* the Neoclassical façade of S. Giovanni. And given the structural similarities (both façades are organized around giant pilasters supporting an upper-story pediment that is flanked by statues and a balustrade), it is almost possible to view the later façade as a reproach to the earlier — an attempt by the architects Domenico Gregorini and Pietro Passalacqua to compete with their rival Alessandro Galilei on his own terms, using the same basic elements to create a livelier and more fluid effect.

If so, the attempt falls flat. The Baroque conventions and motifs that look so engaging on smaller church façades around the city — the curved walls, the nested capitals, the top-hat crown — are here blown up to gigantic proportions, and the extra size creates a problem. The giant pilasters loom, the windows and doorways gape, and everything looks uncomfortably overscaled. The general design would work perfectly for a modest two-story church, but it looks overblown and cartoonish when expanded to basilican size.

Inside the main portal, the entrance vestibule is still large, but far closer to human scale. A simple oval dome is supported by piers faced with pilasters (with columns substituted for emphasis along the entrance axis); between the piers the wall is scooped out to allow for a ring of space — almost an ambulatory — that gives the dome an extra lift, suspending it over an expanded oval area below. The decoration is (happily) understated, limited mostly to column and pilaster capitals that are inventively designed and incisively carved. The lack of profuse decoration grants the architectural elements pride of place, creating a space that is enveloping and welcoming.

Within the church proper, Gregorini and Passalacqua were mostly limited to redecorating, and excessive monumentality again takes its toll. But the baldacchino they designed to shelter the high altar is a remarkable structure. At first glance (from the main entrance door) it may appear quite conventional, its only unusual feature being the flattened and twisted curve of the marble arches that spring from the four columns, which seem almost deformed by the weight of the bronze canopy they support. But a closer look reveals that the flattened arch form is used only at the front and back of the baldacchino; on the sides, an entirely different form is employed. This second form reverses the design of the first — that is to say, where the basic shape at the front and back is a full arch with a broken horizontal base (horizontal fragments that do not span the full gap between the columns), the basic shape at the sides is a full horizontal base with a broken arch (curved fragments of arch rising up to suggest the beginnings of an arch similar to the front and the back). The overall result is a tensely twisted Baroque construction, which may look willfully eccentric from any given single point, but which makes perfect visual sense when multiple viewpoints are taken into account.

8-13   PORTA MAGGIORE AND TOMB OF THE BAKER
Porta Maggiore: 52 C.E.
Tomb of the Baker: ca. 40 B.C.E.
(Piazza di Porta Maggiore / Piazzale Labicano, north of S. Croce in
Gerusalemme and through the arches at the end of the Via Eleniana)

The Porta Maggiore is one of the best preserved of the Roman city gates, and for visitors to Rome approaching from the east down the Via Prenestina, it announces the city in no uncertain terms, just as it did in ancient times. Built by the emperor Claudius around 50 C.E., the structure might at first glance seem quite conventional: two arched openings (for incoming and outgoing vehicular traffic) flanked by three decorative aedicules (the larger central aedicule containing a through passageway for pedestrians at its base), the whole topped by an imposing three-part attic. But a closer look raises some stylistic questions. Why, in a structure that so closely resembles a triumphal arch, are the proportions of the attic so top-heavy in relation to the base? Why is the attic so plain, and its tripartite division so awkwardly unequal? And why are the aedicules such a strange mixture of styles — smooth, traditionally carved pediments supported by rough, crude half columns made of seemingly unfinished blocks?

In fact, the Porta Maggiore is not quite what it seems. It was built by Claudius as part of a new double aqueduct — a wholly utilitarian structure

— and it did not become a city gate until 271 C.E., when it was incorporated into Aurelian's new defensive city walls. The attic was purely functional, carrying within it the pipes of the Aqua Claudia and the Aqua Anio Novus, one atop the other; the travertine masonry and the decorative aedicules were mere architectural amenities, added here only because the aqueduct happened to cross a major road. And the hybrid style of the aedicules reflects a temporary change in Roman architectural taste that was probably initiated by Claudius himself. Before he became emperor, he was a historian, and the rustic, self-consciously primitive architectural style he favored for his Imperial building projects suggests a strong nostalgia for the past.

The Roman aqueducts were eleven in number, and they were famous throughout the ancient world, supplying a city of some 1.5 million inhabitants with constant and abundant running water. The earliest (the Aqua Appia) dates from around 312 B.C.E., the latest (the Aqua Alexandrina) from around 226 C.E.; both originated — as did seven others — from sources to the east or southeast of the city. The volume of water flow was astonishing: at peak capacity, the system was capable of supplying the city with more than three thousand gallons of water *per second*.

Two of the aqueducts entered the city from the west (tunneling through the Janiculum Hill above Trastevere) and one entered the city from the north (emerging from the Pincian Hill near the Piazza di Spagna), but the other eight all entered the city at the Porta Maggiore. Three of these were at ground level or below — around 80 percent of the entire system was underground — but five were aboveground; remains of the three non-Claudian aqueducts survive on the east side of the piazza at the curve in the tram tracks, where the truncated channels of the Aqua Marcia, the Aqua Tepula, and the Aqua Julia can be seen embedded high up in the Aurelian wall.

One further antique survivor deserves special notice: the elaborate tomb of Marcus Vergilius Eurysaces, erected in his memory by his wife, Atistia, around 40 B.C.E. Located just outside the city gate, the surviving fragment commemorates Eurysaces's prosperous career as a baker, with round holes (possibly representing ovens) and a frieze above depicting the practice of bread-making in all its various stages. Discovered in 1838, the tomb survived because for centuries it was encased in and protected by towers that formed part of the city's defenses.

TOUR 9

·

OFF THE BEATEN TRACK I:
THE AVENTINE HILL
FROM THE PIAZZA VENEZIA
TO THE PORTA SAN PAOLO

TODAY THE AVENTINE Hill is primarily residential — it was residential in ancient times as well — and it is the closest thing to a modern suburb that exists within the ancient walls. Most of its buildings date from the 1930s, when the area was developed by Mussolini and his planners, but a few older structures survive. The hill is almost secluded in feel, and the walk from the Piazza Venezia down to the river at the Piazza Bocca della Verità and then up the slope of the Aventine to S. Sabina offers the most dramatic transformation in town, starting at the very heart of the city and ending — still inside the walls, but barely — at one of the most peaceful and beautiful spots in all of Italy, the grave of the English Romantic poet John Keats at the base of the ancient pyramid depicted above.

9-1 THEATER OF MARCELLUS (PALAZZO ORSINI)
Dedicated ca. 12 B.C.E.
(Via del Teatro di Marcello, south of the Via Montanara)

In Imperial times, the Theater of Marcellus was the largest of Rome's three important theaters, with a capacity that exceeded 20,000 spectators. Today its remains are still in use (though not as a theater), and the history of its derelictions and transformations mirrors the long saga of the city as a whole. The Colosseum and the Pantheon are in their separate ways incomparable — one as an antique ruin and the other as an antique survivor — but it is the Theater of Marcellus, battered but unbowed, that is archetypically Roman in its ability to adapt to the vicissitudes of time and history.

The structure was begun by Julius Caesar and completed by Augustus, who in 13 or 11 B.C.E. dedicated it to the memory of his nephew and son-in-law Marcellus, deceased at age nineteen. Similar to the much later Colosseum in its use of stacked arches to support tiers of seats, it quickly became the model for theaters throughout the empire. It was abandoned and neglected throughout the early Middle Ages, and then fortified in the eleventh century by the Pierloni family to serve as a neighborhood stronghold. In the fourteenth century, the property passed to the Savelli family, who in 1519 employed architect Baldassare Peruzzi to construct the palazzo (still intact) that replaced the top tier of seats. Further additions were made by the Orsini in the seventeenth century, and as the city grew, the structure continued to attract barnacle-like hovels and shops outside and inside the ground-floor arches. Between 1926 and 1932, all these accretions were cleared away, and the ground was excavated down to its antique level (the high-water mark of the old ground level is clearly visible on some of the arch piers, about halfway up the lower arches). Today the structure is a maze of rented offices and apartments; during World War II, its owner, the Duchess of Sermoneta, is said to have escaped arrest at the hands of the Gestapo by hiding in its labyrinthine passageways. The three clustered free-standing columns that so arrestingly catch the eye from the Via del Teatro di Marcello once belonged to the theater's neighboring structure, the Temple of Apollo Medico (fifth century B.C.E.).

9-2 SAN NICOLA IN CARCERE
Temple remains: First century B.C.E. and early first century C.E.
Main body: Twelfth century
Façade: Giacomo della Porta, 1599
(Via del Teatro di Marcello, south of the Theater of Marcellus)

Another palimpsest church, but with a difference: here the exterior is more interesting than the interior. The façade is odd enough, but S. Nicola's most intriguing features are the rows of weathered columns carrying eroded entablatures set into the side walls. The two rows are far from identical in size and shape, and neither set of columns matches the single antique column embedded in the left-hand edge of the façade. What could have produced such a strange jumble of architectural relics?

In fact, all of the antique columns are still in their original positions. In ancient times, three different Roman temples stood side by side by side on this spot, all fronting on the *Forum Holitorium,* the city's main market for fruits and vegetables. When S. Nicola was constructed — probably in the twelfth century — the church took over the entire central temple, and spread out far enough to incorporate the neighboring colonnades of the temples on either side. It also took over a fortified tower originally built by the Pierleoni family, whose medieval mansion (now heavily restored and modernized) can still be seen across the Via del Teatro di Marcello.

The façade came much later, in 1599. The architect was Giacomo della Porta, designer of the Gesù façade, and his work here is highly idiosyncratic. The basic motif is not uncommon: the aedicule (that is, a doorway framed by vertical columns carrying a horizontal entablature that is topped by a triangular pediment). But this particular aedicule is anything but conventional. At first glance, it seems to turn the normal order of things upside down. A canonical entablature consists of three sections — the architrave at the bottom, the frieze (which is sometimes carved and sometimes left blank) in the middle, and the protruding cornice at the top — but on the S. Nicola façade Della Porta has placed the protruding cornice *below* the carved frieze, and has allowed the less emphatic base of the triangular pediment to serve as a sort of pseudo-architrave above. The traditional entablature sequence appears to have been willfully reversed.

In actuality, the façade of S. Nicola does possess a traditional entablature of sorts, and in the traditional place. As a moment's further study will show, the protruding cornice is not set directly on top of the columns that support it at either end; between the Ionic capitals and the cornice are short fragments of a conventional architrave and frieze (the latter left blank). But neither architrave nor frieze is allowed (as would normally be expected) to span the gap between columns like the cornice; instead they are limited in size to the width of the capitals below, and thus read to the casual eye as continuations of the columns. As a consequence the eye is fooled, at least initially, into ignoring the true architrave and frieze, and reads the cornice/attic/pediment assemblage above as the entablature instead. In the end, the façade might even be seen as possessing *two* entablatures, one fragmented below the cornice, the other fully but perversely developed above.

Such unorthodox visual games — games that employ Classical elements in ways that undercut or even reverse traditional expectations — are highly intellectual and esoteric, and would have shocked the architects of the High Renaissance a century earlier. But by the last half of the sixteenth century, such heretical gambits had become quite common, and modern architectural historians view them as the defining characteristic of the reigning style of the day: Mannerism. It was Michelangelo who led the way, with his boldly imaginative design for the Campidoglio; other architects followed, including Della Porta, Giacomo del Duca (S. Maria di Loreto, S. Maria in Trivio), Baldassare Peruzzi (Palazzo Massimo alle Colonne), Giorgio Vasari and Bartolomeo Ammanati (Villa Giulia), and many others. As it turned out, however, Della Porta's façade for S. Nicola was one of the last of the quirky Mannerist style. Four years later, in 1603, Carlo Maderno completed the façade of S. Susanna on the Quirinal Hill. With that epoch-making design, the Mannerist era in Rome ended, and the Baroque era began.

9-3   PIAZZA BOCCA DELLA VERITÀ

Temple of Portunus (formerly called Temple of Fortuna Virilis)
Temple of Hercules Victor (formerly called Temple of Vesta)
Second century B.C.E.

CASA DEI CRESCENZI
ca. 1100

The Piazza Bocca della Verità hardly qualifies as a piazza at all — it is merely an amorphous open area with a great deal of traffic, some pleasant greenery, and a scattering of buildings around the edges. But the site is immensely important, for it was here that the Palatine's early settlers set up a market to serve travelers crossing the Tiber, and so began the commerce around which the original city grew. It was also here (at the base of the Palatine on the piazza's extreme eastern edge, according to legend) that the shepherd Faustulus stumbled on the abandoned infant twins Romulus and Remus, who grew up to found the city. And the buildings themselves are notable, for time has spared some venerable works: two Republican temples, an Imperial arch, a medieval church and campanile, a medieval house, and a Baroque fountain (the large palazzo façade, which looks Renaissance, is in fact nineteenth-century Historicist). It is a fine historical cross-section that deserves a better showcase.

Of all these architectural survivors, the two oldest are perhaps the most evocative. Stranded on their island between the streams of traffic on the Lungotevere dei Pierleoni and the Via Petroselli, the little Republican temples are disused and permanently locked, their interiors intact but empty. Their look of lost isolation amid all the modern bustle lends them a special pathos, as if the Roman gods had simply packed up, moved out, and shut up their houses behind them.

The circular Temple of Hercules has lost its original entablature and roof, so the replacement roof sits directly — and awkwardly — on top of its supporting columns like a Chinese rice-paddy hat. The rectangular Temple of Portunus is more complete; best viewed set against the sky from its original ground level (at the bottom of the approach steps), it offers some idea of what Roman architecture was like before the megalomaniacal obsession with size began to infect Imperial architects. Here is strength and power in abundance, but on a human scale, and the temple straightforwardly displays its Ionic order without oppressing or overwhelming the visitor.

The contrast with the medieval Casa dei Crescenzi across the street, built some twelve hundred years later (around 1100 C.E.), could hardly be more extreme. As the inscription over the front door states, the house's owner hoped his building would revive the long-lost splendor of ancient Rome. But the only original architecture he could muster was a set of half columns with primitive schematic capitals, awkwardly set into the exterior wall to visually support a miscellany of friezes and cornices scavenged from deteriorating buildings nearby. The two rows of columns — the temple's and the house's — face each other across the Via del Ponte Rotto, the newer a sad, faint echo of the older. Despite occasional spasms of building, the longed-for revival of the once omnipotent city was not to arrive for another four hundred years.

S. Maria in Cosmedin, showing the Baroque façade decorations that were later removed.

S. Maria in Cosmedin is one of Rome's most venerable churches, but today it is best known for an oddity mounted on the wall inside the entrance portico: a large circular stone face known as *la Bocca della Verità* — the Mouth of Truth. Medieval legend held the face to be a lie detector; anyone who placed a hand in the mouth and told a lie risked losing fingers. The face is in fact an ancient drain cover, once part of the city sewage system. For many visitors, it will call up fond memories of a famously improvised comic scene in the film *Roman Holiday,* in which Gregory Peck briefly feigns amputation (Audrey Hepburn, supposedly, did not know what was going on, and her reaction, captured on film, was entirely spontaneous).

In Imperial times, the building on this site may have been the *statio annonae,* a structure in the center of the area's markets and storehouses that served as an audience hall for the official in charge of food inspection and municipal provisioning. After the empire fell, the Roman Catholic Church moved in to fill the civic vacuum left by the collapse of the Imperial government, and the building was expanded to become a Christian *diaconia,* or welfare center, where food was distributed to the needy. The church was added during the eighth century, incorporating the still-visible colonnade of the *statio annonae* into its interior front wall and using smaller scavenged columns and capitals for the nave.

The marble Cosmatesque flooring, enclosed choir, and Gothic baldacchino over the altar were added during the twelfth and thirteenth centuries.

In the late 1800s, S. Maria in Cosmedin became the first church in Rome to be restored — that is, to be stripped of its Renaissance and Baroque accretions and returned to something resembling its medieval state. The result may at first seem brutally ascetic — bare on the outside and dour on the inside — but a closer look at the interior reveals some unexpectedly affecting details. The tall columns along the left-hand wall remain visibly Roman, retaining a sense of antique strength and presence; the stubby nave columns, by comparison, look sadly reduced in scale, barely adequate to support their arches. The poignancy of the comedown is heightened by the nave columns' capitals; worn and weatherbeaten as they are, they constitute one of the finest scavenged collections in the city, displaying a remarkable range of themes and motifs. As elements in the church's overall design, however, they remain leftovers — sad reminders of an architectural feast long ended and only dimly remembered.

In part, the harsh feel of the interior is due to the modern restoration. The medieval nave frescoes did not survive the Baroque renovation, so the visual interest and warmth they originally supplied is missing, and the upper nave today is delimited by large expanses of cold blank wall relieved only by small, niggardly clerestory windows. The late medieval additions — untouched by the restoration — compound the problem. The enclosed marble choir and the Gothic baldacchino seem to crowd rather than fill the modest nave; they give the interior a cramped, cluttered feel that belies the simplicity of the surrounding architecture. In the end, S. Maria in Cosmedin remains a church of bits and pieces — a patchwork collection of architectural remnants cobbled together to form a modest communal shelter carved out of the prevailing urban decay. As Roman churches go, it is humble and unpretentious, but as a metaphor for Rome during the Middle Ages — midway between the architectural glories of antiquity and the Renaissance — it retains an oddly disturbing power.

9-5   CLIVO DI ROCCA SAVELLA
(South of the Piazza Bocca della Verità, off the Via di S. Maria in Cosmedin south of the Via della Greca)

Just beyond S. Maria in Cosmedin, the cars and buses all turn onto the Via della Greca, but for pedestrians the best way to climb the Aventine Hill is the Clivo di Rocca Savella, one block farther along to the south. The path begins at the sidewalk, climbs a short flight of ten steps, and then angles to the right. At this point the city suddenly seems to drop away, supplanted by a wholly unexpected vista: aged, ivy-smothered walls enclosing a cobbled and grassy path ascending to a beckoning door. Were it not for the noise of the nearby traffic, the climb would seem the entrance to a dream. At the top, reality reasserts itself, offering a fine view of the Capitoline Hill; on the other side of the door, the Parco di S. Alessio overlooks the Tiber and offers a full-blown west-bank panorama: Trastevere, the Janiculum Hill, the dome of St. Peter's, and Monte Mario beyond (if the door to the park is locked, follow the bend in the path to the Via di S. Sabina, then turn right and enter the park farther along at the church).

9-6   SANTA SABINA
Fifth century C.E.
(Piazza di S. Pietro d'Illiria, off the Via di S. Sabina opposite the Via Raimondo da Capua)

S. Sabina's large size, venerable age, commanding location, and parklike setting have earned the church a special nickname among Romans: the Jewel of the Aventine. But in this case the jewel's sparkle — at least as far as the church itself is concerned — has been cruelly diminished by the vicissitudes of time and history.

The structure dates from the fifth century, with ninth-century additions. In the late 1500s, however, the interior was completely remodeled by Domenico Fontana, and most of the medieval mosaics that covered the walls were destroyed during the renovation. The decoration that replaced them was removed between 1914 and 1939; at the same time, the windows and ninth-century enclosed choir were restored, and the renovated vaults were replaced with a medieval-style flat wooden ceiling.

The result is harsh and forbidding, with the ruthless hand of the restorer to be felt everywhere. Something of the interior's lost medieval finery can be seen on the upper wall above the entrance doors, where the original mosaic decoration survives. But elsewhere everything is stripped and naked. A bone-chilling frigidity rules; the welcoming warmth of some of Rome's other medieval churches (S. Maria in Trastevere, say, or the much smaller S. Giovanni a Porta Latina) is nowhere to be found. Restoration — the stripping away of Renaissance and Baroque "improvements" — has uncovered some fine things in Rome, but this bleak and sterile interior is not one of them.*

Human feeling unexpectedly returns in the church vestibule, where the original fifth-century carved wooden doors remain intact in the left-hand doorway. The eighteen panels are carved with scenes from the Old and New Testaments; the panel showing Christ on the cross (upper left corner) is one of the oldest depictions of the Crucifixion in existence.

9-7 PIAZZA DEI CAVALIERI DI MALTA
Giovanni Battista Piranesi, 1764–1766
(South end of the Via di S. Sabina)

A small but shocking surprise. G. B. Piranesi is famous for his etchings of Roman ruins, which took Europe by storm in the late eighteenth century and helped launch the Romantic movement in both art and literature. As a draftsman he was a master of hallucinatory exaggeration, and in his etchings the ruins tower over the landscape, all looming columns and massive arches and huge, crumbling fragments. He made the ancient remains look as if they had been built by a race of giants, and anyone who comes to Rome with Piranesi's etchings in mind cannot but be disappointed to find that the ruins are, after all, merely very large.

Who, then, would expect Piranesi's sole piece of public architecture to be *underscaled?* But underscaled it is: against all expectations, his evocative decorative scheme for the tiny walled Piazza dei Cavalieri di Malta is not in the least melodramatic. Only the cypress trees loom, and against their background Piranesi's artfully arranged bas-reliefs and obelisks (shrunk to a fraction of their normal size) possess an aura of cozy intimacy, as if the ruins had been scaled down, tamed, and domesticated. Opposite the obelisk-topped wall, the arched and pedimented gateway wall enclosing the grounds of S. Maria del Priorato throws Classical correctitude to the winds, blithely making up its own rules as it goes along. All in all, the little cul-de-sac

---

*Probably a minority view, and possibly a blind one as well. The redoubtable *Blue Guide* describes S. Sabina as "perhaps the most beautiful basilica in Rome which survives from the Early Christian period," and Georgina Masson, in *The Companion Guide to Rome,* calls it "the finest of Rome's ancient churches." She continues: "The outside is of the starkest simplicity; in the interior the severe majesty of the fifth-century basilica stands revealed in all its grandeur. Probably in no other Roman church are superb proportions and a magnificent array of twenty-four Corinthian columns allied to such a flood of golden light as pervades the whole of this splendid building."

exudes an air of lighthearted Classicism that is the precise antithesis of Piranesi's powerful etchings.

As an extra fillip, the piazza cunningly conceals its most entertaining treat, not to be missed. It is to be found by looking through the keyhole in the door leading to the grounds of S. Maria del Priorato: a splendidly unexpected and beautifully framed view of the dome of St. Peter's, some two miles away.

9-8 PROTESTANT CEMETERY AND PYRAMID OF GAIUS CESTIUS
Earliest known grave 1738
Tomb constructed ca. 15 B.C.E.
(Entrance off the Piazza di Porta S. Paolo, at the far end of the
Via Caio Cestio)

Rome's small Protestant Cemetery — a misnomer, since other non-Catholic religions are not excluded — lies tucked away just inside the ancient walls of the Porta S. Paolo, in the shadow of the ancient pyramid tomb of Gaius Cestius. The cemetery is celebrated as a place of pilgrimage for English poetry lovers, who come to seek out the graves of the Romantic poets Keats and Shelley. But it is not only the famous graves that give the cemetery its special bittersweet piquancy. It is also the modesty, serenity, seclusion, and dignity of the setting, combined with an extra sense of loss that is all but palpable: not just bereavement and burial, but bereavement and burial achingly far from home and loved ones. "It might make one in love with death," wrote Shelley, little knowing how prophetic his words were to be, "to think that one should be buried in so sweet a place."

According to legend (almost certainly apocryphal), the cemetery was established when a young foreign nobleman, in audience with the pope, described his love of Rome and spoke of his desire to be buried by the ancient pyramid; the young man was killed in an accident several days later and the pope granted his wish. The oldest known grave dates from 1738 — an Oxford graduate named Langton who died at the age of twenty-five — and when Keats was buried here in 1821 (also twenty-five years old and dead of tuberculosis), the cemetery was still an open field. Shortly thereafter, in a halfhearted effort to discourage anti-Protestant vandalism — apparently preserving the view of the pyramid was an equal consideration — the papal authorities surrounded the graveyard by a moat, and fenced in an adjacent field for new graves. Since that time, the newer section has served as the primary graveyard, and burial in the *parte antica* has been purposely limited (the wall that finally enclosed the entire site was not constructed until the 1870s).

In addition to the gravesites of Keats and Shelley — Shelley's ashes were interred in the new section against the upper wall near the *parte antica* — one particular monument is worth searching out, located close by Shelley: the grave of William Wetmore Story, the nineteenth-century American sculptor who lived in Rome for almost forty years and who carved the famous "Angel of Grief" mourning over his wife's tombstone (the angel was his last work, and he was interred beside his wife later in the same year). A full guide to the cemetery may be purchased at the entrance, along with a map showing where many of the graves are located, including those of the Renaissance scholar J. Addington Symonds, the German architect Gottfried Semper, the American painter Elihu Vedder, the medieval scholar Richard Krautheimer, and the Italian politician Antonio Gramsci, one of the founders of the Communist Party in Italy.

The ancient looming pyramid tomb that adds so much to the cemetery's ambience was constructed around 15 B.C.E. in accordance with the will of one Gaius Cestius, about whom nothing is known except what appears on the tomb's inscriptions: that he was a praetor (magistrate), tribune, and one of seven priests in charge of public religious banquets. As required by law at the time, the tomb was built outside the city proper; it was some three hundred years later that it was incorporated into the Aurelian walls. A second antique curiosity, twice as high as the pyramid, is located nearby: Monte Testaccio, a small hill west of the cemetery across the Via Nicola Zabaglia. The mound is entirely artificial, built up of broken potsherds — pottery fragments — dumped on the site through the third century C.E.

TOURS

10 - 11

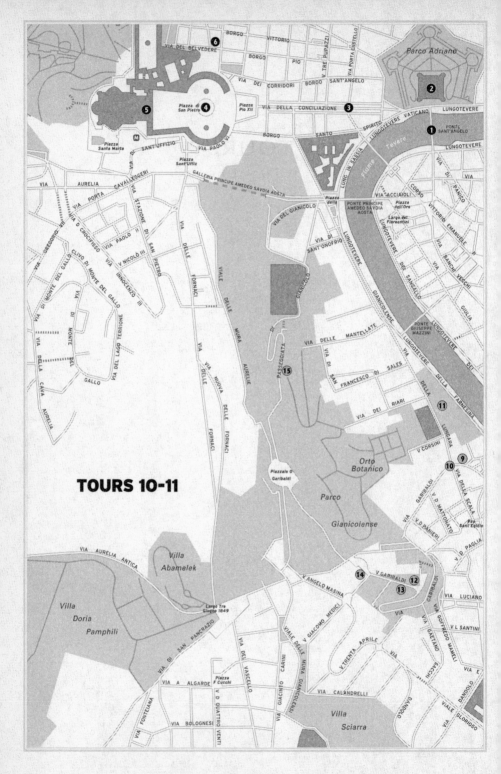

TOURS 10-11

MAP #4
TOURS 10 — 11

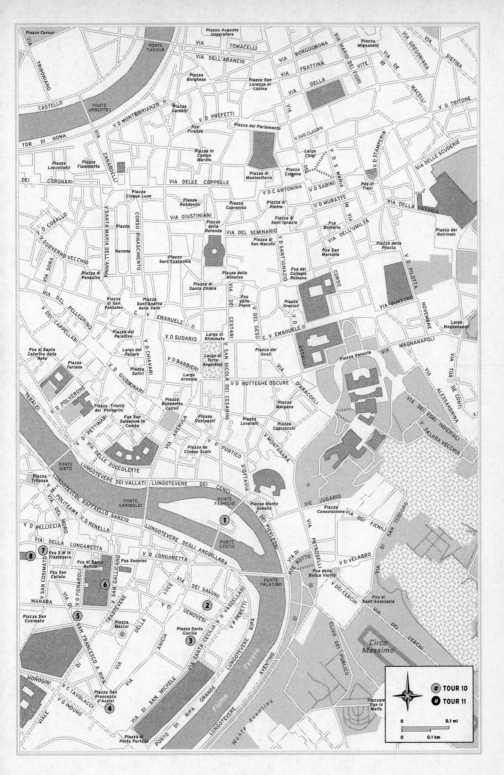

MAP #4

TOURS 10 — 11

TOUR 10

—◆—

OFF THE BEATEN TRACK II:
TRASTEVERE AND THE JANICULUM HILL

RASTEVERE — LITERALLY "ACROSS the Tiber" — is one of the oldest sections of the city, and its residents are famously proud, traditionally viewing the rest of Rome as alien territory. The medieval street plan of the area remains substantially intact (its central square, the Piazza di S. Maria in Trastever, is pictured above), with one significant modern intrusion: the Viale Trastevere, constructed as a wide north-south traffic axis in the late nineteenth century in frank imitation of the boulevards of Paris.

Above Trastevere rises the Janiculum Hill, famous among sightseers for its panoramic view of the city and famous among architectural historians as the site of one of the most influential buildings ever built: Donato Bramante's little Tempietto, tucked away in the courtyard of a minor church set into the side of the the hill. Rome is of course notoriously Baroque, so there is considerable irony in the fact that it boasts among its hidden treasures a building that many architectural historians consider the apotheosis of High Renaissance rationality, clarity, and beauty.

10-1   TIBER ISLAND

An island in the middle of a river in the middle of a European capital city inevitably conjures up thoughts of Paris, but anyone coming to Tiber Island with memories of the Île de la Cité and the Cathedral of Notre Dame is bound to be disappointed. Tiber Island is very small (its only cross street is hardly more than a single block in length) and it contains no architecturally important buildings. It is not even a neighborhood, and never has been. But it is not without special character, for it serves — and has served without interruption since ancient times — a highly specialized purpose: the care of the sick.

According to legend, Tiber Island gained its special status in 291 B.C.E. Rome, ravaged by plague, had consulted the Sibylline books and been advised to send to the Greek city of Epidaurus for a statue of Aesculapius, the god of medicine. As the ship bearing the statue sailed up the Tiber, a huge snake was seen to slither overboard, taking refuge on the island. Believing the snake to be an incarnation of the god himself, the Romans constructed a temple dedicated to Aesculapius on the site, and later built up the downstream end of the island to resemble the prow of the ship (a fragment of the prow survives in the form of a travertine wall set against the base of the modern buildings on the island's left bank). The temple in effect served as the island's first hospital, attracting sick people who would spend the night praying to Aesculapius for a cure. Nothing of the temple remains, although the ancient bridge from the east bank — the Ponte Fabricio, constructed in 62 B.C.E. — is still in use, the oldest bridge in the city. Today most of the island is occupied by the hospital of the Fatebenefratelli, founded in 1548.

Just downstream from the island, the isolated midriver arch of the Ponte Rotto stands as a testament to the past power of the Tiber, untamed until the late nineteenth century. Known in Imperial times as the Pons Aemilius, the original bridge — the first in the city to be made of stone — was constructed in the second century B.C.E. Over the centuries, the structure collapsed several times (the carved dragons that decorate the spandrels of the arch refer to the arms of Pope Gregory XIII, who had it rebuilt around

1575); it collapsed for the final time in 1598. The remains have been known as the Ponte Rotto ("Broken Bridge") ever since.

10-2   VICOLO DELL' ATLETA
(South of Tiber Island, between the Via dei Salumi and the Via dei Genovesi)

Only a block long, narrow at one end and even narrower at the other, with an odd dip and divide in the middle. Formerly known as the Vicolo delle Palme, the Vicolo dell' Atleta earned its current name in 1849, when excavations under the medieval building at Nos. 13–16 uncovered an ancient marble statue of an athlete using a strigil (a tool used to scrape oil off the body). The famous statue — a Roman copy of a fourth-century B.C.E. bronze original by the Greek sculptor Lysippus — is thought to have originally stood outside the Baths of Agrippa, south of the Pantheon; it is currently in the Vatican Museum.

The building itself is characteristic of Trastevere — a medieval structure tucked away in a back alley that somehow managed to survive both bad times and good. It might be taken for a typical dwelling of the period were it not for one peculiarity: the Hebrew lettering carved into one of the exterior columns. In fact the structure was once a Jewish synagogue, thought to have been founded here in the eleventh century by the lexicographer and Talmudic scholar Nathan Ben Jechiel. Since the Renaissance — the Trastevere Jewish community was forced across the river into the Ghetto in 1555 — the building has passed through many hands, and has served at various times as a convent, a bakery, a shop, a private residence, and, most recently, a restaurant.

10-3   SANTA CECILIA IN TRASTEVERE
Constructed ca. 820 C.E.
Portico and campanile: twelfth century
Upper façade and courtyard entrance portal: Fernando Fuga, 1741
(Piazza di S. Cecilia in Trastevere, south of the Vicolo dell' Atleta)

Like S. Maria in Aracoeli on the Capitoline Hill, S. Cecilia is old and venerable, a palimpsest church possessing layer upon layer of architectural features and decorative detail. Unlike S. Maria in Aracoeli, however, the heterogeneous components never quite cohere, and the feel of a unified whole is lacking.

According to tradition, the original church on the site dated back to pre-Christian Rome. St. Cecilia, so the story goes, was a Christian convert of noble birth and great wealth who lived in Trastevere. Because of her status and visibility, the Imperial authorities marked her for death, and imprisoned her in the superheated steambath of her own home. But when the steambath doors were opened after three days, she was found to be alive and in perfect health. An executioner was then dispatched to behead her, but the prescribed three strokes of the ax failed to do the job. She lingered for three more days, during which the story of her martyrdom spread throughout the city and produced hundreds of conversions. Several decades later, Pope Urban I founded the original church on the site of St. Cecilia's home.

The current church was built by Pope Paschal I around 820, when the saint's remains were discovered and transferred from the catacombs of S. Calisto; the entrance portico and bell tower were added in the twelfth century. During the Renaissance a complete renovation ensued from a sensational discovery: St. Cecilia's ninth-century tomb was opened and the body inside (it is said) was found to be intact. Further rebuilding followed in 1741, when the courtyard entrance façade and the church façade above the entrance portico were remodeled, and in 1822, when the antique nave columns, which were found to be dangerously out of plumb, were encased in supporting piers.

All this rebuilding and redecorating has produced a decidedly mixed bag. At first sight, the exterior looks distinctly promising. The central archway of the entrance portal frames a fine view of the church and its garden courtyard; the planted flower beds, the huge antique marble vase that serves as the courtyard centerpiece, the antique columns of the portico, the high and slightly tipsy bell tower — all these serve to tantalize and invite, and to suggest an interior of great age and dignity. Inside, however, the promise of the exterior goes all but completely unfulfilled. Very little of the medieval structure remains visible, and the nave feels more like an eighteenth-century ballroom than a ninth-century church. The piers enclosing the nave columns look both clunky and flimsy (a particularly perverse visual trick) and the rest of the nave is burdened with a decorative scheme that combines pedestrian design with coarse detailing and gilding. The style is nominally Rococo — wall surfaces covered with purely decorative nonstructural gilding — but the lightness and grace and elegance of good Rococo decoration are entirely lacking.

There is one section of the interior, however, that is worthy of attention: the sanctuary, around the high altar. Here the architectural history of the church remains visible, and the various elements combine to produce a memorable set piece. The ninth-century mosaics of the curved rear wall serve as a backdrop for Arnolfo de Cambio's intricate Gothic baldacchino (1293); the baldacchino both encloses the high altar and crowns the niche below, which contains Stefano Maderno's sculpture of the body of St. Cecilia. Maderno is said to have been present when the saint's tomb was opened in 1599, and he was so moved by the sight of the body — supposedly lying on its side and wrapped in a robe of gold cloth, with the signs of the executioner's ax visible on the neck — that he re-created it in marble. The niche below the altar was then specially constructed to display the sculpture. The piece quickly became famous, and deservedly so. Its understated eloquence puts the tawdry glitter of the nave to shame.

10-4   SAN FRANCESCO A RIPA
Façade: Mattia de' Rossi, 1681
Altieri Chapel: Gianlorenzo Bernini and Baciccio (G.B. Gaulli), 1671
(Piazza di San Francesco d'Assisi, southwest of the Piazza di S. Cecilia
in Trastevere)

A neighborhood church, a bit larger than usual but still modest in its pretensions. Mattia de' Rossi's façade follows the Gesù model — wide ground floor and narrow upper story — but with curved pediment sections replacing the Gesù's scrolls to either side of the upper story. Compared to the Gesù, however, the façade of S. Francesco a Ripa is stripped down to bare bones (in this case plain Doric pilasters). The effect, by Baroque standards, is almost puritanical in its plainness, with the pediment sections — presumably meant to soften the transition between the two stories — placed too far away from the upper story to have much effect. The disembodied fragments look like broken wings, amputated and isolated from the main body of a façade that remains ponderously earthbound.

The dingy interior continues the plain Doric pilaster motif, at odds with the fussily marbled high altar and most of the cheerlessly overdecorated side chapels. One of the chapels, however, is remarkable. It is best approached down the right nave aisle, up the two steps to the crossing, and then to the left. The rear wall of the dark chapel opposite has been pushed back to form a niche that is dramatically lit by a side window (or, irregularly, by electric spotlight). In the specially constructed niche is displayed one of Bernini's most powerful works: the statue of the Blessed Ludovica Albertoni.

Ludovica Albertoni was a relative of Bernini's patron Cardinal Paluzzi degli Albertoni, who commissioned the sculpture to celebrate the sanctioning of Ludovica's cult in 1671. She had been a widow who devoted her life to the poor; the day before she died in 1553, she was said to have experienced a holy vision of paradise. Scholarly opinion is divided as to whether Bernini's sculpture represents the agony of Ludovica's death throes or the ecstasy of her vision, but it is entirely possible that Bernini meant to equate the two — to unite them in a single sculptural statement that equates death with new life. The obvious (for some viewers offensively obvious) sexual component of Ludovica's feverish spasm would certainly suggest as much. As a sculptural *tour de force*, the work recalls the more famous *Ecstasy of Saint Theresa* in S. Maria della Vittoria across town, produced some twenty-five years earlier. Bernini was into his seventies when he produced the *Ludovica*, but the work exhibits no sign of such advanced age.[*]

As with the *Saint Theresa*, Bernini's overall plan for displaying the *Ludovica* encompassed all the visual arts, architecture and painting as well as sculpture. The setting was carefully worked out: the dramatically canted walls and arch that frame the statue and lead the eye from the chapel to the niche, the stucco cherub heads that seem to point to the figure of Ludovica on her couch, the Dove of the Holy Spirit hovering above. Often overlooked is Baciccio's luminous altarpiece, painted expressly to accompany and complement Bernini's sculpture. At first glance, the painting would seem a conventional *Madonna and Child with St. Anne* (to whom the chapel as a whole is dedicated). But a different interpretation is possible. Given the unmistakable similarity in facial features and dress between Baciccio's St. Anne and Bernini's Ludovica, the two figures can be seen as the same person. By this reading the painting — in which the figure of Ludovica/St. Anne reaches out to receive the Christ child in a gesture of great tenderness — both symbolizes and illustrates the vision of renewed life after death that is the central theme of the work as a whole. Sculpture and painting are connected in a stylistic way as well: in both works the hands are especially eloquent, and seem to echo each other in their suggestion of spiritual touch.

---

[*]Bernini lived and worked for another nine years, until 1680; shortly before he died, his right arm became paralyzed, leading him to comment that in all fairness an arm that had worked so hard for so long deserved a rest.

10-5 SAN PASQUALE BAYLON
Giuseppe Sardi, 1744–1747
(Via di San Francesco a Ripa, northwest of the Piazza di S. Francesco
d'Assisi, across the Viale Trastevere at the intersection with the Via Luciano
Manara and the Via Fratte di Trastevere)

Designed by the little-known Giuseppe Sardi in the mid-1700s, S. Pasquale Baylon is one of two neighborhood churches in Trastevere — the other is S. Dorotea — that stand out as especially fine. The façade is merely a prelude, although its late Baroque origins can be seen in the way that the normal pilasters have been reduced to wall panels, leaving the door- and window-surrounds to cope on their own. Only the double pediment at the peak follows accepted Baroque precedent, giving the façade as a whole a look that is almost purely decorative. The structural strength and visual clarity of the Renaissance — or even of early Baroque façades like S. Susanna — are a distant memory.

Inside, the rejection of Renaissance rules for achievement of "correct" proportion and harmony continues. The paired sets of pilasters in the nave possess no visual support (not only do they lack pedestals, they are joined at the bottom in a way that transforms their bases into plain wall surface), and their elongated, cherub-topped capitals deviate markedly from accepted Corinthian convention. The arches that top the side-chapel openings are emphatically flattened and squat, the visual antithesis of the "pure" semicircular arches favored by the Renaissance. The pilasters and arches support a full entablature — architrave, frieze, and cornice as prescribed by antiquity — but the straightforward (and straight-lined) conventions of the canonical Classical orders are everywhere violated. The architrave takes a noticeable detour whenever it meets the molding of the nave arches, the frieze is elaborately painted with free-form designs, and the exaggerated projecting cornice rises up at intervals to leap over inserted oval *coretti*, the lower portions of which take bites out of the frieze below.

Against the odds, all these unconventional elements come together to give the interior the feel of a unified whole; at the curved nave corners the interior space seems not so much built up as scooped out, with a Baroque softness and pliability that cares not a whit for Renaissance geometrical rigor. The play of curves continues throughout the rest of the church, and some of the details — the nave upper window-surrounds, for instance — are splendidly inventive. Only once does the rigidity of sharp angles and straight lines intervene: at the high altar, where the upper cornice moldings rise to form a conventional triangular pediment. Amid all the soft, mellifluous curves, the pediment is like a sudden sharp call to order, almost painful in its incisiveness.

But beautiful as all these architectural features are, they cannot survive the mess of jaundiced ocher paint that everywhere defaces the interior. The false marbling of the nave pilasters is crude as well as ugly, and elsewhere the relentless slathering on of painted decoration renders the fluid lines of the architectural elements all but undetectable. It is the same old Roman problem: the architecture is not allowed to speak for itself. A coat of white paint would work wonders.

10-6   OSPEDALE DI SAN GALLICANO
Filippo Raguzzini, 1724–1726
(Via di S. Gallicano, west of the Viale Trastevere at the
Vicolo di Mazzamurelli)

Ospedale di S. Gallicano.

A sprawling building — two city blocks long — with a fine and original late Baroque façade. It should be viewed progressively from three vantage points: first, from the Viale Trastevere at the intersection of the short Vicolo di Mazzamurelli; second, from the other end of the Vicolo di Mazzamurelli where it merges with the Via di S. Gallicano; third, from the sidewalk of the Via di S. Gallicano.

The hospital was founded by Pope Benedict XIII in 1724, and in designing the building's façade architect Filippo Raguzzini faced three separate challenges: how to construct an effective view-stopper at the end of a narrow street, how to integrate the façade of the hospital's church with the façade as a whole, and how to deal with the overall façade's excessive length. He solved these problems by creating three separate compositions of ever-widening width, each of which can be viewed on its own, but each of which blends harmoniously with its successor.

First view: from the Viale di Trastevere at the point where the buildings on either side of the Vicolo di Mazzamurelli frame the high pilasters that flank the church doorway. In creating a visually effective churchfront design, Raguzzini was hampered by an approaching street that is narrow and tunnel-like (and was far more tunnel-like before the Viale di Trastevere was cut through the area in the nineteenth century). He met the problem head-on: he gave the church's entranceway a tunnel effect of its own. He pushed the door proper (and the second-story window above it) deep into the wall surface, and then framed the door not once but twice, first with a high, rounded arch (a tunnel motif in itself), and then with two high pilasters that jut out into the street. The pilasters, especially, work to deepen the burrowing effect; because they intrude into the entranceway's second story — jutting up as well as out — they provide the entranceway with a double shift of scale (from pilasters to archway to door) that accentuates the double recession of the wall plane. As a result, the pilasters serve not so much to frame the church door as to stand sentry beside it, and their emphatic presence transforms the simple doorway into a true and effective view-stopper.*

Second view: from the point on the Vicolo di Mazzamurelli where the full church façade comes into view. The unusual mixed scales of Raguzzini's doorway composition suggest unexpected things to come, but the design of the façade as a whole turns out to be quite traditional. With its wide ground floor and narrower upper story, its progressively recessive wall surface, its flat pilasters and decorative scrolls, the façade clearly and frankly imitates that most influential of all Roman churches, the Gesù. Raguzzini's goal, however, is far more modest than Della Porta's. Whereas the Gesù sought (and achieved) a new and august monumentality in stone, S. Gallicano settles

---

* As repeated visits to S. Gallicano will reveal, the visual effectiveness of Raguzzini's view-stopper varies dramatically according to — of all things — the weather. On sunny days, the tall pilasters catch the Roman sunlight while the doorway (like the approaching street) remains in deep shadow, accentuating the tunnel-like effect; on cloudy days, the entire composition appears to flatten out. Unabashed theatricality is one of the defining characteristics of Baroque architecture, and — like all theater — it requires sympathetic lighting to be seen at its best.

for unpretentious ornament in stucco (a material that had only recently come into general use on building exteriors). Still, Raguzzini clearly relishes his plaster surfaces; by filling the façade's leftover spaces with non-Classical decoration — textured panels between the pilaster shafts and grooves between the capitals — he gives the façade's decorative and structural elements equal weight.

Third view: the entire two-block façade, from the sidewalk of the Via di S. Gallicano. With the hospital's side wings, non-Classical decoration takes over completely. For a full block in either direction, there is not a single pilaster or pediment in sight. The only hint of Classicism — it is the merest whiff — comes from the pilaster-like shape of the narrow rectangular protruding panels that organize the façade into traditional bays. The bay division, in its turn, is developed to offer a simple but effective contrast between upper and lower stories. The lower story supplies variety, with its A-B-B-A rhythm of arched windows and decorative geometric panels; the upper story supplies unity through simple repetition. And at the top, the roofline plays a special role: it ties the entire hospital-church-doorway composition together, continuing from the hospital wings onto the church façade, where it serves as the ground-floor cornice and ends by crowning the pilasters that flank the front door.

Raguzzini was in many ways the most talented and original Roman architect of his generation. He lived an astonishing ninety-one years (from 1680 to 1771), but his effective career in Rome lasted only six, beginning and ending with the papacy of his patron Pope Benedict XIII (1724–1730). Raguzzini's unusual late Baroque style — more stripped down than gussied up, yet sometimes adventurous enough to abandon the Classical vocabulary altogether — looks forward to the death of Classicism in the twentieth century. But in the early eighteenth century, it produced few (if any) imitators, and after 1730, with Roman taste shifting away from the Baroque toward a more severe and monumental Neoclassicism, Raguzzini's architectural practice languished. For the last forty years of his life, he was unable to obtain a single important Roman commission and built very little.

10-7 PIAZZA DI SANTA MARIA IN TRASTEVERE
Fountain: date of origin unknown; reconstructed in 1604, probably by
Girolamo Rainaldi; remodeled in 1659 by Gianlorenzo Bernini;
remodeled again in 1692 by Carlo Fontana; entirely reconstructed in 1873,
retaining Fontana's design.
(West of the Via di S. Gallicano)

Aesthetically, the boxy Piazza di S. Maria in Trastevere falls distinctly short. In the center an awkwardly conceived octagonal fountain — a round peg trying to fit itself into a square hole — fails to achieve much beyond size; on the south side a ponderously undistinguished Renaissance palazzo visually overwhelms its far more interesting neighbor, the ancient and venerable church of S. Maria in Trastevere. Around the rest of the perimeter the façades loom rather than enclose, producing an uncomfortable box canyon feel. The overall effect is more than a little bleak, and during afternoon siesta, when an eerie quiet descends and the light turns harsh, the space can take on the ominous, surreal quality of a Di Chirico painting.

On fine summer evenings, however, the square is transformed. As dusk descends, the buildings around the square seem to lose their forbidding quality, and the mosaics on the church façade — illuminated by spotlight — gradually come into their own, replacing the fountain as the main focal point. The piazza's restaurants and cafés spill out of their doors, creating new boundaries around the perimeter with their outdoor tables and umbrellas, and the steps of the central fountain fill up with idling strollers, students, and itinerant musicians. The whole piazza comes exuberantly and exhilaratingly to life. Darkness, it turns out, transforms the forbidding daytime space into a commodious, welcoming outdoor room teeming with nocturnal activity.

The transformation is an object lesson in the special nature of the Italian piazza. Like so many of the lesser Roman cityspaces, the Piazza di S. Maria in Trastevere only reveals its true character when it is put to use, and to analyze it formally in terms of architecture and design is to miss the point. Not so much an aesthetic set piece as an empty vessel waiting to be filled, the piazza's true character is defined by the interaction between the space and the people who use it.

10-8 SANTA MARIA IN TRASTEVERE
Constructed ca. 1140
(Piazza di S. Maria in Trastevere)

S. Maria in Trastevere was founded in the fourth century — it was probably the first church in Rome to be dedicated to the Virgin Mary — but the structure that exists today dates from a complete rebuilding that took place in the mid-twelfth century. The exterior is something of a mishmash, with a twelfth-century campanile, an early eighteenth-century entrance portico, and a medieval-looking upper façade that dates mostly from renovations made around 1870. The façade mosaic, however, is in large part original and worth a close look. The theme is generally taken to be the Virgin and Child flanked by the Wise and Foolish Virgins, five of whom — according to Christ's parable of spiritual readiness — have wisely prepared their lamps ahead of time and five of whom have foolishly run out of oil.* As Walter Oakeshott describes it in *The Mosaics of Rome*, the mosaic as a whole evinces three different styles, and was probably created in stages over a period of some hundred years beginning at the end of the twelfth century.

The three separate stages are perhaps most apparent in the ten lamps: those held by the figures in the center (the first two figures to the left of the Virgin and the first figure to the right) possess globular reservoirs depicted as decorative concentric circles; those held by the last four figures on the right possess globular reservoirs depicted with naturalistic highlights that make the shape far more visually convincing; those held by the last three figures on the left possess tureen-like reservoirs that are far more complex in detail. Likewise with the figures themselves: the earliest figures (and the Virgin) are schematic in design, with stiff gestures and rigid draperies; the right-hand figures are more subtly handled, with suggestions of light and shadow; the left-hand figures are most naturalistic of all, with rounded bodies, individual hand gestures, and solid, flowing draperies. In its more primitive way, the mosaic mirrors the revolution in painting initiated by Cimabue and Giotto, the most important artists of the Italian proto-Renaissance of the late thirteenth century. As Oakeshott puts it:

> Stylistically . . . the mosaic shows the development of a remarkable new series of conventions, the transition being from a highly stylized, linear representation of the human figure to one that is far freer, far more solid and far more naturalistic. . . . This is, in fact, the transition from Romanesque . . . to Renaissance.

---

*In Christ's parable of a nighttime wedding, ten virgins go forth to meet the bridegroom — who represents the Second Coming — and accompany him to the marriage ceremony. But only five possess sufficient oil to properly trim their lamps; the remaining five miss the ceremony because they are forced to go in search of oil elsewhere. In the mosaic at S. Maria in Trastevere, eight (not five) of the ten lamps are lit, so the significance of the ten figures is open to question.

The church interior remains remarkably medieval in feel, despite the seventeenth-century ceiling and the nineteenth-century decoration of the upper nave. The dominant features are the scavenged antique nave columns and entablature fragments, the Cosmatesque floor (nineteenth-century but constructed of old materials arranged in patterns used by the Cosmati family in the twelfth and thirteenth centuries), and — above all — the mosaics in the apse. On sunny days, the reflection of light off the myriad tiny tiles envelops the high altar in a soft, luminous glow. This is true, deep-down warmth, not false surface glitter, and among the churches of Rome, it is all too rare.

Indeed, the sharp contrast between medieval and Baroque is rendered immediately apparent in the left aisle, where the Avila Chapel (the last chapel before the steps) contains what can only be described as a Baroque explosion. Antonio Gherardi, who designed the chapel in 1678, filled the arches and vault with a veritable encyclopedia of Baroque architectural effects. Bernini's indirect lighting in the Coronari Chapel at S. Maria della Vittoria, Borromini's sensuous wall curves at S. Carlino, Michelangelo's flowerlike Corinthian capitals at the Campidoglio, Borromini's curved and fragmented aedicule pediments at S. Giovanni in Laterano — they are all recalled here, as if in summary of the entire Roman Baroque experience. Unfortunately, the end result is more crowded than composed, and the straight lines necessary to achieve the perspective effect seem to jar against the overwhelming preponderance of curves elsewhere. Compared to the profound dignity of the rest of the church, the chapel seems merely clever — a Baroque *tour de force* that goes too far to achieve too little.

10-9   SANTA DOROTEA
Giovanni Battista Nolli, 1751–1756
(Via di S. Dorotea, northwest of the Piazza di S. Maria in Trastevere)

Nowadays, Giovanni Battista Nolli is better remembered as a mapmaker and surveyor than as an architect. In preparing his famous Plan of Rome, he measured the entire city within the walls, block by block and sometimes building by building; the huge, many-paneled map he produced stands today not only as an invaluable historical document, but as one of the most elegant engravings in the history of cartography. Just before he died, however, he designed the little neighborhood church of S. Dorotea in Trastevere, and it is an extremely accomplished piece of work.

As might be expected from the late Baroque date, the façade is unusually simplified. Four massive giant pilasters fill up most of the wall surface with single-minded resolution; the outermost pilasters are expanded and nested into triplets to supply a framing effect. As at S. Pasquale Baylon, the overall look is reductive, but with a difference: here it is the decoration that has been banished, not the pilasters, and the architectural elements are allowed to do all the visual work.

Inside, the ruling architectural scheme at first appears more conventionally Baroque. The most distinctive feature is the domical vault, which completely dominates the interior. But the power of the vault produces a visual ambiguity. Is this a centralized church or a longitudinal church? That is, are the four arms of the church of equal length, or is the nave-apse axis longer than the transept axis? To the casual eye, the prominence of the vault centerpiece immediately suggests a centralized space. But once the eye leaves the vault and begins to explore the walls and side chapels, the sense of centralization disappears. In fact, the ground plan of the church is longitudinal, but the domical vault — and therefore the transept — is unexpectedly placed at (or very near) the center of the long nave-apse axis. It is an extremely unorthodox shape for a church, halfway between the traditional longitudinal Latin cross and the traditional centralized Greek cross.

This odd melding of shapes produces an unusual visual tug-of-war; as the eye moves back and forth between upper and lower regions — between the implied centrality of the vault and actual longitudinality of the ground plan — the interior as a whole seems to vacillate between the two opposing schemes (or perhaps to teeter perpetually on the edge of both). But the balance is beautifully controlled, creating an overall space that is tense with potential energy. Michelangelo would have approved. It is a shame that the applied decoration — false painted marbling, as at S. Pasquale Baylon — is so dingy; once again, Baroque decoration robs the underlying architecture of its rightful power and works against the very structural elements it is meant to enhance.

10-10   PORTA SETTIMIANA
Constructed ca. 1500
(At the intersection of the Via di S. Dorotea, the Via della Scala,
and the Via Garibaldi)

At the northern edge of Trastevere, just inside the old Aurelian wall, four streets come together to offer a memorably picturesque conjunction: two views that link up one of the city's least imposing gates with one of the city's most imposing fountains. The place to stand is on either side of the Via della Scala just as it ends; the Porta Settimiana is then a few yards straight ahead, and the Fontanone dell' Acqua Paola can be seen on the Janiculum Hill in the far distance to the left, rising above the rooftops up the Via Garibaldi.

The gate is merely a single arch, topped by a machicolated parapet with battlements. Such features were in medieval times defensive. The vertical slabs of the battlements offered temporary refuge to archers between shots, and the projecting arches of the machicolation (directly below the battlements) screened holes through which molten lead, boiling oil, and rocks could be dropped on invaders. In this particular case, however, the protection offered could not have been very effective, for the defensive features face the wrong way — into the city rather than out of it. In fact, they are not medieval at all, and their purpose was always primarily decorative. They were added to the gate by Pope Alexander VI (1492–1503) when he built the Via della Lungara, the long, straight street that prior to the construction of the modern Lungotevere served as the main connector between Trastevere and the Vatican.

The Fontanone dell' Acqua Paola was constructed by Pope Paul V some hundred years later, in 1610. In the interim, Rome had changed dramatically. The Renaissance had produced the city's first true building boom since Imperial times, and Pope Sixtus V, recognizing the need for rational urban planning, had restored the ancient aqueduct of Alexander Severus and had laid out the network of long, straight streets that shaped Rome's growth for the next 350 years. But Sixtus's plan had not included Trastevere, and the Fontanone was built to remedy that deficiency. Its purpose was to receive and distribute the waters of the newly repaired aqueduct of Trajan, and also to mark the starting point of a new avenue descending the Janiculum Hill to a second fountain at the Ponte Sisto. Near the river, the avenue was to cross a new main thoroughfare cut through the heart of Trastevere, from S. Francesco a Ripa to the Porta Settimiana.

In the end, only a portion of Paul V's street plan was carried out (the Via di S. Francesco a Ripa, which runs from S. Francesco a Ripa to the Piazza di S. Maria in Trastevere), and the fountain remained isolated atop the Janiculum. But its distant presence at this spot, overlooking the Porta Settimiana, produces a telling juxtaposition. The gate was built at the beginning of the Renaissance, and its useless medieval battlements look backward in time with an almost palpable nostalgia; the fountain was built at the end of the Renaissance, and its imposing monumentality looks forward to the Baroque city — the city of the Trevi Fountain and the Spanish Steps — with unfaltering confidence. Together, gate and fountain combine to symbolize a momentous sixteenth-century change: Rome, at long last, had emerged from its thousand-year decline to enter a period of renewal and growth that continues to this day.

10-11   VILLA FARNESINA
Baldassare Peruzzi, 1508–1511
(Via Lungara, east side, just outside the Porta Settimiana)

The term *villa* is commonplace in architectural parlance, but its many distinct meanings make it the source of endless confusion. In its customary modern acceptation, it means (mostly in England) a small detached house with a modest garden in a city suburb. But in antiquity it meant something quite different. In fact, the ancient Romans inhabited three separate kinds of villas: the *villa rusticana* (a large and substantial country house, often a working farm, with attendant outbuildings); the *villa suburbana* (a house near a city or town, usually less substantial and lacking outbuildings); the *villa urbana* (a retreat with galleries and sometimes extensive gardens and grounds, often at the edge of town, either with or without living quarters). During the Renaissance, the term took on added connotations of high culture, and came to mean a building of almost any size that functioned as a refuge from the demands of daily life, where like-minded people could spend an afternoon or an evening engaged in civilized discourse surrounded by art and beauty. The Villa Farnesina, constructed in 1508–1511 by architect Baldassare Peruzzi for his patron Agostino Chigi, is the classic example of this type of structure, a Renaissance villa *par excellence.*

Agostino Chigi was banker to popes Alexander VI, Pius III, Julius II, and Leo X, and in the early 1500s, he was reputed to be the richest man in Europe. He owned most of the land between the Tiber and the Via Lungara, and the complex of buildings surrounded by gardens that he constructed included a combination stable and guest house on the Via Lungara and a dining pavilion at the edge of the river. Both of these ancillary structures have since disappeared, and the building that remains gained its current name — although it is occasionally called the Villa Chigi to this day — when it was purchased by the Farnese family in 1579 and became an adjunct of the Farnese palace just across the river.

On initial approach, the villa appears modest to a fault: a simple, understated façade with a simple, understated central entrance door. The basic composition of identical window bays delimited by plain pilasters is repeated on most of the building, and the sole enlivening feature is the stucco frieze beneath the cornice along the roofline. In Chigi's day, however, the effect would have been a bit more flamboyant. For one thing, the main entranceway was on the other side of the building, through the open and arched garden loggia (a far more welcoming façade flanked by short side wings); for another, all the plain exterior stucco wall surfaces were filled with decorative monochromatic frescoes (faint traces can still be seen around the upper portions of some of the arches on the loggia side of the building). Peruzzi himself was responsible for this decoration, which served for the visitor as an appetizer to the feast of painting within.

With the frescoes that adorned the interior rooms, Chigi pulled out all the stops, hiring (in addition to Peruzzi) the artists Raphael, Sodoma, and Sebastiano del Piombo to create one of the most elaborate decorative schemes of the era. The works by Raphael and his studio are the most famous (notably *Galatea,* a single panel showing the sea nymph riding a seashell chariot drawn by dolphins, and *The Legend of Cupid and Psyche,* a full cycle covering the entire ceiling of the ground-floor loggia that faces the garden). But from an architectural point of view, the *pièce de résistance* is the set of illusionistic frescoes by Peruzzi in the Sala delle Prospettive on the upper floor, where the walls have been painted to look as if they opened out onto columned balconies that offer views of the city outside (the illusion is most effective when viewed from the center of the wall opposite the fireplace).

Although the villa did contain an upstairs bedroom, it was used primarily for afternoon and evening gatherings, and its heyday came with the election in 1513 of the famously extravagant Pope Leo X, who supposedly declared, "Since God has seen fit to give us the papacy, let us see fit to enjoy it." The pope was a regular visitor to the villa, and the entertainments given in his honor became famous. The most celebrated of all the villa's dinner parties took place in 1518: a lavish banquet held in the dining pavilion next to the Tiber, at which the servants who cleared each course, to the astonishment of the guests, cavalierly disposed of the silver plate by throwing it into the river (it was not until later that information leaked out about the newly installed underwater nets that were used to catch and retrieve the discarded treasure).

10-12 SAN PIETRO IN MONTORIO
Probably Baccio Pontelli, 1481
Raimondi Chapel: Gianlorenzo Bernini, 1640
Tempietto: Donato Bramante, 1503
(Piazza di S. Pietro in Montorio, above Trastevere, off the continuation of the
Via Garibaldi that climbs the Janiculum Hill; the winding road possesses
loop-connecting stepped shortcuts)

The church itself is unassuming, to say the least, but it possesses some fine art (especially Sebastiano del Piombo's *Flagellation,* after a design by Michelangelo, in the first chapel to the right, and Baldassare Peruzzi's *Coronation of the Virgin,* in the vault of the second chapel to the right), and also boasts a notable Bernini chapel (second on the left) designed around a revolutionary idea: concealed natural lighting. The effect here is not especially dramatic, but it was a critical first step, and out of Bernini's continued experimentation with the concept came two unequivocal masterpieces: the Cornaro Chapel in S. Maria della Vittoria and the Altieri Chapel in S. Francesco a Ripa.

The main attraction, however, is outside in the courtyard: Bramante's little Tempietto, built in 1503, arguably the most beautiful and surely the most Classical modern building in the entire city. Despite its early (for Rome) Renaissance date, there is no feeling of experimentation here, no awkward groping toward a new architectural grammar. This is fully realized Classical architecture — and in some ways a new type of Classical architecture — that is both assured and controlled.

Built to mark the spot where St. Peter was thought (erroneously) to have been crucified, the Tempietto's construction was an act of simple religious commemoration: the building sanctifies the holy space it encloses. Given this function, Bramante's choice of a circular building was especially apt, for his concentric rings of steps, columns, and wall immediately suggest a zeroing in on a central focal point. His choice of Roman Doric for the colonnade — its first appearance since antiquity — was also apt: it is the simplest and most dignified of the Classical orders. And his handling of the detail work — the triglyphs on the frieze, for instance, and the carved liturgical instruments on the metopes between — shows total confidence. For the first time in over a thousand years, the Classical vocabulary is being used with absolute fluency.

But if the architectural vocabulary is old, the rigor of the ruling geometry is quite new. The Tempietto's plan is generated by two concentric circles, which generate two concentric cylinders, one low (the circle of columns) and one high (the walls enclosing the sacred space); the diameter of the outer cylinder is exactly the same as the height of the inner cylinder. These complementary shapes in turn give rise to the hemispherical dome topped by a lantern — an entirely original invention for which there was no precedent whatsoever in antiquity. The strict mathematical relationship of part to part continues throughout the entire building.

To Bramante, such a tight three-dimensional organization would have been more than an arbitrary aesthetic choice. It would have been a philosophical necessity, for High Renaissance scientific theory held that symmetrical shapes and simple proportional relationships by their God-given mathematical nature must be the most pleasing to the eye. Mannerist and (especially) Baroque artists would soon come to question this thesis, but for a short period — the period of the High Renaissance — it reigned supreme.

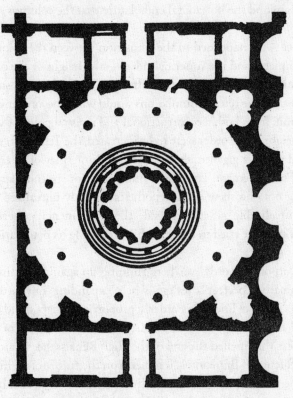

Ground plan of Tempietto and proposed courtyard.

Aside from some minor modifications to the dome and a later (and enlarged) replacement lantern, the Tempietto stands today exactly as Bramante designed it. But his plan for the rest of the courtyard was never executed. As a surviving ground plan shows, he probably intended to reorganize the space into a circular cloister, surrounding the Tempietto with a circular colonnaded portico attached to a circular wall with chapels protruding into the four corners of the outermost square. In effect, the courtyard would then have been a mirror image of the Tempietto's lower half — the Tempietto turned inside out. The viewer entering the courtyard would not merely face a circular building but would find himself surrounded by circles as well, all focused inexorably on the holy spot in the center.

Bramante's plan looks artful and elegant on paper, but in fact it may have presented insurmountable practical problems. In *The Architecture of the Renaissance,* architectural historian Leonardo Benevolo suggests that the plan, which looks so elegant on paper, would in reality have been impossible to execute. He explains as follows (the term "order" refers both to the vertical columns and the horizontal entablature that the columns support):

> If in fact — as happened in the transition between the colonnade of the Tempietto and the inner cylinder — the height of the order was to remain constant (even if the difference in level of the steps were made use of), the intercolumniations would widen beyond any permissible limit, from both a constructional and a visual point of view; but if the height of the order were to be increased, the Tempietto would be crushed inside a gigantic shell, blurring all interplay of internal relations of measurement. The plan ... must therefore be considered as the working out of a theoretical hypothesis not only unrealized but perhaps unrealizable, situated outside the experimental sphere within which Bramante tried to remain while exploring its boundaries.

Bramante, in other words, was here running up against the limitations of philosophically "perfect" design; when expanding outward from the Tempietto's inner cylinder, his orderly proportions, shapes, and rules could be pushed so far and no farther. In part, it was the discovery of limitations such as these that spelled the end of the High Renaissance in architecture.

The influence of Bramante's Tempietto on the future of architecture can scarcely be overestimated, for this little building is probably the most copied Classical structure ever built. Over and over again, the motif of dome-on-drum-rising-out-of-colonnade reappears on the important buildings of the day, regardless of the reigning architectural style. Wren's seventeenth-century St. Paul's Cathedral in London, Soufflot's eighteenth-century Pantheon in Paris, Walter's nineteenth-century U.S. Capitol in Washington, D.C. — these are merely the most famous examples in the most famous cities. The list is virtually endless, and in the United States, twenty-two of the fifty state capitols possess domes based on Bramante's design. Indeed, the influence of the Tempietto has been so pervasive that most modern viewers, understandably jaded by overexposure to cities filled with nineteenth-century Neoclassicism, may have trouble responding to the building at all. But the value of making an aesthetic leap back in time — of imagining a Rome where most new buildings were as rudimentary in their Classicism as the façade of the church next door — is greater with this building than with any other in Rome. The Renaissance Classical revival in architecture had begun to flower in Florence some eighty years earlier, but this was its first perfect bloom.

10-13   MONUMENTO AI CADUTI 1849–1870
Giovanni Lacobucci, 1941
(Via Garibaldi, up the hill from S. Pietro in Montorio on the left)

Built in 1941 in memory of those who gave their lives for the liberation of Rome and the unification of Italy, the Monument to the Fallen 1849–1870 is typical in style (if not in scale) of the fascist architecture of Mussolini and his followers. "Neoclassicism with a cookie-cutter," Robert Hughes called it; rejecting all but the simplest decorative elements, it strips traditional Classical architecture down to its essential lines. The result here is unusual in feel — bordering on Art Deco — because of its modesty; it is one of the very few structures of its day that did not attempt to mirror Mussolini's obsessive heroic posturing. Were it not for the fascist associations the style inevitably conjures up, this monument would be almost all right.

10-14   FONTANONE DELL' ACQUA PAOLA
Flaminio Ponzio, 1610–1611
(Via Garibaldi, just below the Passeggiata del Gianicolo)

From the distant Porta Settimiana down below, the Fontanone dell' Acqua Paola appears to crown the Janiculum slope with dignity and distinction. Up close, however, the fountain is far larger than expected, and not nearly so impressive. Sharp and angular in both outline and detail, it bristles with self-importance, giving pride of place to a long-winded inscription boasting about Pope Paul V's munificence in repairing the aqueduct of Trajan. Moreover, beneath the surface braggadocio runs an unattractive undercurrent of envy. The fountain's design is based upon the much smaller Fontana dell' Acqua

Felice, built some twenty-five years earlier by Pope Sixtus V on the Quirinal Hill across town. Paul V, determined to outdo his predecessor, copied the earlier fountain's basic design but increased the overall size to gargantuan proportions. The result rivals the Trevi in size, but not in panache. One historical note: the fountain's four central columns (flanking the arches) are antique, and were salvaged from the wreckage of the porch in front of the original St. Peter's.

10-15   VIEW FROM THE JANICULUM HILL
(Passeggiata del Gianicolo, east side, beyond the Piazzale Giuseppe Garibaldi at the lighthouse)

The tour buses mass at the Piazza Garibaldi, but a better view can be found a short three-minute walk to the north, at the lighthouse. The path of the mostly hidden Tiber can be traced by following the line of trees that winds through the panorama. The most prominent monuments and domes (from the left and moving always to the right) are as follows: at the extreme left, the Palazzo di Giustizia; moving slightly forward and across the river, the dome and façade of S. Salvatore in Lauro; back, the dome of S. Carlo al Corso, with the Villa Medici behind; forward, Borromini's clock tower in the Piazza dell' Orologio; back, the obelisk and twin towers of SS. Trinità dei Monti atop the Spanish Steps; forward, the squat dome and pedimented façade of the Chiesa Nuova, with Borromini's Oratorio façade between; straight right, the dome and twin towers of S. Agnese in the Piazza Navona; slightly back, the lantern of S. Ivo della Sapienza, with the saucer dome of the Pantheon behind; just to the right and back, the Presidential Palace on the Quirinal; forward, the dome of S. Maria della Valle, with the twin domes and pointed Gothic tower of S. Maria Maggiore far behind and the Torre delle Milizie slightly to the right; forward, the Palazzo Farnese, with the dome of S. Carlo ai Catinari and the Victor Emmanuel Monument behind; back, the Palazzo del Senatore campanile in the Campidoglio; on the horizon, the statues on the roof of S. Giovanni in Laterano; and finally, moving forward and visible at last, the waters of the Tiber as it approaches the Aventine Hill. The huge, many-winged structure at the bottom of the hill in the foreground is Rome's main prison, ironically named *Regina Coeli* — Queen of Heaven — after the monastery that once occupied the site.

TOUR 11

—•—

CATHOLIC ROME:
ST. PETER'S, THE VATICAN, AND THE BORGO

Basilica di S. Pietro in Vaticano

IN 1870, WHEN the Italian army broke through the ancient walls near the Porta Pia and captured the city, Rome ceased to be a papal possession and became the capital of the newly united republic of Italy. The pope, famously, became "the prisoner of the Vatican," and it was not until 1929 that a treaty was signed by which the Vatican City — essentially St. Peter's, St. Peter's Square, and the Vatican Palace and gardens — was created as a tiny remnant sovereign state controlled by the Catholic Church.

The area immediately around St. Peter's — known as the Borgo (borough), from the old German word *borgus*, meaning a small fortified settlement — was enclosed within defensive walls by Pope Leo IV in 850. It had been an important pilgrim destination ever since Constantine built the original basilica over the putative site of St.

Peter's grave around 320, but it did not take on its modern role as an administrative center until the fourteenth century, when the popes returned from their seventy-year sojourn in France to find the medieval papal palace next to S. Giovanni in Laterano uninhabitable. The papal court moved into some ancillary buildings adjacent to St. Peter's, and the papacy has been ensconced on the Vatican Hill ever since. The complete rebuilding of St. Peter's and the construction of St. Peter's Square (pictured on the previous page) in the sixteenth and seventeenth centuries entirely transformed the neighborhood, creating both the most famous church in Christendom and the most illustrious architectural threshold in Europe.

11-1   PONTE SANT' ANGELO
Constructed 134 C.E.; end arches restored and enlarged 1892–1894
Angel statuary: designed by Gianlorenzo Bernini (1668)
and executed by his assistants
(Crosses the Tiber at the Castel S. Angelo)

The idea would seem foolproof: to mark the ancient Ponte S. Angelo as unique by lining it with sculpted angels carrying symbols of the Passion (the sufferings of Christ at the end of his life, from his entry into Jerusalem to his entombment). And from a distance — from the Tiber embankments, say, or from the heights of the Castel S. Angelo — the angels seem to be doing their work with exemplary skill and grace, setting the bridge apart from its peers and proclaiming its special importance as the main approach to St. Peter's and the Vatican.

But up close, things go oddly wrong. The monolithic Castel S. Angelo — more a fortress than a castle — looms over the bridge with a distinctly threatening presence; its hulking shape completely overshadows the dome of St. Peter's, which is in any case too distant to relate to the bridge in any visually meaningful way. And the sculpted angels, upon closer inspection, turn out to be self-conscious and mannered in style; with their contorted body poses, masses of billowing drapery, and ecstatic facial expressions, the figures exhibit all the hallmarks of the Baroque style at its most artificial and extreme.

Part of the problem, perhaps, lies in the execution. Though the statues were all designed by Bernini, they were carved by his assistants and pupils.*

---

*Bernini himself originally carved two of the statues meant for the bridge: the *Angel with the Crown of Thorns* and the *Angel with the Subscription "I.N.R.I."* These statues were never set up, however, because Bernini's patron Pope Clement IX declared them too beautiful to be exposed to the vicissitudes of wind and weather. Clement ordered replicas for the bridge, and Bernini's originals remained indoors, eventually

Bernini made drawings of each of the angels, but beyond these sketches his pupils were free to do as they wished. The results are decidedly mixed; even so fundamental an attribute as the size of the head varies markedly from angel to angel. Moreover, the scale of the statues — a feature that was certainly determined by Bernini himself — does not help matters. Noticeably larger than life-size and placed on high pedestals, the figures seem almost as threatening in their heavy, looming presence as the Castel S. Angelo (compare the pre-Baroque statues of St. Peter and St. Paul at the bridge's south end, which are straightforward in attitude and far less overbearing in effect). In the end, it is probably best to view the angels from the middle distance, where the individual figures merge into a group and meld with the design of the bridge as a whole.

11-2 CASTEL SANT' ANGELO (HADRIAN'S TOMB)
Completed 139 C.E., with much later additions
(At the north end of the Ponte S. Angelo)

According to legend, the massive Castel S. Angelo — built in the second century C.E. as the tomb of the emperor Hadrian — owes its decidedly odd religious name to a miraculous medieval visitation. The year was 590; Gregory I (today known as Gregory the Great) had recently been elected pope, and Rome was ravaged by plague. Praying for relief from the terrible scourge, the pope led a penitential procession through the city streets, and as the head of the procession reached the bridge leading to St. Peter's, the archangel Michael suddenly appeared atop Hadrian's tomb, brandishing and then sheathing his sword. The sheathed sword was taken as a hopeful portent — a sign that God's anger had at last been appeased by the prayers of the faithful. The plague abated shortly thereafter, and a chapel was constructed at the spot where the archangel appeared. Hadrian's tomb has been known as the Castel S. Angelo ever since.

The castle's character as a citadel dates from the end of the third century, when the emperor Aurelian built the city walls and incorporated Hadrian's tomb into the city defenses as a bridgehead. From that time on the castle's function was primarily military, and periodic renovations (and the addition of ramparts) gradually transformed the tomb into a fortress. For centuries,

---

finding their way to S. Andrea delle Fratte, near the Spanish Steps, where they remain today. On the bridge, one of the replicas — the *Angel with the Subscription "I.N.R.I."* — is sometimes ascribed to Bernini because it is in fact a variation rather than a true copy of the original.

the castle also served as a defensive adjunct to the Borgo, and in the early 1400s, the antipope John XXIII began construction of the high wall topped by a covered passageway that connects the castle and the Vatican Palace to this day.

The castle served as a refuge of last resort for a number of medieval popes beset by barbarian invasions, but its most infamous stint as an emergency papal residence came during the Renaissance. On the morning of May 6, 1527, Pope Clement VII fled down the passageway from his palace as Rome was attacked by the troops of Emperor Charles V. From the relative safety of the castle, the pope watched the city being ruthlessly sacked, and he remained a besieged prisoner for the next seven months. Benvenuto Cellini, the celebrated sixteenth-century goldsmith, sculptor, and memoirist, accompanied the pope on the day of the attack (along with at least a thousand other supporters, including thirteen cardinals and eighteen bishops), and in his autobiography he described with characteristic modesty what happened next:

> So there I was in the castle. I went up to some guns that were in the charge of a bombardier called Giuliano the Florentine. He was staring out over the battlements to where his poor house was being sacked and his wife and children outraged. He dared not fire in case he harmed his own family, and flinging his fuse on the ground he started tearing at his face and sobbing bitterly. Other bombardiers were doing the same.
>
> When I saw this I seized one of the fuses, got help from some of the men who were not in such a state, and lined up some heavy pieces of artillery and falconets [small cannon], firing them where I saw the need. In this way I slaughtered a great number of the enemy. If I had not done so the troops who had broken into Rome that morning would have made straight for the castle and could easily have entered, as the artillery was not in action. I continued firing, with an accompaniment of blessings and cheers from a number of cardinals and noblemen. Inspired by this, I forced myself to try and do the impossible. Anyhow, all I need say is that it was through me that the castle was saved.

When Hadrian's remains were placed inside the newly constructed mausoleum after his death in 138 C.E., the structure was far less aggressive in its character than it appears today. It was originally surrounded by gardens, sheathed in marble, and surmounted by an earthen mound planted with trees and ringed by statues. Hadrian carefully calculated the size so as not to exceed the nearby Tomb of Augustus; as a political gesture, he meant his memorial to complement Augustus's structure, not compete with it. Today the more meaningful comparison is with St. Peter's, visible down the Via della Conciliazione to the west, where Michelangelo's magnificent dome serves as a welcome aesthetic counterpoint to the castle's hulking, minatory presence.

Interior Museum: The tomb is open to the public. The interior spiral ramp, which originally ascended to the chamber containing the cinerary urns of every emperor from Hadrian to Septimius Severus, now leads to the former hardship quarters of the pope, which have been well preserved. The view of the city from the upper terrace is superb.

11-3   VIA DELLA CONCILIAZIONE
Construction begun 1937
(West of the Castel S. Angelo)

Schemes for giving St. Peter's Square a grand boulevard approach had been considered, off and on, ever since the square was built in the seventeenth century. Nothing was done, however, until 1937, when Mussolini's city planners demolished most of the buildings between the square and the Ponte S. Angelo and laid out the 150-foot-wide Via della Conciliazione in their place. The result has been much criticized, and rightly so. The new palazzi that line the street are dull in conception and coarse in execution; the two rows of rigid obelisk lamps down the center — added after the fact in an attempt to alleviate the feeling of excessive, barren width — merely heighten the oppressive effect. The new view of St. Peter's is admittedly fine, but probably not so fine as the old, when the huge dome was seen only in tantalizing glimpses above narrow streets and crooked alleyways, looming over the jumbled Borgo like God inspecting His disorderly dominions. There are times when a bit of chaos brings life and energy to the cityscape; to banish disorder as ruthlessly as this is to impose a cure that is worse than the disease.

11-4   ST. PETER'S SQUARE (PIAZZA SAN PIETRO)
Colonnade: Gianlorenzo Bernini, 1656–1657

After Pope Julius II laid the cornerstone for the new St. Peter's in 1506, construction continued for some 150 years. During this period the status of the open area in front of the church was occasionally discussed, but it was not until 1656, when the church was almost completed, that the question was effectively addressed. Some preliminary work had already been done: in 1586, Pope Sixtus V had commissioned architect Domenico Fontana to move an ancient obelisk from the side of the church to the front, and Carlo Maderno had built a fountain to complement the obelisk in 1613. But these amenities merely marked the church forecourt area as important; they did not delimit it or give it a character that was in any way pervasive or unified. The perimeter structures remained an irregular hodgepodge — to the north, the cluster of buildings that made up the Vatican Palace; to the south and west, residential housing — and the church façade lacked any sort of formal approach.

Pope Alexander VII (1655–1667) was determined to remedy this situation. On the practical side, he wanted three things: first, a forecourt that would properly set St. Peter's off from the surrounding city; second, a formal processional approach to the church that would offer shelter from the elements; and third, clear sightlines from the square to the two balconies used for papal blessings, one above the main door at St. Peter's and the other at the papal apartments in the Vatican Palace. On the aesthetic side, he wanted magnitude and splendor — something that would compare favorably with the works of Rome's ancient emperors and reclaim some of the city's long-lost architectural glory.

The fantasy was grandiose even by Roman standards. But Alexander knew exactly where to turn in order to transform his dream into a reality: Gianlorenzo Bernini. As Rudolf Wittkower comments in his survey *Art and Architecture in Italy, 1600–1750,* "Bernini himself was responsible [for the fulfillment of the project] . . . he alone had the genius and resourcefulness to find a way through a tangle of topographical and liturgical problems, and only his supreme authority in artistic matters . . . could overcome intrigues and envious opposition and bring this task to a successful conclusion."

Bernini responded to the pope's challenge with a two-part plan: a matching pair of curved colonnades (made up of four concentric arcs of Tuscan columns) facing each other across an oval area around the obelisk, and two straight enclosed passageways — extensions of the curved colonnades decorated with pilasters — approaching the church façade at either end. The scope of the plan was vast, requiring two-hundred and eighty-four columns for the curved colonnades, eighty-eight pilasters for the straight passageways, ninety-six statues of saints and martyrs for the unifying balustrade, and a second fountain to match Maderno's earlier fountain of 1613.

Overall, it was one of the most ambitious projects in the history of Italian architecture, and (in contrast to St. Peter's) it was constructed with astonishing speed, requiring less than fifteen years to complete.

Bernini's basic design was simple but inspired. The three passageways inside the colonnade — the outer two passages for pedestrians and the wider central passage for carriages — created the desired processional shelter, and the limited height of both the curved colonnade and the straight passageways not only offered clear sightlines from the square to the papal balconies, but also allowed the entire set piece to serve as an optical corrective for St. Peter's (the lowness of the straight passageways as they approach the church at either end makes the excessively wide façade look taller and narrower than it actually is). The apparent simplicity of the colonnade is deceptive; in fact, Bernini's idea was highly original both in conception and in effect. As Anje Scherner explains in *The Architecture of Rome:*

> Bernini selected . . . a structural form unknown to the architecture of his times: it was a free-standing colonnade consisting of four rows. This architectural form, which Bernini justified to his contemporaries by referring to ancient models, concludes the square towards the outside, but at the same time opens it up: it is possible to walk through the colonnade at any point, and it makes the square accessible from all sides. However, inside the square, the view towards the outside is obscured by a forest of columns. Only at two points in the square, namely the centers of the semicircular colonnades . . . is it possible to look through to the outside.

The two points (or at least one, since the effect is identical from each) are worth searching out — they are marked with medallions in the pavement between the central obelisk and the side fountains — for the views drive home Scherner's basic point: Bernini's colonnade is in effect a porous wall, opened and closed at the same time. The effect is so obvious that it is often overlooked, but it is a key element in the piazza's uniquely welcoming character: an incoming visitor, no matter what the approach route, is always free to enter and is never confronted by a solid barrier that necessitates an irksome detour to a prescribed entry point.

Engraving showing Bernini's proposed terzo braccio for the colonnade in St. Peter's Square.

Bernini was well aware of the colonnade's special characteristics, and its openness and embracing overall shape were for him a chief virtue. Indeed, he viewed the colonnade as an architectural metaphor for the Catholic Church itself. "The portico," he wrote, "expresses her [that is, the Church's] receiving in her open arms Catholics to be confirmed in faith, heretics to be reunited with the Church, and unbelievers to be enlightened by the true faith." As originally planned, the sense of protective enclosure would have been further heightened by a third section of colonnade at the piazza's east end; unhappily, Alexander VII died before this section was constructed, and his successors abandoned the plan on economic grounds. But the loss of Bernini's *terzo braccio* — the third arm — is only a minor drawback, and the rest of the colonnade was constructed exactly as Bernini and Alexander envisioned it.

Today St. Peter's Square is so famous and so beloved that it is difficult to imagine Rome without it. But when it was first proposed, the project was highly controversial. Critics charged that the piazza as planned would be too big, would take too long to build, would be too expensive, would rob the poor of much-needed alms, and would be perceived by the faithful as a sacrilegious monument to the vanity of a profligate pope. Advocates answered that the colonnade was appropriately Roman in scale and effect, that construction would be relatively quick, that the project would benefit the economy by circulating money and giving the poor employment, and that the result would be a great civic work of art that would be worth the expense. In the end, only the worries about cost proved justified: at more than a million *scudi* — a colossal sum — the project reduced an already depleted papal treasury to dangerous levels. But in spending the money, Alexander VII gave St. Peter's and Rome one of the most effective architectural set pieces ever created — a bold and dramatic structure that carves an unforgettable space out of the surrounding city, and welcomes all who enter within its enveloping architectural arms.

11-5 SAINT PETER'S (SAN PIETRO IN VATICANO)
Original conception and design: Donato Bramante, 1505–1514
Design modifications: Primarily Michelangelo, 1547–1564,
and Carlo Maderno, 1603–1616
Dome: Michelangelo, 1547–1564, and Giacomo della Porta, 1564–1602
Façade: Carlo Maderno, 1603–1612
Baldacchino and *Cathedra Petri*: Gianlorenzo Bernini, 1624–1666

St. Peter's is certainly the most famous building in Rome; it is also, perhaps, the most problematical. In their massive and comprehensive 1994 architectural exhibition catalogue titled *The Renaissance from Brunelleschi to Michelangelo: The Representation of Architecture,* Henry A. Millon and Craig Hugh Smyth state the basic facts forthrightly:

> St. Peter's is acknowledged to be one of the most important structures in the history of architecture. Enclosing and commemorating the tomb of the first apostle, St. Peter's is the largest, most imposing religious building of the Christian West, the center of the papacy and a goal of Christian pilgrimage. It also incorporates the architectural aspirations and achievements of generations of architects, chief among them Bramante, Michelangelo and Carlo Maderno.

The church, in sum, is a structure to be reckoned with. But its architectural character is far from straightforward. Reactions of first-time visitors vary widely — perhaps more widely than with any other famous building in Europe — ranging from awe to indifference to dismay. When an important building produces such a wide array of responses, how can its aesthetic character be fairly evaluated?

First, some history. Construction of St. Peter's was spread out over a period of more than 150 years — from the early 1500s to the mid-1600s — and the story of its design is dizzyingly complicated. The new church replaced a far older one, originally constructed by Constantine and consecrated by Pope Sylvester I on November 11, 326 C.E. Like most early churches, the Constantinian structure was basilican in form, with four interior aisles (two on either side of the nave) and a curved apse attached directly to the transept; it was approached up steps and through a large, enclosed courtyard. By the time of the Renaissance, it was well over a thousand years old, and despite repairs, down the centuries it was plagued by serious structural problems, including deteriorating masonry, shifting foundations, and walls that leaned alarmingly out of the vertical. Renovation was urgently needed, all the more so because the official residence of the pope had recently been moved from the Lateran Palace on the other side of town to the Vatican Palace next door.*

It was Pope Nicholas V (1447–1455) who began the refurbishment that was to continue for so long. Nicholas's plans were limited in scope; beyond a general shoring-up, new construction was contemplated only at the church's apse end, which was to be substantially enlarged. Construction on the additions was slow, however, and after Nicholas died, most of the fifteenth-century popes who succeeded him preferred to concentrate their architectural attention on additions to the Vatican Palace.

Some fifty years later, in 1503, Pope Julius II revived the moribund church project with a vengeance. His favored architect was Donato Bramante — designer of the peerless little Tempietto in the courtyard of S. Pietro in Montorio — and the two made a formidable pair. Julius's ferocious military ambitions were reflected in his choice of a papal name, which inevitably called to mind the long-lost Imperial Rome of the Caesars (the name *Julius* had been used only once before, in the fourth century). Bramante's architectural ambitions were no less grandiose, and a contemporary satirical verse depicts him after his death confronting an exasperated St. Peter with plans for the complete architectural redesign of heaven. Spurred on by Bramante, Pope Julius put forth a plan that stunned Roman Catholics all across Europe: St. Peter's was to be torn down and replaced by an entirely new and different structure.

As a leader Julius was famously arrogant and autocratic, and his many detractors were scandalized at his plans for a new church. In their eyes, the immense and monumental statue-covered tomb he had already commissioned from Michelangelo was bad enough; the new St. Peter's — thought by some to have been conceived merely as a vainglorious setting for the

---

*The basilica of S. Giovanni in Laterano remains to this day the ecclesiastical seat of the pope as Bishop of Rome. But even during the Middle Ages, St. Peter's was always the primary Roman goal of pilgrims — S. Giovanni in Laterano had no religious relic that could compete with the bones of St. Peter — and at the beginning of the Renaissance the proximity of St. Peter's to the shrunken medieval city on the Campus Martius made it far more convenient as a papal headquarters than the distant Lateran.

self-aggrandizing tomb — was injury added to insult. Its construction would destroy the most venerated church in all Christendom, and at the same time would impiously disturb the remains not only of St. Peter but of many of his papal successors (and this in an age when the spirits of the dead were thought capable of retaliation against the living). Julius's transparently cynical decision to defray building costs by selling indulgences did not help matters, and as construction progressed, the successive deaths of the architects in charge (Bramante in 1514, Fra Giocondo in 1515, Giuliano da Sangallo in 1516, the young Raphael in 1520) was taken by many as irrefutable proof of God's displeasure.

The form the new church should take was much debated. Should it be longitudinal, like its predecessor? Or should it be centralized and symmetrical, and thus totally focused on a central altar that would mark the spot of St. Peter's grave below? There were compelling arguments on both sides. A longitudinal church was by far the more practical, with a nave that more easily accommodated a large congregation. Moreover, a longitudinal structure could be built exactly on the site of its predecessor, while a new centralized church, if big enough to cover the entire footprint of old St. Peter's, would necessarily encroach upon the Vatican Palace. A centralized plan, on the other hand, had long been considered the appropriate form for a martyrium church built to shelter the grave of a martyr or saint, and also called up suggestions of two famous centralized structures in Jerusalem: the Dome of the Rock (traditionally the site where Abraham undertook the sacrifice of his son Isaac) and the Church of the Holy Sepulchre (thought during the Renaissance to be the Biblical Temple of Solomon).

Pope Julius vacillated in choosing between the longitudinal and centralized options, and Bramante was not the only architect to draw up elaborate plans.* The most famous (and ultimately the most fruitful) of the many schemes considered was Bramante's centralized plan of 1505, which combined a symmetrical Greek cross with a square to produce a balanced play

---

*The fierceness of the competition among architects is evidenced by a drawing now in the Uffizi in Florence, probably dating from 1505. The front side of the paper shows a meticulously delineated ground plan for St. Peter's known to have been drawn up by Giuliano da Sangallo; the back side of the paper shows extensive but sketchy revisions by Bramante that manage to overlay the markings on the front side exactly without redrawing them. This startling congruence conjures up a dramatic scene: Pope Julius, worried about the strength and stability of Bramante's favored design, confronts the architect with an alternative plan by Sangallo; Bramante, sensing that his leadership of the project is threatened, holds Sangallo's diagram up against a window and sketches on the back his own impromptu revisions, modifying the plan in a way that both answers Sangallo's structural criticisms and restores the basic geometry of his own plan.

between dominant and progressively more subordinate spaces. Bramante's idea (as he himself is supposed to have stated) was to "raise the dome of the Pantheon on the Temple of Peace [the Basilica of Maxentius]." This idea was audacious enough in itself, but Bramante's plan went even further: given the fact that his dome was to be raised on a drum, what he really wanted to do was raise the *entire* Pantheon — walls, dome, and all. As Stefan Grundmann and Philipp Zitzlsperger put it in *The Architecture of Rome:* "The magnificent . . . feature of the plan was that the main building of the Roman Classical period was to be lifted into heaven on four pillars and no longer rest on the well-founded earth." This conception proved so seductive that a number of medals picturing the ultimate result were produced, which Julius distributed to potential donors.

Pope Julius died in 1513, and Bramante shortly thereafter; as construction continued over the next few decades (beginning at the western altar end of the church and moving slowly eastward toward the main entrance), Bramante's plan was significantly and continually revised by his successor architects. A succession of variant designs followed, most notably a hybrid plan by Antonio da Sangallo that attempted to combine the best features of both the centralized and the longitudinal options. But it was not until after Sangallo's death in 1546 that a definitive plan emerged. Pope Paul III appointed the seventy-one-year-old Michelangelo head architect, and the great master — at that point a figure of immense artistic authority — swept much of the work of the past forty years away. He tore down all of Sangallo's partially finished exterior walls, and reverted back to Bramante's centralized plan of 1505, which he strengthened and simplified.* For the western section of the church (the whole altar end beyond the nave), it was Michelangelo's building that was ultimately constructed.

It was Michelangelo's dome, too, that eventually crowned the church, although his original design was significantly altered after his death. Just as plans for the body of the church shifted back and forth between centralized

---

* From Michele Furnari's *Formal Design in Renaissance Architecture from Brunelleschi to Palladio:* "As newly appointed master architect, Michelangelo went one day to visit the construction site, and there he saw Sangello's wooden model. Numerous former assistants of Sangallo were in attendance — Vasari calls them 'the Sangallo faction.' They were obviously curious to hear the artist's comments on their master's design. At a certain point one of them congratulated Michelangelo on his appointment, adding that the model was of such a rich and complex conception as to be like a meadow where one could endlessly graze. 'You are indeed right,' Michelangelo replied sharply, 'but only with regard to cows and sheep, who do not understand Art!' From that moment on, the 'faction' did everything in its power to obstruct Michelangelo's work, until the Pope finally granted him exclusive control of the St. Peter's project."

and longitudinal, plans for the dome shifted between hemispherical (like the ancient dome of the Pantheon) and elongated (like the fifteenth-century dome of the Duomo in Florence). It is currently thought that Michelangelo at his death favored a hemispherical dome constructed with tapered ribs that gradually narrowed toward the top. Such a structure would have been a conscious hybrid, in that the hemisphere would have recalled the Pantheon and the ribs would have recalled the Florentine Duomo; it would also (as James Ackerman suggests in *The Architecture of Michelangelo*) have been a typically Michelangesque fusion of balance and tension, with the static shape of the dome played off against the dynamic form of the ribs, whose gradual diminution in width would have added an enlivening false-perspective element to the overall effect.

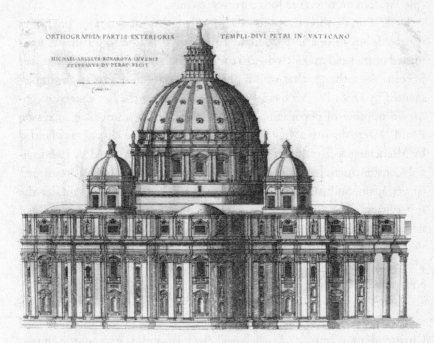

Engraving showing the dome of St. Peter's as designed by Michelangelo (the engraving was made before the entrance façade was constructed, so the view of the church is from the back, showing the rear exterior as designed and constructed by Michelangelo).

But Michelangelo's hemispherical dome was not to be. He died before construction had begun, and his successor, Giacomo della Porta, was apparently not comfortable with the more innovative features of his design. When the dome was actually built, Della Porta increased the height of the drum, elongated the curve of the dome itself so as to form the elliptical shape that exists today, and eliminated the taper of the ribs. The result was still magnificent, but it was also much more conventional than what Michelangelo had envisioned, and much closer in appearance and spirit to the Florentine dome than the Pantheon. It did, however, retain Michelangelo's most important and influential new idea: the use of columns around the circular drum to visually generate and support the dome ribs. This idea took the motifs originated by Bramante with the Tempietto and transformed them, combining a columned drum and a ribbed dome into a single unified whole. In achieving this unification, Michelangelo created what is perhaps the most beautiful dome in the world; he also created the archetypical Classical dome pattern that would rule Western architecture for centuries to come.

Della Porta's modifications to Michelangelo's design are sometimes regretted, but in one important way they were distinctly fortunate. As it turned out, a final major change to the overall design of the church was still to come — a change that would give the increase in dome height implemented by Della Porta a special importance. During the late sixteenth century, a number of popes (and particularly Paul III's immediate successor, Paul IV) were disturbed by the fact that the centralized church, as planned by Michelangelo, would not cover all of the ground occupied by the original Constantinian basilica. So the idea of a longitudinal plan was resurrected yet again, and ultimately (in the early seventeenth century under the supervision of Carlo Maderno) a nave was added at the entrance end. That nave extended the church significantly to the east, and therefore cut off the view of the dome from the main entrance piazza. Had Della Porta not increased the dome's height, it would be even less visible from St. Peter's Square than it is today.

The addition of Maderno's nave left one final problem to be solved: the façade. How should the main entrance to the greatest church in Christendom be framed? Michelangelo had wrapped the rest of the church exterior in a jacket of imposing giant pilasters, thereby achieving the large-scale unified design that had eluded his predecessors. But when he died in 1564, he left no plans for the façade. The job fell to Maderno, and his solution was quite logical: continue the use of giant pilasters at each end of the façade, but transform them into more forceful columns as they approach the center and then top them with a triangular pediment, thus forming a temple front that frames the main door and benediction balcony. Visually, however, Maderno's design is less than successful; the great width of the façade as a whole — the end bays were meant by Maderno to support towers* — detracts from the central temple front, which gets lost in the excessively horizontal expanse of wall surface. The end result is oddly bland, especially when compared to Michelangelo's magisterial dome and Bernini's noble piazza colonnade.

The interior is vast, and its comparative size can be experienced during the walk down the nave, where the lengths of the other great cathedrals of Christendom are marked out on the pavement (along the center of the nave in gold letters). The centerpiece is of course the sumptuous bronze baldacchino designed by Bernini, which marks the spot of St. Peter's grave (many levels below) in the middle of the crossing. The baldacchino's twisted columns are typically Baroque in their flamboyant effect, but they also derive from ancient precedent: set into the upper niches of the four piers facing the baldacchino are similar columns, which were saved from the original Constantinian structure, and which were thought during the Renaissance to have been brought by Constantine to Rome from the Temple of Solomon in Jerusalem.

Bernini's other Baroque *tour de force* can be found at the far end of the church, in the apse. Here, completely enclosed within an elaborate bronze chair-shaped casing that is topped by an explosion of gilded sculpture, sits the *Cathedra Petri*, the original papal throne of St. Peter. Approached from the nave, the baldacchino and the *Cathedra Petri* form a single set piece, with the baldacchino serving as a dark, contrasting frame for the gilt-glittered light that streams into the apse above the ancient throne. As Charles Scribner III lovingly describes it in his monograph *Bernini*:

> The viewer first experiences the *Baldacchino* and the *Cathedra Petri* as a single composition that unites the apostle's tomb (and papal altar) with the apostle's throne. As in the Cornaro chapel [in S. Maria della Vittoria] and S. Andrea [al Quirinale], natural light is transmuted into gilded shafts as the Holy Spirit becomes the agent of creation.... The four Church fathers — Augustine, Ambrose, Athanasius, and John Chrysostom — bridge west and east as they raise the symbol of

---

*Bernini began to construct the left-hand tower in 1638 — Maderno had died in 1629 — but cracks appeared in the façade and the partially finished tower had to be torn down (the modest clock decorations that currently top the façade's end bays were added by Giuseppe Valadier in the early nineteenth century). An official inquiry was held and Bernini was blamed; for a short period he was actually in disgrace, and was not returned to papal favor until 1647, when Pope Innocent X found himself unable to resist Bernini's design for the Fountain of the Four Rivers in the Piazza Navona.

Catholic unity [the throne] on patriarchal fingertips. With only the flimsiest of ribbons linking them to the solid volutes of the chair, their ostensible support is theological, not physical. . . . Contrapuntal gestures and crackling drapery enliven these massive and venerable pillars of Christendom. Five meters high, they were the largest bronze figures to be cast since antiquity — in fact, Augustine's mold broke during the first try in 1661. Two years later they were completed, and work began on the throne itself. Its central relief — "Feed my sheep," Christ's charge to Peter — reinforces the sacramental bridging of heaven and earth by the Eucharist, through which Peter's successors fulfill the divine commission. Against Protestant rejection and Jansenist undermining of papal power, Bernini enveloped the relic of Roman primacy in an apotheosis that dissolves the boundaries of art and suspends the laws of nature.

Bernini's hand can be seen all over the church, for he was in charge of the interior decoration during most of his adult life. But the great wealth — some would say welter — of Baroque detailing can be tiring to the eye, and many first-time visitors experience the interior of St. Peter's as Rome's most significant disappointment. In all probability, however, there is a more subtle negative phenomenon at work here. St. Peter's is vast, but — ironically — it does not look nearly so vast as it actually is. Would anyone, standing in front of the baldacchino and assessing its size, come to the conclusion that it is exactly the same height as the massive and looming Palazzo Farnese across town? It looks far smaller, and the reason must have to do with the carefully calculated proportions of the church interior. Unlike the great Gothic cathedrals of northern Europe, whose relatively narrow naves and aisles contrast so strikingly with the soaring verticality of the walls and the upward-pointing arches of the ceiling, St. Peter's is measured and balanced in its proportions, always as massively wide as it is toweringly high. For every vertical element (the giant pilasters that line the nave, say) there is a countermanding horizontal element (the nave barrel vault, which feels as if it is pressing down rather than striving upward). The result is stately and ordered, to be sure, but it is also disconcertingly inert, producing an effect of size without power or sanctity. Where the Gothic interiors soar, St. Peter's remains stubbornly earthbound.

The feeling of uneasy ambiguity — the sense that St. Peter's in some critical way works against its own architectural best interests — extends to the detailing as well. No expense was spared in the decoration of the interior, and it was all meant to reflect the greater glory of God and the riches of the Heavenly City. But for many visitors (and particularly for those disturbed by the prodigious abundance of costly ornamentation on display), the whole idea of St. Peter's is fundamentally equivocal. Conceptually, it is nothing less than an attempt by man to create God's palace on Earth, with all the positive connotations of splendor and all the negative connotations of excess that the word *palace* implies. And the viewer's reaction — is the interior awesome in its splendor or dismaying in its excess? — is perforce a personal one. In the end, architecture and aesthetics cannot be separated from religion and politics, and it is this very human muddle that makes St. Peter's, for all its grandeur, one of the most ambivalent structures ever built.

Notable Works of Art: St. Peter's contains a great deal of art, some of it extraordinary. The most celebrated work is certainly Michelangelo's *Pietà* (1499, first chapel on the right), the only piece of sculpture he ever signed (on the ribbon descending from the shoulder of the Virgin). Even a brutally abbreviated list of highlights must include Arnolfo di Cambio's famous bronze statue of St. Peter (1296, facing the nave and set against the right-hand pier just before the crossing), Bernini's monument to Urban VIII (1644, in the apse to the right of the *Cathedra Petri*), Algardi's relief *Pope Leo Arresting the Progress of Attila* (1650, at the end of the left aisle, above the tomb of Pope Leo I), and Bernini's monument to Alexander VII (1678, in the left aisle just beyond the transept, on the left). Off the left aisle just before the transept, the Treasury contains a major collection of historical and ecclesiastical artifacts, including the superbly carved sarcophagus of Junius Bassus (found beneath the basilica and dating from the fourth century), plus Antonio Pollaiolo's huge bronze monument to Sixtus IV (1493). Access to the dome and the roof — as might be expected, the views are very fine — is outside the church proper, from the right side of the entrance portico, a spot that also offers a fine view of Bernini's equestrian statue of Constantine (1670, to the right when facing the church).

Vatican Museums: The entrance to the Vatican Museums is not, as many people assume, on St. Peter's Square. It is many blocks away to the north on the Viale Vaticano, at the other end of the Vatican Palace. The collection is vast but well disposed and displayed within the palace. It is virtually impossible to see everything in a single day, but a first-time visit should certainly include the Raphael Rooms (containing Raphael's most famous painting, *The School of Athens*, 1508–1511), the Chapel of Nicholas V (frescoed by Fra Angelica, 1448–1450), and the Sistine Chapel, which contains not only Michelangelo's celebrated ceiling frescoes (1508–1512) and *Last Judgment* (1535–1541), but also wall frescoes by Pinturicchio, Perugino, Botticelli, and Ghirlandaio, among others. Although the fact is not in any way advertised, it is usually possible to exit the museum at St. Peter's Square when leaving the Sistine Chapel; when inside the Sistine Chapel, the door in the right-hand wall (beyond the screen that divides the room) leads to the square, while the door in the left-hand wall leads back toward the original entrance (by a different route from the approach).

11-6   SANT' ANNA DEI PALAFRENIERI
Interior: Giacomo da Vignola, 1565–1583
(North of St. Peter's Square, just inside the Vatican gates off the Via di Porta Angelica; the driveway through the gates is guarded, but access to the church is allowed through the pedestrian entryway to the right of the driveway)

In size and spirit, the very antithesis of St. Peter's. S. Anna dei Palafrenieri is the Vatican parish church, small in scale and intimate in feel. It is also the first oval church interior ever constructed. Designed by Giacomo da Vignola — who also designed the original but unexecuted plan for the façade of the Gesù — it was begun in 1565 but not completed until the eighteenth century, and the delay produced some major modifications to the original plan (principally the Baroque embellishments to the façade and the expansion of the Greek-cross chancel containing the high altar). But the church's main interior space remains much as Vignola designed it.

The oval plan must have been a shock when the church was first built. But the shape became so common during the Baroque era that it seems unexceptionable today, and to the modern eye it is Vignola's recessed columns — rare in any era — that stand out as unusual. By carving out wall space around his columns, Vignola manages to have it both ways: vertically the strength and force of the full column is present to support the entablature and the dome, but horizontally the column's power is substantially diminished (since it obtrudes only partway into the interior space, it functions more like a conventional half column applied to the wall surface than a full column stepping forth from it). The result, visually, suggests an X-ray, and the unusually strong feel of genuine skeletal support — vertical columns-as-bones within horizontal wall-as-skin — serves as a reminder that the original function of columns was to do the heavy lifting, not the heavy decorating. In Baroque and Neoclassical architecture, such reminders are rare — one reason the twentieth century rebelled so implacably against Classicism as a style of unnecessary and irrelevant decoration.

The twentieth-century argument makes its case even here, for in the nineteenth century the entire interior below the dome was painted to mimic marble. Even at first glance the eye senses that something is wrong — the painted plaster lacks the sheen of polished marble, and the attempt at opulence feels forced and false. The dome, happily, supplies some relief; its simple two-color paint scheme is a model of understatement, subtly emphasizing the dome's structural features and allowing the architecture to speak for itself. Vignola's revolutionary design on the ground floor deserves no less.

TOUR 12

—◆—

GREATER ROME:
OUTSIDE THE WALLS

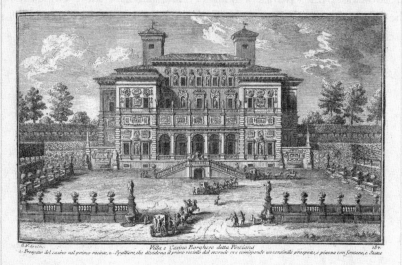

Villa e Casino Borghese detta Pinciana
1. Prospetto del casino nel primo recinto, a. Spalliere, che dividono il primo recinto dal secondo ove corrisponde un consimile prospetto, e piazza con fontane, e Statue

*T*HE FINAL TOUR ventures farther afield — the distances are too great to be walked — to a handful of sites located outside the ancient city walls: two well-known villa museums (the garden side of the Galleria Borghese is pictured above), a lesser-known medieval church, a little-known modern memorial, and a twentieth-century suburban neighborhood famous in architectural circles for sending Modernist purists into fits of scathing denunciation. There is of course a good deal more to be seen outside the walls — inside the walls, too, for that matter — and this short sampling does not pretend to be exhaustive. It is merely a selection of favorites that, because of their locations far off the beaten track, might otherwise be missed.

12-1 VILLA GIULIA (MUSEO NAZIONALE ETRUSCO)
Overall plan: Giorgio Vasari, 1551
Main building: Giacomo da Vignola, 1551–1555
Nymphaeum: Bartolomeo Ammannati, 1551
(Via di Villa Giulia, off the Via Flaminia at the northwest corner
of the Villa Borghese)

For more than a century now, the Villa Giulia has been home to the Museo Nazionale Etrusco di Villa Giulia, one of the most important (and least visited) of the city's archeological museums. Its collection of Etruscan artifacts is world famous — the remarkable Sarcofago degli Sposi (Husband and Wife Sarcophagus) alone is worth the price of admission — with most of the pieces coming from the area between Rome and Florence, where the Etruscans flourished during the sixth century B.C.E. The choice of the Villa Giulia to house the museum was singularly appropriate, for the complex of buildings was built by Pope Julius III in the mid-sixteenth century for precisely the same sort of purpose: to display an extensive collection of antiquities in a suburban retreat that offered a respite from the clamor of city life. Today the antiquities are entirely indoors, but in Julius's time the villa's exterior courtyards were filled with them as well, probably to overflowing — it is said that when the villa was stripped of its treasures a few years after Julius's death, some 160 boatloads were required to carry off the booty.

Oddly, three (or possibly four) separate architects seem to have been responsible for the villa. Giorgio Vasari probably created the overall plan (perhaps with the assistance of Michelangelo), while the main building was constructed by Giacomo da Vignola and the nymphaeum — the fountain-courtyard — was constructed by Bartolomeo Ammannati. Vignola's façade for the main building is not promising; the plain wall surface around the windows contrasts starkly with the overcrowded Mannerist entranceway composition, where the vertical force of the columns and pilasters is entirely undercut by their horizontal rustication. Once inside the building, however, things improve dramatically, with a number of spatial surprises in store.

The first surprise is the size of the main building. Although it looks quite massive on approach, the structure turns out to be only one room deep, with the main ground-floor room functioning as a vestibule leading to the walled garden courtyard beyond. The courtyard presents a second surprise: immediately outside the vestibule, a semicircular portico stretches out to the right and the left, forming a covered walkway that is open to the courtyard on the ground floor and enclosed on the upper floor. The six antique statues of

Roman consuls that originally occupied the niches of the vestibule are long gone, but the frescoed decoration of the portico remains intact, and the intricate vault frescoes, depicting vine-covered trellises tended by *putti* and filled with birds, retain their freshness to this day.

Unhappily, the courtyard is a pale shadow of its former self. Contemporary accounts describe a profusion of stuccoed and gilded wall reliefs — the wall panels flanking the columned loggia at the far end of the courtyard give some idea of what has been lost — with antique statues filling all the wall niches. In the center of the courtyard stood a fountain with a great porphyry basin, now in the Vatican Museum, that supported a statue of Venus holding a swan, from whose beak the fountain's water gushed. None of this decoration remains, and the loss renders the courtyard architecturally naked; its current stripped-down look is a far cry from its original fancy antique dress.

At the end of the courtyard — through the triple-portal loggia (originally a more secretive single portal) — lies the biggest surprise of all: a nymphaeum that is sunk two stories into the ground. Leading down to the middle level, curved staircases to the right and left echo the shape of the courtyard portico; at the lowest level, grottoes burrow under the pavement front and back. In Julius's day, four plane trees offered shade on the middle level, and twin aviaries (later walled in) flanked the colonnaded back-wall loggia on the top level. For Pope Julius and his friends, the nymphaeum must have been the villa's *pièce de résistance;* on walking through the portal at the far end of the main courtyard, visitors found themselves confronted not by the expected panoramic view of the villa's grounds, but by an entire miniature self-enclosed world to be explored on three separate levels, with cool fountained grottoes below and twittering aviaries above.

Pope Julius began constructing his villa soon after his election in 1550, and construction of the main building, courtyard, and nymphaeum progressed quickly. But Julius died in 1555, so the villa's heyday lasted a mere five years. In the succeeding centuries the complex went through several cycles of abandonment and restoration — at one point it was used primarily to store farm equipment — and the buildings that today define the villa's side and back perimeters (and that enclose the side gardens and the back garden beyond the nymphaeum) date from later renovations. The oddest of the later features can be found in the garden to the right of the main courtyard: a reconstruction of the Etruscan Temple of Alatri, built in 1891, when the villa was turned into a museum.

12-2 GALLERIA BORGHESE AND VILLA BORGHESE
Galleria Borghese: Flaminio Ponzio, 1608–1613
Villa Borghese: dedicated as a public park, 1902
(In the Villa Borghese, at the north end of the Viale del Museo Borghese;
the nearest park entrance is on the Via Pinciana opposite the
Via Giovanni Sgambati)

Recently restored, and thereby hangs a tale. Since 1902, when it was purchased by the state, the Galleria Borghese has been one of Rome's most famous museums, containing one of the world's most famous art collections. In 1984, it was closed for a periodic renovation; the usual *In Restauro* signs went up, the disappointed tourists were turned away, and Rome shrugged. Work continued for a year, then two years, then five years, then ten years. By 1996, after twelve years of restoration, there was still no end in sight. Rome shrugged again — who ever went there except the tourists?

But Walter Veltroni, the newly appointed Italian Minister of Culture, did not shrug. After visiting the site and viewing the mess, he decided that enough was enough. He announced that the protracted renovations were a disgrace to the city and the nation, that he himself was taking charge of the project, and that the work would be completed in a timely manner even if it meant setting — his own words — Anglo-Saxon deadlines. Rome laughed. But when the museum reopened on schedule in 1997, the locals thronged to see the result and reservations were sold out months in advance. The Galleria Borghese became the hottest ticket in town.

Today the building sparkles, and a more opulent setting for the art could hardly be imagined. The spit-and-polish shine will not be to everyone's taste — it is all very Baroque, and entirely lacking the patina of respectable old age. But it is safe to say that Cardinal Scipione Borghese, who built the building in 1608 as an elegant suburban retreat, would be immensely pleased to see his legacy so beautifully preserved.

The cardinal's architect was Flaminio Ponzio, who expanded on the precedent set by Baldassare Peruzzi at the Villa Farnesina in Trastevere. Like the earlier building, the Galleria Borghese* possesses two wings flanking an arched loggia opening out on gardens. From the beginning all the main rooms were used to display art — Borghese was one of the most avid collectors of his

---

*Strictly speaking, the building should be called the *Villa Borghese*, a term that would normally encompass both the structure and its grounds (as it does at the Villa Farnesina). But in this case the grounds — now a city park — are so vast that they possess an identity all their own. To distinguish between the two, it is the park that is today known as the *Villa Borghese*, and the museum is known as the *Galleria Borghese*, the *Casino Borghese*, or the *Museo Borghese*.

day — with the ground floor housing the specially commissioned pieces of sculpture that made the young Bernini famous: *Pluto and Proserpine*, *Apollo and Daphne*, and *David* (the works were produced between 1621 and 1625, and are still in place). In the late eighteenth century, a major renovation took place (most of the ceiling paintings date from this period), and in 1807, Prince Camillo Borghese sold part of the art collection to the Louvre. But the core of the collection remained behind and is now once again on magnificent display. It includes works by Raphael, Titian, Andrea Del Sarto, Correggio, Bronzino, Caravaggio (six paintings, including the *Ailing Bacchus*), Rubens, Domenichino, and Canova (the famous statue of Pauline Borghese — Napoleon's sister — as Venus), among many others.

The character of the grounds — Rome's most beautiful and accessible public park after the Forum downtown — was established in the late 1700s, when the old formal gardens were swept away and replaced by a more picturesque scheme that ultimately expanded to include broad avenues, terraces, fountains, tall trees, and sham ruins, including a little Neoclassical temple on an island in the middle of a central lake. After World War II the park was poorly maintained for decades, but in recent years it has been reclaimed, and today it offers a welcome refuge from the clamor of the city around it.

12-3 THE QUARTIERE COPPEDÈ: FROM THE PIAZZA TRASIMENTO TO THE PIAZZA MINCIO
Piazza Mincio: Gino Coppedè (1919–1924)
(Piazza Trasimento: outside the Porta Pia along the Via Nomentana, then left on the Corso Trieste and past the Piazza Trento)

What to do in the afternoon when the city shuts down for its daily siesta? The Forum and the Palatine are the traditional fallback venues, along with the patriarchal basilicas and the major museums, which remain open all day. A more adventurous alternative is the area around the Piazza Mincio known as the Quartiere Coppedè, outside the walls to the north of the Porta Pia. But architectural purists should be warned: there is no high seriousness hereabouts.

The Piazza Mincio neighborhood is architecture on intellectual holiday. The area is solidly residential, mostly constructed between World Wars I and II, and it looks at first glance like a complacent continuation of the Ludovisi and Sallustiano Quarters within the walls. But this particular architectural deck is stacked with more than a few jokers. The first sign that something is up comes at No. 1 Piazza Trasimento; with its medievalizing tower, its glistening Beardsleyesque mosaics, and its inventively decorative stone and brickwork, the building clearly gives not a hoot for traditional

Roman palazzo design. Around the corner on the Via Clitunno, things get odder still. No. 40 is festooned with musical motifs — the capitals are constructed out of musical notes, staves, and clefs* — and No. 45 sports a distinctly non-Italian but delicately lovely band of Jugenstil tiles apparently imported from Austria. At the next corner, things veer sharply toward the surreal: the architecture at No. 13 Via Serchio cannot be assessed because the house is almost entirely enveloped in a monstrous growth of ivy. Turning left, the medieval motif appears again at No. 2 Via Serchio and at No. 11 Via Ombrone (across the street and high up from No. 2 Via Serchio).

But these are merely appetizers. The main course comes a block to the right down the Via Brenta: the buildings in and around the Piazza Mincio, designed and constructed by Gino Coppedè from 1919 to 1924. "Ornament is crime," declared the Modernist pioneer Adolph Loos in 1908, and God knows what he would have said about Coppedè's fantastical centerpiece here. Ornament is everywhere, Classical and Medieval and Gothic and whatnot (Pre-Raphaelite? Art Nouveau? Art Deco? the usual Italian tag for the style is "Floreale") all mixed together without the least regard for historical correctitude or formality. The overeducated eye, perpetually in search of the unified whole while assessing Renaissance decorum or Mannerist idiosyncrasy or Baroque invention, is sure to be offended. But the untrained eye will have less trouble seeing the obvious: these irrepressibly whimsical buildings possess a rambunctious vitality that should produce grins all around. Yes, the result is "merely" picturesque, form without function, retrograde pastiche. But in the face of such infectious gusto, who cares? Coppedè's elaborate main-entrance composition (best viewed from the intersection of the Via Tagliamento and the Via Arno) makes the message immediately clear: around the Piazza Mincio, high spirits must be allowed to carry the day.

12-4   SAN LORENZO FUORI LE MURA
Ca. 590 C.E. and ca. 1225
(Piazzale di S. Lorenzo, outside the Aurelian walls to the east, adjacent to the Cimitero Campo Verano)

The medieval church of S. Lorenzo fuori le Mura stands at the edge of Rome's main cemetery, the Campo Verano, and on the outside it appears pristine in its orderly simplicity: a tall campanile standing next to a plain church with a high nave and a wide narthex supported by six scavenged

---

*The Latin inscription on the wall says: "Small, but suited to my needs, and free of encumbrance, and not displeasing, built as I pass on to my home in heaven."

antique Ionic columns (and containing some fine thirteenth-century frescoes illustrating the lives of St. Lawrence and St. Stephen). But the interior is another matter altogether, and far from simple.

Most medieval churches were organized around a straightforward plan based upon the ancient Roman public basilica: a high nave flanked by lower side aisles, with the nave terminating in a protruding curved apse. The nave at S. Lorenzo conforms to this pattern, but instead of a simple curved apse, the church unexpectedly possesses a chancel — an area beyond the nave that is typical of later cross-shaped churches (where the long arm of the cross is designated the nave, the short cross-arms are designated the transept, and the short top arm is designated the chancel). But there is no transept here, and the unusual size and design of the chancel raise some perplexing questions. Why is it on two levels, one above the other, both of which must be reached by stairs because neither is at the level of the nave? Why is the upper floor level of the chancel hemmed in — bizarrely — by column shafts whose bases reach down to the lower level but whose capitals rise above the chancel floor to support an upper gallery at still another level? Why is there no apse at the chancel's far end? And why is the entire chancel set at a slight but noticeable dogleg angle from the nave? These questions puzzled architecture historians for years, and it was only in the late 1940s, when the nave and narthex of the church were reconstructed — S. Lorenzo was the only church in Rome to suffer serious bomb damage during World War II — that excavations produced reliable evidence of the building's unusual history.

Part of the church, it turned out, did an about-face in the twelfth century, and the whole may even have started out as two separate structures. The oldest section is the chancel, which was originally a church unto itself oriented in the opposite direction (and lacking the floating upper floor in the center). It dates from the late sixth century, a period when the influx of pilgrims wishing to visit the graves of saints and martyrs had swelled to unprecedented heights. As Richard Krautheimer explains in *Rome: Profile of a City, 312–1308:*

> The tourist trade, meaning pilgrimages to Rome, reached a peak in the sixth and seventh centuries. It is not by chance that the three earliest surviving guides to Christian Rome date from the seventh century, two of them prior to 640. Addressed to pilgrims, the guides appeal to these visitors' belief in the miraculous powers of the martyrs' graves, and all follow the same scheme: proceeding along the roads outside the

walls, they list, often with legendary accretions, the venerated graves in the catacombs, the covered cemeteries, the small shrines, the great basilicas. . . . [Reading the texts] one can practically hear the guides at each catacomb crowding in with their spiel for the pilgrims and the whining beggars and the coins dropping in their begging bowls; and one can imagine the gifts donated at the tombs and at the servicing monasteries and the sums left in the hands of innkeepers and tradespeople. . . .

The flood of pilgrims forced on the Church new building activity at the graves of the martyrs. The covered cemeteries of Constantinian date, near the venerated sites, had been abandoned or reduced to secondary importance. The new type of pilgrim demanded more direct contact with the martyr. But a grave far down in the catacomb was hard to reach over steep stairs and through a maze of dark, narrow corridors; the situation was inconvenient, dangerous, and incompatible with the needs of the huge pilgrimage center Rome had become. A solution was found when Pelagius II (579–590) built within the hill [containing the catacomb where Saint Lawrence was buried] a "new basilica of admirable beauty" to enclose the grave of the martyr within the catacomb. . . . Sunk into a pit hollowed into the hill of the catacomb, Pelagius's church had its floor level with the tomb of Saint Lawrence, which was isolated as the corridors of the catacombs round about were destroyed in the scooping operations. . . .

The new basilica form was an ingenious solution to the major problem posed by the recent influx of pilgrims: the grave of the saint was made visible and easily accessible; the ground-floor of the church sunk in the hill would hold large crowds; the galleries, reached from the hilltop, offered space for the overflow and for those unable or unwilling to descend the stairs.

The Pelagian basilica, then, was constructed (at least in part) below ground level because its apse burrowed into the hill of catacombs to enfold the tomb of St. Lawrence, an isolating process that destroyed the section of the catacombs nearby. Much later, at the end of the twelfth century, Cardinal Cencius Camerarius (later Pope Honorius III) ordered an expansion of the Pelagian church, perhaps on the site of an earlier church built next to the catacombs in the fifth century (which would explain the dogleg in the ground plan). It was Honorius who built the current nave — presumably at what would have been the ground level of the Pelagian church had it not needed to burrow into the hillside — and inserted the floating chancel floor, which allowed the high altar to be placed directly above the restored and redecorated tomb of St. Lawrence on the lower level. This renovation shifted the main entrance from the west end to the east end of the building (the traditional orientation), and produced, in effect, a pair of Siamese-twin churches, with neither church possessing a conventional apse because the site of the apses is where the two churches are joined. As might be expected, the configuration is unique.

12-5   MAUSOLEO DELLE FOSSE ARDEATINE
Designed 1948 by a collaborative group of architects that included Nello Aprile,
Cino Calcaprina, Aldo Cardelli, Mario Fiorentino, and Giuseppe Perugini
Stone statuary: Francesco Coccia
Bronze gates: Mirko Basaldella
(Outside the Aurelian to the south, just south of the intersection of the Via
Ardeatina and the Via delle Sette Chiese, west of S. Sebastiano)

On March 23, 1944, during the occupation of Rome by the Nazis, the Italian resistance exploded a bomb that killed thirty-two German soldiers on the Via Rasella, near the Piazza Barberini. The next day the German authorities rounded up three hundred thirty-five men — roughly ten men for every German soldier who died — and took them to a sandstone quarry south of the city. There the prisoners, who were randomly chosen and had nothing to do with the previous day's attack, were herded into a quarry cave and executed. After the massacre, the Germans attempted to hide the mass grave by blowing up the cave passageway.

Three months later, the Allies liberated Rome, and exhumation and identification of the bodies began immediately. In 1949, after the victims were reinterred in a newly constructed cemetery just outside the cave entrance, the site was turned into a national memorial monument and park. The cave — which should be seen first — is straight ahead upon entering the main gate; the cemetery and a small museum are to the left.

In a place as moving as this, detailed aesthetic analysis would serve only to belabor the obvious. Suffice to say that every inch of the lovingly tended park is worth exploring, and that the cemetery enclosure employs modern architecture's most problematical building material — poured concrete — with imagination and power.

APPENDIX A:
THREE-DAY ITINERARY
—•—

ROME'S MAJOR SIGHTS are: the Forum, the Colosseum, the Pantheon, the Campidoglio, the Piazza Navona, the Spanish Steps, the Trevi Fountain, the Piazza del Popolo, St. Peter's Square, St. Peter's, and the Sistine Chapel (part of the Vatican Museums). The three days of morning and afternoon tours outlined below cover all these sites, and a good deal more. All walks except the second and third mornings begin at or near the Piazza Venezia; the walks do not include museum visits unless noted.

DAY 1 *(Morning):* Tour 1, including a visit to the Capitoline Museums. *Pages 15-37; includes the Campidoglio and an overview of the Forum.*

DAY 1 *(Afternoon):* Tour 2, excluding the Palazzo Doria-Pamphili interior, and returning to the interiors of S. Ignazio, S. Luigi dei Francesi, and S. Maria Maddalena after the churches reopen at 4:00, if necessary. *Pages 38-66; includes the Pantheon.*

DAY 2 *(Morning):* Tour 3 through S. Maria della Pace, then part of Tour 4 beginning with Pasquino and ending with the Largo Argentina or (if time permits) the Jewish Ghetto. *Pages 67-102 and 116–139 (or 116–146 if time permits); includes the Piazza Navona.*

DAY 2 *(Afternoon):* Tour 5, returning to the interiors of S. Maria del Popolo and Gesù e Maria after the churches reopen at 4:00, if necessary. *Pages 151-188; includes the Trevi Fountain, the Spanish Steps, and the Piazza del Popolo.*

DAY 3 *(Morning):* Tour 11 walked backwards, starting with the Vatican Museums (during high season it is advisable to arrive at the entrance — which is on the Viale Vaticano, many blocks north of St. Peter's Square — well before the doors open at 8:45 A.M.), then exiting the Sistine Chapel through the St. Peter's Square door to see St. Peter's Square, St. Peter's, S. Anna dei Palafrenieri, the Via della Conciliazione, and the Castel S. Angelo, ending with the Ponte S. Angelo. *Pages 327–345; includes the Sistine Chapel, St. Peter's Square, and St. Peter's.*

DAY 3 *(Afternoon):* Tour 7, excluding the Forum and the Palatine Hill unless the ruins there are of special interest, and excluding the entries on the Appian Way and S. Giovanni a Porta Latina if the walk is too long. The second entry in Tour 6 (S. Maria di Loreto and SS. Nome di Maria, p. 192) may be added at the beginning, since it is adjacent to the first entry in Tour 7 (Trajan's Column). *Pages 233–257 (or 192–194 if time permits); includes the Forum and the Colosseum.*

If there is extra time when the churches are open (before noon or between 4:00 and sunset), the sequence of four small Baroque churches along the Via del Quirinale on the Quirinal Hill (S. Andrea al Quirinale, S. Carlo alle Quattro Fontane, S. Susanna, and S. Maria della Vittoria, *pages 198–210*) should be added. If there is extra time when churches are closed (between noon and 4:00), a visit to the Galleria Borghese *(pages 349–350)* should be added (but calling ahead to make sure tickets are available is advisable). If the weather is fine, a summer evening walk through Trastevere ending with dinner on or near the Piazza di S. Maria in Trastevere is highly recommended *(pages 315–317).*

APPENDIX B:
SPECIAL INTEREST INDEX

———•———

$\mathcal{T}$HE SPECIAL INDEX that follows is intended for sightseers who wish to seek out a favorite architectural style or a favorite architect. The index is in two parts: Part I (Chronological Index) lists sites in chronological order; Part II (Architect Index) lists individual architects alphabetically, with a chronological list of sites under each architect's name.

Baroque (1600–1800)

façade (1641): Giovanni Battista Soria (1581–1651), 195–196

Palazzo Madama (1642): Paolo Maruscelli (1596–1649), 92–93

Fontana del Tritone (1643): Gianlorenzo Bernini (1598–1680), 225

Lantern, S. Ivo della Sapienza (1643): Francesco Borromini (1599–1667), 75–77

S. Ivo della Sapienza (1643–1660): Francesco Borromini (1599–1667), 77–83

Fontana delle Api (1644): Gianlorenzo Bernini (1598–1680), 225

Cornaro Chapel, S. Maria della Vittoria (1644–1652): Gianlorenzo Bernini (1598–1680), 209–210

SS. Vincenzo ed Anastasio façade (1646–1650): Martino the Younger Longhi (1602–1660), 157–159

Collegio di Propaganda Fide façade (1646–1666): Francesco Borromini (1599–1667), 164–166

Chiesa Nuova ceiling (1647–1665): Pietro da Cortona (1596–1669), 114–115

S. Giovanni in Laterano interior (1647–1649): Francesco Borromini (1599–1667), 283–285

Fontana dei Quattro Fiumi (1647–1651): Gianlorenzo Bernini (1598–1680), 86–90

Palazzo Spada false perspective (1652–1653): Franceso Borromini (1599–1667), 128–129

S. Agnese in Agone (1652–1672): Girolamo Rainaldi (1570–1655), Francesco Borromini (1599–1667), Carlo Rainaldi (1611–1691), Gianlorenzo Bernini (1598–1680), Pietro da Cortona (1596–1669), 90–92

S. Andrea della Fratte dome and campanile (1653–1665): Francesco Borromini (1599–1667), 162–164

Palazzo di Montecitorio façade (1653 onward): Gianlorenzo Bernini (1598–1680), Carlo Fontana (1634–1714), 53

SS. Domenico e Sisto staircase (1654):

Vincenzo della Greca (active 1616–after 1650), 195–196

S. Maria del Popolo nave embellishments (1655–1657): Gianlorenzo Bernini (1598–1680), 177–179

S. Maria della Pace façade (1656): Pietro da Cortona (1596–1669), 95–102

St. Peter's Square (1656–1667): Gianlorenzo Bernini (1598–1680), 331–335

Palazzo Chigi façade (Piazza Colonna) (1658): Felice della Greca (ca. 1626–1677), 187–188

S. Maria in Via Lata façade and vestibule (1658–1662): Pietro da Cortona (1596–1669), 48–50

S. Andrea al Quirinale (1658–1670): Gianlorenzo Bernini (1598–1680), 197–180

S. Maria di Montesanto (1658–1675): Carlo Rainaldi (1611–1691), Carlo Fontana (1634–1714), Gianlorenzo Bernini (1598–1680), 180–181

S. Maria dei Miracoli (1661–1679): Carlo Rainaldi (1611–1691), Carlo Fontana (1634–1714), Gianlorenzo Bernini (1598–1680), 180–181

S. Andrea della Valle upper façade (1662–1666): Carlo Rainaldi (1611–1691), Carlo Fontana (1634–1714), 136–137

S. Maria in Campitelli (1662–1675): Carlo Rainaldi (1611–1691), 141–143

Palazzo Odescalchi rear façade (1664): Gianlorenzo Bernini (1598–1680), 45–46

S. Carlo alle Quattro Fontane façade (1665–1667): Francesco Borromini (1599–1667), 198–205

Elephant with Obelisk (1667): Gianlorenzo Bernini (1598–1680), 68

Ponte S. Angelo (1668): Gianlorenzo Bernini (1598–1680), 329–329

S. Carlo ed Ambrogio al Corso dome (1668): Pietro da Cortona (1596–1669), 182–183

Palazzo Altieri façade (1670): Giovanni Antonio de' Rossi (1616–1695), 44–45

Palazzo Braschi (1792): Cosimo Morelli (1732–1812), 118

HISTORICIST (1800–1900+)

Piazzale Napoleone (1809–1814): Giuseppe Valadier (1762–1839), 172–173

Casina Valadier (1813): Giuseppe Valadier (1762–1839), 171–172

Palazzo Wedekind (1815): Giuseppe Valadier (1762–1839), 187–188

S. Cecilia in Trasevere interior decoration (1822): F. Salvi (active early 1800s), 307–309

S. Chiara (late 19th C): Luca Carimini (1830–1890), 70–71

Largo Magnanapoli (1876), 194

Lungotevere (Tiber Embankments) (1876 onward), 111–112

Galleria Sciarra (1883): Giulio de Angelis (1850–1906), 152–153

Piazza Venezia (1883 onward), 16–18

Victor Emmanuel Monument (1884–1927): Giuseppe Sacconi (1853–1905), 18–19

Corso Vittorio Emanuele (1884 onward), 112–113

Via Vittorio Veneto (1886), 224

Piazza della Repubblica (1886–1913): Gaetano Koch (1849–1910), 211–213

Palazzo Odescalchi façade (Via del Corso) (1887), 45–46

Cola di Rienzo Memorial (1887), 24–25

Palazzo di Giustizia (1887–1911): Giuseppe Calderini (1837–1916), 93–94

Piccola Farnesina north façade (1898): Enrico Guj (1841–1905), 117–118

Jewish Synagogue (1901–1908): Osvaldo Armanni (1855–1929), Vincenzo Costa (died 1944), 145–146

Camera dei Deputati (1902–1927): Ernesto Basile (1857–1932), 54–55

Galleria Colonna façade (1916–1922): Dario Carbone (1857–1934), 187–188

Piazza Mincio, Quartiere Coppedè (1919–1924): Gino Coppedè (1866–1927), 350–351

Fontana delle Naiadi (1911): Mario Rutelli (1850–1941), 211–213

MODERN (1900–2000)

Via dei Fori Imperiali (1932), 238

Via della Conciliazione (1937), 331

Piazza Augusto Imperatore (1937), 183-184

Monumento ai Caduti (1941): Giovanni Iacobucci, 325

Mausoleo delle Fosse Ardeatine (1944–1951): Aprile, Nello; Calcaprina, Cina; Cardelli, Aldo; Fiorentino, Mario; Perugini, Giuseppe, 354

Stazione Termini entrance façade (1950): Eugenio Montorio & Associates, 216

Il Roseto di Roma (Rose Gardens of Rome) (1950), 252

Office-Apartment Complex (1963–1965): Studio Passarelli (Vincenzo, Fausto, and Lucio Passarelli), 222–223

British Embassy (1971): Sir Basil Spence & Partners, 220

PART 2: ALPHABETICAL INDEX OF ARCHITECTS, WITH SITES

Ammanati, Bartolomeo (1511–1592)
Villa Giulia (1551), 292
Villa Medici (1576 onward), 171

Angelis, Giulio de (1850–1906)
Galleria Sciarra (1883), 152

Aprile, Nello (active mid-1900s)
Mausoleo delle Fosse Ardeatine (1944–1951), 354

Armanni, Osvaldo (1855–1929)
Jewish Synagogue (1901–1908), 145

Baccio Biggio, Nanni di (died 1568)
Villa Medici (1564 onward), 171

Basile, Ernesto (1857–1932)
Camera dei Deputati (1902–1927), 54

Bernini, Gianlorenzo (1598–1680)
St. Peter's interior decoration (1624–1666), 335
Fontana della Barcaccia (1627–1629), 169
Palazzo Barberini (1629–1637), 226
Raimondi Chapel, S. Pietro in Montorio (1640–1647), 322
Fontana del Tritone (1643), 226

St. Peter's (1564–1602), 335
Il Gesù façade (1575), 40
Palazzo della Sapienza courtyard (1577), 131
S. Maria in Via lower façade (1579), 187
S. Luigi dei Francesi façade (ca. 1585), 56
Fontana della Tartarughe (1584), 139
Palazzo Chigi façade (1588), 187
S. Andrea della Valle body (1591–1621), 136
S. Nicola in Carcere façade (1599), 291
SS. Domenico e Sisto (1628), 195
Dérizet, Antoine (1697–1768)
SS. Nome di Maria (1736–1741), 192
S. Luigi dei Francesi interior decoration (1756–1764), 56
Dominicis, Carlo de (active 1716–1770)
SS. Celso e Giuliano (1733–1735), 106
SS. Bartolomeo ed Alessandro di Bergamaschi façade (ca. 1735), 187

Fiorentino, Mario (active mid–1900s)
Mausoleo delle Fosse Ardeatine (1944–1951), 354
Fontana, Carlo (1634–1714)
S. Maria di Montesanto (1658–1675), 180
S. Maria dei Miracoli (1661–1679), 180
S. Andrea della Valle upper façade (1662–1666), 136
S. Maria Maddalena body (1673), 58
Cybò Chapel, S. Maria del Popolo (1682–1686), 177
S. Marcello façade (1682–1683), 47
Palazzo di Montecitorio façade (1694), 53
Fontana, Domenico (1543–1607)
S. Luigi dei Francesi façade (ca. 1585), 56
Fontana dell' Acqua Felice (1585–1587), 211
Palazzo del Laterano (1586–1589), 280
Quattro Fontane (1588 onward), 205
Fuga, Ferdinando (1699–1781)
Palazzo della Consulta (1732–1737), 196
S. Mara Maggiore façade (1740), 269
S. Cecilia in Trastevere façade (1741), 307

Galilei, Alessandro (1691–1736)
S. Giovanni in Laterano façade (1732–1736), 283
Gherardi, Antonio (1644–1702)

Avila Chapel, S. Maria in Trastevere (1675–1685), 317
Giardini, Francesco (active ca. 1635)
S. Nicola dei Lorenesi (1635–1636), 94
Giulio Romano (1499–1546)
Palazzo Stati-Maccarani façade (ca. 1520), 73
Grassi, Orazio (1583–1654)
S. Ignazio (1628), 51
Gregorini, Domenico (ca. 1690–1777)
Santissimo Sacramento Oratory (1727–1730), 161
S. Croce in Gerusalemme façade and vestibule (1741–1744), 286
Grimaldi, Fabrizio (1543–1613)
S. Andrea della Valle body (1591–1621), 136
Guj, Enrico (1841–1905)
Piccola Farnesina north façade (1898), 117

Iacobucci, Giovanni
Monumento ai Caduti (1941), 325

Juvarra, Filippo (1678–1736)
Palazzo Zuccari entrance portico (1711), 171

Koch, Gaetano (1849–1910)
Piazza della Repubblica (1886–1913), 211

Landini, Taddeo (1550–1596)
Fontana delle Tartarughe (1584), 139
Lippi, Annibale (active 1563–1581)
Villa Medici (1564 onward), 171
Longhi, Martino the Elder (active 1570–1591)
Chiesa Nuova body (1575–1606), 114
Palazzo Borghese courtyard (ca. 1585), 185
Longhi, Martino the Younger (1602–1660)
SS. Vincenzo ed Anastasio façade (1646–1650), 157
Lorenzetto (1490–1531)
Palazzo Caffarelli-Vidoni (1524), 138

Maderno, Carlo (1556–1629)
S. Andrea della Valle body and dome

ACKNOWLEDGMENTS
———•———

IN WRITING THIS book, I have drawn information from many sources, including textbooks, biographies, histories, and the standard guidebooks. But three general references deserve special recognition for having been especially valuable: *The Architecture of Rome,* edited by Stefan Grundmann; *The Oxford Archaeological Guide to Rome,* by Amanda Claridge; and *Guide to Baroque Rome,* by Anthony Blunt. I owe these books (and their authors) a great debt of gratitude; the task of marshalling the necessary information would have been all but impossible without them.

On-site in Rome, my test readers walked their feet off during the day and then talked their heads off during dinner, discussing their reactions and suggesting many improvements. Midge Pendergast, Pat Alexander, Gilbert Vezina, and Sue Landini were all tireless in their assistance, and Arina van Breda, the best sightseer I know, was unwavering in her dedication, accompanying me to Rome three times to walk new material as it was written and then returning a fourth time to walk the entire completed manuscript. Her contribution to the book has been enormous.

On the home front, many friends offered help and encouragement along the way, but four people must be singled out for special thanks. Mel Parker, my agent, took on a problematically quirky manuscript with alacrity, and masterminded the search for a publisher with great assurance and resourcefulness. Deborah Hornblow, friend and fellow writer, reviewed the completed manuscript in its entirety, searching out inconsistencies, redundancies, repetitions, and echoes, not to mention grammatical and syntactical howlers. And finally, Jonathan and Rosanne Cerf, my oldest friends, to whom this book is dedicated. Their support, enthusiasm, and generosity have been beyond measure. They were present in Rome when the project was first conceived, amid the flock of sculpted angels and cherubs at work in Bernini's S. Andrea al Quirinale, and they have edited every word of the manuscript with unfailing intelligence and unflagging patience. The journey that ultimately produced this book has been long and fascinating, and they have accompanied me every step of the way. Every writer should have such friends.

ILLUSTRATION CREDITS

——•——

$\mathcal{F}$OUR PEOPLE WERE especially helpful in procuring the reproductions contained in this book: art researcher Toby Greenberg, who supervised the search for the more obscure engravings; Greg Jecmen and Peter Huestis at the National Gallery of Art in Washington, D.C., who oversaw the reproduction of the Vasi etchings; and Julie Tozer, Assistant to the Curator, Avery Drawings & Archives, Columbia University, who was tireless in her efforts to track down the last few missing pieces.

Piazza del Campidoglio	Giuseppe Vasi, *Delle Magnificenze di Roma Antica e Moderna (Vol. 2, #80)*, Mark J. Millard Architectural Collection, David K.E. Bruce Fund, Image © 2005 Board of Trustees, National Gallery of Art, Washington, published 1747-1761, bound 1 vol: illus.
Piazza Venezia	Giuseppe Vasi, *Delle Magnificenze di Roma Antica e Moderna (Vol. 1, #39)*, Mark J. Millard Architectural Collection, David K.E. Bruce Fund, Image © 2005 Board of Trustees, National Gallery of Art, Washington, published 1747-1761, bound 1 vol: illus.
Piazza del Campidoglio	Reunion des Musees Nationaux/Art Resource, NY
Piazza del Campidoglio	Drawing and Archivies, Avery Architectural and Fine Arts Library, Columbia University

View of the Roman Forum	Giuseppe Vasi, *Delle Magnificenze di Roma Antica e Moderna (Vol. 1, #31),* Mark J. Millard Architectural Collection, David K.E. Bruce Fund, Image © 2005 Board of Trustees, National Gallery of Art, Washington, published 1747-1761, bound 1 vol: illus.
Pantheon	Giuseppe Vasi, *Delle Magnificenze di Roma Antica e Moderna (Vol. 1, #25),* Mark J. Millard Architectural Collection, David K.E. Bruce Fund, Image © 2005 Board of Trustees, National Gallery of Art, Washington, published 1747-1761, bound 1 vol: illus.
Il Gesù Façade (Vignola)	Drawing and Archives, Avery Architectural and Fine Arts Library, Columbia University
S. Marcello	Giuseppe Vasi, *Delle Magnificenze di Roma Antica e Moderna (Vol. 3, #133),* Mark J. Millard Architectural Collection, David K.E. Bruce Fund, Image © 2005 Board of Trustees, National Gallery of Art, Washington, published 1747-1761, bound 1 vol: illus.
S. Luigi dei Francesi	Giuseppe Vasi, *Delle Magnificenze di Roma Antica e Moderna (Vol. 3, #175),* Mark J. Millard Architectural Collection, David K.E. Bruce Fund, Image © 2005 Board of Trustees, National Gallery of Art, Washington, published 1747-1761, bound 1 vol: illus.
Piazza Navona	Giuseppe Vasi, *Delle Magnificenze di Roma Antica e Moderna (Vol. 1, #26),* Mark J. Millard Architectural Collection, David K.E. Bruce Fund, Image © 2005 Board of Trustees, National Gallery of Art, Washington, published 1747-1761, bound 1 vol: illus.
S. Eustachio	Giuseppe Vasi, *Delle Magnificenze di Roma Antica e Moderna (Vol. 2, #113),* Mark J. Millard Architectural Collection, David K.E. Bruce Fund, Image © 2005 Board of Trustees, National Gallery of Art, Washington, published 1747-1761, bound 1 vol: illus.
The Pharos of Alexandria	© Bettmann/CORBIS

S. Ivo Dome Interior with Bee	Drawing and Archives, Avery Architectural and Fine Arts Library, Columbia University
S. Ivo Geometry [line drawing]	After Anthony Blunt, *Guide to Baroque Rome,* redrawn by Kristen Zimmerman, Suzy Rae Design.
S. Maria della Pace	Giuseppe Vasi, *Delle Magnificenze di Roma Antica e Moderna (Vol. 3, #121),* Mark J. Millard Architectural Collection, David K.E. Bruce Fund, Image © 2005 Board of Trustees, National Gallery of Art, Washington, published 1747-1761, bound 1 vol: illus.
SS. Celso e Giuliano	Giuseppe Vasi, *Delle Magnificenze di Roma Antica e Moderna (Vol. 2, #109),* Mark J. Millard Architectural Collection, David K.E. Bruce Fund, Image © 2005 Board of Trustees, National Gallery of Art, Washington, published 1747-1761, bound 1 vol: illus.
Palazzo Farnese	Giuseppe Vasi, *Delle Magnificenze di Roma Antica e Moderna (Vol. 2, #73),* Mark J. Millard Architectural Collection, David K.E. Bruce Fund, Image © 2005 Board of Trustees, National Gallery of Art, Washington, published 1747-1761, bound 1 vol: illus.
Palazzo della Cancelleria	Giuseppe Vasi, *Delle Magnificenze di Roma Antica e Moderna (Vol. 2, #74),* Mark J. Millard Architectural Collection, David K.E. Bruce Fund, Image © 2005 Board of Trustees, National Gallery of Art, Washington, published 1747-1761, bound 1 vol: illus.
Palazzo Massimo alle Colonne	Giuseppe Vasi, *Delle Magnificenze di Roma Antica e Moderna (Vol. 2, #76),* Mark J. Millard Architectural Collection, David K.E. Bruce Fund, Image © 2005 Board of Trustees, National Gallery of Art, Washington, published 1747-1761, bound 1 vol: illus.
S. Maria in Campitelli	Giuseppe Vasi, *Delle Magnificenze di Roma Antica e Moderna (Vol. 2, #117),* Mark J. Millard Architectural Collection, David K.E. Bruce Fund, Image © 2005 Board of Trustees, National

	Gallery of Art, Washington, published 1747-1761, bound 1 vol: illus.
Trevi Fountain	Giuseppe Vasi, *Delle Magnificenze di Roma Antica e Moderna (Vol. 2, #104)*, Mark J. Millard Architectural Collection, David K.E. Bruce Fund, Image © 2005 Board of Trustees, National Gallery of Art, Washington, published 1747-1761, bound 1 vol: illus.
Piazza di Spagna	Giuseppe Vasi, *Delle Magnificenze di Roma Antica e Moderna (Vol. 1, #40)*, Mark J. Millard Architectural Collection, David K.E. Bruce Fund, Image © 2005 Board of Trustees, National Gallery of Art, Washington, published 1747-1761, bound 1 vol: illus.
Spanish Steps [line drawing]	After John Varriano, *Italian Baroque and Rococo Architecture*, redrawn by Kristen Zimmerman, Suzy Rae Design.
Piazza del Popolo	Giuseppe Vasi, *Delle Magnificenze di Roma Antica e Moderna (Vol. 1, #21)*, Mark J. Millard Architectural Collection, David K.E. Bruce Fund, Image © 2005 Board of Trustees, National Gallery of Art, Washington, published 1747-1761, bound 1 vol: illus.
Porto di Ripetta	Giuseppe Vasi, *Delle Magnificenze di Roma Antica e Moderna (Vol. 2, #85)*, Mark J. Millard Architectural Collection, David K.E. Bruce Fund, Image © 2005 Board of Trustees, National Gallery of Art, Washington, published 1747-1761, bound 1 vol: illus.
S. Susanna & S. Maria della Vittoria	Giuseppe Vasi, *Delle Magnificenze di Roma Antica e Moderna (Vol. 3, #148)*, Mark J. Millard Architectural Collection, David K.E. Bruce Fund, Image © 2005 Board of Trustees, National Gallery of Art, Washington, published 1747-1761, bound 1 vol: illus.
SS. Luca e Martina	Print Collection, Miriam and Ira D. Wallach Division of Art, Prints and Photographs, The New York Public Library, Astor, Lenox and Tilden Foundations

SS. Domenico e Sisto & S. Catarina da Siena a Magnanapoli	Giuseppe Vasi, *Delle Magnificenze di Roma Antica e Moderna (Vol. 3, #149),* Mark J. Millard Architectural Collection, David K.E. Bruce Fund, Image © 2005 Board of Trustees, National Gallery of Art, Washington, published 1747-1761, bound 1 vol: illus.
Serlian Arch	© Historical Picture Archive/CORBIS
S. Carlino Geometry [line drawing]	After Anthony Blunt, *Guide to Baroque Rome,* redrawn by Kristen Zimmerman, Suzy Rae Design.
Il Gesù	Giuseppe Vasi, *Delle Magnificenze di Roma Antica e Moderna (Vol. 3, #135),* Mark J. Millard Architectural Collection, David K.E. Bruce Fund, Image © 2005 Board of Trustees, National Gallery of Art, Washington, published 1747-1761, bound 1 vol: illus.
Mannerist Gateway #1 (Villa Grimani)	General Research Division, The New York Public Library, Astor, Lenox and Tilden Foundations
Mannerist Gateway #2 (Villa Sermoneta)	General Research Division, The New York Public Library, Astor, Lenox and Tilden Foundations
Porta Pinciana	Giuseppe Vasi, *Delle Magnificenze di Roma Antica e Moderna (Vol. 1, #2),* Mark J. Millard Architectural Collection, David K.E. Bruce Fund, Image © 2005 Board of Trustees, National Gallery of Art, Washington, published 1747-1761, bound 1 vol: illus.
Colosseum	Giuseppe Vasi, *Delle Magnificenze di Roma Antica e Moderna (Vol. 1, #33),* Mark J. Millard Architectural Collection, David K.E. Bruce Fund, Image © 2005 Board of Trustees, National Gallery of Art, Washington, published 1747-1761, bound 1 vol: illus.
Porta S. Sebastiano (Appian Way)	Giuseppe Vasi, *Delle Magnificenze di Roma Antica e Moderna (Vol. 1, #10),* Mark J. Millard Architectural Collection, David K.E. Bruce Fund, Image © 2005 Board of Trustees, National Gallery of Art, Washington, published 1747-1761, bound 1 vol: illus.
Piazza di S. Giovanni in Laterano	Giuseppe Vasi, *Delle Magnificenze di Roma Antica e Moderna (Vol. 1, #34),* Mark J. Millard

Architectural Collection, David K.E. Bruce Fund,
Image © 2005 Board of Trustees, National
Gallery of Art, Washington, published 1747-1761,
bound 1 vol: illus.

Tomb of Julius II	Bildarchiv Preussischer Kulturbesitz/Art Resource, NY
S. Maria Maggiore	Giuseppe Vasi, *Delle Magnificenze di Roma Antica e Moderna (Vol. 1, #48)*, Mark J. Millard Architectural Collection, David K.E. Bruce Fund, Image © 2005 Board of Trustees, National Gallery of Art, Washington, published 1747-1761, bound 1 vol: illus.
S. Giovanni in Laterano	Giuseppe Vasi, *Delle Magnificenze di Roma Antica e Moderna (Vol. 1, #46)*, Mark J. Millard Architectural Collection, David K.E. Bruce Fund, Image © 2005 Board of Trustees, National Gallery of Art, Washington, published 1747-1761, bound 1 vol: illus.
Porta S. Paolo (Pyramid of Gaius Cestius)	Giuseppe Vasi, *Delle Magnificenze di Roma Antica e Moderna (Vol. 1, #11)*, Mark J. Millard Architectural Collection, David K.E. Bruce Fund, Image © 2005 Board of Trustees, National Gallery of Art, Washington, published 1747-1761, bound 1 vol: illus.
S. Maria in Cosmedin	Giuseppe Vasi, *Delle Magnificenze di Roma Antica e Moderna (Vol. 1, #56)*, Mark J. Millard Architectural Collection, David K.E. Bruce Fund, Image © 2005 Board of Trustees, National Gallery of Art, Washington, published 1747-1761, bound 1 vol: illus.
Piazza di S. Maria in Trastevere	Giuseppe Vasi, *Delle Magnificenze di Roma Antica e Moderna (Vol. 1, #60)*, Mark J. Millard Architectural Collection, David K.E. Bruce Fund, Image © 2005 Board of Trustees, National Gallery of Art, Washington, published 1747-1761, bound 1 vol: illus.
Ospedale di S. Gallicano	Giuseppe Vasi, *Delle Magnificenze di Roma Antica e Moderna (Vol. 3, #174)*, Mark J. Millard Architectural Collection, David K.E. Bruce Fund, Image © 2005 Board of Trustees, National

	Gallery of Art, Washington, published 1747-1761, bound 1 vol: illus.
Tempietto Ground Plan with Courtyard	The Granger Collection, New York
St. Peter's Square	Giuseppe Vasi, *Delle Magnificenze di Roma Antica e Moderna (Vol. 1, #41)*, Mark J. Millard Architectural Collection, David K.E. Bruce Fund, Image © 2005 Board of Trustees, National Gallery of Art, Washington, published 1747-1761, bound 1 vol: illus.
St. Peter's Square showing Third Arm	Print Collection, Miriam and Ira D. Wallach Division of Art, Prints and Photographs, The New York Public Library, Astor, Lenox and Tilden Foundations
St. Peter's Dome (Michelangelo)	The Metropolitan Museum of Art, Harris Brisbane Dick Fund, 1941 [41.72(3.24)] Photograph, all rights reserved, The Metropolitan Museum of Art.
Galleria Borghese	Giuseppe Vasi, *Delle Magnificenze di Roma Antica e Moderna (Vol. 3, #187)*, Mark J. Millard Architectural Collection, David K.E. Bruce Fund, Image © 2005 Board of Trustees, National Gallery of Art, Washington, published 1747-1761, bound 1 vol: illus.

INDEX

———•———